*Dangerous Pregnancies*

*The publisher gratefully acknowledges the generous support of the General Endowment Fund of the University of California Press Foundation.*

# Dangerous Pregnancies

MOTHERS, DISABILITIES, AND ABORTION
IN MODERN AMERICA

*Leslie J. Reagan*

UNIVERSITY OF CALIFORNIA PRESS

BERKELEY   LOS ANGELES   LONDON

University of California Press, one of the most distinguished university presses in the United States, enriches
lives around the world by advancing scholarship in the
humanities, social sciences, and natural sciences. Its activities
are supported by the UC Press Foundation and by philan-
thropic contributions from individuals and institutions.
For more information, visit www.ucpress.edu.

University of California Press
Berkeley and Los Angeles, California

University of California Press, Ltd.
London, England

Library of Congress Cataloging-in-Publication Data

Reagan, Leslie J.
    Dangerous pregnancies : mothers, disabilities, and abor-
tion in modern America / Leslie J. Reagan.
        p.      cm.
    Includes bibliographical references and index.
    ISBN 978-0-520-25903-4 (cloth : alk. paper)
    1. Rubella–United States–History.   2. Rubella in
pregnancy–United States–History.   3. Abortion–United
States–History.   4. Abnormalities, Human–United
States–History.   5. Disability awareness–United States–
History.   I. Title.

RA644.R8R43   2009
614.5′240973—dc22                        2009030996

Manufactured in the United States of America

18   17   16   15   14   13   12   11   10   09
10   9   8   7   6   5   4   3   2   1

This book is printed on Cascades Enviro 100, a 100%
post–consumer waste, recycled, de-inked fiber. FSC recycled, certified, and processed chlorine free. It is acid free,
Ecologo certified, and manufactured by BioGas energy.

*To Jacob and Rosie*

# CONTENTS

# ILLUSTRATIONS

# ACKNOWLEDGMENTS

Like many books, this one is the result of a long and winding trail that took me to unexpected places. For a while, my working title was "Unexpected" because it described both the topic of unanticipated reproductive experiences—pregnancy losses and birth defects in a newborn—and my own experience as I wrote a book on a topic I had not planned. This project began as a result of my own miscarriage and my reaction to the supportive literature that I had received telling me to expect grief and equating a miscarriage with an infant death. I investigated the history of ideas about miscarriage through the twentieth century and found that the overall representation of miscarriages (and thus the feelings prescribed for women) had changed from being regarded as a hazard to women's health in the early twentieth century, when maternal mortality had been high and the birth control movement was beginning its fight for legal contraception; to being regarded as a blessing at midcentury because a miscarriage then meant that Nature had intervened to stop the birth of a child with defects; to being regarded as a tragedy at the end of the twentieth century because miscarriage and the grief women felt were now equated with a child's death.* Since pregnancy loss was explained through birth defects, my project expanded.

I did not realize until rather late that my book would be focused on German measles (also known as *rubella*). Although German measles does

---

* Leslie J. Reagan, "From Hazard to Blessing to Tragedy: Representations of Miscarriage in Twentieth-Century America," *Feminist Studies* 29, no. 2 (Summer 2003): 356–78.

cause miscarriages, stillbirths, and infant deaths as well as serious birth defects when pregnant women contract the virus, when German measles hit the United States after World War II, pregnancy losses and infant deaths received little notice. The chief concern was not pregnancy loss but rather the birth of children with congenital malformations, sensory impairments, and mental retardation. Studying a disease also interested me as a method for looking at science and medicine in practice and from a patient's perspective, and as a means of writing a biography of sorts through mass experience of the body and disease rather than a biography focused on a heroic individual.

I have been fortunate in receiving much support—institutional, financial, and personal—as I have followed this research path. I have many people to thank, with pleasure. The University of Illinois, Urbana-Champaign, has provided essential support for research and leave time for writing. The UIUC Research Board; the Illinois Program for Research in the Humanities (IPRH); a Mellon Faculty Fellowship from the College of Letters, Arts, and Sciences; a sabbatical leave; and a National Institutes of Health–National Library of Medicine grant have supported semesters for research, thinking, and writing. This book could not have been written without this material support for research assistance, travel, and copying and most especially leaves that granted me quiet time for thought and concentrating on the craft of historical writing. Research has been partially supported by NIH-NLM grant number 5G13LM8407. I am deeply grateful to the NIH and my university for that support. This book's contents do not necessarily represent the official views of the NIH. My homes in the History Department and the Medical Humanities and Social Sciences Program in the College of Medicine at the University of Illinois, Urbana-Champaign, have supported my research by generously granting leaves from teaching and giving whatever bits of support they could. I am grateful to the chairs over the last several years for their ongoing efforts to support research; thank you to Antoinette Burton, Peter Fritzsche, Jim Barrett, and Evan Melhado. Thank you also to the staff who have helped me, and special thanks to Tom Bedwell and Tracy McAllister.

I am grateful as well for library and archival grants that have made possible my archival and library research in many different spots. The ACOG-Ortho-McNeil Fellowship in the History of American Obstetrics and Gynecology underwrote a summer of research in Washington, DC, in the ACOG Library and the National Archives. A Rockefeller Archives Center Research Fellowship got me to Yonkers and New York City for a very special month at the Rockefeller Archives and the March of Dimes Archives. The University of California–Los Angeles James and Sylvia Thayer Short-Term Research Fellowship made it possible for me to spend a full two weeks in the library's rich archival collections. I have had the great pleasure of using the wealth of historical resources held in libraries all over the country, including those at the University of Illinois, Urbana-Champaign; the University of California–Berkeley; the University of California–Los Angeles; the University of California–San Francisco; the University of California–Santa Cruz; Yale University; and Johns Hopkins University and the National Library of Medicine. Archivists, librarians, and other staff members at each of these institutions have been warm and helpful. I especially thank David Rose at the March of Dimes Archives and Mary Stuart, librarian of the History, Philosophy, and Newspaper Library at Illinois.

At the tail end of this project, I found Nancy O'Donnell, and we immediately recognized our shared and unusual interest in this disease. Through Nancy, I gained a better sense of the people with CRS and the "rubella moms," and was invited into the Deaf/deaf-blind world. I am grateful for the anecdotes, memories, and stories that strangers and friends have offered about their lives and experiences with German measles. Their insights matter to me. I hope to hear more.

While I was in California on sabbatical, I enjoyed visiting scholar appointments at the University of California–Berkeley in the Beatrice Bain Research Group associated with Women's Studies and at the Science, Society, and Technology Center as well as connections with the history of medicine people at Cal and at the University of California–San Francisco. Every meal and every meeting with these anthropologists, historians, sociologists, nurses, and physicians was an intellectually stimulating pleasure. Carol Joffee, Niranjan Karnak, Tom Laqueur, Anne Nesbet, Barrie Thorne, and Liz Watkins made my time in the Bay Area special.

Audiences at many different conferences and institutions have helped to make this a better book. Earlier versions and pieces have been presented at the University of California–Berkeley; the University of California–San Francisco; San Francisco General Hospital; the University of Illinois, Urbana-Champaign; Indiana University; Washington University; the National Library of Medicine; the American Association for the History of Medicine; the Berkshire Conference on the History of Women; and the Organization of American Historians. All of the graduate students with whom I work in history, in the arts, and in our IPRH medicine/science reading group, an interdisciplinary group of graduate students and faculty, have been the source of camaraderie, intellectual exchange, and inspiration. Thanks to Amanda Brian, Roswell Quinn, Matt Gambino, Brian Hoffman, Kristen Ehrenberger, Dawn Flood, Robin Jensen, Heather Ault, Bonnie Fortune, and all of the others past, present, and future.

My research assistants have done important work, all with enthusiasm and a smile. I thank Dawn Flood, Elisa Miller, Diem Mi Bui, Brian Hoffman, Matt Gambino, Holly Nakamura, and Britta Jewell. Thank you to the many friends and family who have welcomed me and shared their homes during research trips, including Zola Dincin Schneider and Irving Schneider, Paul Lopes, Sherri and Mac Brown, Mary Coughlan, and Elaine Kihara and David Sweet. And thank you to my family in general— Billy, Dorothy, Daniella, Anna, Julia, David, Cynthia, Dad, Laurie, Mom, Doug, Karen, Kate, Phil, June, Geoff, Zola, Irv, Norman, Linda, David, Paul, Ben, Rafi, Peter, Susan, Max, Anne, and Ellis—for their continuing interest in books of all sorts, including mine.

I am immensely grateful to my friends who have read drafts, often more than once; who have listened and offered thoughts and suggestions; and who have helped me keep going. Some of these wonderful people have read the entire book manuscript; others have read a page or a paragraph on demand; all of them have listened and offered encouragement, even enthusiasm, for this book. I am grateful to each of you. (If I have accidentally forgotten to include your name, please forgive me and know that I am grateful.) Thank you to Emily Abel, Sari Aronson, Jim Barrett, Kathy Brown, Eve Fine, Mary Fissell, Karen Flynn, Vanessa Gamble, Linda Gordon, Diane Gottheil, Sandra Hammond, Kristin Hoganson, Ellen Jacobsen, Judy Leavitt, Lewis Leavitt, Sarah Leavitt, Sue Lederer, Mark Leff, Trish Loughran, Nancy MacLean, Laura McEnaney, Sarah Projansky, Naomi Rogers, Walt Schalick, Tim Shea, David Tanenhaus, Anghy Valdivia, and my anonymous reviewers. I was honored to meet the late Ruth Roemer, an expert in public health who organized many of the petitions and briefs analyzed here and decades later offered her encouragement. I am especially grateful to Janet Golden, Anne Nesbet, Liz Pleck, Susan Smith, Siobhan Somerville, Daniel Schneider, and Paula Treichler, who have read the entire manuscript or close to it and who have talked and listened to me throughout the twists and turns of this project.

Thank you to my editors at the University of California Press, beginning with former Director Jim Clark, who wrote the contract for an entirely different project and looked appalled at the idea that I might force myself to write a book that I no longer wanted to write (thank you again for that feeling and for your confidence); through Monica McCormick, who encouraged the transformation; and Niels Hooper, who became my editor—active, thoughtful, helpful, and funny. Thank you also to Nick Arrivo, Kate Warne, Vici Casana, and everyone at UC Press for making this book real.

This book has been a mystery, a surprise, a source of exhaustion and of pleasure. I especially thank Daniel Schneider who, in the final stages that dragged on, pitched in hugely with the work on the home front and also made espressos to help this book reach its conclusion. Thank you. This book is dedicated to my kids—Rosie and Jacob—whom we imagined and who now imagine and make themselves.

# Epidemics, Reproduction, and the Fear of Maternal Marking

WHEN THE GERMAN MEASLES EPIDEMIC crossed the globe and hit the United States in 1963, women were terrified of catching it. For women themselves, German measles meant at most a minor rash and a fever. They worried, however, about contracting the disease during pregnancy, a situation that could cause miscarriages, infant deaths, or serious birth defects in their babies—including deafness, blindness, heart malformations, and mental retardation. Experts predicted that twenty-thousand "damaged" babies would be the result of the German measles epidemic of 1963–65.[1] The disease, which uniquely threatened pregnant women and the developing fetus, could not be prevented or treated. In fear of the potential consequences of German measles (also known as *rubella*), many women sought abortions although abortion was illegal at the time. As *Dangerous Pregnancies* shows, anxieties about reproduction—such as the fears surrounding German measles—have shaped national histories to a profound degree. Although today the significance of this epidemic has been largely forgotten, its legacies have been written into the U.S. social infrastructure; into law, medicine, science, and social movements; and into contemporary politics. German measles became a catalyst for bringing about fundamental changes in the culture, public health, and constitutional law.

German measles was a disease of national importance in the early 1960s. As such, it now provides an opportunity to observe how a country and a people responded to a threatening disease that appeared in epidemic form as well as to see the state's intense interest in reproduction. In striking pregnant women and babies, this disease also struck at the nation's hopes for the future and its newly won sense of security after World War II. Like the Cold War, the German measles epidemic of the early 1960s exposed the fragility of domestic security in the most powerful nation in the world. At a time when threatening diseases—including smallpox, diphtheria, tuberculosis, and polio—appeared to have been stamped out in the United States; when penicillin and antibiotics had conquered deadly infections; and when infant, child, and maternal mortality had all dropped dramatically, this new epidemic was insidious and frightening. The disease marked and reshaped bodies. As it entered the culture, it also reshaped law, medical practices, school policies, public health programs, and patients' rights.

Infectious diseases have never been confined to the body, for diseases are only understood through culture and history. As epidemic diseases race through bodies, they also race through societies, cultures, and the media, producing myriad cultural objects and effects as well as physical symptoms. As cultural studies scholar Paula Treichler argues, novel and frightening epidemic diseases produce a proliferation of language and representations.[2] German measles produced not only rashes, miscarriages, infant deaths, and "damaged" babies but also scientific discoveries, terminologies, jokes, family dramas, legal fights, political contests, and cultural stories. It also contributed to the building of several emerging social movements, including the movements for abortion and reproductive rights, the right to life, and disability rights. This history investigates these cultural products and effects and uses the disease to identify the approaches of American parents to pregnancy and family, the role of ordinary Americans and patients in the creation of law and political movements, the state's relationship to and responsibilities for its citizens, and the development of citizen rights and expectations.

This particular disease had powerful legal and political ramifications; it landed in court and in Congress both because pregnant women sought legal abortions and because parents organized on behalf of their children who had been disabled by rubella. German measles offers an unusual opportunity to look again at some of our current policies and ideas about disabilities, pregnancy and abortion, informed consent, vaccines, and viruses by immersing ourselves at a point in time before children with disabilities were mainstreamed in public schools; before a visible, militant disability rights movement; and before movements for reproductive rights and justice. German measles and the responses to it played a central role in constructing the movements and policies that are now part of everyday life, medicine, and law in the United States.

To study how the general population, health experts, and state officials understood and responded to this frightening disease, I have closely analyzed popular mass media and the visual culture surrounding German measles. Pictures often mattered more than text for producing a shared sense of what the individual and the country confronted in this disease. I have looked at popular materials—such as daily newspapers, magazines, movies, television, and public health educational pamphlets—alongside specialized medical literature, legal records, government documents, and the papers of lawmakers and organizations. The visual and popular materials produced a dominant cultural climate that gave shape to people's understanding of German measles, its consequences, and the possibilities for social change. The media did not do this work alone, nor were their messages uniform. Mass media are not transparent reporters or reflections of reality, but neither are media stories fictional or irrelevant. Instead, mass media's representations, selections, and storytelling skills help create people's understandings of the real world. As such, media presentations of disease may guide decision making and shape not only what audiences and viewers think about events but also what they feel about them. For people facing an unknown disease that threatened pregnancies and might result in the births of children with serious disabilities and contemplating as well unknowns of caring for and educating an "abnormal" child, mass media served as a crucial source for gaining knowledge of what German measles meant.

This book brings together rich fields of scholarship typically treated separately: epidemics and infectious disease; pregnancy, reproduction, abortion, and motherhood; and representations of and people with disabilities. What little history there is of German measles appears either in literature focused on virology, as a rare sentence in disabilities studies, or in passing in histories of privacy, abortion, and tort law.[3] Histories of virology and vaccine development tend to take the pressing need for a vaccine as self-evident rather than treating it as a question. The rubella vaccine is today known for the contemporary resistance to it. Rather than charting the work in the laboratory or vaccine mandates, *Dangerous Pregnancies* instead shows how the cultural and political meanings of this disease pushed scientific research and mass acceptance of the rubella vaccine.

The demographic bump in the population of "handicapped" children that resulted from the German measles epidemic has been overlooked as well. Disabilities studies scholars have closely analyzed the stigmatizing representation of people with disabilities as freaks and criminals, the institutions that segregated them, and the rise of the contemporary disability rights movement.[4] Disability activists make the important distinction between organizations of parents, educators, physicians, and researchers who claim to represent the interests of the disabled for them and organizations composed of people with disabilities who speak for themselves. The perspectives of these two types of organizations are not the same. The parent-professional advocacy organizations, however, represented the disability movement as it existed in the 1950s and early 1960s.[5] Since the movement and its scholars tend to focus most on the militant self-advocates who moved from more polite demands to protests demanding rights in the late 1960s, parent work for disability rights during the same period has been relatively neglected.[6] The people who spoke out for the needs of disabled babies and children were parents, especially mothers. "Rubella parents," as they named themselves, helped win the earliest victories for the right to public education for children with physical, sensory, and intellectual impairments.

There is now a vast literature on the history of reproduction, including childbirth, obstetrics and gynecology, birth control, contraception, abortion, sterilization, eugenics, child rearing, adoption, and more. Historical attention to birth defects, however, is quite recent.[7] *Dangerous Pregnancies* analyzes the political and cultural consequences that followed the personal, medical, and scientific reactions to the children born with "congenital malformations" and the disease that caused them. Finally, although specialists in the field of reproduction are aware of German measles, they have not closely investigated why this disease appears in histories of privacy and abortion law. German measles played a key role in jump-starting abortion law reform. Analyzing why and how it did so is important for understanding the cultural and political processes that brought about fundamental changes in women's reproductive rights and American law.

German measles and scientific knowledge about its effects first brought the complex moral and legal questions about pregnancy, possible disabilities, and possible abortion to the forefront of American medical, political, and media culture and public attention. Indeed, the availability of amniocentesis in the United States today grew out of legal suits brought against hospitals and doctors for malpractice in German measles cases. The widespread use of amniocentesis today, as sociologist Barbara Katz Rothman reports, makes many women (and their partners) think of desired pregnancies as "tentative." Genetic testing technologies require that women consider abortion an option if serious anomalies appear to be present—regardless of what personal or moral views they hold or decisions they make—and thus require that women think about the health status of their own fetuses, their future children, and their values and capacities and then decide what to do. Through her sensitive interviewing and analyses, anthropologist Rayna Rapp documents the "hard thinking" done by pregnant women of all races, classes, and religions in the midst of genetic testing. At the forefront of new ethical dilemmas growing out of new and increasingly more sensitive technologies, pregnant women today are, in Rapp's words, "moral pioneers."[8] The ambiguities, confusion, distress, and hard thinking of pregnant women today and the politics of amniocentesis and abortion are extensions of what pregnant women faced in the 1940s, 1950s, and 1960s when they suspected that they had contracted German measles. For the women who grappled with the knowledge of German measles in the past, however, abortion was illegal.

Perhaps the physicians who provide legal abortions should be seen as moral pioneers as well. These doctors—particularly those who provide late-term abortions—have faced growing hostility and aggression from abortion opponents. Late-term abortions are rare, but when women decide they are necessary, it is often in situations similar to the ones faced by women who contracted German measles during pregnancy. A woman may know of severe conditions that will cause her child to die soon after birth, the fetus may have already died, or the pregnancy may threaten her own life. In the violent context of the turn of the twenty-first century, some abortion providers—most notably Dr. George Tiller, who was murdered in 2009—have taken on roles of moral and civic leadership as they insist on women's rights to abortion and defend diversity, religious freedom, and civil rights.[9]

An epidemic may act as a catalyst for social change. As historian Charles Rosenberg observed about cholera's effects in the nineteenth century,[10] German measles in the early 1960s helped produce new public policies and powers. Epidemics of frightening diseases, numerous histories have shown, have served as occasions for creating social stigma, demarcating difference, and assigning blame. The contagious—typically identified as an already marginalized group by race, class, foreign origin, religion, sexuality, or other stigmatized status—are blamed and excluded in panicked efforts to avoid infection. Frightening infectious diseases had previously been associated with the poor and tenement dwellers; Jewish, Irish, Italian, and Chinese immigrants; Mexican and African Americans; male alcoholics; and women who worked as prostitutes.[11]

The post–World War II response to German measles, however, did not follow the usual pattern of further stigmatizing an already outcast group. The early 1960s epidemic spotlighted a homogenous, white, middle-class, heterosexual, married nuclear family. When this normative population appeared to be injured by the epidemic of the early 1960s, the politics of disease took an unusual turn. Instead of looking for and fingering a nonwhite or other stigmatized group as the source of this contagious disease and aiming control measures at its members, as had been typical in earlier epidemics, a new politics of civil rights and protection of mothers and children developed. The victims of rubella were presumed to be families, mothers, and children of privilege—white and middle class—and the damage done to them received enormous public attention. Indeed, whiteness, together with middle-classness and the normative heterosexual family, opened up new conversations about reproduction and public health and contributed to the creation of new social movements. As German measles appeared to target white families in particular, the racial representation of abortion changed and made abortion respectable.

This book demonstrates the importance of race and ideologies of respectability to the histories of reproduction, disease, and disabilities. Here I aim to highlight that whiteness and middle-classness brought (and continue to bring) privileges. I use *middle-classness* to denote how people might be read as being middle class, respectable, and trustworthy by journalists, doctors, politicians, and the general public through their overall self-presentation—including their whiteness, heterosexuality, and married status—rather than use the term *middle class* to narrowly refer to wealth or type of employment. For many white middle-class Americans, the subtle privileges and political power of respect and trust have been as assumed and invisible as the privileges of health, education, and wealth.[12]

The dominant media representation of German measles as a disease that hurt white middle-class families also helped the nascent disabilities rights movement win attention and social services. The new "handicapped" children born of German measles were pitied not only because they had disabilities but also because their expected prosperous futures had been interrupted. Chris Bell has aptly observed that the field of disability studies is unaware of its own racial stance and its practice of overlooking people of color; he suggests it should honestly call itself "white disability studies."[13] This book contributes to that rethinking of the field by analyzing how whiteness—together with the privileges of middle-classness—shaped the representation of disabilities when today's disability rights movement began to emerge.

The fear of having a child with birth defects did not originate with German measles. Since at least the early twentieth century, the birth of a "congenitally malformed" child was equated with the term *tragedy*. *Dangerous Pregnancies* analyzes the nation's deep fear of this tragedy through the telling of the German measles story. More than scholars have previously recognized, expectant mothers and fathers across all social categories feared the prospect of a "defective" child and hoped for healthy, normal, well-formed babies. Many women worried that they might do something wrong during pregnancy, thus causing deformity in their own babies. They feared, in the language of medical experts, "maternal marking" of pregnancy. By the middle of the twentieth century, it was a truism among doctors that the first question every new mother asked was "Is my baby all right?"[14] At birth, the new mother's first worry concerned the body and health of the newborn. The anxious question and the need for reassurance point to the cultural importance of physical normality and the deep-seated fear of the abnormal and different. The question also simultaneously encapsulated immediate fears about infant survival as well as worries about the future. Parents of children born with malformations saw a lonely, outcast, and dependent future written on the bodies of their children. The body itself, at the moment of birth, was read as a prediction. Disability, like gender and race, was understood to be produced in the body, a fixed biological condition rather than a socially, culturally, and historically produced creation.

### MATERNAL MARKING

By the start of the twentieth century, health reformers, scientists, physicians, midwives, and maternalists were urging women to attend to and care for their pregnancies in order to protect the health of the babies on the way. The prescriptive advice built upon a long tradition of women observing their own bodies and their pregnancies, but now experts asked women to do new things: to follow expert advice and to bring themselves, their own pregnant bodies, to doctors for examination in advance of delivery. Where nineteenth-century women had thought about and planned for the event of childbirth, twentieth-century women were now also being told to think about the health of the baby before it was born. The U.S. Children's Bureau, a federal agency founded in 1912 and charged with implementing the Sheppard-Towner Act of 1921 to improve maternal and infant health, worked to educate all mothers throughout the country through magazines, classes, and pamphlets.[15]

The Children's Bureau's method of encouraging mothers to write and ask for pamphlets about maternal and child health and to ask questions generated up to 125,000 letters each year, some brief and simple requests for a particular pamphlet, others with specific questions, and still others with detailed and intimate narratives of the writers' lives.[16] Writers included educated, middle-class women as well as the rural, immigrant, and barely literate. Some wrote on lovely stationery; others on pieces of old envelopes. Women, and some men too, wrote to the Children's Bureau in the early twentieth century—as they did to birth control activist Margaret Sanger, patent medicine seller Lydia Pinkham, and even the president of the United States— seeking information, reassurance, sympathy, and material help. In writing to state agents, these women developed an intensely personal relationship with the state. Letter writers believed that the officers of the state had a personal interest in the lives of ordinary Americans, that citizens deserved a hearing— even on matters of family, the body, and reproduction—and could reasonably expect assistance. Many women, it appears, felt comfortable talking with other women through the form of a personal letter. Popular women's magazines also developed close relationships with their readers through correspondence and advice columns on family, love, health, and sex. The practice of writing letters for sympathy, information, and advice drew on generations of women's writing to friends and family, their recording of family stories and histories in letters and diaries, and the female practice of both seeking advice from and providing sympathy to each other when it came to matters of health, babies, family, life, and death.[17]

Knowing that sympathetic female experts might be found at the Children's Bureau emboldened some to ask the questions they found shameful. "I planned to go to a doctor several times in the past two years to ask his assistance," wrote one Wisconsin woman, "but somehow couldn't find the courage. I find it much easier to discuss this personal a topic on paper than in person." It was easier to write to a distant person than to speak to a (most likely male) doctor face-to-face. Although this particular woman was asking about how to get pregnant rather than how to protect her pregnancy, her letter expressed the common fear of talking about the body, sexuality, and pregnancy and illustrates her relief at being able to use the letter mode instead.[18]

The Children's Bureau filed letters from worried expectant mothers in folders labeled "superstitions of pregnancy" and "maternal impressions," which are now held at the National Archives in College Park, Maryland. Written between 1914 and 1940, these letters offer an unusual opportunity to glimpse ordinary women's concerns about their pregnancies, bodies, and babies—concerns that might have more typically been voiced to friends and neighbors while cooking or caring for families in conversations long gone and inaccessible to the historian.[19] These letters from all parts of the country reveal women's deep fear of giving birth to a deformed baby and their deep desire to give birth to a healthy one. They also show (expectant) mothers' attentive monitoring of their own bodies and the world, their thinking and suspicions, and their enormous sense of responsibility for the health and well-being of their children.

Fears of harming the baby-to-be were many and varied. Some women believed that attending public amusements threatened their babies on the way. Since many reformers frowned upon sideshows, vaudeville, and movies as dangerous sites of sin and sex, it is no wonder that the expectant mother also felt that she and her child could be injured by popular entertainment. "Would [it] make any difference to a baby, if," asked one woman, "when the Mother was in the first month of pregnancy, she saw a man with a disfigured arm acting on a stage, and it impressed her so much that she became very nervous and had to leave the hall, and has been able to think of nothing else for three days?"[20]

Viewing a disability could frighten. This woman projected disability into her future and onto her future child. That the man "with a disfigured arm" appeared on stage added to the drama of the event and to her trauma. Another mother-to-be who reported herself "anxious about everything" wondered whether her own body's misshapen look might cause deformity. Or maybe the movies could cause it. "My neighbor has a new baby & it is deformed," she explained. "People say picture shows did it—I haven't been to the show since I knew I was pregnant—but I think I went before I knew. Will that deform mine? I am really worried." The Alabama woman asked for pamphlets.[21]

Movies and circuses, the Children's Bureau reassured, would not hurt the baby on the way. In fact, attending such amusements was good for the women themselves. In addition to sending a Children's Bureau pamphlet, Dr. Viola Russell Anderson sent more personal reassurances in letters. Bulges were "perfectly normal," not something to worry about. "You need wholesome recreation and play," the doctor urged. "If you enjoy the movies and can go at times which do not interfere with your eight hours of sleep at night or your hour's rest during the day, there is no reason why you should not visit an amusing picture show now and then, just as you have always done."[22]

"The only way in which a mother can mark her baby is in giving it a healthy body and a healthy mind," Doctor Anderson further wrote. "A mother does this by observing the rules of hygienic living, getting plenty of rest, proper food, exercise out-of-doors, and above all, keeping a sane wholesome point of view on life. This means that the mother does not allow herself to worry because worry interferes with her health. It is not advisable for a mother to talk too much to her friends and neighbors who quite unintentionally frighten her with stories of sad experiences of others. We can assure you that the tragedies of childbirth are very, very rare, if the mother has the proper care before birth and at the time of confinement."[23]

The pregnant woman's job was to be "sane," to follow "the rules" of good healthy living, and to ensure that her own "need" for recreation be fulfilled. Dr. Anderson simultaneously reassured and described the correct path for the expectant mother to take. This official informational letter included a subtle warning that trouble might come to expectant mothers who failed to follow the advice. Yet it should also be noted that this maternal health adviser emphasized that a woman's *own* health deserved care. Caring for herself in terms of nutrition, rest, medical care, and even entertainment paved the way for the health of the baby. Avoiding too much talk with nonexperts and too much worry was part of a good health program. This reassuring advice permitted, indeed urged, pregnant women to take care of themselves and enjoy their lives.

Finally, the doctor addressed the letter writer's central anxiety about "deformed" babies. "*The tragedies of childbirth,*" Dr. Anderson wrote, "*are very, very rare,* if the mother has the proper care before birth and at the time of confinement."[24] The deformed child was defined as a "tragedy." Such a tragedy, however, could be avoided with "proper care." Medical attention, as specialists in obstetrics had long claimed, promised safety for mother and child.[25] It apparently also ensured healthy and well-formed babies.

Modern life threatened in other ways as well. Did riding in a car threaten a pregnancy? As cars became part of daily life for many Americans in the 1920s, some suspected that the bumpy rides might cause harm. You should not ride in an "automobile over rough roads [or] . . . take long fatiguing trips," Dr. Anderson advised one worried mother-to-be. In response to the question of whether the woman herself should drive her own car during pregnancy, the doctor said, "You will have to decide [for] yourself."[26] This worry and the medical advice to avoid driving in order to avoid miscarriage lasted long into the twentieth century.[27]

Others suspected that the mundane events of daily life endangered pregnancy and babies on the way. Could a child "be marked by a dog jumping on the mother before the child is born?" one questioned.[28] A neighborly visit to a new mother might threaten. A friend's baby whose head looked "like a snake" worried one expectant mother. She had "looked" for "about 10 minutes." Would that exposure "make my baby deformed?"[29] she wondered. Perhaps the fact that she had looked at the baby only briefly, a mere ten minutes, would lessen the danger. This Indiana soldier's wife received the hoped-for reassurance. "Scientists," the Children's Bureau's medical expert told her, agreed "that mothers cannot mark their children."[30]

Some queries revealed anxiety that a woman's own body threatened a child—or perhaps the words betrayed the writer's own distress about being pregnant and wishes that she not be so. Could a woman's body "choke" the growing baby within? "Does bending or stooping cause the navel cord to form around the baby's neck and choke it?" asked one expectant mother from South Dakota.[31] Mothers-to-be worried about going to the dentist. Did they imagine that pulling a tooth might be equated with getting rid of a pregnancy? Mrs. Atwater, mother of a six-year-old child, had heard that marking was possible early in pregnancy. She had had eight teeth pulled, she explained, "before I realized my condition, but it has made me so nervous. . . . I wonder if I have done anything to disfigure it [the baby] by worry?" If the dental work was not dangerous, then was her worrying dangerous?[32]

The normal hygienic practice of douching after sexual intercourse might threaten a pregnancy, one woman feared. Pregnant women, as this letter indicates, worried about their future children from the instant of conception. They also believed themselves responsible. Early-twentieth-century advertisers encouraged douching as good hygiene; some women knew that douching might work as a contraceptive method.[33] As more women adopted douching— whether for cleanliness, for avoidance of disease, or as a contraceptive or possible abortifacient—some worried about the implications of its use when they found themselves pregnant. One woman reported that her sister was "depressed with the fear that her child will not be normal." The reason? She had used a douche of water and "25 drops (not more) of iodine" "*immediately* after the time conception must have occurred." She was certain the "iodine has injured the cells, and a child physically or mentally imperfect will be the result." The writer sought "scientific knowledge as to whether or not such injury could possibly have occurred."[34] Dr. Anna E. Rude believed harm to be "unlikely" and anxiety over the question unnecessary.[35] If a woman had douched in order to prevent pregnancy, perhaps she feared that abnormality would be punishment for her efforts.

Living or working in close quarters with the "feeble-minded," some were certain, promised to harm future children. Disabilities and intellectual deficits appeared to be both inherited and contagious. A Connecticut mother could not get her adult daughter, a school teacher for "feeble minded children," to see reason on this point. The self-described "anxious mother of this teacher" believed that her daughter could mark her own child, but her daughter insisted otherwise. The mother went to the experts at the Children's Bureau to sort things out. Dr. Rude told her that she "need have no concern whatever" about her daughter's work.[36] No doubt Rude's answer was a relief to both mother and daughter. (Since Dr. Rude sent a pamphlet on prenatal care, we can imagine that the future grandmother then started worrying and prodding her daughter about other things.)

One husband feared that living with his wife's epileptic sister could be "a fatal mistake" for his wife and child. The Brooklyn man described the situation. His wife, "in a pregnant condition," was being urged by her sister and mother to live with them. He said that he "hesitated," however, "believ[ing] it may be fatal to my wife and child if she should see her sister in one of these attacks of Epilepsy," which tended to occur in the middle of the night. Furthermore, he worried, his wife was older (34) and having her first child, and besides, she had two other sisters and a brother who could help. He asked the experts to tell him "what would be the harm to a pregnant woman and her child if she lived with" and saw "an Epileptic convulsion, especially the shock on being suddenly awakened at night by such convulsions." He added, "I want my child to have every possible safeguard, and I do not want to make a fatal mistake."[37] The man's fears went unnamed. Perhaps he feared that his child might be an epileptic too; perhaps he feared a miscarriage or a premature birth and injury to his wife and the baby on the way. Perhaps he dreaded living in a cramped Brooklyn apartment with his mother- and sister-in-law.

The expert at the Children's Bureau never directly responded to the question of whether living with a person with epilepsy could harm a pregnant woman or mark the developing child; instead, she responded to the family issues. That a man needed expert ammunition in this disagreement underlines the power of women in matters of family, home arrangements, and preparation for childbirth. In this case, Dr. Rude sided with the husband's preferences, agreeing that he raised a "complicated problem" and that it would be best if his wife did "not . . . live with her family during her pregnancy." Although she did not say so, the interpersonal dynamics of sharing an apartment and the power dynamics among the women and between husband and wife appeared to have the potential to create stress and disputes. Instead, Dr. Rude viewed the proposed housing conditions through a medical lens. "Pregnancy itself," she continued, "is somewhat of a tax even under favorable conditions, and there is no doubt that a prospective mother should be freed from all possible shocks, anxiety and excitement."[38]

The power of mothers to shape their children in utero was not only negative, however. Just as many believed that the pregnant woman could harm and deform her developing child through her ideas, actions, and experiences, some also believed she could deliberately give desirable characteristics to her future child. When so many women felt powerless in the face of pregnancy and afraid for their futures, it is fascinating to see that others imagined themselves to have tremendous agency in the future of their children. Of course, that is what motherhood meant: not only enormous responsibility but also enormous power over children and over the context and directions of their lives. "A prospective mother may give her child any talent she fully determines upon giving it," asserted one woman who had educated herself about pregnancy through reading. "This knowledge I am *particularly anxious* to possess," she continued, hoping that the Children's Bureau could help her.[39] "The best medical opinion," however, Mrs. Max West informed her, considered maternal shaping of a baby's talents impossible, for "such characteristics are determined by the hereditary traits transmitted to the baby by father and mother."[40] The mother-to-be did not outline what talents she hoped to impart to her child.

Although a mother could not "influence her unborn baby in th[is] way," Mrs. West continued, the mother did "determine to a considerable extent probably the health and the strength of her baby by the care she gives herself during pregnancy."[41] While advisers told women that they could neither control traits nor "mark" their children (though the Children's Bureau never scoffed at these ideas), they also told women how they did shape the health and bodies of their children. Their eating habits; their submission to medical exams, tests, and treatments; and their habits of rest and exercise affected the developing fetus. Yet this quoted sentence also shows that the woman's commitment to her own health, "the care she gives herself," was what mattered and what affected the future child. In political and cultural climates (like our own) that are suspicious of pregnant women and mothers, the fact that it is women's commitment to themselves *and* to their future children that ensures the health and future of babies is too often obscured. Indeed, women's health has primarily been addressed in reproductive terms, with the unfortunate consequence of women's other health needs being overlooked. Yet at the same time, and paradoxically, women have received more health care and have attended more closely to their own health in order to protect and improve the health of their offspring. Caring for a child on the way often motivates women to take care of themselves.[42]

In the thinking of at least some, a pregnant woman might not only mold her baby's shape and talents; she might also determine its color. "Can you tell me whether it depends on food one eats during pregnancy whether the expectant child is fair or dark skinned? If so," wrote one Georgia woman, "I am anxious to know what food to take, as I would like very much for my baby to have fair skin."[43] This belief, coming out of the South, is an interesting one, and one can see that it could be socially useful. If the word in the neighborhood was that the mother had eaten the wrong foods, that report could explain the birth of children perceived to be either too light or too dark. Such an explanation would put the blame on the mother but would redirect more dangerous questions about her sexual behavior and relationships. When race mattered enormously, loyalty to one's whiteness (as well as sexual loyalty to one's husband) was required, and lack of loyalty could be dangerous, this notion could be quite useful. It might also be desirable for some African Americans when lighter skin tones brought social advantages and useful for a child who might pass despite being a bit dark. If women widely believed that food could determine the color of their baby's skin, we can imagine worried expectant women changing their eating habits in an effort to lighten the color of the baby on the way. This thought harkened back to older ideas, common in early modern England and in antiquity, that mothers could make their babies black or white through their imagination or by looking at paintings at the moment of conception.[44]

Men too feared that their bodies might be the source of ill health or deformity in their children. William Crawford, a soldier in World War I who had married before he shipped out, wrote to the "Better Babies Bureau," as he dubbed the Children's Bureau. The name revealed his hopes and fears as well as his accurate understanding of the national emphasis on producing "better" babies. "Our greatest hope is for a house and babies," he reported, but "the war has broken me, and we will have to start all over again." The man explained, "I was wounded—resulting in atrophic paralysis of the right leg. . . . Will my wound affect my babies?"[45] The bureau's doctor reassured this man who hoped to be a father. "There is no possibility of an acquired injury being inherited or affecting a child," she explained. The wounded soldier could expect "perfectly healthy children."[46]

This man had been a soldier during World War I, a time when the military and the social purity movement had taught men of the need for sexual self-control and had emphasized that sexual depravity would inevitably result in venereal diseases. Physicians and reformers highlighted the damaging reproductive effects of syphilis and gonorrhea: infertility, stillbirths, blindness. Perhaps those teachings were more generalized in the minds of some men. By focusing on the harm to families and babies, reformers and public health officers could address the disease and insist on public action. Public health measures against venereal diseases, however, were most forcefully directed at women and African Americans.[47] World War II health films warned thousands of military men and women that sexual contact with prostitutes or with men with illicit sexual histories would produce sterility or crippled children.[48]

It was commonplace for women to be anxious about their sexual relationships with their husbands out of fear that they would get pregnant once again. Many also worried that sex during pregnancy could be harmful. "Should sectual [sic] intercourse be permitted during pregnancy?" asked one cautious expectant mother. "I would not want to permit anything that would be harmful to my baby, but I have been allowing this, perhaps, twice a month, only when I thought it was necessary. My husband and I are very fond of each other, and sometimes it is very hard to overcome this desire."[49] "Can you let your Husband have it after you are in that kind of shape?" asked another. "Will it injure the baby in any way?" she wondered. She asked for "full information."[50]

Children's Bureau advisers stressed sexual moderation and strict abstinence at specific times in order to prevent miscarriage. "Regarding your marital relations," Dr. Rude answered, "it is very hard to give set rules. However, frequent sexual intercourse should be avoided during pregnancy and," she added, "total abstinence during the time the monthly period would occur."[51] Intercourse during the usual time of menstruation, the bureau advised in personal letters and pamphlets published through the 1940s, threatened miscarriages. In 1915, women had been told that they should have no sex in the month before delivery, but a decade later Dr. Anderson emphatically advised a longer period of abstinence. By the late 1920s, intercourse was considered ill-advised during most of the pregnancy because doctors believed that the sexually active woman risked miscarriage in the early months and risked infection and premature labor at the end of the pregnancy. "Intercourse in the middle three months is of less risk, but," the doctor emphasized, "it is forbidden absolutely in the last two months of pregnancy because it may bring on childbed fever or labor before time."[52] In keeping with the general teachings to girls and women, sex was dangerous. (And one should note the obvious: *sex* was narrowly defined to mean vaginal intercourse with the woman's husband.)

No doubt some women hoped that sexual intercourse during pregnancy would be officially frowned upon. Official government advice might bolster a wife's arguments made to a husband who pressed her for sex. Prohibitions against sex during pregnancy or the time of menstruation could provide a period of relief for some women. Feminists who advocated voluntary motherhood and birth control vigorously objected to men who would not leave their wives alone during pregnancy. Instead of providing tender care and concern during pregnancy, too many husbands pressed for sex and acted as "brutes." Male demands for sex during pregnancy and soon after birth represented the height of male barbarism. This analysis of sexual inequality propelled the voluntary motherhood movement in the nineteenth century and infused Margaret Sanger's critiques of marriage as well.[53]

At times, medical advisers took their cue from parents about the advice and tone needed for the prospective mother. In an agency built upon protective, maternalist movements, it is no wonder that a doctor listened to mothers and advised their adult daughters accordingly. One woman, concerned for her married daughter, asked the bureau to send her "pamphlets pertaining to child raising [and] also correct sexual relations during pregnancy."[54] Her daughter was only nineteen. Warnings about sex, it appears, came quite naturally from mothers and medical women alike. A letter and advice bulletins soon went out to the married daughter. This letter was like others in terms of giving the standard advice, but it was more forceful. Dr. Rude underlined her message (and the mother's message) regarding "sexual intercourse during pregnancy": "*In moderation* it usually does no harm."[55]

The early-twentieth-century Children's Bureau worked to educate mothers and encouraged good prenatal care. Most notably, the health and lives of women themselves were of importance. By the 1930s, however, the tone had changed. Communications became more prescriptive and distant; pregnant women increasingly were regarded as conduits for protecting the health of future children. Funding for the Sheppard-Towner Act and the Children's Bureau's work on behalf of maternal and infant health had been cut thanks to the hostility of the American Medical Association and birth control opponents.[56] The nation increasingly appeared to be most dedicated to protecting future babies *through* the bodies of women and much less concerned about the health of women and mothers themselves. States passed laws making premarital and prenatal syphilis testing mandatory. Such laws intended to protect and save babies and to protect the nation from the costs of caring for children born blind or "defective."[57] The health and lives of the women were secondary at best.

Worrying about the progress of a pregnancy and possible dangers was only the beginning of a lifetime of worrying about children. Once the child was born, it was the mother's job to observe the health of her child, to monitor her or him for physical or developmental oddities, to provide nursing care, to make doctors' appointments, to watch for signs of contagious diseases and other dangers, to immunize, and to insure that the child ate well, slept, and learned proper hygiene habits. Mothers felt for fevers, listened to coughs, and watched for sore throats and rashes; they read advice columns and took classes, applied remedies, asked the neighbor or the corner druggist for help, went to clinics, or called in healers or doctors as needed. They, along with public health officials, doctors, nurses, and teachers, looked for and worried about contagious diseases, poor sanitation, and clean milk and water. The mother's intensive, individual, and primary responsibility for the health and survival of her child had developed first in the nineteenth century among middle-class white Protestants; at the turn of the twentieth century, reformers and experts such as those found in the Children's Bureau pushed scientific motherhood forward. Maternalist reformers and government agencies like the Children's Bureau, departments of health, and public schools increasingly made this work on behalf of child health an official duty of all mothers of all classes, races, and regions. Poor and working-class women themselves also grasped their expanding duties to child health. What good mothers perceived to be evidence of good mothering—and their capacities to carry out new health duties—varied by class and culture. Nonetheless, the expectation that it was a mother's special duty to watch for her children's health—and her pride in doing so—was shared across class, race, region, and culture. The club woman, the immigrant mother, the race woman, the rural mother, and the indigent mother all shared this gendered responsibility. Early-twentieth-century mothers worried about many things.[58] German measles was not one of them.

The title of this book, *Dangerous Pregnancies,* is meant to encapsulate the fears associated with German measles and its effects, the sense of danger, and the emotions aroused by this disease, particularly during an epidemic. This book is about how German measles became a primary worry for (expectant) mothers in the United States and a significant issue for the state as well. Although the fear of German measles was new in the mid-twentieth century, that fear built on age-old anxieties that external events or a mother's actions during pregnancy might harm a baby during its development. Those old fears of maternal marking combined with the modern sense that hazards could be prevented through maternal, social, and state action fueled the cultural, scientific, and political responses to this disease. Indeed, American citizens expected that science and the state would protect them from such devastating danger. The German measles epidemic of the early 1960s revealed and strengthened that expectation.

*Dangerous Pregnancies* begins with the discovery of German measles and ends with the development of a vaccine to conquer it. How people made sense of German measles and responded to it in the 1950s and 1960s forms the middle of the book. The first chapter rethinks the people involved with and the processes of discovering diseases from the nineteenth century through World War II by investigating nineteenth- and twentieth-century U.S., European, and Australian medical and scientific research literature, newspapers, and popular magazines. The chapter shows how women, in their work as mothers who cared for and observed the sick and the well, were essential collaborators in making medical discoveries and knowledge. Chapter 2 examines the mid-twentieth-century cultural encounter with this newly discovered disease as it arose in epidemic form in the United States in 1963. Contemporary representations of German measles built upon other diseases, medical events, and ideas about gender, family, and bodies. This chapter outlines the ideas and practices then current regarding the disabled child and the changing representations of abortion in the context of a new epidemic that threatened to produce tens of thousands of deformed babies. Chapter 3 turns to individual families who discovered that they were unable to act as patients on what they had learned from the media about this disease and therapeutic abortion. Contrary to what the media and medical textbooks taught, decisions that medical authorities suggested belonged to the expectant mother regarding the continuation or termination of pregnancy were, in reality, blocked. By looking closely at two malpractice suits, the chapter shows how the medical system and the transmission of medical information actually worked in the lives of women. The subtleties of inequality become evident only through a close analysis of sources from cases of individual patients. Chapter 4 turns to the political stage, where German measles exerted an unexpected but powerful influence. The effects of the disease contributed to path-breaking changes in law and to the growth of the abortion rights movement as well as to the emerging right-to-life and disability movements. Analysis of the competing actions of various representatives and agencies of the state underlines the complexity and argumentation within the state itself. The final chapter follows the state's interest in this disease down another path: the push to develop a vaccine. This chapter tracks the ongoing commitment to conquering rubella in order to protect mothers and children and in order to avoid both abortion and disabilities. Parents of children harmed by rubella simultaneously pushed for state services for disabled children and supported science and vaccination. The chapter presents a cultural analysis of the mass immunization campaign carried out through television and comic books in 1970. The campaign revised gender expectations and racial understanding of the disease while it also called upon good citizenship, along with fear of disability, to succeed.

And succeed it did. As a result of massive immunization, rubella declined and began to disappear in the Western world. In 2005, the United States CDC announced the successful elimination of rubella in this country.[59] Yet the disease raised new worries in new ways among some parents. Today, rubella is a vague memory, and few know what the *R* means in the MMR vaccine (combined measles, mumps, and rubella) now routine for young children. The epilogue brings the "rubella children," the disease, and its myriad ramifications up-to-date.

German measles/rubella has been known by many names, and as people have gained new knowledge, it has acquired new names. *German measles* was the name most commonly used by both doctors and ordinary people in the nineteenth and twentieth centuries; *rubella* became more important at the end of the twentieth century. By 1965, the children born after their mothers had contracted German measles were identified as having congenital rubella syndrome (CRS). In informal conversations about this project, I have found that present-day awareness of the disease varies by age. People over forty know of German measles, but this name tends to draw a blank with medical students. Instead, they recognize *rubella,* use the mnemonic device *TORCH* to recall the disease as one of several infections that can cross the placenta and cause birth defects or miscarriages, and are trained to identify "blueberry muffin babies," who show the signs of rubella's effects. Some people know of German measles through Agatha Christie's book *The Mirror Crack'd from Side to Side* (or the movie).[60] Parents of young children are most likely to recognize the term *MMR vaccine*.

The children born with the effects of maternal rubella, or CRS, appear here, but this book is more about the responses of pregnant women, mothers, parents, and the larger society to the German measles epidemic and the children they imagined would result. The sources available to me about children born with CRS were more limited, in part because there had been neither a system of national reporting nor a permanent organization devoted specifically to them. But it is also true that the medical diagnosis of CRS in a child did not correspond with the institutions that served children with disabilities and did not designate a lifelong social identity. Instead, these "multihandicapped" children flowed into preexisting groups of the disabled and their schools and communities, namely the deaf, blind, or mentally retarded. Others, perhaps after surgery and perhaps wearing heavy glasses, were identified as normal and entered the regular school system. As a result, the children with CRS and their families became hard to identify and track in historical records. There is more work to be done, including compiling comparative and transnational histories. This study lays the groundwork for future studies and for oral histories of mothers, fathers, and, most especially, the people who live with the physical, medical, and social effects of congenital rubella.

In this book I use the terms of the period about which I am writing, such as *handicapped, crippled, retarded,* and *mentally retarded,* as well as the current, more respectful terminology that has replaced them, such as *disabled people, people with disabilities, differently abled, intellectually disabled,* and *intellectually impaired.* Similarly, I use *birth defects,* a familiar phrase, although its implicit meaning—that a person is born "defective"—and its ties to eugenics make it problematic. Nonetheless, the term *birth defects* is still the standard usage and is more immediately understood by a broad audience. As new languages are being created in order to replace stigma with pride and respect, old terms continue to be used. One pediatrician finds that he needs to use *mentally retarded* and its abbreviation, *MR,* when talking to parents because many have no idea what *intellectually disabled* means.[61] As *MR* disappears because it is perceived as a mean-spirited and derogatory label, to be replaced by *special needs, developmentally delayed, learning disabled,* or other terms, it may nonetheless still be needed in clinical practice when a doctor explains to parents the status of their child—and the new responsibilities that they now have. Using all possible terms in order to ensure understanding is necessary, practical, and sensitive. New and better languages will, no doubt, be created. Although we have yet to settle on perfect replacements, the trend is toward a more respectful language that recognizes the possibilities, capacities, humanity, and legal rights of all people regardless of the workings of their minds or the shapes of their bodies.

"My husband and I both long for the babe and so crave that it will be as nearly a perfect baby as possible," wrote one young woman of their first child on the way. She followed closely all of the instructions she had read and drank "lots of milk and water."[62] Yet she worried, and in 1920 she wrote from Cleveland, Ohio, to the U.S. Children's Bureau in Washington, DC, for further instruction and reassurance. As pregnant women and couples worked to achieve the goal of a healthy "perfect" baby by following advice, many feared doing something wrong and producing an imperfect baby. The desire and the fear went hand in hand. Fear of *maternal marking,* as the experts called it, was by no means ancient or medieval; it was very much part of the modern world. Worried expectant mothers kept an eye out for danger. In order to protect themselves and their babies on the way, women watched the world and avoided threats. In the twentieth century, pregnant women received plenty of advice from doctors, reformers, and public health experts about the need for prenatal care in order to protect their babies. The duties of motherhood began long before birth. Although health experts might have belittled women's fears of maternal marking, the anxieties and insights of mothers contributed to producing scientific discoveries and political change. Women's consciousness of pregnancy and disability, and their practice of scrutinizing the body—most especially their own bodies during pregnancy and the bodies of their children—led to twentieth-century discoveries.

# ONE

# Observing Bodies

THIS CHAPTER IS ABOUT THE DISCOVERY OF A DISEASE. As soon as I write that, I want to fulfill the expectation—mine and my readers, I assume—to give a date and name a person who discovered this disease. However, this disease was discovered many times because discovery of disease was an ongoing process; a discovery had to be researched and confirmed, questioned, and discovered again to be believed. Older histories of diseases and conditions begin by recognizing the person who identified, described, and named the disease. In this chapter I rethink the medical discoveries, the processes of the production of scientific-medical knowledge, and the means by which that knowledge becomes concretized as fact. Discovering a disease entails identifying, defining, and naming the disease as well as winning acceptance of the evidence and the name. This disease was discovered—and named—multiple times throughout the nineteenth and twentieth centuries.

First identified and named in the nineteenth century, German measles was discovered again in the 1940s as a cause of birth defects. The disease came to be understood as a teratogen, an external environmental factor that harms the developing embryo and fetus in utero. Throughout the nineteenth century and much of the twentieth, no one in the medical world imagined such an association. Physicians did not regard the disease as dangerous. Indeed, one of the chief characteristics of German measles was its relatively minor symptoms compared with those of other contagious diseases. In 1941, an Australian specialist in ophthalmology announced his finding that when women contracted German measles during pregnancy, the disease severely harmed the developing fetus, causing congenital cataracts and frequently fatal deformities of the heart. Researchers soon knew that the infection during pregnancy also caused deafness and mental retardation in the fetus as well as miscarriages, stillbirths, and infant deaths. These insights rewrote medical and popular knowledge of German measles specifically and also reshaped the general scientific understanding of viruses, epidemics, and pregnancy. Now known in an entirely different way, German measles was essentially a new disease.

Medical discoveries about German measles in the nineteenth and twentieth centuries grew out of modern practices of observation of the body. As Foucault showed for the late eighteenth century, the rise of "the clinic" in Paris—or the practice of anatomizing a series of dead bodies and then looking at patients in hospitals for the signs of internal pathology—produced a new relationship between the physician and the sick as well as new knowledge and new social practices. In Foucault's analysis of the clinic, the sick (and the dead) became objects of analysis, passive subjects, means for producing information and categorization. Doctors and scientists at the Paris clinic now prioritized the medical eye and the gaze over other senses and other methods of gaining knowledge, such as the ear that listened to the patient's verbal report of her or his own body.[1] Yet the reliance upon listening did not disappear. The habit of observation by twentieth-century mothers and their communication with doctors were essential components of new medical discoveries about German measles. The German measles case shows that both modes—seeing the patient's body and listening to the words of the patient and family observers—coexisted and contributed to the major mid-twentieth-century discovery of rubella's danger to the fetus. This discovery of the 1940s built upon medical listening in a pediatric medical encounter. In collaboration, mothers and doctors produced new knowledge that transformed the significance and meaning of this disease.

Through the mother's observation of a sick body and her decision to show that body to a doctor, a patient is made. The situation surrounding German measles is an example of the central role played by mothers in producing patients, cases, data, and medical discoveries. My analysis of German measles returns another active observer and active intermediary to the process of modern scientific discovery: mothers, as the traditional and most intimate caretakers of the sick body, have been historical coworkers in the production of scientific knowledge.[2] As doctors began to regard a particular type of patient first as an example of a specific disease—as a clinical case—and then as one of many cases—as points in a spectrum of data—they produced new medical and scientific knowledge and made new discoveries in the nineteenth and twentieth centuries. Grounded first in gendered and maternally based observation, knowledge, and insight, physicians translated the sick individual into medical and scientific information and importance.

If we focus exclusively on an individual named as the "discoverer" of a disease, key components of that discovery are lost and left uncredited and untheorized. Both the process of translating gendered and home-based knowledge into scientific knowledge and the concomitant transformation of sick individuals into data and evidence are made invisible. The physical and intellectual work of unnamed female observers of the body was used, even required, but subtracted from publications, public honors, and historical memory of the scientific process of learning, interpretation, and discovery. Since these processes of biomedical discovery were both obscured at the time and then later perpetuated in the thinking habits of subsequent scientists and historians, the knowledge, labor, and civic commitment of women—often as mothers—to science and medicine have been buried and erased. Observing the body, analyzing symptoms, sharing knowledge, and sharing bodies and ideas with physicians and researchers for the development of science were not simple byproducts of maternal responsibility to care for family health. Rather, this active observation and involvement in the development of medical knowledge was a gendered civic and scientific duty that twentieth-century women embraced and upon which medical, scientific, and modern public health advances and practices depended.

DIAGNOSIS. WHAT IS THIS RASH?

Noting the symptoms of rash and fever alone does not describe a disease. Nineteenth-century observers readily saw that there were two, three, or more diseases that included rash and fever and resembled or combined measles and scarlet fever. The question was whether there was something that was distinct from measles and scarlet fever.[3] Although German scientists agreed by the early 1800s that rotheln was a distinct disease, British and American physicians with a range of interests, including dermatology, children, and military medicine, continued to investigate the question throughout the nineteenth century. Discovery of disease was not a moment but rather a process. The medical literature on rotheln did not deal with any inherent danger of the disease itself. Nor did it detail the disease's treatment. Instead, the literature addressed diagnostic differentiation and naming.

Naming a disease is an essential component of diagnosis and treatment. Diseases have many names, however; and naming precisely what condition someone had was difficult in the nineteenth century when there were so many different names used by English physicians for red rashes. Rotheln, rosalia idiopathica, rubeola notha, epidemic roseola, rosella, rosalia, and rubeola, as well as false measles and secondary measles,[4] spurious measles, and rose-rash,[5] were all in use for this disease. It might also be named rosalia spuria or scarlatinea hybrida or dubbed a "bastard" or "hybrid" form of scarlet fever or measles.[6] Reflecting its mildness, the disease was also called "very mild scarlatina."[7] Surely there were also other names used among families, neighbors, and local healers that did not get preserved in the medical literature. A single unifying name for a disease is a modern device. It is a sign of the standardization of knowledge across regions, languages, sciences, and individual experiences. By the end of the nineteenth century, medical researchers had agreed upon a single name, yet multiple names persisted, and new names proliferated with the discoveries of the mid-twentieth century.

Throughout the nineteenth century numerous physicians tried to explain the differentiation among measles, scarlet fever, and German measles. Some declared the diagnosis obvious, but the number of doctors who attempted to describe the disease demonstrated that diagnosis was not simple. William Squire of London observed that it was not at all easy to distinguish this disease from measles by looking at the rash alone. Reviewing a series of cases and carefully noting the color of the rash, the swelling, the condition of the rest of the skin, the day of the rash's appearance, the tongue, and any fever, Squire argued that this was not a mixture of measles and scarlet fever but instead "a specific disease, having its own natural history and laws."[8] "It is most difficult to describe the difference in books," observed another doctor, "but when the diseases are seen in company, the distinction is easy and pronounced." However, another colleague disagreed. "Experienced practitioners," he reported, "have great difficulty in coming to a conclusion" about such cases.[9] The confusion continued for decades. "The more one studied these exanthemata," one physician admitted, "the more perplexing is their differentiation."[10]

Dr. Henry Veale, a physician for the British Royal Artillery, weighed in on these pressing questions with an epidemiological study of an 1866 epidemic in a boarding school in India. Veale tracked cases and carefully differentiated among three diseases—measles, scarlet fever, and rotheln—to prove that rotheln was a distinct disease. Dr. Veale produced a table that outlined the symptoms for each of the three diseases. He differentiated among the three related diseases by incubation period, the type of rash and how long it lasted, and fever and how long it lasted as well as by coughing, vomiting, and sore throat. Even the rash of this single disease, he suggested, varied. In this small epidemic, some of the patients had a "dusky red colour" rash like measles while others, he noted, had a "bright rose" rash like scarlet fever. Clearly, the rash alone could not distinguish one disease from the others. He noted too that the rash's "hue was most vivid on the first and second days and [that] when the face, body, arms, and legs were attacked in succession, the eruption faded in the same order." The number of days that the rash lasted was one indicator of the diagnosis: rotheln rash faded on the third day, scarlet fever faded on the fifth day, and measles faded on the seventh day. A sore throat was typical with scarlet fever, unusual with measles, and occasional with rotheln.[11] These fine distinctions were based on familiarity with all of the diseases.

Veale's analysis and differentiation of the diseases were definitive in the history of German measles. His evidence took advantage of an 1866 epidemic at a Bombay boarding school. Through careful differentiation of the symptoms, collection of data, and the physical tracking of people through time and space, Veale concluded that this disease (rotheln) was contagious and a specific disease independent of scarlet fever and measles. He described thirty "cases," boys and girls between six and eighteen years old, who all "presented the disease in the most distinct form . . . an eruption on the face, arms, and body, very similar to that of measles." Yet the first case, a twelve-year-old girl, had already had measles. Veale closely tracked the chronological appearance of the disease and mapped the location of the children and their beds in the school. When the first child became ill, she was isolated for a week. The next case was another girl who slept only two beds away from the first. The fourth case was a six-year-old boy, but the doctor learned that he had slept near his sick sister and then had taken the rash to the boys' dorms. Since nearly half of the children had already had measles, Veale knew this epidemic could not be measles. Contracting measles a second time was rare. Since scarlet fever had never been encountered in the Bombay presidency, and none of the children showed the "strawberry" tongue of scarlet fever, he ruled out scarlet fever.[12]

The school children in Bombay were not only regarded as sick patients; for Veale and other doctors like him, they also became objects of science, cases that produced new knowledge in the British empire. School, an institution that massed children together, served as a space in which to see disease upon bodies and observe its course over time. Children in boarding schools, orphanages, and other institutions provided opportunities for scientists to plot the disease on individual bodies, to plot the movement of the disease on a map as it moved among individuals, and to plot it on graphs and tables that categorized symptoms, histories, and types of individuals. Young students served as sources for scientific observers interested in working out the problem of German measles and other infectious diseases. The school, like the hospital, and, as we shall see, the military training camp, all served as a clinical laboratory for nineteenth- and twentieth-century medical advances.

The concentration of people who suffered the disease consequences of their massing provided the means for research and for finding the solutions to protect them from the disease-ridden—and at times deadly—results of their congregation. Physicians attending children's institutions—like Dr. Veale in Bombay, Dr. May Michael in Chicago, and Dr. Shuttleworth in Lancaster, England—had a better vantage point for observing, distinguishing, and understanding diseases in general, including German measles. As Dr. Shuttleworth remarked at an international medical congress, it is only upon seeing a "*series* of cases . . . that one becomes convinced of the distinctive character of rotheln." His position as medical officer of an institution with five hundred children made him acutely aware of the differences among these diseases.[13] While others struggled to differentiate and diagnose this disease, Dr. May Michael declared the diagnosis "not difficult" in 1907. Describing an epidemic in a children's institution, she listed the quick onset of the disease, its mildness, the lack of respiratory symptoms, and the look of the eruptions, which all "stamp the disease as rubella."[14] Sick children at home also provided clinical opportunities for their medical parents. In the intimacy and amid the daily routine of home, doctors learned, for example, that a rash need not be apparent for this disease to spread to others.[15]

Veale and other interested physicians were immersed in one important aspect of the epidemiological and scientific work of the nineteenth century: differentiating and identifying specific diseases with their "own natural history and laws."[16] This work was part of the intellectual transition toward disease specificity and etiological specificity and away from notions that diseases arose from miasma, from bad and smelly air, from changes in the weather, or from individual internal physiological imbalances. Furthermore, in this new thinking, disease affected all bodies in the same way—regardless of region, national heritage, race, or sex—and all bodies were to be treated in the same way rather than as unique individuals.[17] Veale observed children in far-flung parts of the British empire to address questions of great interest to physicians and scientists at home.[18] Bacteriologists focused on identifying specific germs that caused specific diseases. Germ theory eventually overturned scientific, medical, and popular thinking about disease causation and prevention and transformed medical practices. The experimental and intellectual work of Robert Koch and Louis Pasteur is well known.[19] Physicians in everyday practice too, however, contributed to this intellectual transformation toward disease specificity from a different direction. As clinicians, they observed patients, collected minute data on those patients, and observed in institutions and in their private practices the progress of a disease and its movement from person to person. With those observations, they began producing a science of diseases that regarded them as separate, specific, "natural" entities, each with its own "laws." This was not mere taxonomy but rather a sea change in the thinking of medical men and in the public too regarding the causes of disease and the appropriate responses to them.

Finally, Veale took the occasion to address the problem of naming. Not only did the proliferation of rashes make diagnosis difficult; so too did the multiple names assigned to the condition. "The name of the disease is always a matter of some importance," asserted Veale. "It should be short for the sake of convenience in writing, and euphonious for ease in pronunciation."[20] "*Rotheln* is harsh and foreign to our ears," he continued. "I therefore venture to propose *Rubella* as a substitute for *Rotheln*."[21] The proposed name took care of the problem of having to read and speak German for both doctors and their patients while simultaneously sounding like both Latin and English. It still hinted at a red rash and an association with measles (generally called *rubeola*). Veale's suggested new melodious name did not register, however, with English-language physicians writing about the disease at the same time.[22] It would be many decades before *rubella* became generally used within the medical profession and a century before the general public became familiar with this name.

Out of all of the various names, the one that came to predominate was a simple one, *German measles*. The name arose in the midst of an 1871 epidemic in Massachusetts as a way to name the disease and distinguish it from the other epidemic rashes of measles and scarlet fever. Dr. A. H. Nichols "hit upon a name which was readily accepted by the laity," reported a Harvard colleague. Instead of using the hard-to-pronounce German word *rotheln,* the doctor simply dubbed the measles-like disease "German." The name worked. When an epidemic of a rash "of no very great severity" ran through Roxbury, Massachusetts, in 1871, medical attendants found themselves confused. Realizing that people who came down with this rash included those who had already had measles and scarlet fever as well as those who had never had either confirmed that this rash was a specific disease. Dr. B. E. Cotting, a Harvard man who reported on the spring 1871 epidemic and an earlier 1853 epidemic, claimed that the new name of *German measles* "originate[d] with us." Apparently a Scottish physician had also coined the term *German measles.*[23] As Veale had observed several years earlier, the English-speaking world found the name *rotheln* "harsh and foreign." Rather than adopting Veale's term, *rubella,* however, more than one English-speaking doctor had come up with the more casual *German measles.*

The new term retained both the association with and the distinction from *measles,* but it now appeared to be associated with a foreign country. However, adding the word *German* to the disease's name in order to avoid having to pronounce a German word (but still giving German science credit for identifying the disease) led to new confusions. Another American doctor, J. Lewis Smith, physician to New York's Infant's Hospital, who wrote about an 1873 epidemic, seemed to think that the disease was a foreign one, new to the shores of the United States. He described the disease as occurring "on the continent, especially in Germany" and rare. Indeed, he believed the New York City epidemic of 1873 to be "the first" outbreak of the disease on the American continent. His older colleagues had seen nothing like it in twenty years and believed it to be "an entirely new disease with us."[24]

Clearly, the 1873 cases of rotheln that Smith saw in New York City were not the first on the continent or in the United States, for Cotting had identified such cases in an epidemic twenty years earlier and in Massachusetts only two years before. On my own initial reading of Smith's article in an 1873 issue of the *Archives of Dermatology,* I thought, "He's wrong; it was not the first outbreak of German measles in the United States; he didn't know about the earlier epidemics and publications." I now see that the Smith report can be read in several ways. First, although he referred to "foreign" medical literatures, Dr. Smith had not read all of the most recent publications on the subject in the American medical literature. The full range of medical journal articles may not have been easily available or read during the nineteenth century. When scholars now analyze previous scientific and intellectual developments, the uneven availability of materials should be kept in mind. Now, at the start of the twenty-first century, through the valuable *Index-Catalogue of the Library of the Surgeon-General's Office,* which indexes medical articles from around the world, and the rich journal collections preserved in university libraries, I have better access to the full range of nineteenth-century medical publications than did most physicians and scientists of the time. Finally, Smith's remarks point to the localism of medical knowledge. None of the New York doctors had previously encountered this disease, and apparently they had neither heard Cotting's 1853 talk nor read his paper published two years before the New York epidemic. It is highly likely that the disease had appeared in years past among New Yorkers. The Smith report's conclusion that rotheln had *not* previously been evident in New York probably occurred because no one had recognized it earlier.[25] There may have been "double diseases" or "hybrid measles" but not rotheln.

Although *German measles* became the standard name for the disease among English speakers, some strenuously objected to it on both scientific and nationalist grounds. Dr. Mulheron called it "positively misleading." "Rotheln," he reminded his colleagues, "merely indicates the existence of little red spots." "German measles," in contrast, he pointed out, "implies a modification of measles through some peculiarity of the German temperament, diet, climate or mode of life, a supposition which is, of course, ridiculous."[26] The appellation *German* brought out both nationalist hostility and pride. Dr. Klein proclaimed *rotheln* to be a fine name. "*German measles,*" he declared, "is [an] unwarrantable American fabrication."[27] To the contrary, another medical observer claimed that the French or English equally deserved credit for identifying the disease.[28]

In 1881, Chicago, Michigan, Missouri, Indiana, and Nebraska reported local epidemics of rotheln (or, as its reporter observed, "German measles, rubeola, measlings, spurious measles, false measles, bastard measles, *rubeola sine catarrho*"). Yet the question of whether this was a separate disease or a mild version of scarlatina or measles and the matter of its name still vexed physicians. "If this be an independent disease, as I believe it is, the first thing we want," Dr. Charles Warrington Earle of Chicago remarked, "is a name upon which we can all agree, pronounce, and understand."[29] In 1881, two international congresses of physicians confronted the problem, declared that the disease existed, differentiated it from measles and scarlet fever, and agreed upon a name. It should be called *rubella.*[30] Despite the international attempts to control the name and the medical understanding of the disease, doubt, confusion, and a variety of names persisted among physicians and the public.[31]

In the midst of the confusion, however, doctors agreed that mildness was a characteristic feature of German measles. "The constitutional symptoms were so mild," Dr. May Michael observed, "that it was difficult to keep the children in bed." In another thirteen-page article on a local epidemic, a single sentence addressed how to care for the person sick with this disease: "Rotheln . . . requires very little treatment. I commonly give small doses of quinine to my patients," ended Smith, physician of New York. "Happily," wrote another, "the disorder is in itself an unimportant one, in that it perhaps never destroys life." Another physician labeled it "an inoffensive complaint."[32]

Despite its mild nature, German measles worried doctors and mothers alike because of its more dangerous, and sometimes fatal, associates, measles and scarlet fever. The correct diagnosis of German measles mattered. "The physician's error in diagnosis," warned one observer, "may be the means of spreading measles or scarlatina throughout a family or an institution."[33] The rash might be confused with smallpox as well. "It was probably very fortunate," a Detroit physician dryly observed in 1881, that German measles "prevailed here before the occurrence of the late small-pox epidemic." Otherwise, he was sure, some of the victims of German measles "would have been sent to the pest house." He told of an infant with eczema whom "certain eminent professors" had diagnosed as having smallpox. "The infant escaped the infected lazaretto, and probably certain death," he continued, "because by mere chance she afterwards fell into the hands of a practitioner who happened not to believe that every eruption during the prevalence of small-pox is necessarily small-pox."[34] As this story underscored, the safety and survival of the sick depended on accurate differentiation of diseases and diagnoses. Thankfully for the child, according to this doctor's story, more skeptical and careful physicians read the rash correctly. This doctor's point was not only about smallpox versus German measles versus eczema but also about competitors and status within the medical profession.

It is unlikely that the doctor had seen the baby girl "by mere chance," however. Instead, a skeptical parent, most likely the mother, had made sure that another doctor saw their daughter to get a second (and preferred) opinion. Parents did not passively follow the directives of medical experts but instead followed their own readings of their children's bodies and medical science. Parental observation, diagnostic skill, and skepticism became "mere chance" in this doctor's account. At a time of intense competition among physicians, parents and patients had a wide variety of doctors from which to choose and actively sought different medical opinions.[35]

Differentiating between the dangerous diseases of scarlet fever and measles and the harmless German measles was difficult, however. Physicians continued to publish long descriptions of their observations of dozens and hundreds of cases; they described in great detail how one might distinguish this disease from its "half-sister" of measles or scarlet fever. All agreed on the presence of a red rash (in most cases); all agreed on the disease's kinship with measles and scarlet fever, but authors varied on the size and shape of the rash, the timing of its appearance, the existence or lack of fever or sore throat, and the incubation period. The best way to determine whether a patient had German measles, it appeared, was knowing if the person had already had measles and scarlet fever. Following the accepted rule that once a person had experienced these diseases, she or he gained immunity and could not contract them again, a doctor could conclude, through the process of elimination, that the patient now faced German measles. Additionally, if the doctor (or the mother) knew well what measles and scarlet fever rashes looked like, then he or she would be able to identify German measles. One of the most succinct descriptions of the disease and its diagnosis characterized it this way: "a disease in which the red spots are smaller than measles and larger than scarlet fever."[36] As these confusing comparative descriptions show, parents and doctors might easily mix up and misdiagnose these diseases.

## IN THE NEWS AND IN THE MILITARY

As a mild disease, German measles was hardly newsworthy in the ways that other, more deadly diseases could be. Bubonic plague epidemics in San Francisco, smallpox in Milwaukee, typhoid and "Typhoid Mary" in New York, tuberculosis in Atlanta, leprosy in Hawaii and among Spanish-American war veterans, and other frightening diseases all filled newspapers at the turn of the twentieth century.[37] Nonetheless, because it appeared in epidemic form, German measles did show up in newspapers in the sections dedicated to sports, entertainment, and schools. The manager of the Washington (DC) Senators baseball team worried about the game against the Boston Red Sox when he learned that his players had been exposed to German measles.[38] Track stars, college basketball players, and rowers were reported stricken with the disease; the tours of opera singers were interrupted.[39] When elementary schools and colleges—including Harvard, with its "rich college boys"—periodically experienced an epidemic, they closed their doors, quarantined the sick, and cancelled classes, shows, parties, and other mass events in order to control the epidemic's spread.[40] As one doctor observed, "German measles is not a serious disease, but it is certainly a great nuisance, particularly in an institution."[41] German measles quickly spread among groups, infecting those who had not encountered it before. The sick did not generate enormous worry, but they nonetheless required nursing attention and isolation.

German measles also posed problems for the military. Bringing together hundreds and thousands of new troops in training camps or at central stations to be shipped out to foreign lands created ideal conditions for the spread of contagious diseases. If one man showed up sick with German measles or another contagious disease, it could easily spread among others who had never been exposed to it. Although soldiers were not lost to this disease, they could be laid low, and troop deployment could be delayed for weeks. For instance, one British army garrison had to deal with a German measles epidemic that ran from February through June of 1913. More than two hundred soldiers came down with German measles. Measles and scarlet fever also struck at the same time. As the soldiers were isolated and treated, the two hundred men offered their doctors another opportunity for analyzing and differentiating diseases. The observing physician used a prevailing metaphor when his words likened the disease to a military attack. During the "invasion period," Major J. G. McNaught observed, the sick felt "out of sorts" for a day or two. For many, the first indication of illness was a rash.[42] Some draftees also endured acute arthritis and joint pain.[43] Although German measles was not the most common disease to strike the U.S. army during World War I— influenza and venereal diseases topped the list—it nevertheless accounted for many days lost. Army hospitals admitted more than 17,000 soldiers for German measles and estimated "211,645 days lost from duty."[44]

Soldiers also spread infectious diseases to citizens of nearby towns. During World War I, the congregation of draftees and National Guard troops "caused epidemics" in the United States. Failure to diagnose diseases, differentiate among them, and isolate cases increased the numbers. German measles and measles both arose at Camp Pike in Arkansas and spread to North Little Rock and Little Rock, resulting in hundreds of cases in both towns. At its peak, Camp Pike hospitalized more than 1,200 men with measles and German measles.[45]

War contributed to the understanding of this disease and even to its (re)naming. During World War I and World War II, the disease took on a more ominous and suspect cast. Jokes about "German" measles indicated the nation's anxiety. Nationalist hostilities during wartime infuse a culture, and diseases and epidemics may also be interpreted through the lens of war. In this case, the disease represented an actual enemy: Germany. German measles in wartime represented war as personalized—the enemy, insidious. Oftentimes German measles appeared as a joke, as when the Beloit basketball player about to go to France in World War I "succumbed to his first German attack" and was quarantined with German measles.[46] Presumably, upon recovery the patriot would be even more determined to get the enemy that had attacked him first. Reporters enjoyed the wordplay of linking disease with the enemy, inventing headlines that declared, for example, that German measles "invaded" the Brooklyn Navy Yard and writing a lead sentence that observed that the navy men had "had their first taste of Teutonic frightfulness." Although the *New York Times* reported on at least twenty cases, doctors downplayed the importance of the disease and explained that this situation was to be expected when the military brought together so many men from different regions. "German measles is an unimportant affliction," observed New York City's health commissioner, "and nothing to make a fuss about."[47]

Other jokes pointed to people's fear of betrayal. A rash might reveal a person to be a traitor. A collection of "Bright Sayings of Children" told this anecdote: "The mother asked the doctor what the trouble was, and he replied, 'German measles.' After the doctor had gone, Bud . . . said, 'Mama, don't tell anyone what the doctor said.' "[48] The child understood the political implications of association with "the Germans" and wanted the cause of his rash to be kept a secret. Women war workers, according to one report, were "perturbed by suggestions of pro-Germanism in their midst. . . . Measles has broken out. Miss Marion Curtis has developed the 'German' kind, to the horror of her friends."[49] The legal surveillance of and violent physical attacks on German immigrants and citizens and the attacks on all things German at the time of World War I were, of course, no joke at all. German measles jokes revealed anxieties about any perceived association with the enemy.

By World War II, the disease had been entirely renamed and made patriotic. German measles was now dubbed "the Liberty itch" by at least one newspaper columnist and "Victory measles" by patriots in New Jersey.[50] Political cartoonists for the newspapers again took the opportunity to joke about disease, fear of the enemy, and the fear of being seen as a traitor. In one, a mother peered at her daughter's speckled face and cried, "Heavens above! I believe you're coming down with German measles, and like as not, the airplane factory will think your pop is a Trojan horse or something and fire him. Oh, you naughty girl!"[51] In this vignette, the child with German measles threatened not the family's health but rather its social, political, and financial security. A bit in a 1941 *Chicago Daily Tribune* reported, "An 11 year old who was informed that her cousin had come down with German measles promptly asked her mother if she would break out with swastikas."[52] The idea of a political insignia marking the body as disease is funny, but it also provoked nervous laughter. Were there Nazis or Hitler supporters in the United States? Could the body expose inner thoughts and political commitments? Paralleling the fear that a pregnant woman's thoughts and emotions might mark her baby, the joke indicates the deep sense that imperfect, marked bodies might be signs of bad thoughts or betrayal.

As the world entered war again, German measles reappeared among the troops and in training camps around the globe. In New Zealand and in the United States, German measles delayed troop deployment.[53] Military training camps quarantined their new soldiers and shut down all social activities, including church.[54] A "severe" epidemic of German measles arose in 1940 among troops in Australia and spread when soldiers went home to wives and families.[55] As the United States entered the war, the problem quickly became apparent at home. The California Department of Public Health, for instance, reported in 1942 that the number of cases of childhood infectious diseases had nearly doubled from the previous year. The jump to almost 200,000 cases by May was attributed to the new concentrations of military men and defense industry workers, many "from rural areas who had not been previously exposed to communicable diseases." Measles, mumps, chicken pox, and German measles were all up.[56]

Babies also arrived in greater numbers in 1942. "Chicago Births Rise 2.6 Per Cent in First 6 Months," announced a *Chicago Tribune* headline. With the Great Depression ending as a war economy geared up, young couples married and had babies. The same health report also noted that "the sharpest increase shown by health figures was in cases of German measles; 826 for the first six months of 1941 and 4,417 for this year."[57] With almost seven hundred cases per month—a number that approached the six-month total of the previous year—it was evident that Chicago was experiencing another epidemic of German measles. The epidemic, however, did not get a newspaper headline. Neither the emerging "baby boom" nor the damaging effects of German measles on babies had yet been identified and named for the public.

With physicians and nurses serving in the military and a limited number of doctors available on the home front, mothers went to doctors only when necessary. Seeing that something was not right with their newborns' eyes, several Australian parents brought their infants to eye specialist and surgeon Dr. Norman Gregg, an ophthalmologist at the Royal Alexandar Hospital for Children in Sydney. Both of her baby's eyes, one mother told the ophthalmologist, had "had conjunctivitis at birth." Several weeks later, "she noticed a white mass in the left pupil."[58] The parents of another baby had seen "a scum over each eye at birth."[59] The infants had "unusual" cataracts that required surgery, a rare condition. Child after child, case after case appeared in Dr. Gregg's office in 1941. Gregg described the unique condition of the infant patients: when a child's pupil was in its normal state, "the opacities filled the entire area. After dilation, the opacities appeared densely white—sometimes quite pearly—in the central area." In older babies (over three months), the eye moved in a "jerky, purposeless nature."[60]

As always, in doctors' offices, clinics, and hospitals, mothers and children congregated in waiting rooms. There, mothers inevitably said hello, admired babies, and compared stories, interpretations, and theories. One afternoon two mothers "chatted" and "expressed concern about the rubella they had had early in their pregnancies." Now Gregg had a "clue."[61] To find additional patients, Gregg queried individual colleagues about whether they had seen infants with cataracts and soon sent a questionnaire to the entire Australian medical profession. More cases were found. Upon physical examination of the children with cataracts (or during autopsies), Gregg and his colleagues often found a less visible, internal rubella-related defect as well, heart disease.[62] Gregg eventually amassed the data to make his case: German measles during early pregnancy caused congenital cataracts and heart lesions in the newborn. Gregg based his conclusions on seventy-eight cases, which included thirteen of his own patients. There were fifteen deaths in the group. Gregg presented his findings at the October 1941 meeting of the Ophthalmological Society.[63]

When local newspapers reported Gregg's findings, several women who had read the news immediately put two and two together with their own pregnancies and children. Three mothers personally picked up a phone and called Dr. Gregg to add to his discovery: German measles during pregnancy appeared to cause deafness as well as the eye and heart problems that the doctor had identified. "During the following week," Gregg later said when describing the progress of his learning about the results of maternal rubella, "I had telephone calls from three mothers, informing me that they had suffered German measles early in pregnancy; each thought that her child was deaf, and each wished to know if this deafness could have resulted from the infection."[64] Gregg paid attention to the mothers on the phone. He and the other Australian researchers soon confirmed that deafness was one of the major results of maternal rubella.[65]

Dr. Norman McAlister Gregg had made an important discovery: a virus, long regarded as minor, was teratogenic. The news was startling. The notion that a virus could harm the developing fetus through the body of the pregnant woman was unexpected. Dr. Gregg's discovery transformed knowledge about German measles, highlighted a new characteristic of viruses, and revealed a heretofore unsuspected threat to pregnant women.[66] Australian Nobel prize winner Macfarlane Burnet declared that "the recognition of the consequences of fetal infection with rubella was the most important contribution ever made to medicine in Australia."[67] Gregg was an extraordinary individual who pursued a problem that other physicians and scientists had not noticed. A good listener who believed mothers, Gregg investigated their suspicions and theories about the disease. Gregg carried out a careful epidemiological study and presented a thorough and thoughtful analysis of his findings. Of the epidemic that the mothers had experienced, Gregg remarked that he had never "seen German measles of such severity and accompanied by such severe complications: . . . the swelling of the glands of the neck, the sore throat, the involvement of the wrist and ankle joints . . . were all very pronounced." He left open the question of whether the mothers had been infected with an unusual form of the disease, possibly in combination with a sore throat coming out of the military camps.[68] Without Gregg, it could well be that the teratogenic effects of German measles might never have been discovered in Australia in 1941 or during the 1940s at all.

The discovery was not Gregg's alone, however. It was mothers who made the intellectual leap that associated German measles during their own pregnancies with the health problems that they later observed in their children. Mothers first thought aloud about German measles during pregnancy and later when noticing eye problems in their infants; a second set of mothers connected their having had the disease during pregnancy with deafness in their toddlers. It was mothers who brought their children to see Gregg and other doctors, who responded with alacrity when asked for a detailed history, who read the newspapers and made connections between diseases during their pregnancies and the health status of their babies. Mothers observed and made the link. Doctors listened. These Australian mothers cared for their children and observed their bodies and their development. It was a mother's job to feed, nurse, clothe, and care for her children. It was also a mother's job to notice potential health problems, to take her observations seriously, to investigate, and to go to experts for help, information, and medical care.[69] Those experts included other mothers, maternal advice literature, neighbors, druggists, public health authorities, social workers, and nurses as well as physicians and medical specialists like Dr. Gregg.

Mothers provided the data. Early reports and tabulation of cases on the effects of rubella during pregnancy were peppered with references to mothers and their observations of their children. "The cataract was noted by the mother," Gregg reported in his first presentation of his findings at the October 1941 Ophthalmological Society meeting. ". . . . In another case the mother gave a history. . . ."[70] As Gregg described the series of cases, unnamed mothers appeared for a moment now and again. As he explained his method of looking for additional cases of this rare condition, mothers again appeared in tables detailing maternal histories. "In each new case," Gregg reported learning, "the mother had suffered from that disease early in her pregnancy, most frequently in the first or second month. In some cases she had not at that time yet realized she was pregnant."[71]

As researchers investigated whether German measles caused deafness, mothers' memories and observations again documented the connection. Parents identified deafness at a later age, when the children were two and a half years old or older. When parents recognized a problem—such as delay in a child's beginning to talk—doctors discovered hearing loss. At the point that "speech development is obviously retarded," observed one expert, "the anxious parents seek advice, and then the true situation, the presence of deafness . . . is revealed."[72] Evidence was also noted in the following: "Case Number 78. Mother believes that child is almost 'stone deaf.' May hear a tray being dropped but not motor-cars, aeroplanes, telephones, or alarm clocks. . . . Case Number 104. When the child was aged 10 months, the mother noticed that he did not appear to hear the sound of cutlery being dropped." Another mother reported that her "child did not cry normally—had a sort of squeal." At almost three years old, he was found to be deaf.[73]

Deafness was suspected and proved through everyday life—in interactions with parents and family, in responses to everyday sounds. What the babies heard and did not hear, what parents and medical observers expected, these reports show, was context and time specific. By World War II, the everyday sounds that a child should have noticed and reacted to included not only the words *mum* and *dad* and the sounds of the kitchen—the movement of the wood stove door, falling forks and knives—but also the sounds of modern means of communication and transportation: cars, airplanes, telephones, and radios. Today, one would expect to also include televisions and computers. The turning of wagon wheels and the mooing and crowing of farm animals were not among the expected sound repertoire of these modern, urban babies. Nor was the city clock or church bells. Hearing had become a particularly important sense during World War II and crucial to survival. Sirens and knocks on the door warned people of air raids and speeding police cars and fire trucks. Unable to hear the warnings, the hearing-impaired child might be left in danger.[74] In this culture, deafness could be perceived not only as the loss of a sense but also as a condition that endangered deaf people themselves.

One pediatrician, inspired by Gregg's queries and findings, reported what he described as "typical German measles backwardness." Dr. Donald Vickery identified a series of problems different from those first identified by Gregg: the baby "is not yet speaking"; the toddler "makes no attempt to put sentences together." Another parent "complained" of—rather, she observed, worried, and reported—her baby's "sleeplessness since birth." The child lay "awake for hours playing at night." Others believed their children were not growing properly and were "deaf," "backward," or "a problem child." Based on observations of fourteen children under his care, Vickery described "typical German measles backwardness" as a combination of "so-called deaf-mutism," microcephaly (in ten), "general instability of their nervous systems, lying awake for hours at night, showing a failure to concentrate and taking a peculiar, fleeting, prying interest in things."[75] None of the children had cataracts or vision problems. Vickery added an important dimension to the growing knowledge about the effects of maternal rubella. His term for describing these conditions, *backwardness,* however, did not become part of the standard medical vocabulary for what by the 1960s came to be called *congenital rubella syndrome* or *CRS.*

The male, educated, professional, medical scientists' names appear on the published papers, and some of them are still remembered; the mothers in this story of the discovery of the teratogenic effects of a virus are anonymous. Yet embedded within each of these reports and further embedded within the raw data itself are parents, and mothers in particular. As mothers brought their babies and toddlers to the experts, as they answered questions, recalled illnesses, observed events, told stories, and filled out forms, the details they shared were transformed into data. Data was amassed and a discovery made and confirmed by other scientists. The individual mothers and children disappeared into memory, story, histories, cases, and data. The point here is to recognize the complexity of the scientific, social, and gendered process of "discovery." This discovery required visual observation and careful listening, insight, confidence, and collaboration among physicians and parents. Gregg himself recognized this truth and singled out parents for appreciation. He and his colleagues were "particularly gratified," he remarked, "by the extreme interest and keenness shown by parents, who are particularly anxious to assist in every possible way."[76]

In his first report of his unexpected discovery, Gregg considered the prognosis. He spoke of the children and the surgeries and technologies that might become available for their care as well as the problem of prevention. "It is difficult to forecast the future for these unfortunate babies," he began. "We cannot at this stage be sure that there are not other defects present which are not evident now but which may show up as development proceeds. The cardiac condition also makes the prognosis doubtful. One baby [who] had survived two operations some months ago suddenly died quite recently at the age of seven months." If these cases "are the result of infection of the mother by 'German measles,'" Gregg asked, "what can we do to prevent a repetition of the tragedy in any future epidemics? . . . The only sure treatment available," he answered, "is that of prophylaxis." Gregg called for educating the public about the newfound danger of this mild disease and working to stop the spread of epidemics to expectant mothers: "We must recognize and teach the potential dangers of such an epidemic . . . and do all in our power to prevent its spread and particularly to guard the young married woman from the risk of infection."[77]

"What can we do to prevent a repetition of the tragedy in any future epidemics?" Gregg asked. Until its final paragraphs, this first paper on the harm caused by German measles is a scientific description of a disease and its manifestations and an epidemiological report. Then, in the final paragraphs of his talk, Gregg alluded to an emotional response to the effects of this epidemic described in a series of seventy-eight "cases." These seventy-eight cases represented seventy-eight children, seventy-eight women, their pregnancies, their babies, and their families. In calling the effects of this epidemic of German measles a "tragedy," Gregg alluded to the sorrows, suffering, and pain felt by parents and their children and expressed empathy for them. At the same time, the existence of a child born with congenital malformations, whose life was expected to be shortened and compromised, was understood, in common thought, to be a "tragedy."

As Gregg and his Australian colleagues collected clinical cases and investigated his initial findings, they quickly identified not only the symptoms of congenital rubella syndrome but also the social issues associated with it. By the time that the children first identified as affected by maternal rubella were two and three years old, physicians were expressing concern about their educational future (no doubt echoing a concern raised by parents). Gregg's prognosis for the children's futures considered not only the children's survival or the shape of their bodies but also the prospects for their education. Deaf and blind children, physicians and state education officials expected, could be educated and capable of economic independence in adulthood. The prospects for the "ineducables," in contrast, were not optimistic. The need to provide for their care was "urgent." Gregg advocated for early "training," especially for the "deaf mutes." Education should begin, he believed, at a young age and in the home. Those who would be teaching the children at home—in other words, the mothers—should "receive proper instruction." The Department of Education of New South Wales rapidly took up the question. It formed a study committee and planned to assess the educational possibilities for each affected child. Notably, in 1944, Australian education officials began planning for the schooling of children affected by rubella long before they entered school.[78] Nevertheless, one expert observed, "The training and teaching of a deaf-mute child are extremely slow and difficult."[79]

Furthermore, this host of medical and social issues affected the family as a whole. Gregg expressed particular concern for the mothers: "In some cases the strain imposed on the mother in caring for the child is more than she should be expected, or permitted, to endure." These words of caution and concern for the mother, like the very discovery of the effects of rubella on the developing fetus, grew out of Gregg's careful listening to mothers in his practice and, presumably, from his own observations of their distress as they coped with babies who slept little, with surgeries, with the difficulty of communication, and with social isolation. "There is a very grave risk not only of undermining the health of the mother," he commented, "but also of ruining the whole atmosphere of the home and disrupting the family. In such cases it is considered that the only solution is to place the child in an appropriate institution."[80]

Institutionalization for the severely retarded was the standard advice of the time. Decisions about whether or not to institutionalize were neither exclusively medical nor exclusively personal, but social and cultural. The disabled child was understood to be a threat to the family as a whole. In the United States in the 1940s and 1950s, new admissions of mentally retarded children to public institutions doubled. Half of all parents of such children reported being advised by doctors to "immediately" institutionalize their children. Many doctors strongly urged parents to separate themselves from their newborns at the time of delivery. Family members, clergy, and the community at large added to the pressure. Families that resisted these pessimistic judgments and resisted placing their children often found that as the children got older, they eventually reached a point at which they felt they had no choice but to place their children in an institution for their education and care.[81] Rearing and teaching a child with sensory losses required special skills as well as moral support and social services. When institutionalization was the norm and support for rearing a disabled child at home minimal, families found it difficult to do otherwise. If moral support, material help, and services did not exist and responsibility fell on the mother, then mothers' distress was going to be a normal and socially produced outcome of having a disabled child, and institutionalization was often the answer.

Gregg's medical colleagues in Australia "congratulated" him on his significant findings and jumped into German measles research with alacrity.[82] They soon corroborated Gregg's findings, but the medical profession elsewhere in the world accepted his discovery more slowly. An abstract in the premier British medical journal, the *Lancet,* on the Australian research pointed to a series of problems in the case presented by Swan et al. in the *Australian Medical Journal.* The unidentified author found the study to be poorly designed, and thus "safe conclusions" could not be made about whether rubella "during pregnancy affect[ed] the chances of the baby being born with congenital defects." The Australian research lacked data for babies born without abnormalities, how these data were collected was unclear, and the very diagnosis of rubella itself, for this *Lancet* critic, was a question mark. Although there was no evidence of incorrect diagnosis, he claimed that "the doubt must remain, for even fever clinicians find rubella difficult to diagnose with certainty." The difficulty of differentiating rubella from measles and scarlet fever that had produced numerous medical articles in the nineteenth century now raised questions about Gregg's findings. As controlled clinical research trials became the new norm in the 1940s, this scientist regarded the Australian findings as dubious because the researchers had failed to meet high research standards.

"More extensive and better controlled observations," he insisted, "must be made before we can be sure of it." Further research, this writer urged, was needed before Gregg's case was "proved."[83]

The *Lancet* reviewer raised further doubts by pointing to the beliefs of generations of mothers. "The lay public," he remarked, "have always held that congenital malformations have an extrinsic explanation—from being frightened by a dog to falling downstairs—and it will be strange if the influence of a minor illness in the first months of pregnancy, accompanied by a rash, has escaped attention."[84] Here, in a strikingly unusual move among members of the medical profession, the Australian physicians' clinical findings were doubted, even scorned, because they did not mesh with the "lay public's" thinking. To point to women's fears of what physicians called "maternal marking" as a source of doubt—for surely if they think a dog can cause birth defects, they would have noticed a rash!—was simultaneously to scorn Gregg and give false credit to traditional "lay" thinking.

The dubious response of the *Lancet* reviewer points to how new and unusual Gregg's discovery was. The fact that it had originated in Australia and arisen during wartime contributed to the medical world's slow uptake of Gregg's finding. But penicillin was quickly adopted worldwide during World War II, so war alone cannot explain the doubt expressed in the *Lancet* article. Although research on rubella, the writer was sure, "is being carried further *out there*," he urged research in Britain as well.[85] Medical colleagues "out there" in Australia first made the intellectual leap and presented early epidemiological findings indicating that the rubella virus caused congenital malformations, but this writer found their research methods deficient. Australia was far away, a former colony, part of the commonwealth, a land of prisoners, cowboys, kangaroos, and the "outback." Medical ideas, knowledge, and research findings from "out there," it appears, were questionable in part because of their foreign and exotic origins.[86] The writer pointed to research in Britain and the United States that suggested that nutrition, maternal age, and environmental factors affected fetal development,[87] but the idea that a virus that infected the pregnant woman could harm her developing fetus was still new and strange to most clinicians.

Gregg's finding forced a conceptual shift in medical thinking, but for scientists working in embryology or pathology who knew that viruses crossed the placenta, Gregg had confirmed what they knew experimentally. For embryologist and expert on the developing eye Dr. Ida Mann of Oxford, Gregg and his colleagues had accomplished something of "far-reaching importance." They had provided "the awaited clinical evidence of certain embryological truths." Dr. Mann's remarks pointed to the segregation of scientific knowledge. Gregg and his colleagues had "focused attention on phenomena which, although well known to biologists, have received too little attention from clinicians. By proving beyond question the causative relation between a virus infection early in pregnancy and the appearance of certain congenital defects in the infant, these workers have laid the foundation for a host of observations of like nature which . . . will probably alter profoundly our views on the causation of congenital anomalies in man." Careful clinical research proved in human bodies "the results of experimental embryology."[88]

As ophthalmologists in the United States confirmed Gregg's findings in their own patients, they wondered if this new menace could be attributed to a far-off, exotic continent and to war. Perhaps it came from Australia, thanks to "increased traffic" with the wartime ally.[89] A California physician who collected reports of scores of cases of cataracts and heart defects in newborns whose mothers had had rubella early in pregnancy wondered whether the disease had traveled from Australia across the Pacific to the California coast and was "now making its way across the country."[90] These speculations suggest the automatic association of dangerous diseases with foreigners and far-off lands, but the remarks also reveal a discovery in process. It was not yet clear what Gregg's report and the accumulating data meant. One possibility, entertained by these authors, was that this was a new version of an old virus since these effects had never been noticed before. Oddly, troop movement itself did not merit scrutiny as a possible piece of the American story although Gregg had indicated the importance of the massing of troops in camps where epidemics started and then spread to civilians.[91] Nonetheless, babies with rubella-related congenital defects had been identified at one "naval hospital" in San Diego, according to one report, and appeared to be concentrated on the West Coast, home to numerous military bases.[92]

Despite the skepticism expressed in Britain's premier medical journal, by the late 1940s, Gregg's discovery of the teratogenic effects of rubella had won international attention and confirmation. Individual physicians wrote to medical journals of one or a handful of cases that corroborated Gregg's findings. The Institute of Medical and Veterinary Science at Adelaide (Australia) researched the effects of maternal rubella in depth and published numerous articles in the *Medical Journal of Australia*. Several years after Australians first learned of Gregg's discovery, it started to become general knowledge among American physicians and to reach the public.

When Australian virologist (and later Nobel prize winner) Macfarlane Burnet toured the United States in 1943, he brought news of Gregg's discovery to the attention of physicians, and the information percolated out through medical meetings and reports. In 1946, Dr. Edith Potter, professor of pathology at the University of Chicago, reported on the discovery in the *American Journal of Public Health,* and in 1947, Dr. Conrad Wesselhoeft, clinical professor of infectious diseases at the Harvard School of Public Health, announced Gregg's findings and commented on the new "serious problem" posed by this minor disease in a major two-part article on "medical progress" in the *New England Journal of Medicine.*[93] Although *Newsweek* and *Time* newsmagazines each reported on Gregg's discovery in 1944 and 1945, popular media paid little attention to it. Neither did physicians who wrote for the public. In the *Chicago Tribune*'s syndicated "How to Keep Well" column, for instance, mention of German measles appeared now and again, but it was not until 1947 that a full column outlined the effects of rubella during pregnancy.[94]

Signaling the acceptance of Gregg's findings and the rejection of the *Lancet's* doubts, the British Medical Association awarded the 1949 Katherine Bishop Harman Prize to Dr. Charles Swan, one of the Adelaide researchers, for his internationally comparative report on rubella's effects on pregnancy.[95] Swan had compiled, summarized, and analyzed all of the existing correspondence, notes, and studies on the effects of maternal rubella. The report appeared as a thorough two-part article in the *Journal of Obstetrics and Gynaecology of the British Empire.* In it, Swan detailed the data that had been compiled in Australia, England, the United States, Finland, Sweden, Switzerland, and South Africa. Studies from around the world confirmed the harmful effects of rubella on the developing fetus and identified the period of pregnancy when the disease caused the most damage. Those effects included congenital blindness and vision defects, heart defects, deafness, intellectual impairment, and "miscellaneous abnormalities" such as skeletal deformities, poor muscular tone, and slowness in the eruption of teeth.[96] During the earliest stages of pregnancy, when a woman might not even know of her pregnancy, the risk of harm from contracting rubella was the highest. The risk of a mother's "giving birth to a child with congenital anomalies following the contraction of rubella in the first 4 months of pregnancy," Swan reported, "ranges from 83.2 percent in the first month to 61.1 percent in the fourth month, with an average of approximately 74.4 percent." In contrast, he continued, the risk of birth defects dropped later in pregnancy: "In the last 5 months of gestation, the risk ranges from 11.1 per cent to 29.9 percent."[97] These rates—over 80 per cent in the first month and more than half for the first half of pregnancy, according to the world reports—were extremely high. Typically, somewhere between 1 and 2 percent of newborns had serious congenital malformations.[98] Researchers found miscarriage and stillbirth to be associated with the disease as well.[99] Given the evidence, Swan believed therapeutic abortion in such cases "entirely justified."[100]

Mothers' responses to this new information about German measles underscored the pervasive fear of deformity and mothers' guilt. Swan described how blaming a disease rather than one's heritage for deformity could alleviate the guilt felt by mothers. Indeed, sharing medical knowledge about German measles with the public could be considered *pronatalist* (meaning the encouragement of procreation as the central priority of adulthood, especially for women). When mothers learned that a disease had caused the congenital malformations that their children faced, he explained, some felt newly freed to have another child. One woman who had read about German measles in *Time* magazine had worried "that there was a family taint somewhere" and had avoided having more children. Now, she realized, she could have more.[101] Swan and his colleagues "reassured" worried parents like this one that they could have additional children without fear of deformity.[102] Identifying a disease as the cause of birth defects made the mother and father innocent. Public knowledge about the effects of this disease could prompt women to try to avoid German measles and, Swan optimistically pointed out, prompt mothers with harmed children to get pregnant again and expand their families. This outcome was, he reported, "contrary to expectation" that if the "laity" realized the dangers of this disease, "undue alarm" would be the result.[103]

Nonetheless, Swan ended with a vision of tragedy—for individuals and for the greater society. "If large numbers of cases of rubella in pregnancy continue to occur," he warned, "they will constitute a social problem of some magnitude, for the consequences are not confined to the affected child. Indeed, the shadow falls upon the family, especially the mother and the other children, on the children as yet unborn, and on the community generally. The lot of children afflicted with a congenital abnormality of eye, ear, or heart is a sad one, but when two or more of these defects are present in combination, and the more so if there is superadded mental retardation, their fate is tragic in the extreme, and death at an early age can be only looked upon as a merciful release. Nevertheless, recent advances in cardiac surgery and in the perfection of deaf-aids offer real hope of the amelioration of these handicaps."[104] This quotation reveals much. These babies were regarded by definition as tragedies. Dr. Swan expressed the culture's feelings about such children. His own meetings with children and their families and observation of the material realities shaped his view. At the same time, "tragedy" was a social construction and cultural assumption. New surgeries and technologies offered "hope," but in Swan's eyes, there was little hope for some. In severe cases, death was "merciful."[105]

The early medical literature on maternal rubella did not emphasize the number of infant deaths or the impact of those deaths on mothers and families. In his first report, Gregg reported fifteen deaths in seventy-eight cases.[106] Children died at one week, three weeks, four months, ten months, and three years or more.[107] For an expectant mother in mid-twentieth-century Western industrialized countries—where infant and maternal mortality had fallen and child survival was the norm—contemplating these early infant deaths would be terrifying. One baby, Gregg reported, "spent most of its short life" in a "hospital. . . . It was always extremely difficult to feed, and remained throughout a tiny wisp of a child. It finally succumbed to an attack of heart disease." Another weighed only six pounds twelve ounces when two months old. At one year, "it could not sit up, had no teeth, and screamed a lot. Death came suddenly from heart failure, but throughout the preceding day the baby continually banged its head on the pillow."[108] These clinical reports, in which the children are unnamed and the doctor retreats to referring to one child as *it,* hint at the pain felt by the children, their parents, and their doctors. Australian state mortality data also revealed the impact of German measles epidemics as infant cardiac deaths reached their highest numbers ever.[109]

These infants had difficulty feeding, presented as "failure to thrive," and experienced repeated surgeries. If "mental retardation" was "superadded," Swan described child death as "merciful." Intellectual impairment appears as *the* tragic characteristic. Swan's words expressed a gloomy forecast for the children's future—especially for the intellectually impaired—a view shared by many in the larger culture and in medicine and among parents. Perhaps he expressed the feelings of grief-stricken parents who felt relief that with death their child's misery had ended. Perhaps his words added to their grief by denying the loss they felt. Perhaps parents felt both emotions simultaneously.

Swan painted a dark picture. He represented the effect of German measles in pregnancy as a "shadow," one that fell particularly hard upon the mother. When the children were "mentally deficient," he quoted Gregg, "homes were disrupted" and the mother's life "ruin[ed]."[110] Yet Swan imagined that things might be different and suggested a pronatalist vision. A vaccine might protect pregnant women and their babies. "It is to be hoped," he remarked, "that . . . in the near future . . . methods of immunization against the disease will render such drastic procedures as the termination of gestation unnecessary."[111] Early students of the effects of maternal rubella endorsed abortion and imagined the creation of a vaccine to prevent rubella among expectant mothers. By preventing disease, a vaccine would prevent both birth defects and abortions. In this imagined future, a vaccine became a miracle cure for complicated medical, social, moral, and legal issues.

The sense that women themselves could damage the bodies and minds of their babies was an age-old fear. Expectant mothers worried that, through their own thoughts, sights, and actions or simply through bad luck, they might produce crippling effects and malformed bodies. Although twentieth-century scientists generally dismissed such ideas, women themselves often suspected that they or the world around them could cause deformities, miscarriages, and stillbirths. By the mid-twentieth century, however, physicians and maternal health advisers warned expectant mothers that an infectious disease could threaten their pregnancies and the bodies of their children. Such an idea would have been dismissed as an unnecessary, even silly, fear and an old wives' tale only a few years earlier. Indeed, when Dr. Van Dellen first reported the effects of German measles on pregnancy in the *Chicago Tribune,* his column began by referring to old wives' tales and included a drawing of such women scaring a younger woman.[112] The new warnings about German measles originated with the observations of mothers. The German measles case is an example of how medical researchers transformed mothers' expertise and everyday observations of pregnancy and children's bodies into clinical data and scientific discoveries. These warnings became part of standard prenatal advice thanks to the observations of unnamed mothers and to a thoughtful ophthalmologist who cared and listened to them.

Why had the effects of German measles on pregnancy never been noticed before? What made 1941 in Sydney, Australia, different from other years in which German measles appeared in epidemic form? What made Dr. Norman Gregg the doctor who recognized the effects of this virus? Gregg was a unique and smart individual; he saw an unusual number of infants with a specific complaint, but he did more than take care of their individual medical needs. He asked why, pursued an epidemiological investigation, and concluded that the rubella virus was the source of the unusual condition. Surely other physicians had previously seen children with these complaints, but they had not investigated them to find a new explanation; others would have dismissed these mothers' remarks as irrelevant while still others never would have connected two completely unexpected events—a virus and the birth months later of a baby with congenital malformations. Gregg, like all great discoverers, was not thinking in isolation but lived in a specific time and place. Intellectual components, including new attention to environmental factors in relation to pregnancy and congenital malformations and a declining reliance upon heredity as an explanation of their cause, were part of the larger intellectual atmosphere.

Equally as important, structural components of medicine and social conditions also contributed to making his discovery possible. Specialization in medicine made it possible for Gregg to notice an unusually high number of cataracts in infants. Because this condition was rare, parents who noticed it in their infants might have gone to various doctors without any one person ever noticing the large number of such cases. But as patients and doctors increasingly turned to specialists, an unusual outbreak of a specific condition might become visible. Because Gregg was a pediatric specialist, he saw a series of individuals in a short time period and realized that he was seeing more patients with this rare condition than usual. Furthermore, as a university researcher, he knew how to pursue an epidemiological question and how to convince his colleagues to distribute and answer a nationwide questionnaire. Gregg's own stature and connections within his profession aided him in each endeavor. Finally, the fact that by the mid-twentieth century, Australian mothers were well trained to observe their children's bodies closely and to bring anxieties, questions, and observations to expert doctors was a necessary starting point for Gregg's discovery.

The fact that the media too helped move Gregg's discovery forward deserves underscoring. Without the early newspaper coverage of Gregg's presentation at a meeting of specialists, the process of learning about the effects of rubella would have been slower.[113] Gregg himself worked with popular news media in order to alert Australian women to the dangers of German measles, appearing on Sydney's 2SM News Radio for instance. Through the news, mothers learned of Gregg's discovery and then contacted him with their suspicions of another effect of rubella. News coverage of medical research led to new interactions among individuals, professionals,

Figure 1. Dr. Norman M. Gregg, ophthalmic surgeon at Royal Alexandra Hospital for Children and Royal Prince Alfred Hospital in Sydney, was known as a kind and empathetic physician who knew how to talk with children and who listened to their mothers. Gregg's profession and nation honored him for his historic achievement in recognizing the teratogenic effects of German measles. He received numerous honorary degrees, was knighted in 1952, and named Australian Father of the Year ten years later. Photo used courtesy of the Royal Prince Alfred Hospital Museum and Archives.

and institutions and to new insights. Most obviously, the media's treatment of medical findings and investigations as news sped the transmission of new knowledge regarding the danger of German measles to the public.

Equally significant, but underappreciated, is the way in which the popular news media helped to speed knowledge from the public back to medical researchers. That collaboration among media, mothers, and medicine in advancing medical knowledge can also be seen in a medical advice column in a Chicago newspaper. Readers typically sent Dr. Van Dellen questions to answer in his column in the *Chicago Tribune*. In 1947, Dr. Van Dellen reversed the usual flow of questions and asked his readers to give him information. The result revealed mothers' interest in health and their commitment to scientific research. Six years after Gregg's discovery, Van Dellen offered the newspaper's first full-length coverage of "defects following German measles." He described the "Australian" findings as "somewhat controversial." Some, he reported, "go so far as to indicate that if rubella occurs in the first month or two of pregnancy, congenital anomalies are certain to be present." The problem with much of the research thus far, Van Dellen explained, was that it started with the children who displayed anomalies, but one would prefer to follow pregnant women who had the disease since "it may be that many . . . gave birth to normal children." The doctor concluded his column with a query to his readers: "If there are any readers who had German measles during pregnancy, we would like to know in what month it occurred and what was the outcome."[114] Nearly one hundred women answered Van Dellen's request with detailed letters full of information. The strong response from Chicago-area women and their thoroughness resulted in an article on the formidable effects of the disease that was published in the profession's most widely read journal, the *Journal of the American Medical Association* (JAMA). The information provided in these letters showed that 87 percent of the children whose mothers had had rubella in the first trimester were "abnormal" and 42 percent of those whose mothers had been infected in the second trimester had congenital defects.[115]

Mothers responded to the doctor's newspaper query with impressive detail. "The caliber of the letters received," Drs. Stuart Abel and Van Dellen remarked, "was surprising."[116] "The majority were written intelligently and included considerable detail," they noted. The responses from busy mothers, many of them caring for children who needed unusual attention because of their health conditions, show a real commitment to their children and to adding to medical knowledge about the disease. "Many" of the letters, the doctors reported, "were written by persons with a professional background."[117] The women who read Van Dellen's column and wrote back appear to have been drawn from a highly educated class of women. Some may have been scientists and medical professionals themselves, perhaps now out of the workplace due to motherhood and gender discrimination, but they contributed to medical knowledge. This is all we know about the women who wrote, but from these bits we can see that there were not only maternal commitments to children and scientific research but also professional and class commitments underlying the letters. By sharing all they knew about their own pregnancies and children and providing that individual information in "considerable detail," these women did scientific work and transformed their personal histories into data for medical research.

Popular news media alerted readers to the newfound "embryo menace." *Newsweek* framed its early reporting as breaking medical news and traced the movement of information from Australia to the United States. American "medical circles," the magazine reported, agreed that "the Australian discovery is of universal importance." It then told the story of Gregg's insights, the doubts of his "fashionable" colleagues, and Swan's confirmation that rubella in the first two months of pregnancy was likely to result in "a congenitally defective child in about 100 per cent" of the cases.[118] *Time* described German measles as a "pipsqueak disease," but new research revealed its dangers. "If pregnant women catch it," the magazine reported, "it can give their unborn babies heart disease, cataracts, bad teeth or even make them deaf mutes or idiots. Many . . . die in the first few weeks of life."[119] This was frightening news. Thanks to this magazine story, the quoted physician received letters from around the country alerting him about other "abnormal babies" whose mothers had had rubella in the first two months of pregnancy, but he did not receive a single report of a normal baby following maternal rubella.[120]

Nevertheless, the media sent a mixed message about German measles. Dr. Van Dellen's health column in the *Chicago Tribune* is a good example. Although he had devoted an entire column to the effects of German measles in pregnancy, solicited information from mothers, and published in *JAMA* on it, his columns generally continued to treat German measles as a mild childhood disease. His 1947 column was one of the first to give sustained attention to the dangers of German measles, but surprisingly, a lengthy column on the disease in the previous year had not included a single word regarding the danger to pregnant women. Instead, the column had focused on children and their care, noting, "It has been said that rubella is our mildest contagious disease." Van Dellen had concluded, "The greatest difficulty the mother has is to keep her little one confined as there are so few symptoms. Would that every infection proved so tame!"[121]

These curiously cheerful remarks on the mildness of this disease and the absence of any information regarding pregnancy reveal the different approach taken by newspapers and magazines compared with that of health advice materials. The news media named German measles a "menace" and alerted the public to its danger while medical experts like Van Dellen downplayed the danger. In advice materials produced for the public, physicians adopted a paternalistic stance. They protected women from worry by not telling them of the hazards. *Time* magazine broke the German measles story by reporting on news heard at a medical meeting. Notably, another physician pointedly remarked later that the reporter had quoted the physician without permission.[122] The 1947 edition of *Expectant Motherhood,* a widely distributed guidebook for pregnant women by Nicholson J. Eastman, chief of obstetrics at Johns Hopkins University, said nothing about German measles. "Pregnancy should be a healthy, happy time," Dr. Eastman declared in the book's first sentence. That happiness, produced through a physician's "proper guidance," included reassuring women by leaving out information.[123] Dr. Van Dellen continued to emphasize the mildness of the disease in his advice column. In a later optimistic column on vaccine research, he remarked, "There would be no need to administer serum against less serious diseases such as chicken pox, German measles, and mumps."[124] Despite the threat to developing pregnancy demonstrated by evidence that he had collected himself through his own newspaper column, Van Dellen still considered German measles "less serious" and a vaccine unnecessary.

Medical advice books and pamphlets for expectant mothers kept silent about German measles and reassured them that things would be fine. Indeed, they directly associated seeing a doctor with having a normal baby. "When your physician examines you early and follows through carefully month by month," a 1947 Children's Bureau pamphlet promised, "the likelihood of your having a normal baby is increased."[125] Calling the idea that bad experiences might mark a baby "old notions," it suggested that the worried mother-to-be place her worries "on her doctor's shoulders. He can reassure you about the extreme rarity of feeble-mindedness or other abnormality."[126] Seeing the doctor offered examinations, paternal reassurance, freedom from worry, and normality. Implicitly, failure to see a doctor and follow his orders threatened abnormality. Since parents most feared that the new child's body or mind might be damaged and abnormal, that equation of medical surveillance with normality served as both a powerful endorsement of medicine and a powerful threat. The fear of unknown abnormality might keep expectant mothers in the doctor's office, following advice and paying fees. By the 1950s, the medical profession had accepted the connection between German measles and congenital malformations, yet 1961 and 1962 Children's Bureau pamphlets for expectant mothers still said nothing about the disease. A picture leaflet, *When Your Baby Is on the Way,* again made the general promise that early surveillance by physicians and nurses would ensure healthy babies. "Most babies are born healthy and all right in every way," it began. "But once in a while a pregnant woman has trouble. Good medical care, starting early, will prevent or control most things that cause trouble. So go to your own doctor or clinic as soon as you think you are going to have a baby."[127]

Although ten years after Gregg's discovery health advice materials sent surprisingly few messages about German measles to pregnant women, plenty of women worried. "This knowledge has been widespread," health adviser Dr. William Brady observed, "and has naturally given rise to considerable apprehension on the part of pregnant women." A woman contracting the disease in early pregnancy, he reported, "stands a 50–50 chance of giving birth to a defective baby."[128] A mother's autobiographical story, told in a 1954 health magazine, clearly named the danger: "German measles handicapped my child."[129]

When Mrs. E. worried that catching German measles during pregnancy "could harm the baby," her husband called her "superstitious." She wrote to Dr. Van Dellen at the *Chicago Tribune* to find out who was right. Mrs. E, the doctor answered, was "not superstitious but modern."[130] The "modern" mother knew what this virus threatened and that her baby could indeed be changed and marked during pregnancy by outside influences. That mothers' age-old fears of the threat of deformity had become real and scientifically endorsed was a surprising change in medical science. Mothers who observed and suspected that events occurring during pregnancy could damage their children's bodies contributed to making this transformation in medical thinking. It would soon be the modern mother's responsibility to try to avoid this disease and to think about its consequences.

# TWO

# Specter of Tragedy

IN APRIL 1964, the U.S. Public Health Service's Communicable Disease Center announced that "a nationwide epidemic of German measles is now in progress" and advised women in the first three months of pregnancy to avoid the disease. Early CDC reports were contradictory, stressing both the danger to pregnant women and the relatively low risk of bearing deformed babies.[1] News reports, however, underscored the threat. If the disease was contracted in the first four to five weeks of pregnancy, "the danger of having an abnormal baby," was 50 percent.[2] "Malformed," "hopelessly deformed," "abnormal," "defective," "dangerous"[3]—these were the words used to describe the babies affected by the disease. Other reports more baldly declared the danger. Headlines in *U.S. News and World Report,* for example, reported that German measles was "spreading" and about to "engulf" the entire country. Rubella was "a killer and a crippler. Its target: unborn babies."[4]

The media described the threat of German measles in vivid terms. The language used to describe the babies born following maternal rubella exposed and reinforced the culture's fears of disability and the "defective" or "abnormal" child. Visually, however, the picture of the harm done was blank. Most media coverage of the disease consisted of narrative only. Lacking photographs of harmed children, Americans turned to other available representations of "cripples" and "crippling disease" to paint the picture of this disease. Americans drew on two key paradigms to comprehend the looming threat: polio and thalidomide. Quickly dubbed "the crippler" by the news media,[5] German measles was understood through polio, the original "crippler," and thalidomide, a drug that caused severe birth defects and infant deaths when women took it during pregnancy. Polio had terrified families since the early twentieth century as it killed and paralyzed healthy children (and adults) every summer. The frightening disease had been beaten ten years earlier thanks to a national effort to develop a vaccine.[6] The world had learned only a few years earlier of the disastrous effects of thalidomide on the developing fetus. Sold over the counter in Germany and England and widely distributed elsewhere across the globe, it was responsible for thousands of babies who died or were born "deformed." The United States, however, avoided a "thalidomide tragedy" on the scale experienced in Germany and England because the Food and Drug Administration had never licensed the drug.[7] The German measles epidemic developed when children were the central focus of post–World War II American culture and deadly childhood diseases appeared conquered. At this moment of national pride in the achievements of both medical science and government protection, German measles loomed as a new and shocking threat to babies, mothers, families, and the nation. As the country learned that tens of thousands of "crippled babies" would be the result of the epidemic, anxiety about pregnancy and future children grew.

Media coverage of the disease provided more than objective medical information; it provided a cultural framework for understanding the epidemic. Popular media represented German measles as a gendered family drama. The German measles epidemic of 1963–65 was played out on the relationships between mothers and children as well as on the children's bodies. As in every frightening epidemic, someone was blamed for spreading disease and misery. The people blamed for dangerous diseases typically come from already stigmatized minority groups. German measles was different. By the time of the epidemic, the identified source of this infectious disease, the ones who spread the contagion to expectant mothers, was not a disliked group but instead a beloved one: young children threatened babies on the way. The spreading of German measles by soldiers during World Wars I and II had been forgotten. In the 1960s schema, children were at once the threatened and the threat, a depiction of children that matched a long historical pattern. Nineteenth- and twentieth-century reformers had long seesawed between seeing children as endangered and seeing them as dangerous threats to society.[8] German measles brought both of these themes together simultaneously. This disease—and the children who passed it on to pregnant women—threatened both "the unborn child" and the postwar nuclear family. The disabled child was thought both to suffer and to be the source of suffering.[9]

(Expectant) mothers were the ones who had to resolve this dilemma. As women learned of rubella's effects on pregnancy, many avidly sought abortions from doctors. This too became part of the German measles story. In a remarkable twist, German measles contributed to a remaking of the post–World War II representation of and public talk about abortion, transforming it from deviant to decent. As previous social and cultural histories have shown, epidemics have often been used to delineate boundaries of class, race, ethnicity, and sexuality.[10] The 1960s epidemic of German measles is unique in the history of infectious diseases for doing the opposite. German measles helped to lift the repression of a sexually deviant practice—namely, abortion—and transform it into an honorable one. Because German measles and abortion appeared to create an inescapable crisis for decent married middle-class white mothers, the procedure gained respectability. Decision making around possibly harmed pregnancies and possible abortion was an extension of family planning and birth control, a responsibility of the married heterosexual couple and, most especially, a married woman's responsibility for her family. It was the mother—represented as white, married, middle-class, and anguished—who, with the cooperation of her husband and doctor, had the responsibility to weigh the scientific information, risks, and moral questions and then make decisions about the future of her pregnancy.

The German measles epidemic first hit the East Coast in the winter of 1963 and then spread to the South and Midwest, where "the epidemic was the largest recorded in two decades." Massachusetts had five times as many cases as recorded the previous year; New York City, seventeen times the number of cases. By early 1964, more than ten thousand cases had been reported in New York City, with two hundred new cases reported there every day. In the first three months of 1964, Kentucky had 60 percent more reported cases. Rubella came to Puerto Rico, the Far West, and the Pacific Coast in 1964 and 1965.[11] In 1965, Oregon reported more than eight thousand cases; the West Coast and Hawaii were enduring the biggest German measles epidemic in twenty years.[12]

An earlier epidemic in 1958 had received little media attention. The key difference in the coverage of the two epidemics was the awareness of thalidomide. The thalidomide tragedy shocked and frightened expectant parents. Thalidomide, a drug used in sleeping pills, cough syrups, and other over-the-counter and prescribed medicines, had been billed as supremely safe, heavily sold in West Germany and England, and marketed around the world by German and British pharmaceutical companies. Although thalidomide had never been available as an over-the-counter or prescribed medication in the United States, more than a thousand doctors handed out pills to their patients.

In 1961, pediatricians in West Germany saw that the number of infants born with a rare malformation (shortened limbs) had tripled from that of the year before. Physicians investigated many possible causes, including X-rays and food preservatives. Although some characteristics of this increase in congenital malformations mirrored those of German measles, investigators ruled out viruses because "viruses know no territorial borders," as Dr. Helen Taussig of Johns Hopkins University observed. She noted that "this epidemic remained strikingly centered in West Germany." By November of 1961, two pediatricians, one in West Germany and one in Australia, had figured out that thalidomide severely damaged the developing fetus and produced infants born with shortened arms and legs (phocomelia) as well as internal injuries. In addition, doctors expected the affected children to be brain damaged. Thalidomide also caused numerous miscarriages, stillbirths, and early infant deaths. The thousands of babies around the world who had been harmed horrified physicians, parents, journalists, and, as the story hit the American news, the public. Photographs of infants without arms or legs circulated widely in the media.[13]

Thalidomide received intense news coverage in the United States and political attention from Congress and President Kennedy, yet relatively few Americans had personally been affected by it. Thalidomide was sold under different trade names in nearly fifty countries, including West Germany, Britain, Italy, most other European countries, Australia, New Zealand, Canada, Iraq, Iran, Israel, Asia, and South America.[14] In the United States, however, pharmaceutical companies had not won the right to sell the drug. Nonetheless, twenty-thousand pills had been distributed in the United States through physicians as an experimental drug supplied by Richardson-Merrell, the company that planned to get in on the booming business. It was not clear who had the pills or where they were. Some pregnant American women did take thalidomide—because they traveled abroad or lived in West Germany (while married to U.S. military men) or were given it by doctors in the United States—and it then affected their pregnancies.[15] Sherri Finkbine was one American woman who had taken a sleeping pill her husband had bought in England, then later realized she had taken thalidomide and feared for her pregnancy.

Finkbine's story—her shock; her plan to have a therapeutic abortion performed by her doctor in a hospital, which was thwarted when her situation became news; her family; and her travels abroad for an abortion—all became national and international news in 1962. Through Finkbine, many Americans learned about the impact of thalidomide and followed her efforts to obtain an abortion given the high likelihood that the fetus would be severely harmed. Indeed, abortion for reasons of fetal deformity was widely accepted by the medical community and, as the response to Finkbine's case revealed, by the society as a whole. Prompted by the media attention and developing religious debate, in which Catholic commentators declared abortion a sin and murder while Protestant clergy and Jewish rabbis deemed it acceptable in some cases, the Finkbines received phone calls and letters from the public, many angry and threatening, others supportive.[16]

Although the media tracked Finkbine's case closely, she was one of only a handful of Americans personally harmed by the drug. In the main, Americans avoided the global experience with thalidomide because of one extremely careful and dedicated scientist, Dr. Frances Kelsey at the Food and Drug Administration (FDA), who resisted the pressure that the company put on her and refused to grant the medication a license. As Congress and the country saw the disaster that had been narrowly avoided, the FDA won greater powers, though these were still more limited than many reformers wanted. The thalidomide experience strengthened American support for, expectation of, and trust in federal regulation of the pharmaceutical industry and regulation on behalf of health.[17]

For a generation that had embraced postwar pharmaceuticals—from antibiotics, vaccines, and tranquilizers to the newly available and instantly popular birth control pill—it was shocking to discover that seemingly safe medications were not safe at all and that what pregnant women ingested could affect the fetus.[18] This news about thalidomide followed upon the heels of Rachel Carson's exposé of the dangers of DDT and other pesticides to the environment and human health, as well as growing awareness of the perils of X-rays, radiation, and nuclear fallout.[19] Living at the center of global power during the Cold War in a country that touted its products, its science, and its security, Americans were learning that their world and their families faced an array of unseen threats. Thalidomide offered many lessons, including the new lesson to expectant women that the pills and syrups they took to cure their ills could affect the fetus. While physicians had previously offered pills during pregnancy to prevent nausea or miscarriage, experts now strongly advised women to avoid all cold medicines, pills, and prescribed medications during pregnancy.[20] Although the dangers posed by German measles to pregnant women had been known since the 1940s, many may have been only vaguely aware of them.[21] Thalidomide "woke people up."[22]

Intense media attention to thalidomide paved the way for new public interest in German measles and shaped the public's mental image of this disease. Photos of babies damaged by thalidomide were seen everywhere and were heavily imprinted in the minds of childbearing women. A black-and-white photo of a baby with big eyes and tiny twisted arms caught the eye of people passing by street and subway newsstands. "Exclusive First Photos [of] 5,000 Babies Born with 'Seal Flippers,'" *National Enquirer* headlines cried, promising more inside. A popular tabloid newspaper sold at newsstands and in drugstores, the August 12, 1962, edition of the *National Enquirer* did important work in disseminating the bad news about thalidomide. The front page visually told the public of the tragedy. For those who might dismiss the *National Enquirer* as a fictional scandal sheet, its text matched that of mainstream news and quoted medical advisories. Its photos of deformity and "freaks" were drawn from the medical journals and confirmed what the more respectable news outlets had reported: thalidomide was indeed a disaster. The *National Enquirer*'s two-page spread emphasized deformity with numerous photos of affected babies with missing or extremely shortened and "twisted limbs." The photos, combined with headlines and captions, underscored the notion that these babies were "freaks," their lives a horror.[23] At the same time, the reproduction of these pictures invited voyeurism and encouraged people to buy papers and magazines. (See figure 2.)

As the media brought thalidomide to the American public's consciousness, it described the contours of the international tragedy and the shape of the babies themselves. The media echoed the reactions of doctors, nurses, and parents who first saw the babies: they reacted with horror and revulsion. The "blighted babies" of Europe, *Time* reported, had "hideous malformations."[24] As Dr. Helen Taussig, the pediatrician known for pioneering heart surgery to save "blue babies," bluntly put it, the deformities caused by thalidomide were "the most ghastly thing you have ever seen."[25] The press generally described the effects of thalidomide as "armless and legless babies" while refraining from describing the babies born with congenital heart problems, intestinal problems, or the lack of an anus. Using the descriptive terms of medicine, the babies had "seal limbs."[26] The lan-

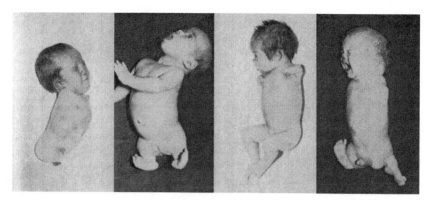

Figure 2. "Thalidomide babies." These clinical images were seen not only by members of the medical profession but also by the public as mass media reproduced and broadcast the photographs in newspapers, magazines, and television news. The nude infants displayed in medical journals in order to show their congenital malformations—as scientific specimens so that physicians could diagnose the syndrome—terrified many. The addition of black blocks across the genitals in popular media photos made the babies look even stranger and more alien as both scientific objects and censored bodies. These pictures were and are disturbing; texts that labeled the children "freaks" or somberly discussed them as "tragedies" made the images even more disturbing and the children seem more hopeless. Helen B. Taussig, "A Study of the German Outbreak of Phocomelia: The Thalidomide Syndrome," *JAMA* 180, no. 13 (June 30, 1962): 1109.

guage dehumanized and frightened. The lack of drug regulation had produced, in the words of *Saturday Review*'s science editor, "the epidemic of infant monsterism in Europe."[27] Thalidomide was a "crippler."[28] The world appeared to agree that the babies' prospects were dim. As *Time* magazine reported on West Germany, "some of the babies promised to be lifelong basket cases. All seemed unequipped to face the uncertain future."[29] At the same time, photos of well-dressed boys and girls with prosthetic arms and legs, smiling and playing with toys, appeared in popular magazines.[30] (See figure 3.) Such photos normalized the children through depictions of gender and typical childhood pleasures. Readers might see and read these images as hopeful or frightful and might imagine the parents and child as overwhelmed and pitiful, optimistic and practical, or a mixture.

Without thalidomide, the German measles epidemic may have received as little public attention as it had in previous years and may have remained a private problem.[31] A national epidemic of German measles *after* thalidomide, however, hit home in a new way that the thalidomide tragedy had

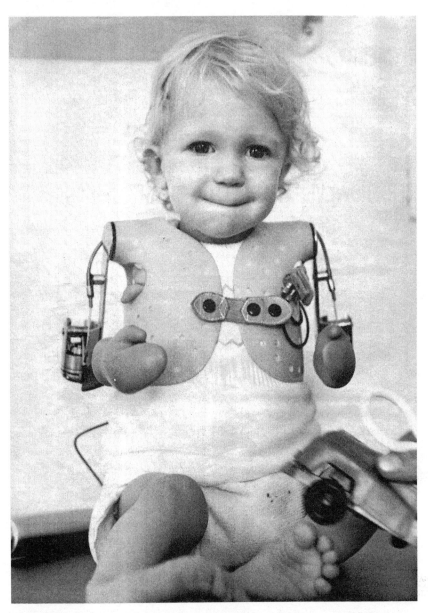

Figure 3. The photo of this bright-eyed German toddler is a portrait of both normality and the benefits of modern prosthetic technologies that allow her to have
arms and hands. At the same time, the need for the leather harness with its electric
plug on one side and leather mitten "hands" frightened and saddened viewers. Even
though "she feels love, she remembers food, she laughs, she cries, she lives," as *Life*
magazine noted, she would still be regarded as a "tragedy." Teenagers and adults
later reported their hatred of these harnesses and prostheses, and many refused to
use them. *Life* 53, no. 6 (August, 10 1962): 36.

not. Thalidomide had severely harmed ten thousand or more children in Germany, Britain, and Canada as well as unknown numbers in Africa, Asia, and Latin America, but it affected few in the United States.[32] In contrast, German measles potentially threatened every woman of childbearing age in the country. As German measles entered public discourse, photos and stories about thalidomide babies were simultaneously in the public eye; news reports on the German measles epidemic in print and on television regularly referenced the thalidomide story and ran stories on both side by side.[33] Thalidomide taught Americans what German measles might mean. German measles had the potential to be a major American tragedy, not a foreign one. Thalidomide was so powerful in people's minds that when one mother whose pregnancy was affected by German measles later recounted the story of her son's birth, she pointed to the fears of thalidomide at the time—though her son was born in 1960 before thalidomide's effects were known.[34] In her own memory, the two had merged. Dr. Virginia Apgar, pediatrician and new medical director of the National Foundation–March of Dimes (which had supported the research, testing, and nationwide distribution of polio vaccine in the mid-1950s) expected the epidemic to produce fifteen to twenty thousand "pitifully damaged children."[35]

### PORTRAITS OF DISABILITY

Although adults with physical handicaps due to war or polio were seen in public with their canes and braces, children with disabilities—most especially those with intellectual impairments—were increasingly invisible to the public as they were institutionalized and segregated from mainstream life. As a result, many people had little personal knowledge of the lives of the handicapped, deaf, blind, or retarded (to use the terms then current) and gained it instead from popular culture. Thalidomide generated frightening pictures of what children damaged during pregnancy might look like. Photos of thalidomide babies generally depicted their bodies as disgusting, suggesting that their minds no doubt were also diminished. Although the mainstream media later redrew this portrait of thalidomide babies as a more buoyant and optimistic picture of children learning to use new prosthetic "arms" and "legs," they were still regarded as different, strange, and woeful. The posters, newsreels, movies, and reports of children with polio that had saturated the culture in previous decades, no matter how optimistic and sunny, made it clear that the life of a "cripple" was difficult and stigmatized. In the words of one ominous educational film on polio, the disease twisted bodies and "specializ[ed]" in creating "grotesques." Even as people with polio proved themselves in high school, college, careers, and the presidency, they continued to be represented as pitiful victims. Heroic achievers modeling themselves on President Franklin D. Roosevelt, people with polio still faced discrimination. Parents of the 1960s surely remembered the fear of polio, the shame of catching it, and the children who died or were crippled as a result of it. They might also remember that when polio victims returned to school using braces or crutches, other kids called them names and left them isolated and dateless.[36] Such memories informed thinking about what German measles might mean for the children affected.

The German measles epidemic entered a culture devoted to babies but ashamed of, unprepared for, and often hostile to children with disabilities. "The birth of a malformed youngster," health columnist Dr. Theodore Van Dellen stated as known fact, "is a hard cross to bear. The parents are upset emotionally, and many feel so conscience stricken for months thereafter that they refuse to mingle with society."[37] The announcement at birth of a newborn's malformation frightened parents who expected healthy babies. The malformed child, this medical advisor recognized, was understood as an affliction to the parents, "a hard cross to bear"— emotionally and socially. "The congenitally defective child," as one maternal health activist put it, was not only a "social and financial problem" but also "himself an unhappy being." As the language of defectiveness revealed, eugenic thinking endured in the postwar period.[38]

Overall, medical advisors and science writers equated disability with tragedy, but they also injected hopeful notes. Hope could be found, first, through parents' realization that they were not to blame and, second, through science and surgery. Mental retardation and physical malformations had long been treated as inherited traits, the fault of the family. These beliefs contributed to family shame and secrecy. In most cases, however, Van Dellen and many other health writers explained that "nature probably can be blamed; something happened prior to birth."[39] Mothers should not feel guilty. Once families understood that they were innocent, the theory maintained, they could accept their child and act on his or her behalf. Second, parents needed to know about medical advances. "Medical science has made rapid strides in the correction of many defects that are present at birth," Van Dellen reassured. With the help of medicine, their child could be fixed and shame eliminated. One *Good Housekeeping* article declared itself to be a "hope-filled report on wonders now being worked by our doctors." "More malformed infants are being restored to health than ever before," it announced, thanks to "a great new weapon[:]. . . . Pediatric Surgery."[40]

Mainstream America has tended to understand disability as a biological defect in the body that can be fixed surgically and to obscure the ways in which social attitudes and structures create "disability." Disability activists and scholars have named this mode of thinking that blames the body and aggrandizes science and doctors for fixing bodies the *medical model*.[41] As energy and resources were poured into scientific solutions, limited resources flowed into programs, policies, and institutions that would make the society different and open to all people—the abled and disabled alike. At the same time, medical, technological, and scientific advances did make lives longer and greater participation in public life possible for people with disabilities. Midcentury medical innovations—such as pediatric cardiac surgery performed by Dr. Helen Taussig, for example—saved the lives of many newborns. Once surgeries or technologies had assured survival, however, the problems of discrimination and exclusion of people with disabilities persisted. The disabilities critique of the medical model for its failure to see and address the social construction of disability perhaps may be best understood as a critique of the entire society, rather than of the medical profession alone, for prioritizing medicine and medical solutions over social reconstruction.

Deafness, blindness, and mental retardation were all highly stigmatized, and the birth of a disabled child was understood to be punishment for deviant sexuality. Movies and novels had long contributed to these ideas. Early-twentieth-century venereal disease films depicted infant death and deformity following upon the heels of a father's depraved sexual behavior. World War II military-made movies for women and men showed that sexual promiscuity and venereal diseases caused sterility and birth defects. One post–World War II novel depicted the birth of a deaf child as punishment for her mother's promiscuous life. Movies about deaf girls, film scholar Lisa Cartwright finds, represented deafness and blindness as horror, nightmare, and shame.[42] Medical experts and educators often equated both deafness and blindness with intellectual impairment. Earlier in the twentieth century, deaf people were sterilized along with other "feeble-minded" individuals. Physicians advised parents to send their blind newborns to an institution and "have another."[43] Some expectant mothers feared causing retardation through their own behavior—particularly through sexual misbehavior. As late as 1968, one worried woman wrote a letter to a health adviser. She knew of a friend who had a retarded child because she had "sex relations" during pregnancy. She feared the same result.[44]

In addition to the difficult emotional responses of shame and guilt felt by many parents of children with physical or intellectual disabilities, the logistics of caring for their children could be extraordinarily difficult and draining. Like child rearing and caring for the ill in general, the work of caring for the disabled child was highly gendered, falling largely on the shoulders of mothers and the women who helped them. Mothers of children born with the effects of congenital rubella later reported the respiratory problems their children had, the need for constant health monitoring, their own exhaustion because their babies did not sleep, and the impossibility of finding babysitters for respite and support. They felt sadness at not knowing how to communicate with their children as well as the frustrations and joys of the intensive training that mothers were expected to give their children every day. Marriages often ended in divorce.[45]

Parents found it hard to locate schools and therapy services for their children.[46] The disabled had no recognized right to education. In contrast to the automatic admissions of most students, public schools routinely required psychological examinations of children with physical disabilities prior to admission. Schools rejected blind children, expecting them to be incapable of learning and difficult to handle. "Many of them are denied admission to [schools] or have been dismissed," one expert reported, for "being too immature, not fitting into the school, [being] uneducable, unable to talk, or in need of more individual attention."[47] Public schools also rejected mentally retarded children. As Chicago's African American newspaper reported, these "excluded children" were then left to "to roam the streets, vegetating, and headed for a life of total dependency." Local charitable groups worked to provide speech therapy, training on the typewriter, psychological services, and more for these "public school untouchables." Lack of funding, however, meant that hundreds of such children had nowhere to go. Half of all retarded children received no education.[48]

Since the early twentieth century, state residential institutions for the mentally retarded had served simultaneously as hospitals and schools. Many parents believed that these institutions were the only place where their children could receive an education. Doctors contributed to that belief by habitually advising parents to institutionalize their disabled children—especially those with intellectual impairments. Doctors urged new parents of children with Down syndrome to institutionalize them at birth.[49] As states built new residential institutions in the 1950s and 1960s and the institutions began changing their policies, the number of institutionalized children grew. Nevertheless, despite the pressure, many parents resisted institutionalization and cared for their children at home. These parents organized collectively, fought for, and created their own special education services in their own towns.[50] Still, a pediatrician's negative assessment of her child's potential could kill a mother's "optimism" and bring her to tears.[51]

In short, having a disabled child not only meant shame but also meant that the parents were highly likely to lose their child to an institution. The imagined happy home filled with children could be transformed by German measles into a home with a child missing. Furthermore, that missing child might be forced to live in terrible conditions. News media investigations of such institutions revealed them to be not only inadequate but also filthy, dangerous, and cruel. "It *could* be your next baby—feeble-mindedness strikes in the finest families," warned one 1948 women's magazine. "Yet thousands of such children and adults still live almost like animals in inferior institutions. . . . Most of our seventy-eight state institutions for mental deficients are not training schools—they are little more than wretched zoos."[52] Many of these "children," (as the writer described all of them, for they were considered children in terms of their mental ages though they were adults) "could be trained to be self-supporting." Instead, they were neglected and condemned to a dull life in an institution. Beds were crowded; toys and playrooms scarce; "jail-like discipline," including the chaining of "a little girl" to her bed, was the norm.[53] Although institutions improved during the 1950s and parents increasingly turned to them, by the mid-1960s, popular magazines and television documentaries again reported and photographed the terrible conditions of state institutions.[54] As President John F. Kennedy's family shared the story of their sister's mental retardation (including her eventual institutionalization as an adult), they too exposed the horrors of state institutions with urine-soaked floors and an atmosphere like that of "medieval prisons."[55] Exposés like these, part of urgent familial and professional campaigns to improve the treatment of the intellectually impaired and to change public prejudice, were alarming. A "feeble-minded" child would be destined not only to go to an institution but also to live in a world of neglect and cruelty.

## STORIES OF GERMAN MEASLES

"Many families meet an occasional catastrophe," began a 1956 Chicago newspaper column on family finances. "This is the story of a Chicago couple whose catastrophe is continuous. Harold and Jane Rivers . . . have a mentally retarded child."[56] A "dollar-and-cents" column on Chicago living made it plain that the costs of caring for a retarded child were staggering and beyond the capacity of a white-collar worker's salary. "Because of Harry," it bluntly stated, "the Rivers are in debt." The writer named the son Harry as the cause of the Rivers's problems and their debts, but she also named a disease and a mother: "The Rivers are not in debt because of extravagance. . . . They are in debt because Jane, now 38, contracted German measles in the first month of pregnancy 13 years ago."[57]

Retardation equaled "catastrophe," and German measles had caused that catastrophe for the Rivers family. The damaging effects of German measles—physical, financial, and social—were chronicled in health columns, news accounts, women's magazines, and financial columns like this one. This *Chicago Tribune* newspaper column alerted its readers to the fact that German measles in pregnancy meant disaster and shame: the sorrow of retardation, the stress of financial crises. The column detailed the family, its budget, and the bills for the surgery, therapies, and education of the Rivers's now twelve-year-old son. It noted, "Not until Harry was 6 did anyone have the courage to tell his parents he was retarded." Prior to that time, his difficulty in walking had been attributed to poor vision; he was expected to talk eventually. As a baby, Harry had had three operations on his eyes, then speech therapy for two years. At a specialized speech clinic, a doctor informed Harry's mother that he was mentally retarded. "The only thing you can do for this child," he told her, is to provide "permanent hospitalization."[58]

Disability threatened the class location of the entire family. Although this story did not analyze the difficulties arising from German measles as structural problems, it showed how a social structure that placed the financial responsibility for much of the medical care and education of a disabled child on the individual private family could easily impoverish a middle-class family. For the Rivers, their son's retardation meant not only "sorrow" but also no family vacations and homemade clothing for all because paying for Harry's care and education absorbed the family income. Providing for their retarded son's special needs also threatened the education of Harry's sister and brother—and thus threatened their futures. These powerful effects—not only the fear of deformity or the actual shape of the child's body—help to explain the depth of anxiety people felt about having disabled children.

The problem of the educational neglect of Harry and others like him appears as almost a footnote to the budget problems detailed in this article, but the education of her children was clearly a primary concern for Harry's mother. When advised to institutionalize him, the parents discovered that schools designed around one "handicap," such as schools for the deaf, were not prepared to take children like their son, who also had vision problems. Finally, Harry was admitted to the Illinois state school for "retardates," where he learned how to write his name and "wash dishes." When the state began charging parents for training and institutionalization, however, the Rivers family fell into debt and could not climb out. After five years, they brought Harry home. "We have a little fellow coming up," his mother explained. "We had to think of him, and of Janet, who wants to go to nursing school somehow."[59]

"There are many of us in this boat," Jane Rivers remarked. "A year or so ago some other mothers and I told a state welfare official we thought our children should receive equal consideration with normal children who share, without charge, in the benefits of public schools and playgrounds."[60] In the early 1950s, Mrs. Rivers and other mothers with retarded and handicapped children initiated the local movements to demand public education for their children—as the right of all citizens, whether "normal" or not. These efforts, invisible to most parents, eventually grew and merged with those of adult disability rights activists in the 1960s, 1970s, and 1980s and resulted in court decisions and federal laws that granted the right of public education to people with physical and intellectual impairments.[61]

In contrast to mothers like Jane Rivers, who pointed to the harm done by the lack of public education for their children, comic-strip doctor Rex Morgan, MD, suggested that the real threat to the retarded child was his mother. Dr. Morgan expressed the belief that the overprotective mother who refused to let her child go undermined her child's life. Speaking frankly to one mother, he outlined the correct attitude that mothers of the retarded should have. She was "far too overprotective of Jerry!" he told her. "You must give him a chance to grow emotionally and mentally!" The doctor taught that German measles could cause mental retardation, but he also urged adopting a more optimistic attitude: "Many retarded youngsters can be trained to be self-sufficient . . . useful citizens" IF the mothers can let go and give them a chance. The mother in this strip, however, was insistent, telling Morgan, "I won't let him be sent away!" The comic strip's final frame depicts both the mother who could not do the right thing for her retarded child by sending him to an institution for training and the growing resistance among parents to this practice. In it, the doctor remarks that he also "prefers" that the child remain with his family—but only, he warns the mother, if she "will permit him to become a member of the community, not just an inmate of this house!"[62]

Dr. Rex Morgan did not speak of the tireless work of mothers to secure education for their disabled children. Instead, written by a psychiatrist, the comic strip expressed the era's psychological analysis of mothers as insecure and inadequate.[63] The overprotective mother, not discrimination against the retarded and disabled, threatened her child's future. Expected to devote their intellectual and emotional energies to their children, women in the post–World War II period found themselves simultaneously blamed for being too involved with and too attached to their children. Good mothers, as Dr. Morgan made clear, had to let their children go— either by permanently institutionalizing them or by sending them to school and out of the house. As in many 1950s magazine stories, memoirs written by parents of retarded children, and movies about deaf girls, the good mother sent her child away.[64]

News reports explained to potential parents what German measles meant. Many listed blindness, deafness, and mental retardation without elaboration; a few told in detail what those disabilities meant in real life. The one-month-old daughter of "a young and pretty Negro woman" in Baltimore exhibited common features of congenital rubella syndrome. The baby girl's eyes were cloudy from glaucoma. "The infant form [of glaucoma] progresses so rapidly," the science writer reported, "that it must be treated as a surgical emergency lest it rupture the eye." Even with prompt surgery, however, "only 35 percent of these babies have normal vision even after a cataract operation." Rubella and modern medicine also marked the baby's body in other ways. The infant had a scar on her chest from having had heart surgery when she was only two weeks old.[65] Of the rubella-damaged children at Willowbrook School on Long Island, the *Saturday Evening Post* reported, "Most have defective hearts, few can walk or talk, and all . . . have the overwhelming brain damage that brought them to Willowbrook after their distraught parents had tried everything else."[66] Rubella syndrome meant multiple surgeries in infancy, permanent medication, and for many of the most severely affected, institutionalization and separation from their families.

Successful surgical operations and new vision technologies that promised these babies sight were celebrated in the news. Photos of babies affected by German measles were rare, but in 1965, untold thousands of newspaper readers saw white infants Grace Bump and, a few months later, Dale Crosby. Baby Grace wore big glasses after undergoing surgery to remove cataracts. "Six-month-old Grace Bump shows off her new glasses at St. Mary's Hospital in Troy, NY," read one newspaper caption.[67] Who was showing off what? It is hard to know how to interpret this picture. Grace Bump is not showing off, but her hospital and doctors are showing off their successful surgery. Probably the baby's parents shared the pride—and the hope for a new, better, seeing future for the child. Certainly the news photos celebrated relief and faith in medicine's abilities. Grace Bump is a cute baby—presumably something always a pleasure for newspaper readers to see—and the photo demonstrated that medicine could counteract vision defects. Likewise, news photos of eight-month-old Dale Crosby showed him having his cornea measured and being fitted with contact lenses at Orange County (California) Children's Hospital. Two "delicate operations and a tiny pair of contact lenses" changed this baby's life. "When you first place the lenses in his eyes, the change in his behavior is amazing," observed his mother. To the clear delight of his mother, "he brightens up [and] looks around, and you can tell he is enjoying what he sees." Creating contacts of this size was also an achievement. Before leaving the hospital, Mr. and Mrs. Crosby learned how to insert the contact lenses.[68] This was a rare mention of a father's active involvement in learning new skills to care for the affected infant. Surely plenty of fathers had learned to care for their children, but their gender-crossing into infant and child care tended to be overlooked and erased. In-depth media coverage of specific individual children like these, however, was unusual. Most coverage of the disease trumpeted death and deformity.

Despite the celebration of medical achievements and the babies' futures, Grace Bump looks odd in her photograph because she wears enormous glasses—called "specs" in the headline—that appear sized for an adult. Indeed, fifty years later, this newspaper photo is now labeled "hilarious" and is catalogued under "Freaks" on an Internet site. The Internet poster clarifies that "it's not that it's a baby wearing glasses. It's a baby wearing *these* glasses."[69] From the perspective of the twenty-first century, the glasses of the 1960s do look odd. But this reaction is not only about style. Filing this newspaper clip under "Freaks" bluntly states how the image appears to viewers. The baby in big glasses is a freak. I suspect that many—perhaps even the photographer and her parents and relatives—saw baby Grace, at least initially, as a bit freakish. One woman today vividly remembers that as a child she saw news photos like this one of a baby in glasses; the disease frightened her.[70] Kids with glasses were called names. On women, glasses were a detraction and antisexual. It is still a regular trope in movies today that smart girls, librarians, and professors wear glasses, and when they finally find a lover and come out of their shell—he takes off her glasses, revealing her beauty and her heterosexuality. Starting life with glasses was to start out as abnormal. Cataract surgery, glasses, and contacts fitted for small children meant that they could see and participate in the regular world. Yet the baby girl in glasses might still be seen as a freak.

Celebratory news photos did not express the emotional toll of infant surgeries, though. In a later account of her own child rearing and her son's successful path to "autonomy," Mary Jean Beaton outlined the reality. "We knew the time had come for Eugene's many operations," she recalled. It was 1967; her son was nearly a year old when the Beatons prepared for his cataract surgery. "We hated to have him suffer, and," as a nurse and a doctor, Eugene's parents "knew that hospitals . . . were painful places to be." Her son was hospitalized for several days and had one eye patched and his arms restrained so that he could not poke his eye. Four weeks later, the family went through the entire process again with surgery on the other eye. Yet Eugene still could not see. "Much to my disappointment, these children do not see immediately when the cataracts are removed," Beaton explained. "They have to learn to see." One night, feeding the baby, she broke into tears. "He still can't see anything," she sobbed to her husband. "I was really depressed. We tried showing him bright, colorful objects, but he did not show much interest." When her son finally looked at her one evening, she was "thrill[ed]." A month later, their doctors told them he needed heart surgery. At a year old, Eugene did not roll over or sit up. Now they knew why: "he needed all of his energy to stay alive. . . . 'If we ever needed you, Lord, we need you now,'" prayed Eugene's mother. The friends who stuck by them, a superb surgical team, and prayer got Mary Beaton, Eugene, and her family through the crises.[71]

Reports of successful efforts to teach children affected by maternal rubella offered reasons for hope as well as reasons for worry both to parents of "rubella babies" and to potential parents. Alongside the first CDC report in *Newsweek* announcing the epidemic, for instance, appeared an article about "'the boy who tuned out'—five-year-old Danny seemed destined for an institution" for the mentally retarded. Danny did not talk; he had aphasia, an inability to speak that was frequently caused by fetal exposure to rubella.[72] The article intended to be sympathetic and to show that the condition was treatable. However, an aware parent would also immediately realize that the intensive, individualized daily therapy available to only twenty-five children at Stanford (which had a six-month waiting list) must be hard to obtain and probably expensive. Readers likely wondered whether the state or health insurance provided for such therapies or whether the individual family had to rely on its own financial resources. Would they have to move in order to gain access to treatment or special education? Families, educators, and policy makers all knew that families might move to find the services that their children required.[73]

In the midst of a major epidemic, CDC officials reassured women that they should not think birth defects inevitable, but the information about risk, consequences, and expenses might overwhelm optimism for many expectant parents.

## WHAT WAS A PREGNANT WOMAN TO DO?

Many women were immune to the disease and need not worry, health officials tried to reassure. "Only one in twenty women of child-bearing age [was] susceptible to rubella," and, according to authorities, "birth defects following infection were not inevitable."[74] Individual women, however, did not know whether they were immune (and no test to determine immune status existed). This disease required that women scrutinize their own bodies and the bodies of everyone, especially children, around them for signs of disease. The minor colds, fevers, or rashes they had had during pregnancy or during the few weeks before they knew of their pregnancy might have been rubella. Worse, it was possible to contract the disease and never notice it at all. The characteristic mildness—sometimes invisibility—of the disease made it particularly insidious. No one could rest easily knowing that the epidemic had spared her; perhaps she had failed to recognize the disease. Few pregnant women could know with certainty that they were *not* at risk for the disease and its consequences. The scientific and medical information about the possible consequences of German measles, which could not be ascertained with certainty for individual women, terrified many. In epidemic years, the specter of tragedy hung over virtually all pregnant women.

The only protection available to pregnant women was to have had German measles in childhood—thus gaining immunity—but, as commentators observed, women often did not "remember" whether they had previously had the disease. The word *remember,* however, covers up a more complex process and may imply irresponsibility on the part of those who "forgot." First, the demand that women "remember" required recalling an innocuous childhood illness. Since the disease concentrated among young children, adults would have to remember the rash and fever that (perhaps) had sent them to bed for a few days when they were perhaps four or eight years old. Many adults would not remember all of the various sicknesses of their childhood. In families that told stories or otherwise remarked upon diseases and epidemics, memories might be formed. Health advisers encouraged mothers to keep records, and some educated, highly health-conscious, and well-organized women did so. No doubt many others had incomplete records or none. Those who kept track noted measles—but not the relatively unimportant German measles—in their baby books.[75] For most, memory would require that the mother of the now-adult woman accurately diagnosed and recalled the diseases of her children. One worried mother who had been exposed to German measles by her daughters' babysitter (note the pathway of transmission and the near im-possibility of avoiding this disease during an epidemic) told her doctor that she was not "sure" whether she had had German measles as a child. "I had an illness when I was about eight, she said. "They always spoke of it as measles. Nobody ever said what kind, though, and my mother died when I was ten." The remark pointed out the obvious: the person likely to know was one's own mother. Without her, health information could be spotty. When this woman asked her father, he remembered that "Mother" had kept her "in bed in a dark room until the rash had gone away."[76]

"Too bad a doctor wasn't brought in, for the sake of establishing a definite diagnosis," her doctor responded. "[For] girls, it can be so important to know, in later life."[77] The doctor spoke of the past but, more importantly, also to the future. The readers of *Ladies' Home Journal* should learn that they needed to take care and to record correct, medically diagnosed diseases for their daughters. The doctor implicitly placed a bit of blame on patients and family members: a mistake had been made; a doctor should have been called. When this woman was eight, however, the significance of German measles may have been unknown or only recently discovered.[78] Calling in a doctor did not ensure a correct diagnosis, either. Diagnosis of German measles was not simple, as clinicians and researchers knew, since it was easily confused with measles and scarlet fever, and not all sufferers had a pink rash and three-day fever. In the midst of an epidemic, the vagueness of the symptoms that might go unrecognized further increased anxiety. Pregnant women, one re-porter observed, "often panic, [thinking,] 'Was I really immune, . . . or do I have a case without rash, and is the virus injuring my baby?' "[79]

To protect themselves, public health officials advised women to avoid the group of people in which the disease concentrated: children.[80] Advising pregnant women to avoid preschoolers and young schoolchildren appeared logical, but it was absurd. None of the advice literature of the time addressed the logistical difficulties of keeping potentially pregnant women away from potentially infectious children. It is essential to analyze the gender arrangements of the household and care of the sick and to bring these problems to the fore in order to understand this epidemic, the growing anxieties of pregnant women, and the government and scientific research agendas in response to this disease. Avoiding children was virtually impossible for women of childbearing age, who tended to be surrounded by children in daily life as mothers, female relatives, and neighbors and in gender-segregated occupations as teachers, nurses, or retail clerks. Many men might have been able to avoid children since they worked in male-dominated workplaces without children present and did not have the responsibility of caring for children whether they were sick or well. Rubella, however, did not threaten men.

The pregnant woman, one medical adviser suggested, should "be isolated from the child who has the disease for at least twenty one days."[81] Aside from the fact that isolation is generally used to remove the infectious, not to hold the healthy,[82] carrying out this suggestion would be extremely difficult. In the early 1960s, when families had several children born close together and many expectant women were already mothers of young children, isolating the mother from a sick child would be difficult. In earlier years, families had faced quarantine for infectious diseases. Generally, that meant sick children, husbands, and relatives stayed at home to be cared for by the wife or mother. Occasionally, particularly in the case of tuberculosis, if the mother was infected, she left the home to go to an institution for care and to avoid exposing others. By the 1960s, however, if pregnant women were expected to remove themselves rather than quarantine the infectious family member, where would they go for three weeks? If a hospital was the place to isolate the healthy patient to prevent exposure, it would cost a fortune. A woman might remove herself to her own mother's home, but then the grandmother could not help with the grandchildren. Did the woman have a sister or neighbor who could take on the children for three weeks? A father might get the kids off to school, make lunches, and do more, but he risked losing income or his job if he left work early to pick them up after school or missed work to care for a baby all day long. In Buffalo, New York's Irish Catholic community, in which families of ten, eleven, and twelve children were common and the mothers always pregnant, one woman recalls that the mothers also always feared

German measles and exposing someone else.[83] There was no way, no matter what health experts might advise, for women to avoid sick children. No wonder anxiety and worry increased.

Americans not only feared bearing children damaged by rubella; they also came to fear the affected newborn. When "rubella babies" were discovered to be infectious for months after birth, they became "dangerous babies" who threatened pregnant women. New York University Hospital discovered that babies born with visible defects had infected the health-care workers attending them. A completely healthy-appearing baby could be, in fact, an infected and dangerous baby who would go home and then infect unsuspecting women of childbearing age who came to "coo over him."[84] This surprising finding strengthened the representation of the child or, in this case, the newborn infant as dangerous to adults, especially expectant mothers. Babies born with congenital rubella syndrome, themselves victims of the virus, were labeled "contagion" and " 'Typhoid Marys' " of rubella, transmitting infections to hospital personnel and other contacts for a period of at least six months.[85] The latter label called up old cultural memories of an insidious individual who secretly infected the unwitting.[86] This baby was no innocent. Instead, the adults who cared for him or her were the innocent victims.

### THERAPEUTIC ABORTION

Once the international medical world understood Gregg's discovery of the terrible impact of German measles on pregnancy, many physicians accepted maternal rubella as a medical indication for legal therapeutic abortions. In the 1940s, Norman Gregg, Charles Swan, and other early researchers strongly endorsed abortions in such cases.[87] Gregg and many of his U.S. medical colleagues regarded it as the obvious answer in every case.[88] "I," Sir Gregg himself declared at a 1955 meeting of U.S. specialists in ophthalmology, "would not allow the pregnancy to continue if the circumstances arose in my family."[89] As the physician who had discovered the link between the disease and congenital abnormalities and had been knighted for his discovery, Gregg's words carried weight. Although there had been some international medical debate on the question of risk and abortion in the early 1950s, by the end of the decade, mainstream medicine largely agreed that the fetus was likely to be injured when the mother had German measles in early pregnancy and that abortion was medically (and morally) justified in these cases. *Williams Obstetrics,* the standard medical school textbook in the United States, endorsed therapeutic abortion for maternal rubella in the first trimester when the risk of "defects" was high "if the mother and her husband [did] not want to assume the obvious risks involved."[90] Indeed, according to one health writer, an expectant mother who contracted rubella was "entitled" to a therapeutic abortion.[91]

Awareness of the disease's dangers drove many women to seek abortions, but they did so within an increasingly repressive context as police stepped up their raids of illegal abortion providers and hospitals cracked down on the legal practice of therapeutic abortion.[92] It was not at all new for married women to turn to abortion, but obtaining abortions was becoming more difficult in this period. During the economic crisis of the Depression, American women sharply cut the birth rate through delayed marriage, contraceptive use, and abortion. Safe abortion clinics had practiced openly. In the more politically conservative and pronatalist 1940s and 1950s, however, abortions came under greater surveillance. At the same time, the number of birth control clinics expanded even as their legal status continued to be challenged.[93] As Dr. Robert Hall, a Columbia University specialist in obstetrics, later recounted, conservative hospital abortion review committees initially rejected cases seeking abortion because the pregnant woman had contracted German measles. At first, only "the wives of insistent physicians" received therapeutic abortions for rubella. As the public learned more about "rubella deformities," however, growing numbers of more ordinary women also became "insistent" and pushed obstetricians and hospital abortion committees to permit therapeutic abortions.[94]

Post–World War II media coverage of abortion emphasized its criminality and deadliness. Newspapers printed mug shots of men and women accused of providing criminal abortions and covered police raids of abortion clinics. Women died in magazine and newspaper abortion stories of the 1940s and 1950s. Abortion, popular accounts emphasized, was a crime associated with the Mafia, prostitution, illegal drugs, and gambling.[95] A 1951 *Ebony* article on "the abortion menace," for example, included a series of photos depicting a woman meeting an unknown connection on a dark corner, the abortion procedure being performed in an apartment, and, finally, several police officers standing in a circle around a bed and pulling a sheet over a dead woman's body. The headline announced that abortion "claims 8,000 lives of desperate mothers-to-be" every year, including "several thousand Negro women."[96] A decade later, a three-part investigative series on abortion in the mainstream *Saturday Evening Post* followed the same pattern. Headlines declared that "every day thousands of American women risk their lives" by having abortions. *Ebony* depicted the death and victimization of an African American woman; photos in the *Saturday Evening Post* featured young white women who had died. Both included photos of the abortionist's equipment and guilty abortionists.[97] Avid readers learned that abortion was deviant, dirty, and dangerous; those who might know otherwise endured shame and secrecy.

The media representations of women who had had abortions at mid-century stressed and magnified not only the women's likely demise but also their promiscuity and problems. Late-nineteenth- and early-twentieth-century newspapers had sympathized with the "seduced and abandoned" girls whom they portrayed as the victims of nefarious men and of abortion. Newspapers and turn-of-the-century feminists alike told this story of the victimization of unwed women, though the truth was that most of the women who had abortions were married, and most survived.[98] The abortion story of the 1950s and 1960s, in contrast, painted the picture of young women who had abortions differently, emphasizing their psychological problems more than their innocence. In this period, women who had abortions—like women who miscarried, adoptive mothers, unwed mothers, mothers of autistic children, infertile women, employed women, overpowering mothers black and white, and lesbians—were analyzed as psychologically immature or deficient.[99] In keeping with the period's tendency to psychoanalyze women, *Saturday Evening Post* journalist John Martin investigated the psychological stability of women who had had abortions and found it wanting. Of the "aborted women" whom he interviewed, he reported that "all . . . feel unwanted by their fathers. Moreover, many have suffered childhood deprivation, divorce, spontaneous miscarriage, severe emotional disturbance, and other sociomedical traumas. At least in the United States, abortion," he continued, "seems often to be only one pathological symptom in a whole constellation of sociomedical symptoms. As one authority said, 'Whenever you have an abortion, you have a sick person in a sick situation.'"[100]

Further underscoring the deviant nature of abortion and the women who had them, black and brown men entered this report either as sexual intimates of white women or as criminal abortionists. Abortions could hide interracial sexual relationships. Women who had abortions thus were violating not only the law but also the gender and racial codes governing female sexuality. White women went into "colored" neighborhoods for abortions performed by dirty, drunk "colored" men, according to mainstream publications. One "sweet, blond girl" originally from Illinois told of a Mexican lover and her need to hide that interracial relationship. To bear and care for a racially mixed brown child, her mother made clear to her, was unacceptable.[101] (This situation would be most true in white communities. Black and other communities of color sometimes absorbed mixed race children and families, though not always easily.)[102] Not only was interracial marriage between whites and people of color socially unacceptable; it was also illegal in many states, and thus children of such marriages could not be legitimatized. Health officials also considered interracial sex a sign of feeble-mindedness and a reason for sterilizing women. Single mothers, low-income black women in particular, endured intrusive surveillance as state welfare authorities hunted for men in their homes and denied them needed benefits to pay for food and shelter for themselves and their children. Single mothers also risked losing their children to state child protection agencies: their unmarried status proved their immorality, and they could easily be charged with neglect if their children remained alone at home while they went to work.[103]

Black men and white women appeared in the abortion stories in both the *Saturday Evening Post* and *Ebony,* but the racial dynamics played out differently in the two magazines. In the predominantly white magazine, a "colored" man threatened the "white" girl; in the black magazine, a white woman threatened an African American man's professional reputation and career. *Ebony* reported on a black physician-abortionist and the white woman who came to him for an abortion. In the black magazine's account, it was a young white secretary's death that resulted in manslaughter charges and the doctor's nineteen-year sentence at a Tennessee prison.[104] Although the article did not say so directly, black readers would be likely to read between the lines and suspect that a prominent African American man—a physician and owner of a Negro-league baseball team—had been prosecuted and convicted in a southern state because of the perceived sexual nature of his medical relationship to a white woman. In his autobiography, Dr. Ed Keemer, an African American physician who practiced in Detroit, pointed to this dynamic to explain his own conviction for abortion in the 1950s. The prosecutor had emphasized that a young white woman had been examined, touched, and aborted by a black man. As soon as the prosecutor framed the case in this way, Keemer knew he would be convicted. Black men with economic and political power had long been threatened and lynched on the pretext of their sexual violence toward white women, and white juries had easily convicted African American men in rape cases in which white women were the victims while white men who had raped black women went free. Convictions for abortion with this racial portrait echoed the history of rape.[105]

Abortion was deadly and criminal, and the women who had abortions were sexually deviant, racially suspect, and psychologically sick, according to the representations of abortion available to the general public. Yet throughout the twentieth century, it was not unusual for women in the United States—married and unmarried alike and of every class, ethnicity, and religion—to seek abortions regardless of the law or to talk about abortion with selected family members and friends. Women did not voluntarily talk about abortion in public, however.[106] What was highly unusual—even "shocking"—in the early 1960s was to speak in *public* spaces and mainstream news media about the decision to have an abortion as one to be made by women.[107] Media attention to women's perspectives, abortion, and disabilities appeared in major news forums, including national network television news shows and *Life* magazine as well as women's and health magazines. These subjects held significance for the nation. The intimate conversations and soul-searching about the question of abortion that took place in doctors' offices, in kitchens, in beds, in churches, in diaries, and among friends and family as women and their husbands made decisions were out of the public eye. A few, however, were reproduced in public formats in the early 1960s as German measles and thalidomide brought the dilemmas of married women to the forefront.

I closely examine a set of texts that appeared in magazines and on television that focused on the married pregnant woman in crisis and her thought processes and decisions concerning whether to carry a pregnancy to term or have an abortion. These accounts indicate the great popular interest in the plight of married women who wanted babies but might have to give them up by having abortions. I analyze these accounts both as "real"—as expressions of the situation that women faced when they realized what a German measles epidemic might mean for them—and as representations because these accounts are also stories for reading and viewing audiences. The shared conventions within these accounts, their emphases, and their emotional tones are as important as the fact that the women avidly sought (therapeutic) abortions with medical support. These narratives tell a certain type of story that shaped perceptions and had cultural and, eventually, political import. They reconstructed the representation of abortion, transforming it from the act of a sick and depraved woman into the act of a responsible, thoughtful married middle-class white mother. The distress and thinking of these married white women, whose motherhood was glorified, received respectful attention—in contrast to the concurrent demonization of black and Latina mothers, who were blamed for crime, poverty, and overpopulation. The demonization and the glorification were closely linked and cocreated. The demonization of the women of color sustained the glorification of white motherhood.[108] (White) women took their pregnancies extremely seriously, these texts demonstrated. Their decisions to abort or even to consider the question of doing so were not taken lightly. At the same time, the solemnity projected into these accounts made serious thinking about pregnancy, family, and abortion a social norm. *Williams Obstetrics* suggested and the magazines confirmed that whether to have a therapeutic abortion was a serious decision to be made by the expectant mother in consultation with her doctor and her husband.

Given that the decision was presented as one to be made by wives and husbands, one might expect the marriage to be a strong emotional focal point in these narratives. Instead, the relationships between married women and their husbands appear as a minor note compared with the prominence of the relationships between mothers and their children. German measles exposed the intensely linked child-mother world of the postwar period. In these accounts we see that children played many roles in the life of a mother: they posed danger because they could infect her with German measles, they expressed the mother's emotions as their own, their health and agility provided her with norms against which she could compare the capacities of an "abnormal" child, and they made prior claims upon the mother. Today German measles provides us with a window into internal family dynamics, power, emotions, fantasies, fears, and realities.

German measles frightened expectant mothers, but, the media taught, they could look to doctors for support. One doctor told the story of Mrs. Bassett for the edification of middle-class readers.[109] Its lessons covered both maternal rubella and proper patient behavior. Believing that she had been exposed to the disease, Mrs. Bassett called her doctor, who acted as doctor, scientist, educator, and marriage counselor. He reassured her and asked her to investigate her own childhood exposure. Two weeks later, Mr. Bassett phoned the doctor to report that his wife had gone "all to pieces" when their pediatrician had diagnosed German measles in his wife and two daughters. "She's been begging me to call you, says she'll have to have a therapeutic abortion right away," he continued. "I'm afraid this hysteria is bad for her." When the doctor arrived at their home, the husband reported, "She keeps saying that if we let our baby be born, it will be defective—blind, deaf, maybe feeble-minded! It sounds to me as if she's delirious." "Sob[bing]," Mrs. Bassett appealed to the doctor for a therapeutic abortion. She told him, "I can't make Harry believe there is any danger at all." As the husband's words conveyed, he perceived his wife's anguish as crazy. He neither believed her nor grasped the seriousness of the situation. The obstetrician understood his patient's agony and validated the wife's knowledge of the impact of maternal rubella. But he also corrected her. Doctors now believed, he explained, that "damage" occurred less frequently than had been initially thought and that the greatest danger was during the first five weeks of pregnancy. Mrs. Bassett, however, he calculated and reassured, had been in her tenth week of pregnancy when she contracted the disease. When the husband astutely asked whether the doctor was telling them that physicians no longer performed therapeutic abortions for German measles, the doctor answered in circuitous fashion that if a woman already had four children, had a definite case of German measles in the first five weeks of pregnancy, and was so worried that her own health was threatened, an abortion might be justified. He concluded, however, "*Your* chances of having a perfectly normal baby are 90 percent or better. I would not consent to a therapeutic abortion under such circumstances, though you might be able to find someone who would." "Those odds sound good to me," the husband responded. "But Marguerite is the one to consider. How about it, honey? Will you be worrying yourself sick until the baby is born?"[110]

In this scene in which information is considered and a decision made, we see the trio—male doctor, husband, and wife/expectant mother/patient—considering the situation. We can also see how unequal power operated to define the situation and its parameters and to control the probable outcome. The men appear as concerned and sympathetic advisers who leave the decision to the pregnant woman. She has to assess the situation and make a decision. In this case, Marguerite/Mrs. Bassett rethinks her original conviction and decides that she will accept the minimized risk and have the baby. The husband interprets "the odds" as being good, as the doctor intended he should. Yet the 10 percent odds of having a child with serious birth defects in this case were five to ten times more than usual.[111] Notably, the doctor did not describe the "odds" in these terms. For the expectant mother, her decision making included considering the conditions of her motherhood, information about the potential effects of maternal rubella on a future child, reassurances that the likelihood of her having "a perfectly normal baby" was 90 percent, her doctor's refusal to provide an abortion, and her husband's optimistic outlook. Her decision was overdetermined. She decided against abortion. "I've been thinking," she said. "This may be the boy we've been wanting, and we may never have another one. If he's born with a defect, maybe it can be corrected. If it can't, we will love him just as much and do all we can to help him have a good life." "Her decision made," the doctor concluded his story, "Mrs. Bassett went through the rest of her pregnancy serenely." The Bassetts had another girl, not the hoped-for boy, but "any disappointment her parents might have felt on that score was more than counterbalanced by the fact that the newborn was healthy and perfectly formed."[112]

This installment of the *Ladies' Home Journal's* "Tell Me, Doctor" column educated those who knew nothing about German measles as well as those who, like Mrs. Bassett, thought they knew all about it. It reassured readers by ending with a woman who previously insisted on having an abortion deciding against it and then giving birth to a "healthy and perfectly formed" baby. As the column focused on the facts of German measles and corrected both husband and wife, it simultaneously modeled and taught women of the authority and paternalism of their doctors. The magazine's female readers, the column taught, not only could trust their doctors' information but also could count on his respect, his empathy, and his unusual capacity to enter into a family and speak judiciously to husbands. The pregnant woman's job was to listen to her doctor. The column provided a model of the anxious but reasonable mother who took responsibility for the health of her children and listened to her doctor, the caring husband who listened to the doctor and showed concern for his wife, and the paternalist, responsive, and caring physician.[113]

The conscientious mother also accepted a new medical responsibility for her daughters. "Wise mothers," as one health adviser observed of German measles, "hope their little girls will have it."[114] At the end of the story about the Bassetts, the new mother promised to expose her new baby daughter to "every case I hear of in the neighborhood."[115] Doctors and mothers tried to protect future pregnancies by exposing girls to German measles so that they could gain immunities in childhood, prior to adulthood and pregnancy. Recognizing the danger of rubella, doctor and mother both imagined a brand-new infant as a future mother. The immediacy of gender assignment could not be more evident. Girls, all girls, will become mothers, doctors and parents assumed. At birth, newborn bodies were inspected, their sex identified and named, and their futures projected.

Some parents held "German measles parties" for girls in hopes of preventing the damages of maternal rubella in the future. An English physician-father first publicized this idea in 1948, and in the 1950s health advisers emphasized that girls should catch German measles "before marriage" in order to protect their presumed futures as mothers.[116] Newsmagazines reproduced a photo of Dr. Charles Stevens and his daughter at a German measles party. (See figure 4.) Dr. Stevens's authority as a physician and a father dignified the practice of hosting German measles parties and spread it. Although other health authorities had doubts about the wisdom of this method because it could spread the disease to pregnant women, popular magazines promoted the idea.[117] "Spring 1964 is the best of times for a German measles party. The rules call for lots of kissing games," Time magazine's article giggled, "so that all the little boys and, more especially, all the little girls get the infection."[118]

The magazine's health advice played with child sexuality and with the children's implicit futures, not only as "mothers" but also as sexual beings and heterosexual couples. Although Time imagined the boys participating in "kissing games," boys and men were largely irrelevant to these enterprising efforts to avoid disease and deformity, for it was women who would become pregnant and who would have the gendered responsibility for the health of their babies. Medical advisers, led by Dr. Virginia Apgar of the March of Dimes, now advocated that "pre-natal care . . . begin in girlhood" since "most little girls are going to grow up to be mothers."[119] The biological futures of boys as fathers received no comparable attention. German measles quickly turned into another health responsibility of girls and women, who were advised to "have your rubella before marriage."[120]

Although the "Tell Me, Doctor" column about Mrs. Bassett downplayed the need for therapeutic abortion in cases of German measles during pregnancy, it nonetheless alerted readers to the possibility. Indeed, the magazine drew in readers with a pull-out quotation that highlighted therapeutic abortion: "I have come down with German measles, Doctor, and I know what that can do to my unborn baby. Surely you will perform a therapeutic abortion?"[121] Even though the doctor's answer in the end was "No," the article broadcast the (possible) availability of therapeutic abortion, the differences of opinion among doctors on this point, and the conditions that made it a likely or unlikely option. Most important, the narrative framework of the story emphasized that this was a decision that belonged to the pregnant woman.

Figure 4. A German measles party could be as much fun as—and combined with—a birthday party, as demonstrated in this photo of a children's party outside London. Dr. Charles Stevens and his wife Betty were "delighted" to be able to expose their young daughter and son to the infected birthday girl. They hoped their children would soon have "the spots" and be able to infect their older sisters. The father appeared to cross a gender line by serving the children, but he acted as a doctor. At the same time, he violated the rule of isolating the contagious and instead encouraged the birthday girl to spread the disease to her friends in order to protect future pregnancies and future babies. "Catch It If You Can," 70, no. 4 *Time* (July 22, 1957): 53. Photograph by Paul Popper.

Sherri Finkbine was the first woman to deliberately share with the public her decision to seek an abortion. Her public presence, soon to be followed by others, indicated a startlingly new daring on the part of individual women to talk about abortion in their lives as mothers. Finkbine was a white married mother who talked openly with the press about her happiness at the prospect of having her fifth child, her sadness as she realized that thalidomide had probably severely harmed her developing baby, and her sense that an abortion was necessary even as her doctors denied her the scheduled therapeutic abortion. "There is only a 50–50 chance the baby would be normal," Finkbine explained to reporters and the public. "His life would probably be tragic and so fruitless." Her husband worried about the toll that "a deformed child" would take on the rest of the family.[122] As Finkbine's private decisions became public and part of an international debate about abortion, she explained her feelings and her thinking in greater detail. Finkbine told of long conversations in the middle of the night with her husband, Bob, about what to do. "Naturally, I had misgivings," she explained to *Life* magazine. "There is life there. . . . But is it life when you can't dress yourself, run, walk, dance, play games, have dates? If I had no choice, I would have the baby. But I have the way to prevent this tragedy, this sadness."[123]

Finkbine's attributes made her an ideal media representation of the American mother caught in a reproductive dilemma, for she represented the ideal mother and "every woman." She was the culture's portrait of the child-centered woman: attractive, white, heterosexual, and a married mother of four. Finkbine's religious identity was left unnamed (at her request), thus contributing to the construction of white middle-class homogeneity. Her situation invited everyone—from the experts to the ordinary, from the most powerful to the least, men and women alike—to talk about reproductive and family issues that typically did not reach the national news.[124] As Miss Sherri, Finkbine led *Romper Room,* a television show for preschoolers. She and her husband welcomed the neighborhood's kids into their home. *Life* magazine photos showed many aspects of Finkbine's roles and personality—as a properly dressed but tormented woman at home, as a good mother with children in her lap. (See figure 5.) Above her photo on one page, several men in shirts and ties were shown passionately discussing her case. That photo of serious discussion among men about law, medicine, morality, and what would be permitted in her specific case matched the mode of official reproductive decision making and policies in hospitals and in law—decisions to be made by male experts. In the photo, Finkbine's husband served as her advocate as he met with their lawyers. The photo also showed that her husband approved of the abortion and that this couple acted together as they thought about and created their family.

The hierarchical placement of these photos on the page may serve as a metaphor for the gendered power arrangements, but the story is more complex. Sherri Finkbine speaks emphatically for herself in another full-page photo.[125] This strong image presents her as a woman who knows her own mind, can speak it, and will follow it. These decisions about pregnancy, children, and motherhood were hers to make. She clearly spoke for herself about what was right for her and what she had decided was necessary. (See figure 6.) Many supported her; others argued with her in angry letters, phone calls, sermons, and radio shows.[126]

Figure 5. Sherri and Bob Finkbine opened their home and shared their family and life with the media. The Finkbines' bodies showed their distress and the intensity of their belief that they should be able to have a legal abortion performed by a physician, a procedure they both wanted. This picture of Finkbine surrounded by several small children also emphasized that she was a typical mother. *Life* 53, no. 6 (August 10, 1962): 33.

Having seen photographs of children without legs, arms, or both and having had personal experience with a child's disability, the Finkbines had a picture of the future. Because of a problem with her hip socket, their first child had worn a "formidable-looking apparatus of leather rings and metal encasing the entire length of her leg." This experience contributed to the Finkbines' vision of what the future might hold. They remembered their deep anxiety for their daughter, the time spent on doctors' appointments and therapies, and the expense. When they envisioned the consequences that thalidomide would have for the expected child, their four children, and themselves, the Finkbines found that avoiding tragedy was the path to take. They knew what caring for "a deformed child" required. "I could be only a partial mother to the other four," Finkbine explained. "Much, much time and effort, and much money too would have to be lavished

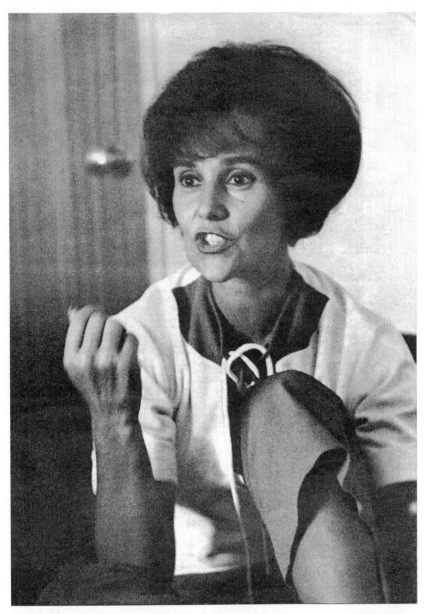

Figure 6. In a previous photo also accompanying this article (not reproduced here), Sherri Finkbine is shown covering her face with her hand, weeping. In this large magazine photo, she is shown speaking emphatically to a reporter and to the public about thalidomide and her decision to have an abortion. She appears as a well-dressed, thoughtful, and determined woman. *Life* 53, no. 6 (August 10, 1962): 31.

on the helpless one, and the others would be cheated of part of their birthright." The child would require lifetime help for all functions. "Would he be grateful to us someday . . . for giving him life," Sherri Finkbine wondered, or would he "look about him at people with arms and legs, at children running, at boys and girls walking hand in hand, and curse us for letting him be born?" The Finkbines thought long and hard and imagined the possibilities. Sherri Finkbine pursued an abortion on behalf of her family and with the belief that God had offered her "the power to prevent" the birth of a "malformed baby."[127]

The media closely followed the Finkbine story, as did the public. Finkbine wanted to warn other women of the danger of taking this medication during pregnancy, but her story also broadcast the news that a married woman could not obtain an abortion that her husband and doctors agreed was needed when malformations and/or early infant death was likely. Polls showed support for Finkbine's decision to seek an abortion. In a Gallup poll, 52 percent of Americans believed that in having an abortion, Finkbine had done "the right thing."[128] Sherri and Bob Finkbine bravely moved through the political firestorm surrounding her pregnancy, but, as she later recalled, when her doctors cancelled the planned abortion for fear of prosecution, "I did not do much deciding." They did.[129] The German measles epidemic brought the same dilemma to tens of thousands of other women just like Finkbine.

As CBS Television News announced, the German measles epidemic was "a far more widespread threat to unborn babies" than thalidomide. The threatening disease appeared in a 1965 CBS News documentary that analyzed laws around the world and the emerging abortion law reform movement in the United States. The show aired twice. Dr. Saul Krugman, a prominent pediatrician and infectious disease specialist at New York University, described for viewers the "malformations" German measles caused and explained that the "risk is approximately 50 percent." Although the possibility of having a "deformed baby was not a reason" for a therapeutic abortion, viewers learned that some hospitals permitted therapeutic abortions for maternal rubella. Following the doctor, another expert, a mother, talked about why she and her husband decided to have a therapeutic abortion after she had contracted maternal rubella. "The child had very few chances of being a healthy child," she recalled. "It was terrible. . . . I love children." In the midst of her traumatic situation, she kept telling herself, "Although we were stopping it now, we would have a healthy baby later."[130] Embedded among the comments of supporters and opponents of abortion law reform, this white married woman's testimony alerted still more expectant mothers and married couples to both the danger of German measles and the possibility of therapeutic abortion. When television newsman Walter Cronkite informed his audience that six weeks earlier this woman had given birth to a healthy baby, the report stressed for its viewers that a bleak story like this one might turn out to be happy in the end.[131]

Jesuit commentators criticized the CBS News documentary for downplaying the use of abortion by married women. The show, they complained, overemphasized the sad stories of young rape victims told by reform advocates and shamed unmarried mothers when, as Cronkite himself reported, 80 percent of the women who had abortions were married. That "cold statistic," in the view of *America,* a Jesuit magazine, was too easily overlooked.[132] The "coldness" of married women who sought abortions, this reviewer believed, would garner no sympathy. *America*'s commentators and abortion law reformers apparently agreed that teenage girls were an emotional draw and thus had potential power to secure legal reform. *America*'s writers seemed to suggest that if the public realized that *married* women had abortions, it would disapprove. These observers would soon learn differently.[133]

The cover of *Life Magazine* in June 1965 featured a white woman, her fist curled as a technician drew her blood. The current German measles epidemic, the headline warned, "will damage 20,000 babies."[134] The full-color cover of the anxious but resigned and strong-looking woman is vivid. For those who recognized that the photo depicted a new blood test, the cover itself raised questions. What will science tell this worried woman? And what will she do? Inside, the magazine explained that the worried "expectant mother" would have to wait two weeks to get her answer.[135] Laboratory analysis of her blood samples could tell whether the woman had antibodies for rubella and whether she was immune to or had recently caught the disease, thus exposing her developing pregnancy to the dangerous virus.

The striking photo showed a woman in the middle of a deeply medicalized and deeply personal—and at the same time deeply public—moment. *Life* magazine's use of this photo for its cover underscores the national importance of German measles and reproductive subjects. (See figure 7.) The young woman holds her fist tightly closed, looking up as though waiting to hear an answer. She looks worried, yet the fist hints at possible protest and an emerging women's rights movement. After all, two years earlier, Betty Friedan's *The Feminine Mystique* had named the dissatisfaction of a generation of white middle-class suburban mothers.[136] The book sold millions of copies. As could be seen in the free speech movement that rocked the University of California at Berkeley; the police beatings of black protesters in Selma, Alabama, shown on television; the civil rights and black power movements; the growing opposition to the Vietnam War; and marches on Washington, DC, dissatisfaction and frustration ran deep across the nation. *Life* magazine's cover photo was a marked contrast to an image of the rubella blood test shown in the *Chicago Tribune*. The central focus of the newspaper's sketch is the needle and the apparatus for drawing blood from the female patient's arm. She and the doctor are on either side. It is a picture of a medical event controlled by the physician, with the patient passive.[137]

*Life*'s portrait of this technology was different. An arm of the technician is visible, but the expectant mother appears to be alone. She is taking the test, she is aware of its purpose, and she—apparently alone—contemplates the outcome. She is agonized but also appears strong. Once armed with information, she will make decisions. Her fist clenched for the blood test might implicitly suggest that she will raise her arm and insist—echoing Finkbine and the changing culture—that she has the right to determine her reproduction, the shape of her family, and her life or that she, along with many others, might claim that right.

The test represented a significant new development in the power of science to control the disease and the power of women to determine their reproductive futures. The first test for German measles had been developed a year earlier, and as soon as the announcement of it was made, Dr. Stanley A. Plotkin reported, his lab was "'deluged' with requests for help."[138] Observers pointed to the test's value to pregnant women for providing emotional reassurance: the test would show immunity, thus eliminating women's worries. The real value of the test, however, lay in its opposite result—its potential to give bad news. The test was immediately touted as potentially "useful" for knowing when a therapeutic abortion should be contemplated. It took a long time to get results, though. The first test required taking two blood samples—one soon after a woman's exposure to the disease, the other two weeks later—and it could take several weeks to get results. Two samples were required in order to compare antibody levels and then determine whether an infection was recent or older (the latter indicating immunity). NIH researcher Dr. Paul D. Parkman called the early tests "very cumbersome."[139] As Parkman and his NIH colleagues worked to develop a vaccine, they announced a quicker test in 1966. "One

Figure 7. The young woman looks up during her blood test—worried, alone, waiting for an answer. This image of an ordinary expectant mother on a magazine cover and the headline above it surely made many empathize with her and grab the magazine. Coverage of German measles was at once news, health education, and a warning. "German Measles and Pregnancy," *Life* 58, no. 22 (June 4, 1965), cover.

Figure 8. These women tucked into their hospital beds are waiting for abortions "performed by conscientious doctors." The lighting emphasizes the loneliness and "agony" of their situation. This picture was a contrast to the images of deceased women that typically accompanied reports about illegal abortion. "The Agony of Mothers About Their Unborn," *Life* 58, no. 22 (June 4, 1965): 24.

of the chief benefits of the new test," newspapers reported, "will be . . . eliminating the distressing period of anxiety of pregnant women who have been exposed to the virus."[140] In three hours a pregnant woman could know whether she was immune or whether she had recently contracted the virus and the fetus had been exposed to the disease.[141]

*Life's* evocative cover photo featured the blood test; the story of this disease, its emotional meanings, and the quandaries faced by mothers and medicine continued inside in four double-page photo spreads. "The Agony of Mothers about Their Unborn" read the headline above a stark black-and-white photo of two women lying in hospital beds. (See figure 8.) Both had "decided to give up their unborn children" after contracting German measles. Side by side in a white room divided by a white curtain and electrical cords, the women appear alone and lonely "awaiting surgery." The emptiness of the room emphasizes their isolation. "Fearful of the almost 50–50 chance that their babies had already been severely damaged, these two women underwent therapeutic abortions." Although their doctors had advised them to have the therapeutic abortions, the magazine described the abortions as "technically illegal." These "conscientious doctors of highest integrity . . . acted in defiance of community convention and state law."[142] These abortions, *Life* declared, violated both "community convention and state law." But this pronouncement overstated the situation. The medical community's convention was to permit therapeutic abortions in such cases, and the law was unclear. The legal status of therapeutic abortion was a question in the process of becoming contentious.[143]

The next spread showcased Mrs. William Stonebreaker in her relationships, talking with her twelve-year-old son, her doctor, and her priests. Readers had seen this mother on the previous pages waiting for her abortion; they now saw her reassuring her tearful son "that it was not his fault she [had] caught German measles and promis[ing] him there will be another baby someday." This child understood his own role in bringing home the disease and harming the much-anticipated sibling-to-be. Infected during the first two weeks of her pregnancy, when the likelihood of severe birth defects was high, she and her doctor discussed therapeutic abortion. For Stonebreaker, the magazine reported, "the dilemma was cruel: she is a Roman Catholic." [144]

American press coverage of reproductive rights frequently assessed the Catholic perspective and Catholic practices, as it had since the early years of the birth control movement. The reason for this focus seems to have been a mixture of voyeurism and interest in exposing both the Catholic Church's power in public policy regarding sex and contraception and its powerlessness to control the growing numbers of its members in their attitudes toward and practice of birth control. Politicians and journalists alike regularly named Catholics without naming their own or others' religious identities. By 1963, Catholic distress and internal debate about church teachings on contraception appeared in Catholic publications and became highly publicized in mainstream media through the Pill's coinventor, Dr. John Rock, an observant Catholic who argued for reform.[145] Dolores Stonebreaker reported mixed responses among the priests: a priest who had visited her in the hospital had called her abortion "murder," but when she asked her own priest whether she would be excommunicated, he was "compassionate," *Life* reported. He heard her confession, gave her communion, and reassured her that she would not be excommunicated.[146]

The magazine named Dolores Stonebreaker and printed several photographs of her. I want to think a bit about that time in contrast with the present. What seems surprising to me, even "naive," nearly fifty years later when I look at this issue of *Life* magazine is the apparent lack of concern about possible retribution—in the form of relentless harassment or violence—that a woman might receive for having had an abortion. That feeling indicates how much our own thinking (mine) is shaped by the current social and political milieu. In 1965, abortion was illegal. Yet here were women having (therapeutic) abortions who allowed their photos and names to be used. These mothers and doctors acted as good citizens; they shared their personal stories and difficult decisions with the public and hoped that their telling of them might encourage both scientific research and legal reform to help others in the same situation. From the vantage point of the present, the representation of the need for therapeutic abortion as unfortunate yet matter-of-fact is striking for its seeming lack of concern about the informants' becoming political targets—for its innocence of the pro-life movement's tactics.

The magazine did not name anyone other than the Stonebreaker family, however. Indeed, of the women having abortions and the doctors providing them, Dolores Stonebreaker alone bravely permitted the use of her name. Although initially concerned about their reputations, she and her husband decided to allow the magazine to use their names rather than retain anonymity. She had already been castigated by one priest and might expect further criticism, yet she did not retreat into silence and secrecy. Instead, in the interest of "help[ing] other women" she told her story and permitted the magazine to use the family's names and photographs.[147] Her forthright courage exemplified and strengthened the growing public debate among Catholics nationwide about Catholicism, contraception, abortion, and citizenship. There is no innocence here. The more I look at this magazine, the more I recognize the quiet and deliberate bravery in these photographs. Abortion was stigmatized and criminalized, yet the Stonebreakers and other women and their doctors shared their stories with the public.

The journalists left the physicians, the city, and the hospital where the abortions had been performed unnamed, presumably in deference to the possible legal questions raised by the article. The first target, however, was not the doctors or the hospital but the magazine itself. Five Catholic priests contested the story, filed a five-million-dollar suit, and won a retraction from the magazine.[148] The magazine issued "A Correction" saying that it had been "misinformed" regarding the priests.[149] These are the public reports; we do not know more about what may or may not have in fact been said in private conversations or confessions or whether the priests and penitents both may have been censured in the wake of this publicity.[150] Californians and the nation would soon learn the lengths to which some antiabortion Catholic physicians and the emerging antiabortion movement would go to suppress therapeutic abortion.[151]

"The nightmarish part of it is not knowing" declared the third set of pages as the story returned to the question raised by the blood test depicted on the magazine's cover. The surrounding photos showed the unnamed anxious mother of the magazine's cover clutching her small towheaded son in a doctor's office. As she listened to a technician tell her about the possible consequences of the disease—and learned that she would have to wait two weeks for the test results—she cried in despair. Her son and the female technician hugged her. As stark as the hospital room appears, physicians and technicians here show empathy for the women who face the dangers and dilemmas posed by maternal rubella. Like Stonebreaker's son, this child too attends to his mother's grief.[152]

The new technology of blood testing offered to give answers and relieve anxiety. Yet technology alone could not assuage anxiety. The time required before receiving results of the early tests caused stress. For some, the test told that they could stop worrying about German measles. For others who received news of recent infection, these blood tests did not resolve the dilemmas. The test could not tell precisely what the effects of the virus would be for an individual woman, but clinicians did know that in the early weeks of pregnancy, the disease had severe effects in a high proportion of cases. Furthermore, by 1965, researchers knew that the disease caused a long list of health problems.[153] The decision around whether to continue a pregnancy or terminate it was the final uncertainty, but long before reaching that stage, plenty of pregnant women feared that the disease might have struck them and the baby on the way and considered what they might do. Some knew in advance that they would have an abortion, even if they later discovered that they were immune and had not needed to have one. As women and physicians used the test, new uncertainties, anxieties, and questions arose as they considered the next step. Many moved to arrange therapeutic abortions.[154] We know little about the women who knew they had contracted German measles early in pregnancy but did not pursue an abortion. A few later reported worrying constantly during pregnancy, envisioning babies with no fingers or toes, accepting gamma globulin and reassurances from their doctors, and hoping for the best.[155]

In the end, in *Life* magazine's narration of the epidemic, all of the personal, medical, religious, political, and legal crises provoked by rubella

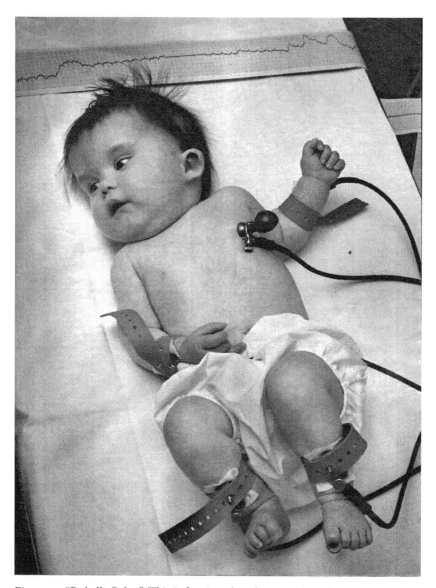

Figure 9. "Rubella Baby." This infant is tethered to machines for monitoring and testing. This process too was one of the agonies experienced by mothers and fathers who tried to provide what their children needed and hoped that medical experts could help. "The Agony of Mothers About Their Unborn," *Life* 58, no. 22 (June 4, 1965): 31.

would be resolved by science. A woman at the microscope surrounded by hundreds of test tubes and an infant attached to electrodes are the final full-sized photographic representations of German measles in the *Life* magazine story. "Test-tube search will stop the human damage," *Life* concluded. Scientists were determined to produce a vaccine to prevent further "damage." All of the questions, doubts, debates, lost pregnancies, abortions, disappointed mothers, and disabled children documented in *Life*'s pages, the final scene suggests, will all be resolved by scientific hard work and discovery.[156]

Oddly, though, on these pages that suggest science will triumph, the "damaged" baby is alone with technology (see figure 9). There is no parent, no comforting adult, in sight. Is this the future for "damaged babies"— isolation and technology? Already diagnosed with vision and hearing impairments, this four-month-old infant was being tested for "heart abnormalities."[157] Just as scientific technology seemed to solve and erase larger social problems, it also seemed, as this photo essay suggests, to erase the humans who provide care. Technology is not as comforting as its promises.

Another woman who had contracted German measles told of her "Tragic Pregnancy" in *Good Housekeeping*.[158] The account focuses on a mother making a difficult decision about an expected future baby, yet it also shows a mother and child sharing pain and guilt. The autobiographical article highlighted the decision that "the doctors left . . . up to" the woman. She asked, "Should I let them end my pregnancy, or should I risk bringing an abnormal baby into the world?" The maternal narrator immediately gave her answer: "I have made the most difficult decision any woman can make. When I was two months pregnant, I decided not to have my baby." Her explanation of her decision and the therapeutic abortion drive the narrative, but the subtext focuses on the complexity of maternal emotions and the mother-daughter relationship. The author, who never gives a name for herself other than "Mummy," contrasts her own confidence and ease about her pregnancy with the attitude of her friend who worried excessively about German measles. Then, one morning her eight-year-old daughter Betsy woke up sick, and the doctor diagnosed German measles. The author waited nervously through the incubation period—trying to isolate her daughter and searching herself for rashes—and thought she had come through safely. When Betsy wished for a baby sister or brother at her birthday party, her mother announced her good news, and the girls, the mother reported, went into a frenzy of baby preparations. Despite "Mummy's" confidence, however, she soon found red bumps.[159]

At this point, the narrator turns from the discovery of her own rash to her discussions with her doctor and husband about what to do, her "horror" at the word *abortion,* the agony of deciding, and the miserable process of going though a therapeutic abortion committee for "permission."[160] State criminal abortion laws had always allowed physicians to perform abortions for medical reasons; those reasons had historically been left to physicians themselves to determine without legal scrutiny or interference. Therapeutic abortion committees, a new creation in the 1940s that became standard hospital policy in the 1950s, required that physicians who wanted to provide a (legal, therapeutic) abortion submit their patient's case to a committee. Originally designed to restrict the numbers of abortions, these committees brought the medical practice of abortion under greater peer scrutiny, drastically reduced the number of abortions, and discouraged both doctors and women from seeking legal, medically legitimated abortions in hospitals. Physicians submitted records; women might have to submit to examinations—gynecological and/or psychiatric—and might be examined by the committee as well in the effort to secure an abortion for medically acceptable reasons. Many women decided to avoid the system. At the same time, it was widely known (and documented through surveys) that different hospitals treated the same types of cases differently. Some hospitals rejected all cases, so doctors learned to go elsewhere when they believed an abortion necessary; others tried to find ways to provide abortions for women in order to protect them from the illegal abortion trade. Hospital abortion committees both restricted and legitimized abortions. Regardless of the intention, though, women patients who needed an abortion found the process intrusive and often humiliating.[161]

In the *Good Housekeeping* story, the decision was the woman's alone to make, she and her husband concluded, but she did so not by thinking about herself but rather by thinking about others. The mother considered the future child, her husband, and her other children as she reached a conclusion about her pregnancy. She wondered, if "he were born with heart or brain damage, would he thank me for the gift of life? What about Joel, and the other children? Had I the right to shadow their lives with suffering and grief?" As a parent, she understood that one could not protect oneself from all risks; children might be damaged, and "one accepts the situation." In this case, though, she knew the risk and could decide in advance. In the end, she declared, she "could not willingly bring into the world a handicapped child."[162]

Once her decision and the hospital review committee's decision had been made, the mother returned to her responsibility to her daughters and the need to explain why she was going to the hospital. "Darling, I have to tell you," she recalled saying to Betsy. "And then," she wrote, "with the some-times extraordinary intuition of the young, [Betsy] said 'It's about the baby, isn't it? Something's wrong. Oh, Mummy, was it the measles? Was it my fault?' " Her mother reassured Betsy that it was not her fault: "This baby could not be born because it wasn't healthy." The daughter asks, "But we can have another baby, can't we?" After going through the distress of the abor-tion and depression, the mother ends her autobiographical narrative by telling about a "brand-new baby, coming very soon." Betsy checks, "A nice healthy baby?"[163] The story ends in the way that magazine stories about preg-nancy loss through miscarriage and a mother's grief usually did—by telling of a baby on the way or a healthy baby being born.[164]

This article tells about more than the consequences of the epidemic; it leaves clues about gender and family in this period as well. The daughter knows what is going on at home without being explicitly told and, like Mrs. Stonebreaker's son, understands her own role in this family drama. Despite the efforts of the responsible mother, she cannot shield her daugh-ter from knowledge or from the shared sadness and guilt about an aborted pregnancy or the excitement about a new one. The mother has imparted the truth and her feelings; her daughter shares and reflects them. The fa-ther's relationship with his daughter is left unwritten; he appears as a hus-band to speak with the doctor about maternal rubella, to raise the idea of a therapeutic abortion, and to support his wife's decision. Though in the ar-ticle communication between husband and wife appears minimal, the ac-count suggests that in a good marriage, decisions about pregnancy and abortion were understood to be the woman's to make and the husband's to support. The parents considered the possibility of a "handicapped" child within a family context and found the possibility potentially devastating for the entire family. The child's severe birth defects, the mother con-cluded, would mean suffering both for the future child and for the rest of her family. Therapeutic abortion was best for the family.

"Tragic Pregnancy" again brought into public view the responsible mar-ried mother who decided upon abortion. This portrait of a woman's re-sponsibility and decision making about abortion within the complexity of family life matched a long history of married women seeking abortions.[165] It, along with other media coverage, significantly remade, however, the *public* representation of abortion. The photo accompanying this article shows a worried young white mother, her downcast daughter in pigtails close to her side. "Mummy" packs a suitcase—preparing for a trip to the hospital for an abortion instead of delivery. "I was in seventh heaven" about the pregnancy, the author recalled, and she remembered "the events of last May with great sadness," adding, "but I'm not regretful or ashamed. I'm convinced that I took the right course for a woman who discovers, at a critical stage of her pregnancy, that she has German measles."[166] German measles stories expressed panic, anxiety, and despair as well as the strength of mothers (and, less visibly, fathers) in the face of adversity. Mothers bravely made decisions.

Neither doctors nor the nation could safeguard mothers and babies from German measles, a newly dangerous disease. Furthermore, children themselves, through their contagious bodies, were the ones who threatened expectant mothers in the drama of German measles. The epidemic would produce, health authorities warned and the media amplified, tens of thousands of "damaged" and "deformed" babies. The panic of expecting mothers, their husbands, and the larger society grew out of what people knew about disability and what they imagined. In imagining their child and the future, expectant parents and the population at large drew on pictures from the thalidomide tragedy, on images and awareness of polio and the handicapped, and on information about German measles. Such knowledge of disabilities was likely to be pessimistic and negative since doctors tended to expect the worst, institutionalization had become standard practice, and the society as a whole offered few accommodations and services—in school, in the workplace, or in public spaces—to assist disabled people, particularly deaf, blind, and/or retarded people, in being part of public life. In spotlighting the fears and desires of potential parents, the epidemic illuminates American life in the 1960s.

However, the language that described the offspring of German measles as "abnormal," "crippled," and "deformed" is more complex than simply being an expression of an unexamined desire for the perfect or hostility toward the disabled. Potential parents imagined the future: they imagined how they would care for such a child, the suffering of an affected child, and what having a "damaged" child would mean for them and for their other children.[167] This type of thinking in terms of the needs and hopes of the existing family—as imagined, as fantasized—was not unique to the case of a potentially severely harmed child but rather was typical of that of many, perhaps most, American families. In a culture that had learned to think ahead about children and family, in which "birth control" was the norm and married couples were encouraged to consider whether, when, and under what conditions they wanted or could have children, potential parents also considered what the birth of a "malformed" child would mean. "Birth control," as historian Linda Gordon has argued, is more than the production and use of specific contraceptive technologies; it is an idea, a cultural attitude, and a practice of thinking about family and childbearing.[168] It includes a range of methods, from abstinence and delay of marriage to the use of contraceptives and abortion. All of these decisions are simultaneously about birth control *and* about parenting—whether there is a pregnancy or existing child or not. Parents of all classes, religions, ethnicities, and races in the twentieth century considered whether they were "ready" for children and whether they could have more children. Their thinking included consideration of marital status, finances, education, (un)employment, emotional preparedness, family size, health, and more. Answers to these questions and the sense of their readiness for children varied by the (potential) parents' class, religion, marital status, race, age, and education.[169] Part of this calculation considered whether an addition to the family would mean less for existing sons and daughters—whether measured at the dinner table, in schooling, or in the quantity of clothing, space, or maternal attention available. Anticipating having a child with severe birth defects brought all of these issues up and intensified them; a child with major physical, health, and/or intellectual problems, and the educational and social demands and difficulties associated with disabilities would involve more time, more work, and more money. Potential parents who suspected that a pregnancy had been harmed by maternal rubella measured their expectations, their current realities, their probable expenses, and their own abilities.

This capacity to imagine and make decisions about the shape of the family and the timing of pregnancy and childbirth reflected the mid-twentieth-century world of "family planning," to use the phrase favored at the time by Planned Parenthood and birth control advocates. In the post–World War II period, the cultural mandate to plan for the future extended to the family. Federal and local agencies planned suburban development, college expansion, and financing for returning veterans; individuals planned marriages, families, mortgage payments, and their children's futures. *Planning*—from the perspective of the birth control movement since the 1930s as well as from the perspective of the March of Dimes and its new movement to prevent birth defects—was a prerogative and a responsibility of the married woman and her husband. Many Americans embraced testing, counseling, analysis of family trees, and early blood and genetic testing as a family and public duty in order to prevent the transmission of mental retardation, malformations, and specific inherited conditions such as hemophilia or Tay-Sachs disease.[170] Couples, many agreed, should plan families based on information about health, finances, and the family's future as well as the couple's and the mother's own desires.

*Desire* describes part of this process of planning and thinking, but perhaps *hopes, dreams,* and *wishes* would be better terms. Using the terms *wanting* and *desiring children* and their reverse, *not wanting children* or *the unwanted child,* may suggest that desire exclusively drove family formation, childbearing, and the use of birth control.[171] These decisions were not simply about wanting or not wanting children, however. Did the family have the money and the emotional and physical ability to provide for a potential child? As we see in the stories about German measles, responsible mothers assessed the future and their own capacities and, at times, made decisions that went *against* their desires. Imagining the future and picturing reality was work and a responsibility of parents, especially mothers. This sense of responsibility and their evident distress made these married mothers the picture of responsibility and made their abortions decent.

New testing technologies pushed the process of decision making and planning into the medical realms of the hospital and clinic and into the public eye. But new technology itself did not create the practice of evaluating scientific and social knowledge and determining the future of a pregnancy. The use of this new blood test for rubella antibodies on pregnant women—and the personal, medical, and social anxieties that it engendered—were forerunners of the widespread use of amniocentesis and the accompanying dilemmas faced by women at the end of the twentieth century. Today, pregnant women increasingly know of possible "birth defects" in advance through genetic screening techniques like amniocentesis, visualization technologies like ultrasound, and blood tests. Anthropologist Rayna Rapp offers a superb study of the routinized use of amniocentesis in the United States and women's decision making about whether to carry to term or to abort a pregnancy that receives a "positive diagnosis." Pregnant women today, Rapp argues, are "moral pioneers." "Situated on a research frontier," she explains, "they are forced to judge the quality of their own fetuses, making concrete and embodied decisions about the standards for entry into the human community."[172]

As we have seen, however, contemporary women are not the first to find themselves in the complicated position of having to assess scientific information about the probability of birth defects and to decide whether or not to carry a pregnancy to term. Epidemiological knowledge, the accidental combination of pregnancy and disease, and social knowledge made women who contracted German measles "moral pioneers" as well. The epidemic concentrated the number of women forced to contemplate the uncertainty of the situation and to make "concrete and embodied decisions" about pregnancy, children, and family.

German measles, together with thalidomide, produced a new image of abortion as respectable and as a need of married middle-class white women. It was not that only privileged white women needed, sought, or obtained abortions because they had contracted rubella during pregnancy or for other reasons. That was not the case. The point here is that whiteness—as an idea, as a picture, and as privilege—coupled with heterosexuality, marriage, motherhood, middle-class status, and the fear of disabilities helped to repaint the portrait of abortion and change the politics of abortion. Mid-twentieth-century media had emphasized the criminality, deviance, and deadliness of abortion. As married mothers—pictured as middle-class and white—came face-to-face with the implications of maternal rubella, talked publicly about it, made difficult decisions, and sought abortions by the thousands, they made abortion respectable. In the process, the representation of abortion was changed from a shameful, thoughtless, and sick action to an ethical and responsible one.

THREE

# *Wrongful Information*

WOMEN WERE "ENTITLED" TO THERAPEUTIC abortion when they contracted German measles in early pregnancy, according to one popular magazine; it was "justifiable" if the pregnant woman and her husband had decided upon it, *Williams Obstetrics* advised doctors.[1] Yet, as many women discovered in the 1950s and 1960s, the decision whether to carry a possibly affected pregnancy to term or to have a therapeutic abortion was not clearly in their hands at all. Physicians refused to perform therapeutic abortions, their legality was uncertain, and hospitals designed policies to limit their number. An unknown number of women who knew they had contracted the disease and understood the implications were denied therapeutic abortions and later gave birth to severely harmed children. Some of them sued their doctors for malpractice. Barbara Stewart and Sandra Gleitman, with their husbands, brought two early cases, *Gleitman v. Cosgrove* (1967) and *Stewart v. Long Island College Hospital* (1970 and 1972),[2] that challenged the medical system that provided—and refused to provide—legal, therapeutic abortions. At a time when abortion was a crime and contraception illegal in some states before *Griswold* (1965), these women were not only "moral pioneers," to use Rayna Rapp's phrase; they also bravely became legal pioneers.

The original suits aimed to right specific wrongs: they were brought against physicians and hospitals for giving inaccurate information, for falsely reassuring patients, and for preventing the patient—the pregnant woman—from making decisions about her own family and her own health care. The failure to provide accurate information—about disease and the possibility of abortion—then resulted in the birth of a malformed child. Barbara Stewart and Sandra Gleitman went to court for themselves and for their children, insisted on patients' rights to accurate medical information and self-determination, sought recognition of the needs of disabled children, and advanced reproductive rights. In the process, they developed a new area of tort law that later came to be known as "wrongful birth" and "wrongful life" suits, torts first articulated during the German measles epidemic of the early 1960s.

Although treated as bizarre by some in the judiciary when they were first brought, within a decade these types of cases had revised law and medical practice.[3] In the wake of the nationwide decriminalization of abortion following *Roe v. Wade* (1973) and *Doe v. Bolton* (1973), these suits gained legitimacy. Indeed, the *Stewart* case exemplified the hospital system of abortion review committees that *Doe* found unconstitutional for violating a woman's right to privacy and a doctor's right to practice medicine. Today, most states permit "wrongful birth" suits claimed by parents; a few allow "wrongful life" suits on behalf of the child.[4]

A wrong that has never before been taken to court requires special work to be translated into law and to be understood as an injury that requires redress. For the person who believes herself or himself injured, the perceived wrong has to be presented in legal terms and through a formal legal process. The formal legal complaint is a translation of an ordinary person's sense of having been mistreated. This chapter is about that process of translation as it is represented in court. Historians have tracked long-term trends and the growth of malpractice suits through hundreds of judicial opinions.[5] Legal scholarship on "wrongful birth" and "wrongful life" has focused primarily on the validity of these torts in relationship to the legality or morality of abortion and secondarily on the implications for the disabled.[6] This history places two early precedent-setting cases in context and illuminates the experiences and expectations of ordinary families caught in the dilemmas of German measles. I look in detail and in depth at the original trial records of *Gleitman v. Cosgrove* and *Stewart v. Long Island College Hospital* in conjunction with medical and media materials to illuminate legal and medical practices. The legal records analyzed here include a trial transcript running more than seven hundred pages, briefs submitted by opposing attorneys, and published appellate opinions. In closely analyzing these cases, we may observe an expansion of medical malpractice and medical protection in the making.

The complete trial record offers unusual opportunities both to learn what ordinary people thought about the rights of patients and to analyze the subtleties of physician-patient communication and physician decision-making. These cases provide intimate insights into the experiences of specific individual women and their families and into the practices of specific physicians and hospitals. They are more than stories about individuals, however. They also offer in microcosm a rare view of the intricacies and power dynamics of medicine. As such, these trial records are invaluable for understanding the era. Detailed documentation of patient-physician interactions is rare. First, most medical interactions and decisions are not recorded except in terse (and often closed) medical records. When there are medical errors or disputes, few of these events ever go to court. Even today, most people who contact an attorney soon give up, and fewer than 2 percent of patients with a valid complaint file a suit.[7] Few go to trial, and very, very few are appealed and thus required to produce a printed trial transcript that will be held permanently in the state archives and will be available to the historian later. Malpractice suits may thus represent other similar experiences and people's deeper dissatisfaction with medicine that may be lost to the public record.[8]

As much as these records show how the legal process forced light upon medicine and revealed some of its inner dynamics, the legal process also suppressed critical information. The limitations of the legal record become apparent when they are put in conversation with the popular media of the time and put in the larger social, medical, and political context. Close textual and contextual analysis of these rich and intricate records produces a more complete picture of the subtle ways in which manners, reputations, class, religion, and race shaped medical practice (and malpractice). Knowledge and information about bodies, disease, and the medical system are actively revealed and equally actively hidden in different venues and different types of texts. Analysis of what is said and not said—in the doctor's office, in the courtroom, in magazines, and in the news media—demonstrates how the spaces themselves and the social hierarchies and rules of power and communication shape what is known at the time as well as the historical record and what is understood later.


Seeing that her fifteen-month-old daughter, Robin, had a fever and "fine bumps all over her body," Barbara Stewart took her to the emergency room at a nearby Brooklyn hospital in April 1964. Robin had German measles.

Soon Barbara Stewart herself had a rash all over her body, and a few days later she saw Dr. Wolf J. Domsky, who found that she had German measles as well. Her period was also two weeks late. Dr. Domsky told her to come back in a week for a pregnancy test. In April 1964, the U.S. Public Health Service announced that the entire nation was in the midst of a German measles epidemic and advised women in early pregnancy to avoid the disease and to avoid schoolchildren, who could spread it. "For a woman who catches the virus in the first three months of pregnancy," *Newsweek* reported, "there is the risk of a retarded or malformed child." New York City had two hundred cases per day, twenty times more than it had recorded the year before. The Stewarts read the news reports with alarm. When she saw her doctor again, Mrs. Stewart recalled, "I told him . . . I had read an article concerning German measles and the pregnant mother." Her husband also talked with the doctor about the newspaper reports; the doctor "confirmed" the information and told him that his wife should have an abortion, a therapeutic abortion."[9] With knowledge drawn from the newspaper and "confirmed" by her doctor, Barbara and Robert Stewart understood that her having had German measles early in pregnancy could mean dire consequences for their future child. With this knowledge, they turned to their local hospital for a therapeutic abortion. And so began their entry into the labyrinthian world of hospital abortion committees.

This is almost all we know about these early moments of learning of the implications of German measles and about the Stewarts' decision to seek an abortion for a pregnancy they wanted and a child they had hoped for. One would like to know more. What were Barbara Stewart's feelings early on; did she walk into Dr. Domsky's office hoping that he would not corroborate the news she had read? What did she think about therapeutic abortion—did she face it with dread, reject it, or immediately see it as necessary? Unfortunately, after testifying in a later malpractice suit that Dr. Domsky had written a letter detailing his diagnosis, Mrs. Stewart was not allowed to say more about her conversation with him or anyone else. Her testimony was reduced to yes or no answers. What she had said, what her views and worries had been, and what advice her doctor had given her could not be told in the courtroom and are missing from the record. From her husband, we have one tiny hint of the Stewarts' concern and thinking: "We thought about it, and we discussed it with the minister of our church, and we discussed it with other members of our family."[10]

Through Robert Stewart's remark, we get an inkling of the hard thinking that anthropologist Rayna Rapp finds and documents among those who contemplate or use amniocentesis today.[11] We do not know the pain expressed, what they weighed, how conversations swayed, the strength of feelings—the legal record discloses little emotional content, texture, or nuance. We know the Stewarts talked and talked, thought and thought, and then went together to two hospitals for an abortion. The limits of the legal transcript as a historical record are evident. More important, the enforced silences in the courtroom masked the social processes of thinking and talking in "private" spaces. It is up to us to use our imaginations, as the jury surely did, to better comprehend the Stewarts' situation.

Although the trial record reveals only a bit of the Stewarts' pain upon discovery of the ramifications of rubella, it highlights their personal commitment to obtaining an abortion. The Stewarts were not alone in their sense that abortion was the appropriate response to the dangers of maternal rubella. Popular magazines and newspapers reported on the situation and explored the difficulties and dilemmas of abortion for married women who had welcomed their pregnancies. Pregnant women aware of the dangers of rubella came to doctors seeking abortions. When pregnant women learned that the normal background risk of "severe deformity" was 1 percent compared with a 50 percent risk when German measles had been contracted in the first month of pregnancy, Dr. Robert Hall of Columbia University testified, "I have yet to see a patient take the risk who was informed of the facts. I have never seen a person take that risk."[12] Medical textbooks taught physicians that maternal rubella was an accepted indication for abortion, many hospitals permitted and provided "therapeutic" abortions for this reason, and a survey by Hall of New York State specialists in obstetrics found that more than 85 percent supported liberalizing the law.[13] A prospective study of more than three hundred cases of maternal rubella in New York City found that nearly two-thirds of the women later had therapeutic abortions.[14] For many, abortion was the obvious answer in such a situation. A small minority of physicians, however, strenuously opposed therapeutic abortion for fetal damage, and this view was just entering public debate.

The Stewarts' malpractice suit shows that access to legal therapeutic abortion was systematically arbitrary and sensitive to individual bias. Dr. Domsky first sent the Stewarts to the closest hospital, Kings County Hospital, which wanted a certificate from the health department confirming the diagnosis of German measles and then, after receiving it, refused to provide a therapeutic abortion three weeks after her first visit. Dr. Domsky then suggested turning to the hospital where Mrs. Stewart had delivered her first daughter, Long Island College Hospital. He gave her a letter describing her symptoms and his diagnosis. On June 8, 1964, Mrs. Stewart checked into a semiprivate room at the hospital, and over the next several days the therapeutic abortion committee examined her and noted their conclusions on her medical record. The Stewarts signed a paper consenting to a therapeutic abortion, and six days after her admission, Mrs. Stewart received an injection of Demerol in preparation for surgery and was wheeled into an operating room. After some time, a nurse returned, told her that she was going home, and wheeled her back to her room to dress. At the last minute the procedure had been canceled. A doctor, Mrs. Stewart recalled, had told her that she did not need an abortion. He had said, "Don't worry; . . . the baby will be all right. And not to go any place to try to have one."[15] Unknown to the Stewarts, at least two doctors had approved the abortion, but the hospital's director of Obstetrics and Gynecology, Dr. Robert Gordon, decided against it. Dr. Gordon, as he explained in court, had read Dr. Domsky's letter as ambiguous, concluded that his own committee had split 2–2 (without talking or meeting with the physicians), consulted with another doctor who had earlier disapproved the abortion at Kings, and believed the pregnancy to be further along than it was, thus requiring an unfamiliar procedure. The Stewarts were informed of none of this. Nor were they advised that they might go to another hospital. Instead, the Stewarts understood the therapeutic abortion to be unnecessary and felt reassured. They did not consult further with Dr. Domsky, their general practitioner, but trusted the decisions and words of the specialists. As Mr. Stewart said, his views had changed after listening to the hospital physician. "I was concerned, but I relied on the doctors. I believed them," he testified, "and when he said that she would be all right, my wife had been there and they had examined her; they had performed tests. . . . I took their word. I believed it."[16]

Barbara Stewart gave birth to her daughter Rosalyn on January 4, 1965. From birth, records presented by the Stewarts in court show, Rosalyn had been identified as a "newborn female with Rubella syndrome"; her mother had "had rubella in first trimester."[17] Giving birth to a "Rubella baby" was precisely what the Stewarts had tried to avoid. When they learned at birth that Rosalyn had a congenital cataract in her left eye and cardiac murmurs and later realized their daughter was also deaf, intellectually impaired, and unable to communicate, it was the culmination of all of their fears. Two and a half months after their daughter's birth, the Stewarts initiated their suit against Long Island College Hospital for failing to give Barbara Stewart accurate information about the dangers of maternal rubella and for taking away her right to make her own decision about her pregnancy and whether to pursue a therapeutic abortion. They sued on behalf of their daughter Rosalyn; the mother, Barbara; and the father, Robert. The Stewarts sued for prospective medical expenses for their daughter and for damages for the "mental and emotional havoc" wrought on the family.[18] In 1968, almost four years after Rosalyn's birth, the suit came to trial. Barbara Stewart testified about the events that had occurred during her pregnancy and about the circumstances of her own life and her daughter's. Rosalyn, she told the courtroom, never slept more than three or four hours at a time, cried often, and did not communicate or play with her parents, her sister, or other children. As Rosalyn got older, caring for her was getting more difficult. Furthermore, because no one was willing to watch Rosalyn and her mother had to constantly attend to her, Barbara Stewart found herself "upset" and "irritable."[19]

In its almost-but-not-quite nature, the Stewart case reveals some of the elements involved in securing or not securing a therapeutic abortion. By the 1960s, in order for a physician to perform an abortion that was recognized as legitimate and legal by the medical profession, it had to be performed in a hospital with the approval of an abortion review board or committee. This system was a product of police crackdowns on abortion and medical conservatism and fear in the 1940s and 1950s.[20] The creation of the therapeutic abortion review system represented a narrowing of access to abortion. The first circumstance to note in the Stewart case is that her doctor was an unknown to the physicians who acted as gatekeepers to therapeutic abortion. Dr. Domsky was a general practitioner without admitting privileges to any hospital. As such, he was unknown to the more privileged men who were specialists; who had reputations, hospital connections, and connections with each other; and who made decisions about therapeutic abortion. As the products of an unknown GP, Dr. Domsky's letter and diagnosis were suspect. Kings County Hospital treated them that way—by demanding verification from the health department—as did Dr. Gordon by his reading of Dr. Domsky's letter as "not 100 per cent certain that she had German measles." Dr. Gordon did not attempt to consult Dr. Domsky but instead contacted Dr. Cohen, whom he knew at Kings, and then used the outcome at the previous hospital to help determine and justify his own decision.[21] Hospitals had their own reputations to worry about as well, and public hospitals like Kings could be especially vulnerable to newspaper exposés and political threats. Taking care to avoid trouble by avoiding abortions and possibly dishonest patients made sense from their perspective. Physicians and hospitals had their own worries, but from the perspective of the patient, having had an unknown general practitioner as her physician appeared to hurt her case.

Connections were key. A woman who did not go to a well-respected, well-connected specialist in the first place would be likely to have a tough time having a therapeutic abortion considered. Women in the know—through friends or medical connections within their own family and friendship networks—as well as those who naturally saw the most well-to-do and well-known physicians because of their privileged and wealthy status, would be most likely to learn about German measles and therapeutic abortion and to get quick action at the appropriate private hospital. Yet most women—working-class as well as middle-class women, women who received public aid and/or went to public hospitals, women of color, and immigrant and non-English-speaking women—would not have had those connections to elite physicians or typically see specialists. Indeed, at trial, a physician explained that Kings County Hospital's ob-gyn department required that a pediatrician diagnose rubella in the pregnant woman. As the Stewarts' attorney pointed out, few adults would go to pediatricians or realize that the hospital demanded diagnosis by a specialist.[22] It seems likely that Dr. Domsky suggested going to the Long Island hospital because Mrs. Stewart would be known as a previous patient and might thus be trusted and granted an abortion. The need for trust based on personal or prior relationships with highly regarded members of the medical profession in order to win approval for a therapeutic abortion would ensure that almost all therapeutic abortions would be for privileged white women with private hospital rooms.

The need for connections may explain much of the documented differences in therapeutic abortion rates among women. National surveys and New York City studies showed stark differences in the number of legal therapeutic abortions performed for those with private rooms and those on public wards and performed for white, black, and Puerto Rican women. Private patients received four times as many therapeutic abortions as did ward and public hospital patients. White women received more than 90 percent of these legal abortions in hospitals.[23] Class inequality in access to hospital-performed abortions may have been built in structurally as well. In one San Francisco–area hospital, private cases required the approval of one staff obstetrician; "clinic cases," in contrast, were "reviewed by the entire OB-GYN Staff at a meeting and the vote taken by the nine professors on the staff."[24]

The details of Stewart's experiences at the Long Island College Hospital reveal the subordinating and humiliating practices built into the therapeutic abortion system. Since abortion had been made a crime in the nineteenth century, the profession had learned to distrust women who sought abortions and to assume they faked illnesses and lied. Operating on these assumptions and afraid for their own legal vulnerability, members of the profession constructed various means of ascertaining the truth, including reviews by therapeutic abortion committees.[25] One excruciating method is detailed in the Stewart case, that of repeated gynecological examinations by different physicians. In the hospital for six days, Barbara Stewart had four gynecological exams—all by male doctors she had never before met. Pregnancy had already been confirmed by test; did each man have to know and confirm by his own individual touch, by his own hand, the state of her pregnancy? Not only did physicians act within a system that distrusted pregnant women; the need for the examinations also suggests that physicians did not trust one another's diagnoses. More broadly, perhaps, the routine indicates that the knowledge a physician needed in order to make a recommendation was, in the end, individualized, even intimate. Probably most women, even in the 1960s, when gynecological examinations by male physicians had become the norm, would have felt uncomfortable with this process.[26] Plenty would avoid enduring so many examinations if they could. In fact, it was well understood that no woman would go through the process of psychiatric, medical, and gynecological examinations demanded by therapeutic abortion committees unless the medical indication was real and her situation desperate.[27] For at least some physicians, the examination process was a deliberate method of reducing the number of requests for abortion.

The judge in the Stewart case, Charles J. Beckinella, expressed this distrust of pregnant women himself when he insisted on the need to substantiate a German measles diagnosis. As the judge commented, one could not have "any pregnant woman just walking in and saying, 'Listen, perform a therapeutic abortion upon me because I contracted German measles'" when as a matter of fact, she never did." The witness, Dr. Irvin Cushner of Johns Hopkins, replied dryly that in the midst of an epidemic doctors in fact had done exactly that if a patient had come in and "described a classic picture" of the disease.[28]

Perhaps the reader has noticed that I have not given any sociological information about the Stewarts. Robert Stewart worked as a machinist at the Brillo Soap factory, and Barbara Stewart was a bookkeeper who worked nights at Chase Manhattan Bank. The Stewarts, originally from North

Carolina, regularly attended a Pentecostal church in Harlem. They were African American.[29] Did their race matter in this case? Up to this point, race has been invisible in this discussion of German measles, birth defects, and the Stewart case. The media's portrayal of German measles painted the woman with a "tragic pregnancy" and the (expected) children harmed by the disease as white and middle-class.

The courtroom and legal processes produced a color-blind legal record. Race is invisible in the legal commentary on wrongful birth cases, invisible in the published opinions on this case, and virtually invisible in the more than seven-hundred-page transcript of the civil trial. The Stewarts' attorney attempted to raise race and class, but prejudice and privilege were not directly discussed or named. The courtroom constrained the ability of expert witnesses to speak directly about racial and class differences in access to abortion. Dr. Christopher Tietze, an expert in medical statistics, was ready to detail the different abortion rates in public versus private hospitals and the "ethnic distribution" of therapeutic abortions in New York City, where nonwhite patients received far fewer legal therapeutic abortions than did white patients, but the court excluded his testimony.[30] Dr. Robert E. Hall illuminated a great deal on medical support for and practice of therapeutic abortion for rubella, but he could not bring out that private paying patients received four times as many therapeutic abortions as did the poor women in wards.[31]

For Barbara Stewart, however, having private health insurance did not guarantee access to therapeutic abortion because race helped determine access. To be more specific, blackness was a barrier. The fact that her physician lacked a relationship with the physicians and hospitals that approved therapeutic abortions hindered Mrs. Stewart's ability to obtain a therapeutic abortion. Additionally, because of the history of racism in medicine as well as income differences, African Americans would be more likely to have physicians who lacked those necessary connections. In a culture that regarded African Americans as deceitful and suspect, how were they to gain the trust of unknown doctors? Simply being black and being seen could be enough for a series of negative associations of blackness with poverty, criminality, and distrust to come into play, with the result being that very few nonwhite women ever "qualified" for a therapeutic abortion. Furthermore, the historical treatment of black women as highly sexualized objects undermined African American women's claims to medical trust and kindness based on their respectability.[32]

Where race and color were brought into the trial was over the question of diagnosis. Much of the case revolved around the diagnosis of German measles itself. For a diagnosis of maternal rubella, textbooks included not only the physical symptoms experienced by the woman herself but also the existence of an epidemic at the time of pregnancy and the contraction of German measles by other family members as indicators of maternal rubella. Long Island College Hospital staff neither registered the fact that Mrs. Stewart's daughter had had German measles nor took into consideration the fact that New York State and the country as a whole were in the midst of a serious epidemic. Furthermore, although Dr. Domsky had written that Mrs. Stewart "evidently" had German measles, Dr. Gordon treated the letter's diagnosis as less than positive and focused on the fact that no doctor documented seeing a rash. Where the social relevance of skin color was never discussed, the medical relevance of color was. When the Stewarts' attorney asked Dr. Gordon about the "color of the rash," an interesting discussion of the colors of rashes and people began.

> THE COURT: What is the color of the rash?
>
> THE WITNESS: Red.
>
> MR. [NORMAN ROY] GRUTMAN: On Caucasians, isn't that right?
>
> THE COURT: What?
>
> MR. GRUTMAN: On Caucasians it is red?
>
> THE COURT: On Caucasians it is red.
>
> . . . . THE WITNESS: That's true.
>
> THE COURT: Have you ever seen it on non-Caucasians?
>
> THE WITNESS: Do you mean on—
>
> THE COURT: A colored person, an oriental or Negro.
>
> . . . THE WITNESS: I have seen regular measles. I don't think I have ever seen rubella in a Negro.

Grutman then pulled out a textbook, Holt's *Diseases of Infancy in Childhood,* and read of the diagnosis of rubella: "Its identification in Negroes is almost impossible."[33]

The judge's active involvement in questions regarding race, to the extent of answering the questions himself and defining a "colored person," reveals the high social interest in race. In 1968, in the midst of local and national struggles for black freedom, it would be hard to ignore race as much as the law tried to do so. We see here how social and political questions were biologized and raised through circuitous routes. Dr. Gordon took a rigid stance on the diagnosis of German measles, insisting on physician observation of a rash, a requirement made by no authority or textbook and scoffed at by other witnesses, in order to say no to an abortion in Mrs. Stewart's case. Indeed, research at the time showed that some people never had a rash even though they did have German measles.[34] Yet Dr. Gordon insisted on proof of medical observation of a rash. Medical textbooks, however, declared seeing a rash to be virtually "impossible" among "Negroes."

The trial did not occur on paper, though; it occurred in a courtroom where everyone could see each other. The law and witnesses were silent on the matter of color, but it was all in plain sight. The Stewarts were African American, and a newspaper article reported that the jury included two black men.[35] Presumably, then, the other ten (male) members of the jury were white. Since the writer did not report on the race of the judge, attorneys, or physicians who appeared, we may safely assume they were all white. The contrast deserves to be noted: the legal system had adopted the convention of color blindness while the media presumed whiteness as the norm and pointed out deviation from the norm. The legal system's protocol represented equality under law, yet the practice of maintaining color blindness also meant silencing witnesses and blinding the law to the social relevance of race.[36]

The Stewart case and the ways in which information was shared, repressed, exposed, and not mentioned also permit us to see the subtleties of how race and racism operated in medicine and within the larger culture. It has long been known that there were differences in therapeutic abortion rates by race and income (and evidence of racial differences in treatment today). Yet there may be little or no evidence of overt racial discrimination. There is no evidence of obvious discrimination in the Stewart case.

The media's open interest in race offers a corrective, not only by providing useful demographic information but also by exposing ongoing racial prejudice hidden by the legal world's efforts to maintain equality. An opinionated article in *Harper's* magazine expressed support for the Stewarts (given pseudonyms in the article) and analyzed the racial and class inequalities in abortion practice and laws. Nevertheless, the article began with racist stereotypes. A TV producer, Marion K. Sanders wrote, might choose the "handsome couple" to star in a "documentary about upward[ly] mobile young blacks in the urban jungle. Beatrice is small-boned, with the delicately rounded features of an elegant African carving. . . . They still speak in the accents of their native North Carolina. Their strapping six-year-old daughter . . . ," he continued.[37] This article about a case concerning how the disease of German measles presents itself on the body and its role in producing a "defective" body began by observing the Stewarts' black bodies. The writer described their bodies as beautiful, "elegant," and "African." Their older daughter was "strapping"—a key word right out of racist tracts describing slaves as well as criminal trials of black men. The bodies of the black family are simultaneously placed in the naturalized, stereotypical, Africanized, and dangerous "jungle" of the city and in the romanticized pastoral South. The Stewarts lived in Brooklyn, but they are still "other." The exoticized family served as the opening for a lengthy article on the Stewart case, on abortion practices in public hospitals, on abortion law reform, and on the "right to be born with a normal body and mind."[38]

In contrast to the Stewarts, the Gleitmans had color on their side. The Gleitmans were white. Sandra Gleitman had not been able to obtain a therapeutic abortion, either, however, and had given birth to a son severely damaged due to maternal rubella. The Gleitmans too sued their doctors for malpractice for failing to inform them of the effects of German measles.[39] Neither insurance coverage nor race alone explained the course of events for Barbara Stewart and Sandra Gleitman. Religion, together with race and income, was shaping medical decisions, information given to patients, and patient access to medical procedures.

In both cases, the religious views of the specialists to whom they went for therapeutic abortions played a decisive role. The Stewarts were Pentecostal Christians; the Gleitmans, Jewish; the doctors were Catholic. In identifying the religious beliefs of doctors and patients, these cases implicitly raised questions about the religious underpinnings of medical decision making and whether patients have a right to religious freedom in their medical decisions. The *Stewart* and *Gleitman* cases both alluded to religious differences between patients and doctors and to the power of physicians to shape information and prevent access to abortions. In Stewart's case, a Jewish physician, Dr. Cohen, also had denied her an abortion at Kings Hospital. Although there is no testimony from Dr. Cohen as to why he had denied the procedure, we know that public hospitals rarely performed abortions and had to be carefully attuned to the political consequences of doing so. Only a few years earlier, in 1958, controversy had erupted when a physician there had prescribed contraceptives, thus breaking an unofficial anti–birth control policy at Kings Hospital. Cardinal

Francis Spellman had led a campaign against the physician and hospital commissioner, other religious organizations had joined in the fray, and "after five months of uproar," the hospital board had voted against banning contraceptives.[40] Perhaps Dr. Cohen and his colleagues hoped to avoid starting another controversy. The Stewarts had consulted with their minister in the process of thinking about a therapeutic abortion. Sandra Gleitman reported having "no religious scruples or objections to a therapeutic abortion."[41] Both Barbara Stewart's physician, Dr. Gordon, and Sandra Gleitman's, Dr. Robert Cosgrove Jr., adhered closely to their church's antiabortion teachings, and the physicians' decisions against therapeutic abortion grew out of those beliefs.

These doctors' disapproval of abortion, rooted in their Catholic faith, shaped their representations of medical knowledge and practice in such a way as to mute their patients' concern about the consequences of German measles. The doctors at Long Island College Hospital had assured the Stewarts that an abortion was not needed and had never informed them of the difference of opinion among the hospital's doctors. The Stewarts had trusted the doctors' assessment. They did not know that Dr. Gordon disapproved of abortion and had never himself performed a therapeutic abortion because he was Catholic.[42] In March 1959, Sandra Gleitman of New Jersey had had German measles; a month later she saw Dr. Robert Cosgrove Jr., who confirmed her pregnancy. Two doctors saw her initially, but neither Dr. Robert Cosgrove Jr. nor his father, Dr. Samuel Cosgrove, Mrs. Gleitman testified, had warned her of the consequences of maternal rubella. When she later asked Dr. Jerome Dolan, part of the Cosgrove practice, specifically about blindness, he reassured her that it would have "no effect." The physicians claimed they had informed her. She testified that she had asked about German measles during repeated visits but had been repeatedly reassured that German measles would not affect her child.[43] When her friend, a nurse, expressed surprise that she was still carrying her pregnancy after German measles, Sandra Gleitman became alarmed. By then, two months before delivery, it was far too late to seek an abortion, but Dr. Dolan, she reported, also had told her that her infection would not affect the baby.[44] In November 1959, she gave birth to her son, Jeffrey, and her doctors declared him to be "normal." A few weeks later, the new mother noticed that "he couldn't see and couldn't hear." The baby was blind, deaf, and intellectually impaired.[45] As I read the fragments of the Gleitman case, it seems possible that both sides of the suit told the truth.

But truth is no simple matter—truth includes power, interpretation, silence, and speaking. Here we can see how the power of the physician—power that drew on his medical expertise, his cultural authority, and the paternalistic and hierarchical form of the physician-patient relationship—shaped (and misshaped) understandings and events. Dr. Robert Cosgrove Jr. may have informed Mrs. Gleitman of the disease's potential effects, but he had downplayed the risks of damage and had not informed her of the debate among physicians on this point. He said he had told her of a 20 percent likelihood of damage. In the 1940s, the first physicians researching and reporting on rubella believed that a very high proportion of infants were harmed when women contracted rubella in the first trimester—perhaps up to 100 percent in the first few weeks of pregnancy—and they supported therapeutic abortion in such cases. Abortion for rubella was not unusual in Britain, Australia, or the United States.

In the 1950s, however, an international debate developed as researchers attempted to ascertain the incidence of birth defects from prospective studies (that followed pregnant women exposed to German measles and tracked the outcome of their pregnancies) rather than from retrospective studies (which began with affected children and then went backwards to search for a cause).[46] As one 1957 report in the *Journal of the American Medical Association* (*JAMA*) concluded, "Rubella appears to increase the likelihood of malformations, but the high rates of incidence set by early authors are exaggerated. The recommendation of therapeutic abortion because of rubella should not be routine."[47] This study by the New York City Department of Public Health of 104 pregnant women who had contracted rubella showed that "congenital deformities among the live-born babies of women with rubella during the first trimester" were evident in 9.7 percent of the cases. This figure was much lower than originally estimated, yet the report also showed that of the total number of cases, only 27 percent of the women had given birth to normal infants. There were a number of women of whom the department had lost track and somewhat higher rates reported for miscarriages and stillbirths, which received little attention. Finally, almost half of the women had had therapeutic abortions. This last point deserves to be underscored: *almost half of the women identified had had therapeutic abortions.* This fact makes it obvious that many pregnant women, with the help of their doctors and hospitals, acted decisively to avoid the possible damaging effects of German measles. Although the authors emphasized that the risk of malformations was much lower than earlier researchers had expected and that "blanket advocacy of therapeutic abortion" when women contracted the disease in early pregnancy was "unjustified,"[48] they did not suggest that therapeutic abortions should not be considered or should be restricted.

Instead, this New York study suggested that women be apprised of the research and the "risk" of deformity. Then, it was up to the woman to consider that risk. "Risk" was not about the likelihood of malformations alone. Risk and the possibility of aborting the pregnancy in such cases depended on the likelihood of "deformity," on the individual's assessment of her own fertility, and on her own willingness to continue the pregnancy with this knowledge of possible damage to the fetus due to rubella. "If the woman is young, has a child or two, and does not find it difficult to conceive, she may not want to take the extra risk, even if it is not large. On the other hand," the authors suggested, "an older primipara [first-time pregnancy], particularly one who has found it difficult to conceive, will be willing to take the risk."[49] Risk, then, had two components: first, the probability of rubella's harming the fetus (about which there was much disagreement and which varied with the timing of infection and the stage of pregnancy) and, second, the expectation of how easy or difficult a future conception would be. Most important was not the physician's or statistician's assessment of risk and what was reasonable but rather the woman's self-assessment of her risk—of both birth defects and infertility—and what she could accept in her future. She would decide whether she was willing to continue the pregnancy with the knowledge of possible damage to the fetus due to rubella or whether she would have a therapeutic abortion. The authors expected different assessments based on ease of conception, but personality, faith, husbands, and other factors could also shape individual assessments. The article emphasized that the danger of maternal rubella had been exaggerated, but it still adhered to the medical consensus of giving the pregnant woman information and letting her make decisions about therapeutic abortion for rubella in the context of her personal, reproductive, and family life. The *JAMA* article was apropos to Mrs. Gleitman's experience in 1959, but the doctors at Margaret Hague Hospital did not follow the protocol advised in this *JAMA* article that analyzed the situation in neighboring New York City.

Other medical commentators also reported lower rates of malformation than originally thought and suggested that few therapeutic abortions for rubella should be performed. The Royal Women's Hospital in Melbourne, for instance, had decided on a "non-termination" policy in rubella cases.

The *Medical Journal of Australia* argued that the most important finding in recent research in Dublin, Ireland, was "the fact that even among those women who developed rubella in the first trimester, seven out of ten had perfectly normal babies." Revealing a division of opinion among Australian physicians about the danger of rubella to the developing fetus, the editorial emphasized that the majority of babies were normal.[50]

The numbers could be presented differently, however. The original researchers in Dublin reported "that 30 per cent of the women who actually had the disease during the first trimester gave birth to abnormal children."[51] To grasp the risk involved, one needs to know what the likelihood of congenital malformations was in normal pregnancies. The Dublin researchers had previously studied that question and found that 1.6 percent of the babies born in normal pregnancies were "abnormal." Clearly, if an expectant mother had German measles in early pregnancy, the odds of malformation were much, much higher than usual.[52]

Dr. Robert Cosgrove Jr. had also mentioned outcomes to the Gleitmans that may have seemed fixable to them—cataracts and heart problems could both be repaired through surgery. If he or Dr. Jerome Dolan—who also cared for Sandra and later delivered her son—had discussed possible blindness, deafness, and mental retardation and had mentioned that a baby might face all of these conditions simultaneously, the mention of these permanent conditions may have sounded stronger warning signals for Mrs. Gleitman. Instead, Dr. Robert Cosgrove and Dr. Dolan had reassured Mrs. Gleitman throughout her pregnancy.[53] According to Robert Cosgrove, he had told her that he did not believe in doing a therapeutic abortion based on the numbers. Performing therapeutic abortions for German measles, he asserted, would be "destroying one baby that was perhaps deformed and at the same time destroying four perfectly normal babies."[54] This analysis of risk emphasized the risk of aborting an unharmed pregnancy that would become a normal baby rather than the higher than usual risk of having a child with serious congenital malformations. Dr. Cosgrove did not tell his patient that as a Catholic he opposed abortion and would not perform one.

Nor would he have informed her of a larger medical-cultural context that shaped his own representations and his thinking. Sandra Gleitman had happened to fall into the middle of a decades-long, religiously inflected battle among physicians over the practice of therapeutic abortion. In fact, Dr. Cosgrove's family and his hospital had long worked vigorously to cut the number of therapeutic abortions: in the 1940s, his father, Dr. Samuel

Cosgrove, had been a leader in attacking, stigmatizing, and repressing the medical practice of therapeutic abortion. Therapeutic abortions were legal at that time and an accepted part of medicine. Dr. Samuel Cosgrove, with Dr. Patricia A. Carter, had calculated therapeutic abortion "rates" of individual hospitals by comparing the numbers of therapeutic abortions to the numbers of deliveries. They then had listed and published the hospitals by name and challenged those with higher "rates" to explain why they had performed more therapeutic abortions. The Margaret Hague doctors then declared that therapeutic abortions should be severely limited and performed only when "the pregnancy threatens the life of the mother *imminently*." This proposed standard would drastically revise accepted medical practice. The doctors further stigmatized the procedure by renaming it *abortion-murder* and associating it with Communist Russia.[55] The scrutiny of hospital therapeutic abortion rates in the 1940s and 1950s contributed to new pressures to restrict access to abortion. Sandra Gleitman had gone to a hospital highly committed to rejecting therapeutic abortion requests and to physicians who believed it was their duty to prevent such abortions and to make these decisions for pregnant women. Doctors at this hospital had been reassuring women and prohibiting abortions for years. Dr. Robert Cosgrove Jr. had testified that hospitals in Jersey City "just don't do abortions."[56] Certainly, the hospital did not have an ethos of providing a patient with the information and letting her decide what risk she was willing to take, nor did it inform her of what doctors knew well. Indeed, the elder Dr. Cosgrove had documented the fact: if she went to a different doctor and a different hospital, she might get a different answer and a therapeutic abortion.

Beyond the opposition of Mrs. Gleitman's doctors to therapeutic abortion, the patient's duty to listen to and trust her doctors' medical expertise (and goodwill) also contributed to the outcome. The inequality and paternalism of the physician-patient relationship lent itself to misrepresentations, misunderstanding, and misplaced trust. As newlyweds of only twenty and twenty-three, Sandra and Irwin Gleitman, their attorney pointed out, "were new to marital life and young in years" and thus "relied upon the defendants more so than older, more experienced persons may have." In trusting their doctors and following their advice, these good, compliant patients were "lull[ed]" into false confidence.[57] They believed that their baby would not be harmed.

The Gleitmans and the Stewarts were not the only ones to be falsely reassured and denied therapeutic abortions. Mrs. Kent, a schoolteacher whose husband was an air force captain, knew what German measles during early pregnancy meant. She appeared on a 1969 television news show to tell her story (after these cases had gone to trial). She reported getting rubella from her students during the first two weeks of her pregnancy. She had gone to seven doctors during the first two and a half months of her pregnancy, but she said, "Each doctor told me not to worry. . . . My hands were tied." As the film showed the Kents' son lying in a crib, unresponsive and unmoving, Mrs. Kent recalled her pregnancy: "Everything I read on my own indicated that a therapeutic abortion was necessary. Each doctor told me not to worry. . . . I used to lay awake at night, as many pregnant women do, wondering about this baby. . . . If a child was going to be malformed, would it be better for him to be blind and be able to hear? . . . to be deaf?" In a dead voice, she continued, "We never expected multiple problems with Kevin." Kevin was born with five "major malformations" and was severely retarded. Doctors told the Kents that he would have to be institutionalized; he would "always be dependent . . . [and] in diapers."[58]

Even though this expectant mother precisely knew the consequences of German measles, even though she persisted in seeking the therapeutic abortion that medical textbooks and the majority of the medical profession agreed was legitimate in such a case, the power to make decisions about the course of her pregnancy lay in the hands of doctors and the legalistic abortion committee system. She was not at all "entitled" to a therapeutic abortion when infected by German measles during early pregnancy. Nor did her respectability and privileges as a married white schoolteacher help her find a physician who would respond to her needs. Unable to end the pregnancy of her first "planned-for baby," she "lay awake at night" worrying.

Calculating the risk of possible danger to the expectant mother and the developing fetus was something physicians tried to do and debated. Weighing those risks, mainstream medicine agreed, was preeminently the job of the mother-to-be. In the Kent, Gleitman, and Stewart cases discussed here, the doctors took away precisely what the women deeply believed to be their decision. National polls in 1962 found that more than half of the public thought that abortion should be legal when "the child may be deformed."[59] This was a decision that even the conservative specialty of obstetrics agreed was up to the potential parents. *Williams Obstetrics* in 1950 had declared therapeutic abortion "justifiable if the mother and her husband do not want to assume the obvious risks involved."[60] By the late 1960s, the majority of the medical profession, including nearly half of

Catholic physicians, followed the abortion rights and feminist movements and supported not only an expansion of the indications for therapeutic abortion but also repeal of the criminal abortion laws.[61]

The harm that German measles did during pregnancy, the harm that it had done to Rosalyn Stewart's body specifically, was described for judge and jury by physicians who read charts and explained diagnoses, technologies, tests, and terminology. Rosalyn Stewart was also displayed for the jury. The jury observed her through their own eyes and through the eyes and expertise of a specialist in pediatrics and in congenital rubella syndrome in particular. Rosalyn's father brought her up and handed her to the doctor. Dr. Louis Cooper, of New York University, held Rosalyn as he pointed out the effects of congenital rubella on her body. He told the jury, "I think you can see Rosalyn's left eye is much smaller than her right eye, and . . . it has a dense, pearly looking cataract which films her pupil and prevents her from using that eye." The other eye, he explained, was also marked by the virus. "The other thing that is striking is," he continued, "you will notice her behavior. She is interested in the lights. She is interested in keeping her head back. . . . Instead of talking, which you would expect for a child of this age, her sounds consist of just some noises. She has no speech." Although brain damage could not be seen, mental retardation could be seen by observing strange, developmentally inappropriate behaviors. Rosalyn was tipping back to look at the lights rather than at the room or the person holding her. "She is paying attention to me as a body," the doctor remarked, "but you know,"—as the jury members had themselves *seen*—"though I am a stranger to her, she went fairly readily to me. That is to say, she didn't really distinguish between handing to her father and my picking her up. . . . This is, of course, not a response that a child who was intact in all spheres would have."[62] "I don't think you have to be a doctor to see," he added, that "she does not function in any sphere up to age level and that she has serious handicaps."[63]

This display of Rosalyn must have been gripping. A little girl, almost four years old, sat in a doctor's lap in a courtroom as he showed her physical and mental condition to the jury.

I want the reader to pause here.

To imagine.

I imagine complete silence. Careful listening. Close observation. The jury saw a child whose behavior was developmentally inappropriate, who did not appear to see or hear, who wore a leg brace and a hearing aid. By observing her behavior, they could "see" that she was brain damaged.

Dr. Cooper further explained that Rosalyn could not communicate at all. She might eventually walk with a crutch, but never "normally," and he considered her "disabilities . . . so severe," her care so demanding and "so disruptive" to the family, that he believed she should be institutionalized. Institutionalization was the standard—virtually automatic—advice given to parents at the time. Rosalyn's life was likely to be long. Barbara Stewart, I imagine, made sure that her daughter's hair was done well, that her clothing was clean and pressed—a well-cared-for, loved, respectable daughter. A deserving child who was worthy of being treated well. A deserving black child.[64] I imagine that the jury—many surely parents themselves—felt the sadness of Rosalyn's parents and possibly the depth of anxiety, perhaps hopelessness, of parents caring for a severely disabled and intellectually impaired child. How would they manage? How would they pay to institutionalize her? Could they survive the situation?

I assume that the defense attorney disliked this scene. Nevertheless, he expressed no objections to the display of the harmed child. Only when the doctor tried to describe the institution to which many children like Rosalyn Stewart had been sent, Willowbrook State School on Staten Island, did the defense attorney object. It was the school, Dr. Cooper started to explain, that "Senator Kennedy visited and was appalled by." The court sustained the defense's immediate objection and instructed the jury to "disregard that." Rosalyn lived at home, but her doctors advised institutionalization. This line of presentation suggests that the Stewarts' attorney hoped to win an award big enough to cover private care rather than forcing Rosalyn Stewart into an underfunded and appalling state institution (for which she was on a waiting list). Though instructed to forget the description of Willowbrook as immaterial, jury members may well have recalled Robert Kennedy's description of the place as a "snakepit," the exposés of this institution and others like it—and their horrors. In an understatement, Dr. Cooper declared that Willowbrook did not provide "optimum" care.[65]

The body of the impaired child served as evidence. She herself, her body, her behavior, and her lack of emotional reaction to the stranger were all exhibited. Her body was emotionally evocative. Rosalyn was Exhibit A although she did not appear on the list of exhibits. The official exhibit list included the notes of Dr. Cooper, hospital records, and letters from Dr. Domsky and the public health department.[66] Rosalyn did not testify, but she may have provided some of the most powerful evidence. Rosalyn's parents were prevented from verbally expressing their emotions. By showing Rosalyn's body, the Stewarts' attorney invited the jury to feel and imagine parental and child emotions. The use of the person herself may offend some—perhaps the child was exploited by her lawyer or by her parents. This display of the disabled child inevitably called upon both voyeuristic "freak shows" and the pity induced by March of Dimes "poster children" and Jerry Lewis's telethons for muscular dystrophy.[67]

This conscious display of a disabled body in court violated the rules of politeness that taught people to avoid looking at the retarded and disabled by insisting that the jury look. The courtroom was a public space in which the rules of politeness and privacy were broken routinely. As in scientific research and the freak show, the jury and the courtroom were invited and required to look and to stare. Rosalyn's body served as evidence; she was a specimen. Displaying the person and body parts in the courtroom was not unusual, however. Courts required criminal suspects to show their bodies, to display the size of their feet, and to submit to blood tests; individuals seeking damages for injuries done brought their bodies and their injuries to the stand, along with medical records, X-rays, and medical testimony.[68]

The trial, which had begun with Dr. Cooper's testimony about the impact of maternal rubella and the display of Rosalyn Stewart, ended two weeks later after covering much medical ground concerning diagnosis, rashes, doctors, and abortion committees.[69] The jury listened to the attorneys' closing arguments. The defense focused on abortion; the Stewarts' attorney focused on the information not given to Mrs. Stewart and the results for Rosalyn and her family.

"The plain truth of the matter," declared the hospital's attorney, James Hayes, "is my client has been condemned for allowing a child to live. That is the issue here. For allowing a child to live at a time, namely June of 1964, when she was only an embryo, a fetus. . . . We did not destroy the child." Grutman objected to the term *child.* "Call it what you will," Mr. Hayes continued, "she now lives, and there was life in June of 1964, and we were asked to do away with that life, and I say that the charge in that regard is horrendous."[70] In calling the request, the expectation of abortion, "horrendous," the defense relied upon the shame and illegality of abortion, the word itself, to provoke horror in the jury.

In equating abortion with infanticide, the defense attorney used a traditional antiabortion tactic. He referred to abortion as "death" and personified the fetus, who "wants life." When doctors "make a decision of this magnitude," Hayes argued, "they are in effect playing God. They are determining life and death over a potential human being." Should that decision be made, he asked, "in favor of the mother who wants the abortion because of her fears, or do you resolve it in favor of the child who wants life?" Furthermore, association with abortion, the defense attorney implied, was in itself suspicious. The Stewart's attorney and several witnesses, the defense attorney pointed out repeatedly, were members of the Association for the Study of Abortion (ASA). Dr. Hall, said Hayes, had "avowedly admittedly associated himself with abortion for some twenty years."[71] (By the time of this trial, it should be noted, the medically oriented ASA was relatively conservative in its fight for reform rather than for repeal of the criminal abortion laws.[72]) Hall had talked about abortion, and thus, the defense suggested, he was suspect; in the view of the defense, to support abortion was to advocate the "death" of the fetus who "wanted life."

The defense attorney sympathized with the Stewarts' plight and avoided directly attacking any plan they might have had for abortion. A direct attack on the parents' morality might backfire. Instead, he suggested that any doctor who would carry out an abortion in such a case would be a "callous human being, . . . a callous doctor, . . . [not] a good human being." That judgment of callousness as opposed to goodness and decency could be extended to expectant mothers who might seek abortions and to juries who might permit it. The doctors at Long Island College Hospital had "hope, good hope, that all would be well." In contrast to the "callous doctor," they were good doctors, good human beings. Their actions were "not negligence."[73] In the defense's final outline of the case, there was no misinformation, no failure to provide standard care to the patient. Instead, there were good doctors, good because the defendant doctors had saved Rosalyn's life.

"This is the last opportunity that I will have to speak to you on behalf of the child who will never speak," the Stewarts' attorney, Grutman, began. Both attorneys claimed to speak on behalf of Rosalyn Stewart, a child who could not express any views and whose parents were not allowed to speak on her behalf. The Stewarts' child, who "was compelled to come into life by the action and omission of this defendant was deprived of those basic fundamental human rights of life, liberty and the pursuit of happiness, which should be the birthright of any healthy human being. You all saw," the attorney reminded them, "that child when she was here, and I am sure that you will all be haunted by the recollection of that blighted and destroyed and mutilated piece of humanity. . . . Her brain has been damaged, and yet she lives, and her parents said to you, 'The first thing is, we love her very much.' . . . But let it also be clear that in June of 1964 that person whom you saw in this courtroom was not a person. . . . cells in organization, but not yet a person." He reminded them that their duty as jurors was to judge the case on facts and law, not on "any moral or theological basis."[74]

Defense attorney Hayes had avoided, Grutman charged, "the crucial issue of the advice and the direction and the alternatives and the intelligent disclosure which should have been made to Mrs. Stewart." The suit before the jury was about the physician's duty to give information to the patient. When "Dr. Gordon decided that his hospital wouldn't perform the therapeutic abortion, at the very least," the Stewarts' attorney insisted, the doctors "owed the Stewarts an explanation in specific detail. 'Madam, we are not going to do your therapeutic abortion,' for whatever reason." This was the standard expectation in the United States, he argued. "They should have told her of the risks of continuing the pregnancy . . . so she could make an intelligent decision as to what she would want to do, and more than that, they owed her a direction to places where the procedures could be done, and they didn't do that." The doctors' duty was to inform the patient; their negligence lay in failing to give her a correct picture of the possible harm and in failing to inform her about where she might obtain a therapeutic abortion. The Stewarts, he reminded the jury, had said, " 'If we had been told, we would have gone.' "[75]

"That pregnancy would have been replaceable," the attorney urged. "Mrs. Stewart wanted a child. This was a planned child, but they wanted . . . to have a healthy child, and living as we do, gentlemen, in the last third of the twentieth century, people have a right for themselves to take advantage of the knowledge and strides . . . science has made in order to avoid bringing into the world a child to whom the boon of life will be no life, but the curse of perpetual and unending torture."[76] These closing remarks brought out an incredible array of ideas—from the notion that a pregnancy is replaceable to the idea that a child like Rosalyn was living a life of "unending torture." In the middle of the baby boom, when it appeared that women easily and often got pregnant and had babies, pregnancies appeared readily achieved and replaceable to many. Infertility was invisible. Today, when treating infertility has become a booming medical business and the grief of infertile women and miscarrying mothers receives public attention, it is hard to imagine such a facile assumption.[77] Similarly, the belief that a child like Rosalyn was destined to a life of "unending torture" because of her body rather than seeing the ways in which the society produced discrimination against the disabled has since come under attack from the disability rights movements.[78] Describing the situation of the parents who cared for their daughter, the attorney was on firmer ground. He reminded the jury that the Stewarts' daughter would never speak and would probably always be in diapers. Parents, psychologists had discovered, found their children's inability to learn how to use the toilet embarrassing and depressing. Finally, Rosalyn needed constant attention and, because she slept so little, her mother never got more than four hours of sleep every night. The Stewarts' lives, their attorney concluded, were a "continuous unremitting nightmare."[79]

"I didn't want you to decide this case on sympathy," Grutman declared, though, of course, the attorney had shaped for the jury a sympathetic portrait of a respectable, hard-working married churchgoing family and their "mutilated" daughter. This case was not only about sorrow and grief but also about the material consequences of the negligence of Mrs. Stewart's doctors. "Don't close your eyes to the damages, the damages which are so colossal, so enormous, that they are almost incapable of being conceived at one time," Grutman told the jury. "When you contemplate what it means to these people in dollars and cents, which is the only civilized way by which, in our society, we can make up for wrongs which are inflicted, what it means to them for what they must suffer, and carry with them, that gets worse as the child gets older, which is disruptive of their family life, what it means to them in terms of their daily living, and most pointedly of all, what it means to that silent central victim, who is the principal figure in the tragedy before you, what it means to that unfortunate child. If right had been done," he ended, none of this suffering would "have come into existence." In his closing, Grutman pointed both to the emotional pain and to the financial expense of "tragedy" and reminded the jury not to be afraid of thinking in financial terms because in this society awarding money is the only way to rectify wrongs of this sort. The Stewarts' attorney asked the jury to award damages of $250,000 for the child and $100,000 each to Mrs. and Mr. Stewart.[80]

"Don't close your eyes," Grutman told the jury. Look, use your eyes, see, and remember "the damages which are so colossal"—look, see, remember Rosalyn Stewart. A "tragedy."

The two-week trial thus ended, and the jury was given the case to consider and decide. At its request, the jury listened to Mrs. Stewart's testimony again through the stenographer's reading of the record. After discussing the case for another hour, the jury of twelve men unanimously found Long Island College Hospital negligent. When polled by the court, the jury affirmed their verdicts and answered three questions: "1, Did a doctor in the defendant hospital tell Mrs. Stewart that she did not need a therapeutic abortion?" The twelve jurors unanimously agreed "Yes." "2, Did a doctor . . . tell Mrs. Stewart that the baby would be born normal?" The jury voted no, with two jurors dissenting. "3, Did a doctor in the defendant hospital tell Mrs. Stewart that she should not seek an abortion elsewhere?" The jury unanimously answered "Yes." The jury awarded damages of $100,000 to Rosalyn Stewart, $10,000 to Barbara Stewart, and $1 to Robert Stewart.[81]

The jury understood the Stewarts. Like the Stewarts, jury members probably also knew about the dangers of German measles from the media and, like the majority of the country, they likely agreed that in such cases abortion involved a decision belonging to the expectant mother and should be legal. By the time of this trial, repeal of the criminal abortion laws was part of the national political and legal conversation and was particularly visible in New York.[82] Furthermore, despite prohibitions and active organizing by the state's bishops against abortion, Catholic jurors participated in this unanimous decision. Five jurors and the judge, *Harper's* magazine reported, were Catholic.[83] The jury awarded much less money than had been requested, but it found that the child, Rosalyn, deserved damages, which would help pay for her medical care, and that the mother deserved damages for the hospital's misinformation and failure to live up to medical standards of the time. The father received a token one dollar— the jury's way of recognizing that a wrong had been done to him but that the damages were small or nonexistent. Perhaps the jury of twelve men recognized that the burdens of caring for her child fell most heavily upon the mother. Or perhaps they suspected that Rosalyn's father would not be present. Under the stress of stigma, grief, and social isolation associated with having a child with disabilities, along with the work of providing for her or his physical needs, marriages often suffered and sometimes fell apart.[84] A subsequent news report told that the couple had separated and that Robert was now a student at Lincoln University outside Philadelphia.[85] Perhaps the jurors recognized the injury as one done to Barbara Stewart, first as a pregnant woman who had been wronged by her doctors and then as a mother with gendered responsibilities to her children. A jury of women, themselves aware of the dangers of German measles and possibly sharing similar frustrations with doctors and hospitals, may have awarded more. However, at that time women rarely served on juries, and some states automatically excused them.[86] We cannot know how the makeup of the jury affected its decisions or how it arrived at these numbers, but we know that the jury believed Barbara Stewart and found the hospital negligent. The jury's verdict was a "landmark decision," the Stewarts' attorney declared; the hospital's attorney called it "illegal."[87]

That was not the end of the case, however. Indeed, if the Stewart case had not been appealed, there would be no transcript and no testimony to analyze. All that remained would be the short accounts in *Harper's* and the *New York Times*. The legal controversy and the appeals left a record behind, however, thus making possible the analysis of the courtroom, the shaping of information, and the differences in the way that the law and the media represented people and events.[88] Without the trial transcript, there would be almost no information about Barbara Stewart other than a brief statement of her predicament and a description of her "elegant" African features. Acting on the defense's motion asking the court to dismiss the judgment, the presiding judge overturned the jury's finding on behalf of the infant Rosalyn and let the verdicts regarding her parents stand. Although he himself found the proof "questionable," Justice Charles J. Beckinella found the jury "justified in finding that the hospital breached duties it owed."[89] Both sides appealed.

The Gleitmans also appealed when the presiding judge dismissed their case without its ever going to a jury. In 1967, the New Jersey Supreme Court affirmed the trial judge's decision: neither the parents nor the child could claim to have been wronged. The suit on behalf of the child, the court remarked, required the child to say that "his very life is 'wrongful.' . . . If Jeffrey could have been asked as to whether his life should be snuffed out before his full term of gestation, . . . our felt intuition of human nature tells us he would almost surely choose life with defects as against no life at all." Although the judges felt sympathy for the parents, the majority concluded that "the sanctity of the single human life is the decisive factor in this suit in tort."[90] Yet the court was divided. One justice found himself personally divided; he joined the majority of four in disapproving the suits brought by the child and the father, but he argued that the mother had a case. Two other justices dissented.[91]

The language of the opinion and the divisions on the court indicate that in the judiciary, as in the medical profession, religion highly influenced opinions regarding (therapeutic) abortion. The opinion's very words—pointing to the "sanctity" and "preciousness of human life"—along with its use of the phrase "snuffed out"—highly charged for its association with murder—betrayed the developing religious debate over abortion. One dissenting justice argued that the nineteenth-century state legislature had written vague laws regarding contraception and abortion because agreement was impossible when views differed depending on religious belief. "Whereas in most areas of criminal prohibition the fact of evil is evident to most people," Chief Justice C. Weintraub observed, "here there is evil or none at all, depending wholly upon a spiritual supposition."[92] The court also disagreed on the legality of therapeutic abortion for maternal rubella, though it did not rule on the question.[93]

The dissenting judges in *Gleitman* insisted that these suits had merit and that damages could be calculated. Weintraub dissented in part from the majority in favor of the mother. He argued that the defendants had failed in "their clear duty" to tell Mrs. Gleitman of the "high incidence of abnormal birth" associated with German measles. Evaluating damages was difficult because "the pain of the parents must be measured against the joy they find in him as he is," Justice Weintraub wrote. Nonetheless, the mother's injury should be recognized, he argued, "in order to support the woman's right to choose whether to risk this misfortune." She alone had the right to decide her future and whether "to risk this misfortune." Justice Jacobs dissented entirely, rejecting the court's assertion of the impossibility of assessing compensatory damages. In fact, he maintained, the law did this every day. "Surely a judicial system engaged daily in evaluating such matters as pain and suffering, which admittedly have 'no known dimensions, mathematical or financial,'" he argued, "should be able to evaluate the harm which proximately resulted from the breach of duty." Furthermore, although the duty breached had been to Mrs. Gleitman, Jacobs continued, the entire family had been harmed. "When Mrs. Gleitman told her obstetricians she had German measles (rubella), they were placed under a clear duty to tell her of its high incidence of abnormal birth. That duty was not only a moral one but a legal one," he declared. "If the duty had been discharged, Mrs. Gleitman could have been safely and lawfully aborted and have been free to conceive again and give birth to a normal child. Instead she was told . . . that her child would not be affected. . . . While the law cannot remove the heartache or undo the harm, it can afford some reasonable measure of compensation towards alleviating the financial burdens. In declining to do so," Jacobs argued, the court "permits a wrong with serious consequential injury to go wholly unaddressed. That provides no deterrent to professional irresponsibility and is neither just nor compatible with expanding principles of liability in the field of torts." In rejecting these suits, he concluded, the court allowed physicians to evade their legal duties and permitted "professional irresponsibility."[94]

By the time that the New York state appellate courts heard the *Stewart* case in 1970 and 1972, state criminal abortion laws were being overturned in state and federal appellate courts and repealed in some states, including New York. Nonetheless, the New York courts followed New Jersey's earlier decision in *Gleitman,* deciding that neither the parents nor the child had a cause for action. New York State's highest courts overturned the awards to the parents and affirmed the trial judge's rejection of the claim on behalf of Rosalyn Stewart.[95] Although the jury in the Stewart case had found itself able to make assessments about the damage done to the child and to the parents—even as it had observed the love of the parents for their child— New York's Appellate Court (affirmed by the New York Court of Appeals) quoted *Gleitman* and declared that it was "virtually impossible to evaluate as compensatory damages the anguish to the parents of rearing a malformed child as against the denial to them of the benefits of parenthood."[96]

Although appellate courts rejected the very premise of these malpractice suits, that did not stop parents from bringing them against hospitals and doctors. Following the U.S. Supreme Court decisions in *Roe* and *Doe* in 1973, many states permitted "wrongful birth" suits brought by the parents. In 1979, New Jersey became one of the states that allowed wrongful birth suits. "Wrongful life" suits brought by the child have been a different matter, however. Many states still reject these suits, and *Gleitman* continues to set the standard for a court's rejection by relying on the "intuition" that the child "would surely choose life."[97] The New Jersey court had relied upon "intuition," but for many pregnant women, their partners, and their families, their consciences told them that potential parents had the need for and the right to information and had the ability to make decisions about their futures. By the end of the twentieth century, most states accepted "wrongful birth" cases. The success of these malpractice suits in the 1970s and 1980s spurred American medicine to advise genetic testing.[98]

These civil suits exposed the arbitrary nature of the medical system of therapeutic abortion in the decades before *Roe* and *Doe.* However, as the legal process exposed, it also masked. Law and the media made information, ideas, and practices visible and invisible in a shifting process. That process of producing and erasing information in specific ways shaped knowledge. Most notably, race disappeared in the legal transcripts but showed up in news reports. Religion—most specifically, Catholicism— was brought out in both the Gleitman and Stewart cases and appeared in some news stories but disappeared almost completely in medicine. Religion had long been part of medicine, but by the mid-twentieth century its public presence remained visible in the buildings and names of hospitals while professional medical science, education, and clinical practices were increasingly secularized and standardized. Medicine, with its power rooted in science and professional authority, made religion invisible even as religion contributed to shaping medical beliefs, practices, policies, and communication.

However hidden or denied, race and religion were of central importance in organizing access to a medical procedure. The role of class, on the other hand, was a bit different. It was well known at the time that women with money and family medical connections were able to get abortions from careful physicians. Today, students of abortion often remark that during this period middle-class (white) women could get abortions when others could not. This statement is sometimes said as though the process had been automatic, even easy. Yet only the most elite and fortunate (at times, only a woman with a male medical relative on her side) could have assumed access to a therapeutic abortion. As we have seen, neither middle-class status nor health insurance, whiteness, education, or money guaranteed access to abortion. Here I want to repeat an earlier observation: the malpractice suits brought by the Stewarts and the Gleitmans make it plain that the medical system of providing legal therapeutic abortion was systematically arbitrary and sensitive to bias, not only to the biases of class and privilege but also to those founded in race and religion.

These suits concerned the problem of restriction and inequity in the existing abortion system. The early abortion law reform movement worked on many fronts; these suits were one tactic among many.[99] However, to read these cases as being only about abortion would be to miss their full significance.

The suits brought by the Stewarts, Gleitmans, and others like them have often been mistakenly treated as expressing a wish that the child had never been born. Yet the record shows that anxiety about possible birth defects and active efforts to terminate pregnancy did not mean that the parents rejected their child or did not love her once the child was born and in their family. Quite the opposite. When asked her feelings about her child's "future," Barbara Stewart told the people in the courtroom, "It is very hurtful to me because I can't really see a future that she has." Mrs. Stewart reported that she hurt "all the time."[100] When asked if he was "disturbed" to learn of his daughter's cataracts and cardiac problems at birth, her father clarified, "I was hurt." Asked to describe "the difficulties" that his family faced, the father began, "Well, it is pretty hard to describe. . . . It is just that we really don't know how to do what we should, and I think that she needs a lot of attention, and she needs a lot of understanding that we don't have." Of his feelings, Rosalyn's father declared, "I think the most important thing is that we love her very much."[101]

These suits may also be seen as pioneering efforts by parents on behalf of their disabled children. In suing their doctors and hospitals, the parents sought recognition of the poor treatment that they had received at the hands of their doctors and of the price their children were paying in suffering.[102] The parents also sought a portion of the tremendous resources needed to provide for their disabled children. The concrete conditions for parents caring for a disabled child were difficult and demanding. As Barbara Stewart testified, she alone accompanied and cared for her daughter; she took her to therapy and medical appointments.[103] As the Gleitmans testified, by the age of seven, their son had had several eye operations and had been seen by "many doctors" and twenty special institutions and hospitals.[104]

"Rubella parents," as a group of parents in Los Angeles had named themselves, had to deal with much more than social shame. Two-year-old Christina Robles, her mother reported, had already been to the hospital eighteen times. In addition to having heart defects, Christina was blind, deaf, and brain damaged; her mother took her to St. John's Hospital every week for physical therapy. Mrs. Lynn Garcia drove at least four hours every day to take her two-year-old daughter to sessions with physical therapists and hearing specialists. Mothers, as the parents with primary, daily, physical responsibility for their children's care and upbringing, had much work to do. Expenses mounted as well. Someone who drove her child to multiple appointments all day long could not earn wages herself; health insurance did not cover physical therapy or hearing aids. Fathers took on additional jobs to cover the needs of their multiply handicapped children.[105]

That two of the three Los Angeles–area mothers featured in this 1968 *Los Angeles Times* article about rubella appear, by their surnames, to be Latinas deserves notice. Unfortunately, the lack of detailed data makes ascertaining demographic patterns in the profiles of the women who sought therapeutic abortions and who had "rubella babies" impossible. However, as this chapter has analyzed, we do know that the few women who received legal therapeutic abortions in hospitals were white and middle-class while the women who had illegal or self-induced abortions included great numbers of women of color and working-class women. If women of color had less information about German measles, less access to the physicians who performed therapeutic abortions, and—*perhaps* among Catholic Latinas—somewhat less willingness to turn to abortion,[106] it may have been that the disabled children of rubella were concentrated among non-white working-class and poor families. Many Latino and Latina parents had known nothing of the dangers of rubella until they heard about them from doctors late in pregnancy or during their children's infancy. A study of CRS in New York attributed the high proportion of Puerto Rican families in the study to a lack of available information about rubella in Spanish, crowded living conditions that spread contagion more easily among this poor population, and the lack of "the sophistication and money" needed to find an illegal abortion.[107]

The Stewart and Gleitman suits were another aspect of an emerging disability rights movement. While the Stewarts and Gleitmans sued for damages that could help with the medical care and education of their children, parents of physically and intellectually disabled children struggled to obtain decent schooling for their children. Parent organizations for the disabled fought for equal access to schools and for state and federal funding.[108] Individual parents evaded their doctors' automatic advice to institutionalize their children, and some physicians challenged what one doctor called "Instant Institutionalization (I. I.)." Dr. Donald Kerr Grant, of Buffalo, called physicians' practice of immediately advising the parents to institutionalize a child whenever they saw severe mental retardation, "a disgrace." As "a physician intimately involved in the management of retarded children" who "spen[t] hours helping parents care for a handicapped child at home," he was appalled to see "infants arbitrarily admitted" to institutions without any attempt to keep them with their families at home. Furthermore, "the parents," he observed, "have been given little chance to assist in a most vital decision."[109] Many physicians assumed the worst, and as a result, as this doctor's remarks make evident, they actively contributed to separating children from their parents and helped to create hopelessness among parents of retarded children. Dr. Grant identified precisely the same problem that the Stewarts, Gleitmans, and others also faced: parents were being left out of a "vital decision" about their children and their own lives.

Labeling these suits "wrongful birth" and "wrongful life" cases diverted attention from the wrongs involved and forced parents (then and now) to proceed in the legal arena as though they would have preferred that their children did not exist and to argue that their children would prefer nonexistence.[110] The labels are misnomers. The suits concern whether doctors have the same duty to their pregnant patients that they have to patients in any other case: the duty to give accurate and complete information, including discussing all treatment alternatives, so that patients can make decisions in an informed way. Indeed, these kinds of malpractice suits may be seen as one of the roots of "informed consent" in patient care, a guiding principle of contemporary health care and health law.[111]

In challenging the subtle deceptions of downplaying risk and failing to inform patients of the possibility of abortion, these malpractice suits represented a pioneering effort to realign power in the physician-patient relationship. Since the nineteenth century, the nation's criminal abortion laws had included exceptions that allowed physicians to perform abortions that they determined to be necessary. The therapeutic abortion committee system was the formalized manifestation of the right and responsibility of physicians to adjudicate whether and when women could receive legal, medically legitimate "therapeutic" abortions. In the medical system of the time, although women had to consent to an abortion, they did not decide. These cases challenged the medical power to decide and a history of medical deception of women who sought abortions. Although many physicians sympathized and helped women obtain abortions, antiabortion physicians had long encouraged each other to prevent abortions by deceiving women by, for example, refusing to reveal the outcome of a pregnancy test. It is worth pointing out that this type of suit is predicated on the problematic assumption of consumer choice among physicians and the legal availability of abortion. Neither the individual doctor nor the larger health care system is expected to implement the patient's decision. They are only required to give accurate information and point the patient to other physicians and hospitals who might perform an abortion, a procedure that is increasingly inaccessible in the United States and may also be expensive, both for those who do not have insurance and for those who do since health insurance often excludes abortion.

We need not accept the view of present-day tort reformers who regard those who bring malpractice suits as deceitful and in search of money rather than as people seeking to redress real violations to see that these earlier suits addressed both the financial needs of the injured and the need for changes in medicine. In a society that provided meager services for the disabled, lacked a universal health care system, and relied upon private family resources—both financial and physical—to care for the disabled, civil litigation could be the only means for securing high-quality care and education for a disabled child. The parents of the severely disabled stood almost alone, with inadequate funding and social support available to provide medical care, social services, and special education for the child or assistance for the parents and family caring for the disabled child. The need for individual suits grew, in part, out of the larger society's failure to meet the needs of its disabled citizens, a problem that suits alone could not solve. The commitment of the parents to their unexpected disabled children is apparent in their efforts on the children's behalf—in seeking medical care and educational services and in bringing malpractice suits.

Even though the Stewarts and Gleitmans lost their suits, these ordinary families of the working class, black and white, were pioneers in advancing patient rights, reproductive rights, and disability rights. In public legal forums, they insisted that the decision to bring a child into the world—and more specifically, the decision of whether to bring a pregnancy to term with knowledge of possible health problems or to abort—was not a decision for doctors to make. This was a decision to be made by the pregnant woman, by the potential parents. The doctor's duty was to provide accurate medical information; the responsibility for making a decision about the patient's health care and about reproduction rested with the patient herself. In failing to give information, in downplaying the consequences of disease, in following their own religious values rather than consulting with the patient and being guided by her (or, as in these cases, the couple), doctors and hospitals, these suits charged, treated their patients negligently and failed in their duties to their patients. The malpractice for which these suits were brought should be called "wrongful information." Today, the responsibility of physicians to provide accurate and complete information to patients and to respect patient autonomy is a basic principle of medical training and a hallmark of patient rights.

# FOUR

# Law Making and Law Breaking in an Epidemic

WHEN MRS. ELAINE BOETTNER WENT to cast her ballot in California's June 1964 primary, she presented a problem. She was eligible and she wanted to vote, but she had discovered that morning that she had German measles. Informing the precinct officers of her situation, she waited while they consulted. The problem was so well known and self-evident that the newspaper report said nothing about why this disease had provoked a discussion at the voting station. Precinct workers at the Fullerton voting station and newspaper readers all knew that German measles could cause birth defects if caught by pregnant women. And clearly there would be more women coming to vote, perhaps some of them pregnant. No one wanted to be exposed to the disease or to spread it. "We discussed the situation at great length, the five of us," precinct clerk Mrs. Freda Murphy reported. "We finally decided we should not prevent her from voting. So I took a can of disinfectant and sprayed everything in sight—the booth, her ballot, her hand, and the marker. It was a clean vote."[1] (See figure 10.)

Public consciousness of this disease had reached such a high point that it caused a dilemma at a voting station. The news story joked that this vote was "the most sanitary ballot in the state's primary" and included a photograph of the booth being sprayed with a can of disinfectant. The precinct clerk punned when she declared it "a clean vote." Perhaps the column laughs a bit at the hypervigilance of women. Nevertheless, that hypervigilance reveals how well the general public understood the ramifications of German measles and the great care that women took—as citizens, as representatives

Figure 10. A California election clerk sprays a voting booth with disinfectant after a citizen with German measles has used it. "Measles Can't Keep Woman From Voting," *Los Angeles Times,* June 3, 1964, p. E8.

of the democratic system, and as the traditional guardians of health—to prevent the spread of this disease.

Officials had long paid attention to epidemics and had attempted to prevent their spread. Infectious diseases could be the basis for excluding immigrants from entering the country, for barring them from becoming new citizens, and for limiting civil rights. This disease, however, affected women most directly. The attention given by the precinct workers—all of whom may have been female volunteers—to Mrs. Boettner's German measles underscored the importance that women attached to ensuring that other women were protected from this disease. As they served as clerks and assisted in the mechanics of running an election, these women made it possible for citizens to vote. In keeping with the long history of exclusion and denial of the right to vote, the precinct committee members also considered whether the disease might bar this citizen from her basic right to enter the voting booth and cast her ballot. They ultimately decided against following that course. In a year of heightened attention to the systematic denial of blacks' voting rights and African Americans' struggles to secure the right to vote, precinct workers and voters had to be keenly aware of the significance of their decisions. This precinct leader turned to a housewife's tool to solve the problem—she used a disinfecting spray to clean away dirt and germs.[2] Humorous in its way, but serious too. The precinct workers found a solution that simultaneously reassured those afraid of exposure to the disease and upheld the citizen's fundamental right to vote.

This incident exemplifies a moment when disease, citizenship rights and duties, gender, and democracy all came together in a literal way. Here, at the voting booth, women citizens worked to protect the public's health and pregnant women while they simultaneously protected, facilitated, and acted upon the right to vote. German measles also offers an opportunity to examine democracy in action in a larger sense. As the epidemic fostered new discourses, social movements, political action, law making, and law breaking, it also fostered women's expression as citizens of their needs and their expectations of the state. Although epidemics have often led to the expansion of public powers—frequently at the expense of civil liberties[3]— German measles did not curtail a woman's right to vote. Instead, like the Voting Rights Act of 1964, German measles ultimately contributed to the expansion of women's constitutional rights.

In 1964, there was little that the state could do to protect women against this dreaded epidemic that threatened infant deaths and crippled children, even if precinct workers disinfected the voting booths. Departments of public health could do no more than issue warnings, count cases, and observe the epidemic's progress across the country.[4] The federal government supported scientific research, but a vaccine remained a hope for the future. Physicians might offer reassurance; gamma globulin, a therapy whose efficacy was a question mark;[5] or therapeutic abortion to those who contracted German measles during pregnancy. As the possibility of contracting German measles and the need for a (therapeutic) abortion became a situation that women and their families could all too well imagine happening to them, the law governing abortion became acutely relevant to a broad section of the population at the same time. Abortion law reform was no longer merely a technical issue or one of interest only to a handful of doctors, lawyers, and priests.[6]

Because epidemics concentrate and intensify the collective awareness of the dangers of disease, they may infuse new meanings and urgency into contemporary conflicts—from revolutionary politics to religion to racial boundaries and debates over civil liberties.[7] The German measles epidemic fueled an emerging political debate about abortion law. "Abortion is a shocking subject—shocking," a *Parents* magazine article declared in 1965, "because there are some million or more abortions performed each year under illegal, distasteful, and often dangerous conditions." Nevertheless, the "shocking" and "distasteful" matter had become a topic requiring discussion and reevaluation of the law, the authors declared, because "millions of wives and mothers are driven to seek illegal abortion." Although "many factors" came into play in rewriting abortion law, "surely" they concluded, "the primary consideration should be to do what is best—medically and morally—for the health and well-being of the whole family."[8] As abortion came to be associated with respectable mothers and families in the midst of this epidemic, the law came under attack from respectable citizens, including doctors, religious leaders, fathers, and mothers.


Mainstream medicine agreed that abortion for rubella in early pregnancy was legitimate and performed therapeutic abortions. Yet the law was not completely clear on the point. Although physicians and journalists often declared therapeutic abortions performed because of German measles to be "illegal" or in "violation" of state criminal laws at the time, this assessment should not now be accepted at face value. These labels should be properly understood as part of an effort to draw a new line between the criminal and the respectable and a new battle line within the medical profession over therapeutic abortion. In the late 1950s, a number of leading physicians and attorneys called for reform of the state abortion laws; the prominent American Legal Institute (ALI) framed a new "model law" that would clarify the law, protect doctors, and narrowly expand the legal practice of (therapeutic) abortion. By the early 1960s, reform bills had been submitted in several states, including California. The German measles epidemic coincided with this nascent professional effort to reform the nation's abortion laws.

Both those who favored liberalizing and expanding the medical practice of abortion and those who wanted to further criminalize abortion by banning all therapeutic abortions had begun to describe therapeutic abortions for reasons other than preserving the physical life of the pregnant woman as "technically illegal."[9] Medical reformers themselves began framing the conventional, mainstream medical practice of therapeutic abortion as illegal. Physician-attorney Ralph J. Gampell, who surveyed his colleagues on therapeutic abortion, for instance, declared, "the laws are being broken widely across the country."[10] At a medical school forum on the topic, another prominent Los Angeles physician "implied that the law is broken every day by legitimate doctors practicing in respectable hospitals."[11] But these therapeutic abortions were not clearly illegal; if they had been, hospitals would not have permitted them, and physicians would not have performed them with the approval of their colleagues. It makes more sense to consider these therapeutic abortions legal since doctors openly performed them in hospitals, and prosecutors (who vigorously pursued underground practitioners and criminal abortion cases at the time) did not investigate hospital abortions.[12] As reform advocates publicized the idea that therapeutic abortions were illegal, and a backlash against abortion law reform developed, physicians felt increasingly vulnerable. That uncertainty and sense of vulnerability were the result of remarks made in the midst of a political battle to control the definition of *therapeutic* and *legal abortion.*

In 1966, to the shock of physicians in the midst of the crises posed by German measles, California state officials suddenly charged a group of physicians with breaking the law for having performed medically justified abortions in hospitals for women exposed to the disease early in pregnancy. In the fight to redraw the lines governing legal abortion, California state officials had targeted reputable medical men and respectable married women. The state's actions struck at the historical understanding between the state and medicine that the law did not intervene in regular medical practice. The Board of Medical Examiners, charged with regulating medical licensing in California and composed of physicians, initiated the official investigation. The Board of Medical Examiners was a state body, but it was also a professional body, and physicians expected it to protect the profession as well as patients. When a powerful and actively antiabortion Catholic board member instigated the official state investigation of therapeutic abortion by specialists in the state's premier hospitals, the long-standing trust between medicine and the state was broken.

This official state investigation represented a new stage in the century-long disagreement between Catholic antiabortion physicians and their medical colleagues about the appropriate practice of therapeutic abortion. Other scholars have also recognized these events in California as a turning point in the progress of abortion law reform. Sociologist Kristin Luker described it as a breakdown in the "medical consensus" that governed abortion practice, a breakdown arising from physicians' discovery that they did not agree about abortion at all—not about when life began, when abortions were medically permitted, or what the definitions and limits of therapeutic abortion were.[13] But this disagreement was not new. It was a continuation of a long-running religious battle within medicine over abortion that had moved into the public sphere.

The unprecedented investigation by the state, which had begun as a backlash within medicine, contributed to remaking American political culture and energized both the emerging pro-life and reproductive rights movements. Antiabortion physicians' use of a state regulatory apparatus to restrict the medical practice of legal abortion outraged the early abortion law reform movement. The use of an official state body in the service of a particular political and religious perspective appalled many physicians and California citizens as did the intervention of religious leaders into state politics. Together, they represented a dramatic break with the postwar ideal of an ecumenical political culture exemplified by John F. Kennedy's presidency.[14] The battle in California turned out to be a key stage in the progress of, first, abortion law reform and, then, the decriminalization of abortion nationwide and in the transformation of the relationship between women and the state. German measles had unforeseen political power.

In an astounding breach of medical loyalty, the former chief of medical staff at Palm Harbor Hospital in Garden Grove, California, turned in his own hospital and colleagues for performing five therapeutic abortions for maternal rubella. Dr. J. D. Leggett, a general surgeon and the former chief of staff of the Orange County, Southern California, hospital, reported the abortions to the district attorney.[15] In previous years, antiabortion physicians had tried to restrict the number of therapeutic abortions in their own hospitals or had complained in medical journals of hospitals' high numbers of abortions. Going directly to the press and prosecutors was a newly aggressive method of trying to control their colleagues. The battle over abortion in medicine reached unprecedented levels in 1965. When these charges reached the local newspaper, the hospital objected to being equated with an "abortion mill." The hospital watched its staff carefully, and only "ethical doctors" performed therapeutic abortions. As the current chief of obstetrics pointed out, "The operations are common medical practice in every non-Catholic hospital in the country." Dr. Leggett, the newspaper explained, was "a member of [the Catholic] church."[16]

While these charges and countercharges between physicians played out in Los Angeles–area newspapers, a small group of professionals organized to win medical support for abortion law reform. Dr. Keith Russell, a specialist in obstetrics who was prominent in Los Angeles and in California medicine, sent a personal letter to more than two thousand of his medical colleagues asking for their support for the Humane Abortion Act, an abortion law reform bill submitted to the California legislature by Assembly member Anthony C. Beilenson. The California Committee on Therapeutic Abortion (CCTA), a group of physicians, attorneys, public health professors and others with ties to the University of California at Los Angeles (UCLA), worked for the Humane Abortion Act. The reform bill, based on the model law proposed by the American Law Institute in 1959, had been submitted before in California without success.[17] By spring 1965, Beilenson's bill had gained impressive support from California's leaders in medicine, health, and law. More than one thousand California physicians and eleven hundred clergymen had listed their names to support reform legislation.[18]

The *Los Angeles Times* focused on possible law breaking in its coverage of the growing support for legal reform. The paper identified "four leading hospitals" in the L.A. area that performed abortions for German measles in "open defiance of California law." But these hospitals and physicians had done no such thing. They had not advertised the abortions to the press or the state in "open defiance." They had merely practiced medicine in accordance with the system that had been cemented as standard practice nationwide in the 1950s. A hospital committee reviewed requests to perform therapeutic abortions and permitted some that met the criteria agreed upon by the profession. Therapeutic abortion for maternal rubella was one of those. Media coverage made public what had been done through normal, quiet hospital routines. Hospitals, and particularly their attorneys, were surprised to find themselves named in the newspaper as being among those institutions where physicians "were being forced to act outside the law," as reform leader Dr. Russell put it. Only the hospital at UCLA confirmed that it performed therapeutic abortions.[19]

Physicians operating within the therapeutic abortion committee system felt confident that the law conceded their right to perform abortions, and, in the main, they were right. "Law enforcement agencies," the president of the Orange County Medical Society observed, "do not consider [abortions] a crime when done by reputable physicians at reputable hospitals and when controlled by the committee."[20] The key word here was *reputable.* When presented with the information about Palm Harbor Hospital, the Orange County prosecutor, Kenneth Williams, found himself in a "dilemma" and unable to act on the complaint against the respectable physicians at the respectable hospital. He "ponder[ed]" the problem for two months. The question for him, as one local newspaper put it, was whether "to be or not to be the first DA to put reputable doctors on trial for performing therapeutic abortions, which are clearly illegal . . . [and] almost as certainly justifiable by medical ethics." As the DA waffled, he wondered whether it would be "fair or practical" to enforce an "archaic" law. (In terming the law "archaic," the DA used the language of the reformers.) He compared his situation to the 1925 Scopes "monkey" trial on the teaching of Darwin and evolution and remarked that "agents of law enforcement shouldn't be made to look like a bunch of asses." Testing the waters, the prosecutor had convened several mock juries of his own, including women in a "coffee klatch," prosecutors, and attorneys. He saw the impossibility of resolving the issue in a criminal trial: in each case, the group members divided in their opinions. He feared that enforcing "an archaic, foolish law" would make him and Orange County into a worldwide joke.[21]

Despite reassurances from local and California state authorities, physicians nonetheless felt vulnerable in a new way. The legality of their therapeutic abortion practices was beginning to look more gray than it had before. Hospital attorneys now worried about the ramifications of announcements to the press that linked their institutions to abortion; doctors "fear[ed]" that the lawyers might force them to give up therapeutic abortions in all except technically legal cases."[22] As later events showed, they had reason to worry. The remarks of the Orange County prosecutor prompted the investigators for the Board of Medical Examiners to forward the newspaper article to the California Department of Justice and to the board's executive secretary in Sacramento.[23] When a few months later *Life* magazine published its story about the heartbreak of German measles for pregnant women and the kind doctor who performed therapeutic abortions at a San Francisco hospital, it added fuel to the fire.[24]

Disgusted with the *Life* magazine news story and prosecutors like the one in Orange County, the California State Board of Medical Examiners began quietly pursuing its own unprecedented investigation of hospital medical practices. "That article," said Dr. James V. McNulty, a member of the Board of Medical Examiners and a Catholic physician, "put the board in an awkward position. Doctors were publicly breaking the law, and the article made a point of this in the most blatant way."[25] McNulty pointed to *Life* magazine for provoking an official investigation of the state's physicians and their practices of therapeutic abortion, but a better way to understand it is to see the *Life* magazine coverage as the straw that broke the camel's back. Dr. McNulty and other activist Catholic doctors had been struggling for several years against legal reform, but Beilenson's bill and the reform effort were nonetheless gaining strength as they won the support of thousands of physicians, thousands of clergymen, and many others. The struggle also hit close to home. The outspoken medical leader of the reform effort in California, Dr. Keith Russell, was a colleague of Dr. McNulty. Both men were prominent obstetricians in Los Angeles and in state medical circles. Russell was chair of the committee on maternal and child health in the California Medical Society as well as regional chair of the American College of Obstetricians and Gynecologists (ACOG). McNulty was a member of the California Board of Medical Examiners. Both Russell and McNulty were clinical professors at the University of Southern California (USC).

This was a long-running battle within the profession and within the specialty of obstetrics; it was also a disagreement among colleagues on their home turf. When USC medical students invited leading reformers, including Dr. Alan Guttmacher, president of Planned Parenthood, to speak at the university, their actions must have irked Dr. McNulty.[26] When the state's physicians and medical school deans signed on to support the Humane Abortion Act by the hundreds, it was clear who was winning. Neither local prosecutors nor the state attorney general showed any interest in investigating hospitals when abortions for German measles came to light. Like the Orange County prosecutor, the Los Angeles–area district attorney, Evelle J. Younger, reassured doctors and hospitals that he had no plans to prosecute.[27] Support for reform accelerated in the spring of 1965, and at the end of May, after hours of testimony lasting into the night, the reform bill was voted out of the California State Assembly's committee for the first time.[28] The article on California in *Life* magazine published in June infuriated Dr. McNulty once again. (See figures 7 and 8.) He then turned to the power he had. As a member of an official state board, he prompted an official investigation of his colleagues. The Board of Medical Examiners formed a committee to look into therapeutic abortion and appointed Dr. McNulty its head.[29]

The systematic investigation of the hospital practice of therapeutic abortion initiated in 1965 was unprecedented. This chapter analyzes, for the first time, the process of this investigation through the official records of the California state investigation together with the public charges, appeals, and political events that followed.[30] State officials looked for possible criminal activity in standard, mainstream hospital routines and treated law-abiding, careful physicians as suspect. The investigation revealed unexpected official distrust of the medical profession and of the regulatory systems that hospitals had established in the 1940s and 1950s to ensure adherence to the law. It also represented an unprecedented intrusion into patients' lives and an expansion of the state's interest in and willingness to invade patients' medical records, lives, and privacy. The state's investigative records not only reveal the path of the state's investigation but also permit an analysis of the reasoning of pregnant women and their doctors.

In July and August of 1965, two-man teams of state investigators traveled throughout California and appeared at the doors of hospitals and doctors' offices to ask questions about therapeutic abortion. The investigation concentrated on the two most populous areas of the state and the homes of the state's premier medical schools, Los Angeles and the San Francisco Bay Area. State agents questioned people at twenty hospitals and investigated more than forty physicians. As required by the California State Archives, I do not include any names or identifying information from these confidential investigative records.[31] Investigators collected newspaper articles for leads, then sought patient records from hospitals. No official warnings were made or charges brought for many months, but the very fact that an investigator had shown up at any hospital served as a warning to all; many hospitals ceased permitting abortions for German measles.

State investigators uncovered not only the practice of providing therapeutic abortion for rubella but also the strength of the medical feeling that doing so was medically correct and morally upstanding.[32] Even as he was coming under investigation, one specialist told investigators that he and his hospital planned to continue to provide abortions for rubella while they sought legal changes. "He hated to be a test case," the investigators recorded, "but felt that good medical practice called for abortions in cases of the type at hand."[33] The chief of obstetrics and gynecology at this hospital "stressed that it is the feeling of the hospital staff that good medical practice requires the physician to practice the type of medicine the public believes to be good medicine, whether or not it conforms to written law. He claims it is the belief of an overwhelming majority of obstetricians that the archaic abortion law does not permit good medical practice, . . . that the public does not want 'vegetables' born so as to become public institutional charges, and that this group of physicians will continue to practice what they determine to be 'good medicine' until the law is changed." The chief, the report continued, said, "that the Staff's feeling is that by doing therapeutic abortions for Rubella, they are doing the people of California a service [and] that cases involving radiation exposure, drugs producing fetal damage, rape, and incest are other reasons for doing therapeutic abortions, as opposed to the legal 'maternal' reason of saving the mother's life."[34]

This statement by the hospital's chief of ob-gyn illuminates not only his confidence in the face of legal challenges but also the members of his specialty's sense of their duties to both their patients and the public. The reasons for performing these abortions went beyond the decision of the pregnant woman to avoid having a child with severe birth defects. Here we see the long-standing presumption among specialists in obstetrics that they practiced medicine not only for their patients but also for the good of society. As was the case with coercive sterilization carried out by physicians and legitimated by the state, some doctors considered performing therapeutic abortions to be for the good of the society as a whole, which, in the specialists' eyes, neither wanted "vegetables" nor wanted to pay for them.[35] This may well have been an accurate reading of public sentiment regarding the severely retarded and the disabled. These ideas fit with the twentieth century's history of sterilization as well as with a developing resentment of state welfare expenditures for the needy. The difference between abortion and sterilization is that physicians did not perform therapeutic abortions coercively. These abortions for German measles, which accorded with the profession's belief in their legitimacy and with this doctor's belief about the public's wishes and the value of preventing the birth of "vegetables," were only performed upon the decision and permission of the pregnant woman herself. (Standard policy required her husband's approval as well.) Physicians sterilized thousands of Latina, African American, and Native American women without their knowledge or under threat of losing medical care or state welfare benefits. Other women were forced to agree to sterilization in order to receive an abortion. Access to therapeutic abortion and the respectful attitude toward women's decisions—which a few women experienced—were in part granted to them because of their class and racial privileges.[36]

While the medical performance of these therapeutic abortions challenged a newly rigid interpretation of the law, they did not challenge medical control and the power to determine when abortions were medically and legally justified for specific reasons. Although women made decisions about their pregnancies, unless their requests fell into specific and narrow "medical" categories, were vouched for by physicians, and were passed through a medical review process, women's own decisions to terminate their pregnancies were not considered valid. Those who could not obtain therapeutic abortions had to go outside the legal hospital system for abortions or carry pregnancies against their own judgment.

This particular hospital had performed nineteen abortions for rubella in 1964, and with the height of the epidemic then hitting California, it expected to perform forty or fifty in 1965. Furthermore, the doctor knew that prosecutors did not want to pursue this kind of case; they only prosecuted "cases in which abortions are done for venal reasons." Interviews by investigators with local district attorneys confirmed the doctor's report. Although this doctor expressed confidence about the correctness of his position and his legal safety, state investigators were ready to take on this hospital's staff. "It appears," they concluded, "that subject has violated Sec. 2377 B & P Code by performing an abortion when it was not necessary in order to save the patient's life." The investigators recommended action by the state attorney general.[37]

In other hospitals, different rules applied. In some, therapeutic abortions were permitted only when women expressed suicidal feelings in reaction to the fear of birth defects. Abortions for psychiatric reasons, in this common interpretation, were legal because they were performed to save the woman's life. As one administrator explained, "The fear and anxiety of the mother that the child might have defects because of her contact with Rubella could lead her to attempt suicide."[38] The chief of ob-gyn at another California hospital explained that in addition to a physician's diagnosis of rubella, two psychiatrists had to agree that "fear that she would give birth to a malformed baby" made the patient suicidal. The doctor related the history of a woman whose request for a therapeutic abortion had been refused. In the fifth month of her pregnancy, the hospital finally allowed an abortion to be performed because "the patient developed suicidal tendency from fear and worry of giving birth to a malformed baby." This woman must have been in agony. Once she became desperate and suicidal enough to meet the hospital's criteria, she qualified for an abortion that months earlier she had known she needed. The hospital's legal counsel had advised this policy. State medical authorities apparently agreed that abortions for psychiatric reasons were legal. "Recommend case be closed," was the investigator's conclusion, "because there is no evidence of any illegal abortions being performed at the hospital."[39]

As in Orange County, investigators found that district attorneys in other areas were also disinclined to bring criminal charges against physicians for performing therapeutic abortions. First, as one district attorney told investigators, if there was any evidence of a woman's "suicidal tendencies," it would seem to make an abortion legal. MDs and DAs understood each other. Second, he knew that abortion rights advocates might *want* a physician to be prosecuted in order to challenge the law. Investigators noted that this district attorney "was not going to accommodate" them. Finally, in the DA's eyes, bringing a criminal case of this sort was a losing proposition.[40] Juries, prosecutors believed, would not convict a reputable physician in such a case. California district attorneys refused to do the work that antiabortion physician-activists pushed upon them. Neither individual complaints nor Board of Examiners' investigations prompted local prosecutors or the attorney general to bring criminal charges against highly respected physicians. Indeed, several county grand juries explicitly supported abortion law reform.[41] Failing with prosecutors, the State Board of Medical Examiners pursued physicians through its own methods.

Investigators also found and questioned patients at home. Women who had already gone through the trauma of learning what German measles meant for an expected baby, made difficult decisions, and endured examinations from multiple doctors to obtain a therapeutic abortion now had to explain themselves to state officials. Although their feelings about being questioned by two male investigators about their pregnancies and abortions do not come through in the concise investigation reports, one imagines they felt surprise and apprehension about what the investigations might mean for them personally. Known to state officials and actively involved in abortion, they were vulnerable and could be forced, as other women like them had been, to testify in public courtrooms against their doctors.[42]

Yet in the investigative reports the women appear to have been composed and firm about the rightness of their decisions. As they answered the state's questions, they revealed their thoughtfulness and their deep sense that the decision of whether to abort or carry a pregnancy to term was theirs to make. They had consulted with their doctors and their husbands and made decisions about their pregnancies and potential children. These mothers-to-be had decided to abort because they knew the dangers that rubella posed early in pregnancy. That information, as one mother observed, was "rather frightening." The investigators noted, "Mrs.——— repeated several times that *the decision to have this operation performed was entirely her own.* The doctors simply gave her the figures on the possibility of her having a child born with serious birth defects." Furthermore, "when she learned . . . the child could be born 'mentally retarded' due to her exposure to rubella during the early weeks of her pregnancy," she stated, " 'That closed the door.' "[43]

Knowledge of the likelihood of mental retardation "closed the door" for this mother. Mental retardation loomed particularly large in the minds of parents. It was not disability or abnormality in the abstract that worried them and that they decided to avoid but rather mental retardation. As one newspaper report on German measles explained, "A substantial fraction of the afflicted babies are mentally retarded, some grossly so. For these, nothing can be done. And, of course," the reporter observed, "each mother fears the worst for her child."[44] The retarded child, in the eyes of Americans at the time, represented shame and heartbreak.[45]

As surprising as it may seem in light of church opposition to abortion, Roman Catholic women and men were among those who turned to abortion when they found themselves in dire circumstances. Upon learning that "there was a risk of her child['s] being born deformed," one woman told investigators, "she and her husband decided to have . . . a therapeutic abortion." She was Catholic, the mother of two young children, and a teacher.[46] Another, whose husband was Catholic, said "that she had wanted the child very badly prior to learning of its possible deformity." (Her case confirmed that schoolchildren posed a threat to schoolteachers. It also verified that women with personal medical connections had better access to safe, physician-induced abortions: her father was a pharmacist, and she went to her mother's doctor.)[47] Questioned by investigators, California women provided context to explain why they had had therapeutic abortions. For the investigators, this was evidence of a crime.

Having pried open patient histories and hospital practices up and down the state, the Board of Medical Examiners brought charges against well-known doctors. In May 1966, the state attorney general's office announced that the board sought charges against twenty-one San Francisco doctors for criminal abortion and that more were under investigation. The doctors had performed therapeutic abortions for German measles. By June, nine prominent physicians had been named and charged with professional misconduct and violation of the criminal abortion law. The news shocked many and soon galvanized the abortion law reform movement. These physicians were among the leading medical men of the state—specialists in obstetrics and gynecology, chiefs of divisions, professors of the University of California's prominent medical school.[48] The abortions had each gone through the medical system's process of review for abortion and had each been carefully considered by several physicians and approved by committees in advance. The abortions now being treated as criminal and unprofessional had been neither secretive nor the now-stereotyped "back-alley" abortions. Rather, these abortions had been the most highly reviewed and legitimated type of abortion performed: done by a specialist openly in a hospital with the review and approval of peers. The physicians faced serious charges: they could lose their licenses to practice medicine and could be subject to criminal charges as well. Their names were in the news and associated with crime and the stigma of abortion. "Expectant mother[s]" planning on therapeutic abortions because they had contracted German measles immediately felt the consequences when hospitals cancelled their appointments.[49]

The doctors became legal pioneers by default. Once fingered by the state, they came to understand that they had been thrust into an important role—one they had not anticipated. They stood on principle on the standards of the medical profession and on the right of their patients to decide on abortion in specific, serious cases. As Dr. J. Paul Shively, chief of obstetrics and chair of the abortion committee at St. Luke's Hospital in San Francisco, remarked, "My primary interest at first was to preserve my license to practice. . . . But then the greater, overriding issue became clear—the need to modernize the law to provide protection for the people we treat."[50]

The board's powers, it was immediately understood, were being used by one powerful physician who intended to punish his medical colleagues for their opposing interpretation of medicine. San Francisco physicians quickly signed up to support their embattled colleagues. Thirty-three obstetricians in the Bay Area agreed "to testify that they performed similar abortions."[51] In a profession that had long denied and covered up its abortion practices—both legal and illegal—and at a moment when physicians' licenses were being threatened, this response was impressive. At a time of dissent and in the San Francisco Bay Area, in particular known for its political radicalism and protests against the Vietnam War, the state had provoked a rebellion among doctors. Instead of remaining silent, refusing to allow their names to be used, or disappearing on the days of trials, a large group of physicians announced their readiness to stand side by side with their colleagues who had been charged with a criminal action and to declare that they had done the same. The public support given to the San Francisco doctors in 1966 contrasted enormously with the experiences of Dr. George Loutrell Timanus in 1951. A highly respected physician who since the 1920s had performed abortions openly in his private Baltimore office, often for patients referred by medical men at Johns Hopkins, Dr. Timanus believed he had acted within the law and was performing therapeutic abortions. In 1950, his office was raided by police who arrested the doctor, his patients, and his staff. His colleagues abandoned him, however, when they failed to show up for his defense at his 1951 trial for illegal abortion. As Dr. Timanus later said, "The profession . . . convicted me."[52] Fifteen years later, however, the situation had changed dramatically. The prestigious American Law Institute, along with some members of the medical profession, advocated abortion law reform; reform bills had been presented in several states, including California; and the California Committee on Therapeutic Abortion (CCTA) actively pressed for legal change.[53]

This early reform group articulated the need to revise the abortion laws in terms of mothers. Mothers needed abortion; mothers' needs legitimated limited legal revision. As German measles hit the West Coast in 1965, CCTA collected petitions in favor of the "Humane Abortion Act" proposed by Assembly member Anthony Beilenson. The petition never used the word *woman* to describe those who needed an abortion; it spoke only of "the mother." The use of *mother* in this petition could be read as a conservative evasion of the word *woman,* references to sex, and women's rights to reproductive freedom, but I think we should read this choice of language differently. The emphasis here really was on *mothers*—and their responsibilities, needs, and rights. This is how early legal reform moved forward. "Our present law," the petition declared, "fails to recognize the importance of the mother's health to the well-being of the family. It does not take account of the possibility opened by modern science of determining in advance the likelihood of a damaged fetus." Everyone, it pointed out, needed this law, for "no family is immune from the fear of a defective or deformed child. All families are subject to the possibility of a seriously sick mother whose pregnancy may further impair her health. The bill would give assurance to all families that, should the need arise, physicians would be authorized to provide proper medical care."[54] The Humane Abortion Act, its supporters urged, would protect mothers, families, and children.

The abortion law reform movement expanded phenomenally, growing into a popular movement when CCTA linked the defense of the San Francisco doctors with an attack on what it called the state's "archaic" abortion laws. The problem, the physician-supporters and legal reformers declared, lay not in the physicians' conduct but in the law. CCTA carried out a multipronged and masterful campaign. Members collected petitions. Ruth Roemer, professor of public health at UCLA, reported that "these signatures were collected at the drop of a hat. Thousands more could have been collected." Organizers mobilized prominent medical, legal, and religious leaders to speak on behalf of reform; garnered publicity and supportive editorials; and arranged hundreds of small meetings with civic organizations in order to develop active, statewide public support for legal reform. A press conference announcing the plight of the San Francisco physicians and the effort to change the abortion laws yielded extensive press coverage. National news outlets—including ABC and CBS television news, AP, UPI, and the *New York Times*—as well as California newspapers, radio, and television reporters all covered the story; more interviews, special news reports, and a CBS documentary team followed.[55]

CCTA worked methodically. Organizers identified a handful of leaders in specific professional groups who wrote a resolution in support of abortion law reform; then the leaders sought support and circulated the resolution among their colleagues. In this way, CCTA developed long lists of names, many of them among the leadership of professional societies, in support of reform. Physicians, attorneys, social workers, ministers, and sociologists all joined and signed resolutions in support of reform. Civic organizations wrote letters supporting the abortion reform bill to their representatives, sent supporters to state hearings, and encouraged their members to support Beilenson's bill. Less than a year after the doctors had been charged, supporters of reform included the California Medical Association, the State Board of Public Health (revealing division among the state health agencies), the State Bar Convention, half a dozen county grand juries, the California Federation of Women's Clubs, the Parent Teacher Association (PTA), the Young Republicans, the State Junior Chamber of Commerce, and the American Association of University Women. National medical, public health, and legal associations had also endorsed reform.[56]

The enthusiasm of different women's groups for a new law—from lawyers to grocery store clerks—signaled the emerging importance of reproductive rights to working-class and professional women alike. "Women lawyers jumped up" when they heard about the legislation, saying "we will back it," reported one woman attorney at a 1962 state hearing.[57] When 350 delegates of the California American Association of University Women (AAUW) met, they expressed enthusiastic support for Beilenson's Humane Abortion Act. There was a "tremendous burst of applause" when the motion carried. One member summarized the feeling: "The women of this state want that bill passed!"[58] The Retail Clerks Union, Los Angeles Local 770, urged its members to write their legislators in support of abortion law reform. Women made up more than half of the clerks' union.[59] Their active support for the bill is a corrective to the simple assumption of too many scholars and activists that the law governing abortion and access to safe procedures was a matter of importance only to middle-class women.

At the same time, a small group of working-class women developed a more militant approach to abortion law. Furious at the "censuring" of the San Francisco doctors in May 1966, Patricia T. Maginnis announced to San Francisco police and the press her plan to distribute names, addresses, and phone numbers of abortion "specialists" outside the country. She went to the streets with her flyer naming a dozen abortion specialists, mostly in Mexico. That simple flyer turned into "the List" and a long-term project to break the law and guide women to safe abortionists. Maginnis never focused on fetal defects or "deformed" children to justify abortion. She trusted women and insisted on their right and their moral capacity to make decisions about pregnancy and family. Several years earlier, Maginnis had become the earliest advocate of total repeal of the criminal abortion law. After collecting signatures for the earliest reform bill introduced in 1961 by California Assemblyman John Knox, she concluded that "reform" would not help the majority of women who needed abortions since, as she knew, most did not seek abortions for reasons of rape, incest, or health. Maginnis criticized reform as bad for women and insisted on total repeal. Although the professional and more moderate reform movement would eventually adopt Maginnis's perspective, in 1966 they opposed each other. Maginnis actively opposed Beilenson's reform legislation.[60]

Religious leaders also joined the fight for abortion law reform and defended the San Francisco doctors. In a case provoked by the outrage of an activist Catholic physician, questioning the very grounds upon which the charges had been brought was politically astute. Through sermons, prayers, panels, and publications, religious leaders and congregations publicly displayed religious support for abortion law reform. Religious support for the California abortion reform bill came from the Episcopal Church, the Northern California–Nevada Council of Churches, the California-Nevada Conference of the Methodist Church, the Council of Jewish Women of Los Angeles, and more than one thousand clergy and rabbis in more than three hundred cities and towns of California.[61] California Episcopal Bishop James Pike and the Reverend Lester Kinsolving, both of whom had joined Martin Luther King Jr. in the March on Selma, immediately announced their support for the San Francisco doctors (two of whom were Episcopalian). The Episcopal Grace Cathedral of San Francisco, known for holding services against the Vietnam War, held a "Service of Witness" on behalf of the San Francisco physicians. During the service, Rev. Kinsolving, vicar of the Episcopal Church of Salinas and vice president of CCTA, gave the sermon titled "Honor a Physician." The Episcopal priest praised the San Francisco physicians "who have chosen to violate an archaic and evil California law." Their commitment to their patients, he urged, "deserve[d] to be saluted rather than persecuted."[62]

Since the 1980s, the broad religious support for reform (and later, religious support for law breaking and the complete legalization of abortion) has been silenced by the convergence of Catholic, Christian evangelical, and Mormon antiabortion activism, overlooked by the media, and increasingly erased from historical memory. For Rev. Kinsolving and many others, the criminal abortion laws were the "evil" to be fought because they prevented physicians from caring for their patients and prohibited women from making moral choices about their pregnancies and childbearing. When religious opponents of legalized abortion today frame abortion as "evil," it is worth noticing that religious leaders have used the same word to describe the laws banning abortion. Clergy did more than give sermons in support of legalizing abortion. Within a year of the surprising events in California, clergy and rabbis around the country openly defied the law by giving women the names of physicians who performed abortion through the Clergy Consultation Service (CCS). Like Maginnis's California organization formed in 1966, CCS linked women with abortion providers. CCS, however, counseled and ministered to women represented as "troubled"—a judgment that Maginnis and the developing feminist movement rejected as patronizing. Nonetheless, advocacy for reproductive rights and women's rights was visible and strong in many churches and synagogues.[63]

While many avoided directly confronting the Catholic Church, Rev. Kinsolving believed it important to debate the Catholic position. It was not "anti-Catholic" to do so, he declared.[64] Kinsolving insisted upon religious pluralism and freedom in the United States. A single church neither defined morality for all nor had the right to impose its religious views on others. Kinsolving judged the Catholic effort to control abortion law to be as "outrageous" as laws that "would ban blood transfusions in deference to Jehovah's Witnesses" or "pork in deference to Orthodox Judaism."[65] The Catholic attack on abortion, Episcopalians pointed out, used the same language and arguments offered thirty years earlier against birth control, which was by 1966 not only widely accepted and used but also protected under the Constitution. Only the year before, the U.S. Supreme Court had ruled in *Griswold v. Connecticut* (1965) that married couples had a right to "privacy" in the bedroom and in their use of birth control. Even members of the Catholic hierarchy had become more liberal in their attitude toward the law governing birth control use by married couples. As abortion's stigma and criminality came under question, however, the Catholic Church now fought abortion just as it had fought the open discussion and legalization of birth control for the entire twentieth century.[66]

The state's Roman Catholic leaders and professionals led the opposition to abortion law reform. Through organized Catholic networks Catholic priests, physicians, attorneys, teachers, and parents spoke against reform at state legislative hearings, and in their Sunday sermons priests urged their congregations to write letters in opposition. "The taking of fetal life involves the slaying of an innocent human being," Catholic bishops declared.[67] As reform bills reached the state legislatures in California and New York in 1967, the church's hierarchy coordinated its efforts. Every bishop in New York signed a pastoral letter "condemning abortion," and priests read the letter at all Roman Catholic masses across the state in February. "It was the first time in the history of the state," the newspaper reported, "that a joint pastoral letter was read to congregations at all Roman Catholic masses."[68] This was the first time that bishops, the archbishop, and priests had coordinated their masses statewide on any topic. The move revealed the significance of abortion and the church's new equation of antiabortion politics with Catholicism. The church's leadership also nurtured grassroots opposition to abortion law reform.[69] In California, on the day of Easter Sunday mass, priests across the state spoke against the reform bill and urged Catholics to write their legislators. Thousands of letters flooded the capitol in opposition to the bill. "I . . . hope and pray," wrote one citizen to her representatives, for your "support of the complete criminalization of abortion" rather than reform. "All of us will agree," she continued, "that human life begins approximately nine months before a child is actually born." Others wrote more angry letters. One referred to the Ten Commandments and declared, "If you sign this bill, you will become a *murderer* in God's eyes!"[70] The tactics that would be seen all over the country during the next several decades were already apparent.

Early on, Catholic priests began developing a graphic language that equated abortion with the historical murder of blacks and Jews. At a 1962 hearing on the proposed legislation, Father William Kenneally of St. John's Seminary in Cabrillo called therapeutic abortion a "lynching in the womb." At a hearing a year later, he denounced therapeutic abortion as "a betrayal of maternity, turning the mother's womb into a butcher shop . . . decapitating children in the womb."[71] These highly charged political metaphors equated pregnant women who aborted with the KKK and lynch mobs. Reversing women's fears of the deadly abortionist who might kill them, the woman herself became a murderer. "From the first moment there is human life, there is a basic right to life," argued another Catholic priest. "Making a mistake [by reforming abortion law] can be as far-reaching as killing 6 million Jews in the ovens of Dachau and Buchenwald."[72] The metaphors were brutal and violent. Individual women, thinking hard about their families and their own lives from different religious viewpoints, were equated with murderous mobs and genocidal dictators. The strength of the hostility indicates the significance of the changes.

The Catholic Church had long fought political and social changes that upset male power, including divorce, birth control, and the Nineteenth Amendment that granted women the vote in 1920. The church battled against public health discussions of venereal diseases and sex education as well. Since the early twentieth century, "Catholic puritanism" had organized on many fronts to limit and prohibit the dangers found in modern American culture.[73] The apparent respectability of abortion and the possibility of legal reform threatened the Catholic Church's vision of the world and its political power.[74]

The German measles crisis, however, like the Pill, exposed a divide within the Catholic Church over sexuality and reproduction and—equally important—a struggle over the separation of religion and politics. Catholic women wrote in opposition to their church's political views, but, as one woman dryly observed, Catholic supporters of abortion law reform "do not . . . have an organized letter writing program."[75] "Please don't let the Catholic Church sway your vote on this issue," urged a Catholic mother of three who told of going to Mexico with her husband for an abortion. "I think if you could determine the real truth, most Catholics are for the new law. God bless you," she concluded.[76] Another reported that she had almost "walked out" during the Easter mass because the sermon on abortion had been "in such bad taste." She wanted her representatives to know that she supported the abortion bill.[77] (A year later when Pope Paul VI issued the *Humanae Vitae* encyclical declaring the Pill in violation of church teachings, many disappointed Catholic priests and laity did walk out of mass in protest.)[78]

In San Francisco, a group of Catholic women formed Catholic Mothers for Merciful Abortion and planned to support the San Francisco doctors at public hearings. The coordinator of the group, Mrs. Philip Foster, was a mother whose two children attended parochial school, a catechism teacher, and a former newspaper reporter. Actively recruiting other Catholic mothers, she announced her plans at her local parish and called women active in state politics and in the African American Catholic community. Patricia T. Maginnis herself was an ex-Catholic.[79] Several Jesuit priests and Senator Robert F. Kennedy favored liberalizing abortion laws, and Irish-Catholic Chicago expressed strong support for reform as well.[80] A nationwide survey of forty thousand physicians found that almost half of the Catholic physicians also agreed upon the need to liberalize the nation's abortion laws. It reported that 49.1 percent of Catholic doctors and 93.3 percent of non-Catholic doctors supported liberalizing the abortion law.[81]

Polls soon documented that most Californians believed that abortion was justified in order to avoid the "tragedy" of bringing a severely harmed child into the world and supported liberalizing the law.[82] A 1967 poll of Alameda County voters (including the cities of Oakland and Berkeley) by their state Assembly member found "an almost unanimous vote in favor of a liberalized abortion law." The surprised Assemblyman planned to vote for the Beilenson reform bill this time around instead of against it, as he had in previous years.[83] The California Junior Chamber of Commerce (the Jaycees), an organization of more than 250 local organizations and more than eleven thousand members, had strongly supported the Beilenson bill since 1964. After an "extensive process" of listening to panels of opposing speakers across the state, the Jaycees passed a resolution in favor of the Beilenson bill by more than 80 percent, to their own "surprise." As a representative of the Jaycees explained at a legislative hearing, their support of the Beilenson bill was rooted in the concerns of "ordinary citizens, most of them family men. . . . The thalidomide cases were very much in mind." The men agreed that abortions "should be left to the judgment and religious beliefs of the individuals involved." The Jaycees hoped that their "overwhelming endorsement . . . by typical citizens [would] lay to rest the fears of legislators." The Jaycees urged that this "statewide lay-man's verdict" pointed to popular support for reform.[84]

"I am all for your therapeutic abortion bill. I have an eight-month-old son who is perfect," wrote one young mother. Her letter to Senator Beilenson concisely summarized the widely held desire for perfection, belief in mothers' rights and agency, and sense that this legal debate was a religious debate. "I know that I would never bring a deformed baby into this world if I could do anything about it," she continued. "I further feel that the Pope has no right to enforce his laws on us non-Catholics. . . . Having abortions legal does not make them mandatory!"[85] This young mother gloried in her "perfect" child. The larger culture had long taught not only that perfection was something desirable but that seeking the "perfect" healthy child was the mother's responsibility. As this one vigorously asserted, she would do "anything" to avoid "bring[ing] a deformed baby into this world"—the responsibility was hers. Furthermore, she understood differences on this subject to be religiously based and, thus, in a country based on freedom of religion, to be illegitimate in law. Finally, she expressed the liberal faith that legalization would not result in coercion. She did not imagine, as others might have because of their awareness of the hostility to the disabled, of sterilization abuse, or of the hundreds of years of coercion of African American women's sexuality and reproductive capacity, that legal abortion might be pressed upon less powerful, more stigmatized groups.

Among the many voices, some disabled citizens chimed in. One thoughtful woman opposed the reform law precisely because it permitted abortions for birth defects. She had cerebral palsy, though, she explained, "a mild case . . . not to be compared to the seriousness of some of the defects resulting from German measles or thalidomide." Despite her own "anguish" at times, she would not have wanted to be "deprived of the great gift of life." To decide upon abortion was to "play God" and to overlook the contributions of "so-called 'defective' individuals."[86] This letter brought together Catholic theology that recognized conception as human life and an emerging disability rights sensibility that asserted the value of people with disabilities and defended their rights.[87]

A few parents of the disabled also spoke up in favor of permitting abortion when German measles threatened a pregnancy. Because the expression of their views is a rare find, I quote them at length. One Pennsylvania mother of a rubella child wrote to the *Wall Street Journal* and to pregnant women of her eight-year-old "mentally retarded" and "completely bedfast" daughter. She had rejected a therapeutic abortion, she wrote, because "a strong religious background made me feel it was a terrible thing to do to an unborn child." Yet over the years, she had "wonder[ed]" about the child's "effect . . . on [her] two normal children." She knew full well of her daughter's effect on her own life, she noted. "My thinking" now, she said, "is that abortions legalized would be a blessing, because since my daughter is mute, I play God to her very existence daily. I do not feel bitter for my decision, for through it I have learned much, but my advice to any mother faced by a decision on abortion would certainly be to have it without question, fear, or lingering conscience."[88] Just as health advisers considered a spontaneous miscarriage a "blessing" because it meant that something had been wrong with the embryo, this mother suggested that an abortion could be a blessing too. Another mother of a "handicapped" child asked, "Who can countenance bringing deranged, deformed, and handicapped children into this world if we know that it is almost certainly their fate? Not those of us who have experienced the frustration of not being able to make whole happy children and citizens out of the offspring we produce, especially when we love them so dearly."[89]

These rare letters expressed a mother's love as well as her pain. With firsthand knowledge, this mother too endorsed access to abortion when "deformity" was likely. "Should therapeutic abortion be allowed when the fetus has been proved abnormal?" another mother asked. "Sorrowfully, but with conviction, I must answer yes to this question. When it has been proved that an abnormal child is on the way, I believe that parents have the right to make a careful assessment of their resources and responsibilities and then to choose whether or not to continue the pregnancy. As the parent of a Mongoloid child (as well as three normal children), I wholeheartedly accept my child as an individual, but I cannot accept Mongolism itself nor any other abnormality that signals lifelong dependency. If serious disorders cannot be prevented or cured, then we must surely allow parents to detect and eliminate—or should I say spare?—those afflicted innocents for whom the normal patterns of life are forever beyond reach."[90] Parent members of the National Association for Retarded Children also expressed support for abortion law reform. No parents wrote of their opposition in their organization's newsletter.[91] Some "rubella mothers" were ready to join legal challenges to the criminal abortion laws.[92]

The abortion reform bill had failed three times since 1961, but now powerful men in the state of California and in medicine wanted the law changed. They rallied around the accused doctors and pushed legal reform. Three "distinguished Californians" formed the Citizen's Defense Fund on Therapeutic Abortion to raise money for the doctors' legal expenses. The group's officers included a regent of the University of California and two physicians, one a past president of the American Association for the Advancement of Science and current chairman of the Department of Pharmacology at the University of California, San Francisco (UCSF), the other the past president of the San Francisco Medical Society.[93] The Defense Fund framed the problem of the San Francisco Nine in terms of the right of patients to the best that medicine could offer and in terms of the right of professionals to practice the best medicine possible. The law, they argued, prevented physicians from practicing good, ethical medicine—which included therapeutic abortion. "Every person has a stake in this case," the Defense Fund urged.[94] "As obstetricians," Drs. George K. Herzog and Edmund W. Overstreet wrote to colleagues in their specialty, this legal defense "really amounts to a symbolic defense of most of us in the specialty." Every specialist might suddenly find himself or herself under state investigation and suspicion; the specialty needed to defend itself. They called upon their colleagues in obstetrics to contribute to the legal defense of the San Francisco physicians.[95] The Defense Fund was announced in March 1967; three months later it reported raising more than $20,000.[96] In their legal battle, the San Francisco doctors won a delay of the state board's scheduled hearing. Their legal team took the case to the California Supreme Court, arguing that the defendants had a right to discovery of the evidence to be used against them as in any criminal trial and that the state's abortion law was unconstitutional.[97]

The doctors' appeal demonstrated national medical support for the accused doctors and for therapeutic abortion for German measles. The amicus brief, written by attorneys Zad Leavy, a Los Angeles assistant district attorney, and Herma Hill Kay, a professor at the University of California's Boalt Law School in Berkeley, included as amici more than 120 medical school deans, including every single medical school dean in the state of California, and more than two hundred physicians, mainly specialists in obstetrics and pediatrics, from around the country. The "overwhelming majority" of the medical profession, the brief showed, agreed that therapeutic abortion was indicated when pregnancy threatened the woman's health and when there was a "strong likelihood of the birth of a seriously deformed child." In addition, 77 percent of the board-certified specialists in obstetrics and gynecology in California agreed that "material risk of fetal abnormality" was a valid reason for abortion, and 75 percent of the non-Catholic hospitals in the state would approve an abortion for this reason. The state, the attorneys argued, should not be involved in abortion decisions. They pointed as well to the *Griswold* birth control case decided one year earlier; the state should not interfere with the rights of married couples to make decisions about family. "In contrast to the dubious interests of the state in interposing itself between doctor and patient," the attorneys argued, physicians had "a sacred obligation to their patients," and the law violated their rights. The California Supreme Court unanimously agreed that the physicians had a right to discovery of all the potential evidence to be used against them.[98] The court did not address the medical or privacy issues, but this case laid the groundwork for another legal challenge in California, which would soon prove momentous for the nation.

As the physicians' attorneys prepared for the hearings before the Board of Medical Examiners, the reform bill was again presented to the California state legislature, but in entirely changed political circumstances thanks to the "San Francisco Nine." The existing law, Senator Beilenson declared, was "archaic, barbaric, and hypocritical" and often led to "tragedy." In advocating reform, the senator described his bill as "most conservative and most reasonable" because it would "simply bring the law into conformity with . . . medical judgment and public opinion," which supported abortion for a limited number of reasons, including rape, incest, and probable fetal deformity in addition to saving the woman's life.[99] The bill also wrote into law for the first time the abortion committee system created by hospitals.

This legislation, new in 1959 when the American Law Institute first wrote a model abortion reform law and when first presented in California in 1961, was by 1967, as Senator Beilenson himself remarked, "conservative." By then, support for outright repeal of the criminal abortion laws and for an end to differentiating among the reasons (the "therapeutic indications") for abortion in order to permit some but not others had grown enormously. Maginnis (and her allies in the Society for Humane Abortion and the emerging women's liberation movement) had a highly developed critique of the hospital committee review system that was being institutionalized in the Beilenson reform bill. (See figure 11.) The Therapeutic Abortion Act, Maginnis argued, "legislates economic discrimination" by "favor[ing]" women with the money to pay for multiple visits to physicians and hospitals and "legislates a complex system of harassment and red tape for both the physician and the patient" by requiring that two physicians seek permission for abortion and a committee of five unanimously approve it. In cases of rape and incest, the new law required that the case

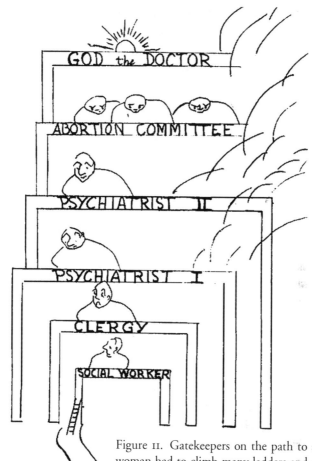

Figure 11. Gatekeepers on the path to an abortion. A woman had to climb many ladders and get the permission of many men before she could obtain a legal, safe medical abortion. Patricia T. Maginnis's cartoon clearly made her point about the indignities of the then-current hospital abortion committee system. Through her cartoons and organizing, she voiced her criticism of the Beilenson bill and other reform measures. This cartoon is an example of movement artwork that urged and taught a political perspective. Maginnis's cartoons and newsletter had wide national circulation to other reformers, ranging from more moderate physicians to the most militant of young feminists. Patricia T. Maginnis, *The Abortees' Songbook,* copyright © 1969, folder Position Papers Part 2, Women's Ephemera Folders, Special Collections, Northwestern University Library, Evanston, IL. Reprinted with the permission of Patricia T. Maginnis.

be submitted in advance to the police or district attorney for approval. Finally, the new law retained the penal code prohibiting abortion.[100] This bill, Maginnis feared, would make things worse.

The bill passed in both houses of the California legislature. Governor Ronald Reagan had agreed to sign the bill, but at the last minute he came under pressure and insisted that the provision allowing abortions in cases of expected fetal deformity be removed. Most concerned about getting a bill through and convinced that winning more was impossible, Beilenson immediately agreed. Governor Reagan signed the bill reforming abortion law in the State of California in June 1967.[101] Senator Beilenson and the CCTA celebrated.

Not all of Beilenson's supporters considered the new law a victory, however.[102] For many, the law was not liberal enough. Furthermore, as everyone realized, the new law did not permit therapeutic abortions in cases of maternal rubella—the issue that had spurred activism and massive public support for legal change. The issues that had animated public support for reform in the mid-1960s—the threat of a child's being born "deformed" due to German measles or a drug like thalidomide and the inability of the expectant mother to obtain a legal abortion in order to avoid that outcome—were left unresolved. What the accused San Francisco doctors had done was now, for the first time, explicitly illegal. The San Francisco doctors did not comment.

In 1968, the Board of Medical Examiners found all of the physicians guilty of performing and advising illegal abortions. In its first findings, the board publicly "reprimanded" Dr. J. Paul Shively and Dr. Seymour Smith. It found Dr. Shively guilty of performing three illegal abortions for German measles and suspended the doctor's license to practice medicine for ninety days, but it stayed the suspension during a year of probation. District attorneys could pursue criminal charges if they chose. These heavy and embarrassing penalties given to upstanding physicians sent a strong message to all of California's doctors. As the president of the board remarked, he "personally" would feel this to be "a severe penalty." Furthermore, he announced, the board planned to "ascertain . . . whether the practice of teaching that such abortions are sound medical practice still continues at the medical schools in the state."[103] By the end of the year, the board had similarly punished the other seven San Francisco doctors.[104] The penalties punished individual doctors, warned the rest of the profession that they could be prosecuted and lose their right to practice, and warned the state's professors that medical education would be scrutinized by the state. The board intended to teach a lesson. Practitioners and professors—in California and across the country—no doubt got the message.

But while some became more careful in their practices, others became more resistant and more vociferous in their challenges to the law. Other doctors stepped up their demands for complete decriminalization of abortion. By 1968, it was clear that the new law intended to make abortion more available and to ease doctors' worries had done the opposite. The reform law in practice showed Maginnis to be entirely correct in her critique of reform. Hospitals and doctors did not feel freed by the new law—they felt more enchained. They worried about legal trouble and about their public reputations. Some hospitals reduced the number of abortions performed; some refused to consider the cases of unmarried or poor women; others refused to perform any abortions. Although the law permitted abortions for women who had been raped, district attorneys did not always allow them. One young woman, for instance, who sought an abortion because she had been raped on a date was refused an abortion by the prosecutor because her date denied raping her.[105] Only a year after the reform law's passage, Beilenson's supporters convinced him that his own law had to be changed, so he submitted a new bill to allow abortions when there was "substantial risk of grave physical or mental defect in the fetus"—the very reasons that had pushed reform in the first place.[106] Doctors, Beilenson learned, were "*extremely* anxious to put that [stipulation] back in."[107]

Dr. Shively appealed. He won, and the board's findings of guilt were overturned. In issuing his opinion, Superior Court Judge Andrew J. Eyman expressed the common sentiment that severe birth defects harmed not only the child but also the mother, the siblings, and the family as a whole. In reviewing the case, the judge remarked on the "heartbreak and disruption" in a family when a mother faced the prospect of bearing "a deformed child" as a result of having had German measles. "Has the family had a normal life?" Eyman asked. "Would there be a malpractice case against a doctor if a normal child were left alone because all of his mother's love and all her attention had gone to the malformed child?"[108]

In 1970, Beilenson submitted a bill to repeal the law whose passage he had celebrated only three years earlier. By then, twelve states had passed reform laws, and that year New York, Hawaii, Alaska, and Washington had entirely repealed their criminal abortion laws.[109] Beilenson now took the position long argued by Patricia T. Maginnis and the Society for Humane Abortion. "Abortion should not be a matter of legislation and control by the state," he now maintained, "but should be left as a matter of individual conscience and choice." The arguments had changed dramatically; the senator now rejected specifying a narrow list of indications for a medically approved "therapeutic" abortion and rejected requiring that a committee of physicians review and approve abortions. Women had a right to privacy and "a right to *not* to bear children as well as to bear them." "We must," he now urged, "end compulsory pregnancy." The right to abortion in order to avoid bearing "severely defective children" had become a minor note.[110] Beilenson had heard women's voices. The California legislature, however, did not vote to decriminalize abortion.

The defense of the nine San Francisco physicians charged in 1966 provided the model and momentum to build a united medical defense of another physician, a Beverly Hills gynecologist who had been convicted for his role in a criminal abortion. Dr. Leon Belous had referred a patient to an illegal abortionist. Having already demonstrated medical support for the "San Francisco Nine," CCTA knew how to put together impressive medical support for Belous and for a state constitutional challenge to the California abortion law. CCTA coordinated three amici briefs filed on Belous's behalf; one, written by Zad Leavy, represented 179 leaders of the medical profession, including medical school deans, all of the deans of California's medical schools, deans of schools of public health, and professors and specialists in obstetrics, gynecology, pediatrics, and surgery from California and forty other states. The medical brief covered much ground, but it emphasized the vagueness of the law and the duty of physicians to provide the best medical care in their judgment, which the law prohibited. It also pointed to the deaths due to criminal abortion and to the safety of properly performed medical abortions. It argued as well for the rights of women to privacy and bodily integrity. A woman could not be "required . . . to use her body as a baby factory."[111] CCTA founding member and attorney Norma Zarky wrote the brief submitted by the American Civil Liberties Union, and University of California law professor Herma Hill Kay submitted the third brief on behalf of preeminent attorneys and law professors. Dr. Leon Belous's appeal resulted in the stunning 1969 California State Supreme Court decision that found the California criminal abortion law to be unconstitutional.[112] *Belous* spurred attorneys around the country to file cases challenging the constitutionality of state abortion laws.

The pace of change in medical thinking and the legal status of abortion astonished many. A model abortion reform law had first been discussed and drafted in 1959. When first submitted to the California legislature in 1961, it had gone nowhere. Only a few years later, a reform law passed, but by then many of the nation's physicians, including many of the most prominent, had become supporters of total repeal. Dr. Keith P. Russell of Los Angeles, an early advocate of repeal who had organized his profession on behalf of *Belous* in 1969, was named president of the American College of Obstetricians and Gynecologists (ACOG) in the same year.[113] That he became president of ACOG indicates that the specialty had completely reversed its century-long antiabortion stance. Only a few years earlier, individual physicians and politicians had avoided public association with abortion (though many doctors had made referrals to illegal practitioners, and some had quietly performed abortions). Now medical leaders lent their names to an appeal in a criminal abortion case and argued for overturning the very abortion laws that had been crafted by men in their specialty a century earlier.

The powerful role that the German measles epidemic had played in making abortion respectable and in making possible the medical argument for the rights of women and physicians to legalized abortion appeared only as an echo in the physicians' brief.[114] German measles was no longer the reason for talking about abortion or reforming the law. The problem was not birth defects and women's anxiety in the face of German measles; it was now much bigger than those issues. By 1969, most of the medical profession had come to reject the path of legal reform and supported repeal of the nation's criminal abortion laws. African American physicians, public health authorities, and psychiatrists had supported repeal earlier.[115] Furthermore, militant feminists, reformers, and some clergymembers all openly offered illegal abortions to all who sought them via "the Service" (later known as "Jane") in Chicago, "the List" provided by the Association to Repeal Abortion Laws (ARAL) founded by Maginnis in San Francisco, the nationwide Clergy Consultation Service, and numerous other local grassroots groups.[116] Through the process of fighting for reform and in the midst of a growing women's movement that insisted on outright repeal, physicians and attorneys who had originally sought limited reform to clarify the law and to protect doctors became advocates of repeal.

When *Belous* found the California abortion law unconstitutional, Dr. Russell, the new President of ACOG, informed the signers of the physicians' brief of the victory and urged them to do more. The national medical leader called on his colleagues to put the new legal interpretation into practice. "The *Belous* decision is but a single episode in a long endeavor to obtain appropriate freedom for women and licensed physicians. Concerned physicians," Dr. Russell continued, "will have to carry on that endeavor in hospital committees, medical school faculties, professional societies, boards of medical examiners, . . . legislatures, and the courts." This doctor was an activist who recognized that the work continued and that changes of heart, procedure, and policy still needed to be made. "The need for change is so great. . . . We should promptly seek and employ enlarged therapeutic powers in our own practices."[117] The *Belous* decision was about more than precedent or discourse or change in representations; it was about real-life clinical practice. It had to be acted upon. Lawyers in every state framed cases and wrote briefs. Doctors needed to clear the path and provide abortions.

A prominent St. Paul, Minnesota, obstetrician, past president of the Minnesota Obstetrics/Gynecology Society, and clinical professor at the University of Minnesota was one of the "concerned physicians" who acted to make abortion available and legal. In 1970, Dr. Jane Hodgson deliberately broke the law by performing an abortion on Nancy Widmyer, informed the police, and was prosecuted. Although Dr. Hodgson had performed a therapeutic abortion because Widmyer had contracted rubella during pregnancy, it was not her goal to expand the legal definition of *therapeutic* to permit abortions for fetal indications. Instead, Hodgson wanted the Minnesota courts to interpret the law narrowly and convict her so that she could appeal her case and bring her challenge of the criminal abortion law to the U.S. Supreme Court. German measles and its harmful effects on the developing fetus were no longer the issue but were now used as a path to win abolition of the nation's criminal abortion laws.[118]

As it did with other female professionals at the center of policy questions of national interest, the media presented Dr. Hodgson as a mother and wife. This representation downplayed her professional expertise and prominence while also providing the seemingly only legitimate platform from which women could speak on public matters at the time—as a mother speaking for mothers. In a lengthy headline, the *New York Times* described her as "Minnesota Gynecologist, Mother"; the headline itself revealed journalists' confusion about representing women in the news. The article mixed her professional and maternal credentials: "Dr. Hodgson is a prominent and highly respected St. Paul gynecologist and obstetrician, a University of Minnesota professor, the mother of two daughters, and the wife of a successful cardiac surgeon."[119] It is hard to imagine the newspaper detailing a wife's career in an article about a prominent male physician.

The Hodgson case was one of many in the nationwide work to bring cases to the U.S. Supreme Court regarding the constitutionality of the nation's criminal abortion laws.[120] An advocate of repealing her state's criminal abortion laws, Dr. Hodgson had been thinking about a possible test case for a while. Widmyer had contracted German measles from one of her three children early in her pregnancy (confirmed at four weeks) and was concerned about the 50 to 60 percent probability of serious birth defects as well the impact of a disabled child on the rest of her family. Widmyer and her husband, a construction worker, wanted an abortion. Dr. Hodgson agreed. Dr. Hodgson determined that a therapeutic abortion was necessary, consulted with several colleagues who concurred, and sought a court ruling for emergency relief so that she could perform an abortion early in the pregnancy. The court delayed responding and after five weeks still had not ruled on the matter. As the pregnancy progressed and the legal wheels slowly turned, Dr. Hodgson decided that her patient could not wait, performed the abortion, alerted the sheriff, and challenged the criminal law through her own arrest. The district attorney then prosecuted her.[121]

During the previous century many physicians (and nurses, midwives, and others) had been arrested and prosecuted for performing abortions in violation of the criminal laws, but Dr. Hodgson was the first physician to be arrested and prosecuted for criminal abortion after performing a therapeutic abortion in a hospital with the concurrence of consulting physicians (*seven*). She did what Sherri Finkbine's doctors had avoided. Dr. Hodgson was unique within her profession for seeking arrest and criminal prosecution for performing a therapeutic abortion.[122] Equally notable, neither she nor her attorneys focused on "deformity" or advocated an expansion of therapeutic abortions on narrow grounds. Instead, they aimed to have the abortion laws of Minnesota and the nation declared unconstitutional. Dr. Hodgson included four case histories of patients who had sought abortions from her and noted the health and social consequences of having denied them abortions. Some went on to illegal abortionists and ended up in her hospital needing emergency care for their injuries. Abortion, she intended to show, was a medical procedure that the medical profession endorsed and whose members had the right to perform according to their judgment. She also intended to show that it was a procedure that women needed and that these women's feelings should be respected. Dr. Joseph Pratt, the nationally prominent senior gynecological surgeon of the Mayo Clinic, as well as Doctors Christopher Tietze and Lewis Cooper of New York University and Dr. Irvin Cushner of Johns Hopkins University testified on Dr. Hodgson's behalf, and extensive medical data and literatures were presented. Through her trial, she hoped to educate the judge and the legislature. She imagined that the state legislature would see the light and immediately pass a new law.[123] (It didn't.)

Nancy Widmyer acted as Sherri Finkbine, Dolores Stonebreaker, Barbara Stewart, Sandra Gleitman, and other women had in making public her desire for an abortion when the likelihood of serious birth defects was high. Widmyer could have afforded to fly out of the country to Mexico or England for an abortion, but she and her doctor knew that other women could not. "We both knew we could not dodge the issue," Dr. Hodgson remarked.[124] Patient and doctor decided together to challenge the law openly in order to change it. Widmyer took a risk too, for she could have been arrested under Minnesota law and, if convicted, imprisoned for one to four years. However, states had rarely prosecuted women for having abortions performed upon them, and Minnesota did not in this case, either.[125] At Dr. Hodgson's trial, Widmyer discussed her thoughts about her children, her responsibilities as a mother, and her reasons for wanting an abortion. Giving birth, she believed, "would be cruel to the baby. . . . I couldn't make a child suffer, and I couldn't live with myself knowing that I could have done something about it." Furthermore, she reported that she was also concerned about her other three children: "I didn't feel I could give them the care all children need and still properly care for a deformed child."[126] Her thoughts about the baby on the way, her determination that bringing it into the world would be "cruel," and her concern for her existing children echoed the feelings of other women who had faced the threat of German measles specifically and the long history of mothers who had turned to abortion and contraception. She had made her decision as a mother.

As a white married mother of three who had contracted German measles and faced what she perceived to be possible tragedy, and whose husband approved of the abortion, Nancy Widmyer fit the media profile that had developed in the early 1960s with thalidomide and German measles. She was a respectable woman who deserved a legal, legitimate abortion. When Dr. Hodgson imagined being involved in a possible test case, she knew that the plaintiff would have to be married and a "model mother." Nancy Widmyer presented a "once-in-a-lifetime perfect case."[127] Widmyer fit the portrait, but with a husband who was a construction worker, she should be seen as a working-class woman. In this period, however, whiteness and a respectable job, along with home ownership and a nuclear family, conferred middle-class status.

The civil rights and reproductive rights movements of the 1950s and 1960s similarly assumed the necessity of respectability, heterosexuality, and marriage for legal victories. As in the Montgomery bus boycott against racial segregation; *Loving v. Virginia* (1967), which overturned state laws banning interracial marriages; and *Griswold,* which found a right to (sexual) privacy for married couples and overturned laws banning birth control, Dr. Hodgson chose a married woman and avoided bringing unmarried pregnant women into the legal eye.[128]

However, as Dr. Hodgson made quite clear to reporters and on the stand in court, she did not intend her legal challenge to benefit the respectable woman only. As a doctor, she had seen what the inability to control pregnancy and reproduction meant: stigma and shame, "forced marriages," and injuries and deaths resulting from "criminal" abortions.[129] All women, Dr. Hodgson had learned from her patients, needed legal, safe, available abortions. Dr. Hodgson's own thinking had undergone a spectacular transformation from her views of only four or five years earlier.

In a courtroom filled with spectators listening "in church-like silence"— but without a jury—Dr. Hodgson was tried, convicted by Judge J. Jerome Plunkett for performing an abortion in violation of the criminal law, and sentenced to thirty days in jail. The judge praised Dr. Hodgson, nevertheless, for her "forthright[ness]" and "courageousness" in challenging a law she believed wrong. Recognizing the medical community's esteem for her, he stayed the sentence, placed her on probation for a year, and stayed that too while she appealed her case. Her medical license was suspended.[130] In her appeal to the Minnesota Supreme Court, Dr. Hodgson challenged the constitutionality of the Minnesota abortion law and expected that her case, along with many others, would be heading for the U.S. Supreme Court. The Minnesota Supreme Court, however, never considered the case and instead let it languish as it waited on the U.S. Supreme Court's decisions on *Roe v. Wade* from Texas. On January 22, 1973, the U.S. Supreme Court announced its ruling finding the nation's criminal abortion laws and the hospital therapeutic abortion system to be unconstitutional in *Roe v. Wade* and *Doe v. Bolton.* Women, the Court found, had a constitutional right to "privacy" to make decisions concerning pregnancy and family (without state interference in the first trimester and with only limited state intervention in the second trimester), and physicians had the right to practice medicine according to their professional judgment. Dr. Hodgson's conviction was overturned following *Roe v. Wade.* She returned to medical practice, challenged

Minnesota law again in the 1980s when the state mandated parental consent for an abortion for a minor, and well into her 70s traveled hundreds of miles to provide abortions in rural counties of Minnesota.[131]

The *Hodgson* case, like *Belous,* represents the evolution of the thinking of doctors, lawyers, and the entire movement for abortion law reform. The process of learning and transformation was speedy during this period. Although German measles had played a critical role in the political and legal processes leading toward the decriminalization of abortion, the Supreme Court's rulings did not rest upon the argument that abortion was justified in cases of expected birth defects or upon other specific medical "indications" for abortion. The legalization of abortion was decoupled from deformity and disease by women in the process of public debate and legal struggles for change. What began as a small movement among professionals for extremely limited legal reform to allow doctors to perform abortions in specific cases—for reasons of fetal defects, rape, and incest as well as the woman's health—had been transformed into a movement for complete repeal of the criminal abortion laws. Dr. Hodgson had learned from her thousands of unnamed patients of the necessity of abortion and the cruelty of forced maternity. Her views on abortion had completely changed from the hostility that she had learned in medical school in the 1930s to believing that abortion was a woman's right and the provision of safe procedures a doctor's duty.

State investigations of highly respected physicians, revocation of medical licenses by state regulatory agencies, criminal trials, and medical malpractice suits all spotlighted the legal dangers facing the medical profession. The state of California's investigation into hospital abortion practices was an innovative and unprecedented invasion of medical practice, patient records, and the privacy of patients' lives. As it became clear that the state board could be used by a minority of the medical profession—namely, in this case, activist antiabortion Catholic doctors whose religious beliefs guided their actions—to change the long-standing rules governing the medical practice of legal therapeutic abortions, the mainstream of the profession—the doctors used to authority, respect, and deference—revolted. As they mobilized and fought for their own perspective on medical ethics and the morality of abortion—also religiously inflected—and for their right to practice medicine according to their own careful and reasoned judgment, they came to learn from their opponents, feminists, and their patients that expanding the legally recognized justifications for therapeutic abortion through reform law would not resolve the problems. In a way that no one could have predicted, the majority of men and women in medicine came to advocate complete repeal of the nation's criminal abortion laws in order to protect their own rights to practice medicine and to support the right of patients to make their own decisions about reproduction and medical procedures.

However, in 2004, Attorney General John Ashcroft revived the tactics that nearly fifty years ago had shocked physicians and much of the public and propelled abortion law reform forward. Ashcroft subpoenaed thousands of patient records from hospitals and Planned Parenthood clinics in New York, Philadelphia, Chicago, Michigan, Missouri, California, Nebraska, and elsewhere in search of evidence that physicians had performed "medically unnecessary" abortions in violation of the new "partial-birth" abortion ban passed by Congress the year before. Hospitals refused to provide the records, citing a violation of patient privacy and the privacy of medical records (privacy that President George W. Bush had declared a "fundamental right" and written into law only the year before as part of HIPAA, the Health Insurance Portability and Accountability Act). Individual physicians and reproductive rights organizations sued; Democrats in Congress protested Ashcroft's actions. Courts gave conflicting opinions on the privacy of patients' medical records, though eventually the federal government withdrew the demand for records. In *Gonzales v. Carhart* (2007), the U.S. Supreme Court upheld the ban on "partial-birth abortion," a nonmedical term written into law and broadly described in such a way as to include a specific procedure, D&E (dilation and evacuation), that was typically used in second-trimester abortions. The American College of Obstetricians and Gynecologists, along with other medical groups, filed a brief supporting their colleagues and opposing the ban. This time, however, the political context and the increasingly conservative Congress and Supreme Court did not rule in favor of medical autonomy or women's reproductive rights. The decision threatened the already eroded protections articulated in *Roe* and *Doe*.[132]

As this book went to press, Dr. George Tiller, an obstetrician-gynecologist who had performed abortions in Wichita, Kansas, was assassinated on Sunday, May 31, 2009. He was killed while serving as an usher at his church. The doctor had performed not only early abortions—by far the most common in the United States—but also the late-term abortions that were then under attack.

The reasons for late-term abortions are to preserve the pregnant woman's life in cases in which the fetus has already died and to terminate a pregnancy because tests show that the baby is destined to die almost immediately after birth due to congenital anomalies. The women who have late-term abortions today are much like many of those who had (therapeutic) abortions for German measles in the mid-1960s: they and their partners want to have babies, but unfortunate circumstances make them decide that termination of their pregnancies is essential.

For years, Dr. Tiller had been targeted by prosecutors, grand jury investigations, and legislators and subjected to harassment, threats, and violent assaults at his clinic and his home. His murder highlighted—again—the terrorism that physicians face when they perform abortions to honor women's requests and to save women's lives. It reminded Americans of the bravery of abortion providers, a type of bravery not required of other health-care providers. Dr. Tiller was mourned in vigils across the country for his gentle medical practice, his absolute commitment to serving his patients in need, and his trust in women (as a placard in his office declared).[133] These were more than memorials, however. The candlelight vigils signaled a new struggle against domestic terrorism emanating from the extreme Right as well as a renewed commitment to reproductive justice. The political, medical, and legal ramifications of Dr. Tiller's murder are in progress.

It is ironic now for feminists who battled physicians and medical control in the 1960s and 1970s, but it is evident that the cultural and political authority of physicians at the time—and physicians' belief in their own autonomy and judgment—helped women win constitutional protection of the right to make decisions about pregnancy, reproduction, and abortion. That right, as described in *Roe v. Wade* (1973), was framed as one shared between a woman and her doctor and limited by trimester and the medically determined viability of the fetus, but in practice and in the words of the leaders of obstetrics and gynecology, abortion was a decision for the woman herself to make. Since the initial legalization of abortion, however, that right to make a decision and the ability to carry it out have been severely curtailed by the passage of myriad restrictive laws upheld by the Supreme Court as well as by restrictions on federal and state welfare assistance, insurance, and funding and by the refusal of many physicians and hospitals to provide the legal procedure. Most counties in the country have no abortion providers; in some states young women are forced by law to inform their parents of their abortion plans; insurance plans often exclude abortion; Catholic-owned hospitals ban the provision of abortion and birth control. And antiabortion activists harass and threaten patients, physicians, and clinic staff; bomb clinics; and kill abortion providers.

Reproductive rights activists at the time of the *Roe v. Wade* decision foresaw and tried to prevent restrictions and inequitable access to abortion. They did not anticipate, however, that the personalized harassment that had been on the fringe of the antiabortion movement would become the norm and that anti-abortion activists would turn to harassment, violence, terrorism, and murder. As many observed in the aftermath of Dr. Tiller's murder, even as abortion remained legal, decades of terrorism had effectively stopped some doctors from providing abortions and prevented many women from obtaining a legal procedure that they deemed necessary. In many counties and states today, it is so difficult and expensive to obtain an abortion that the present is little different from the pre-*Roe* era.

Mothers—middle-class, married, and almost all white—were the first to go public in the early 1960s and talk about their need for abortion. They spoke of their agony when they had realized that a hoped-for child might be severely damaged by infectious disease and of their decisions to abort when it had appeared that carrying a pregnancy to term would spell tragedy for their children, their families, and themselves. As they spoke to the press, to courtrooms, and to the public, these mothers displayed their strong sense that having an abortion was the right thing for them to do in that situation and was their decision to make. The strength of that view and their resolve at a time when abortion was a crime and highly stigmatized in public representations point to the long-standing moral position held by women that it was their responsibility as mothers, as potential mothers, and as the lifelong caregivers of children to think carefully and to decide whether to bring a child into the world.

These mothers represented one expression of the mobilization of different groups of mothers in this period to gain rights, benefits, and respect for their lives, their work as mothers, and their decisions. The welfare rights movement of poor African American, Latina, and white mothers; mothers' struggles for education for their disabled children; and the reproductive rights movements of women of color who fought sterilization and asserted their right to have children all emerged in the mid-1960s and early 1970s as well.[134] When white married, middle-class mothers confronted the dilemmas of German measles, they not only made abortion respectable; they also made respectful discussion of abortion possible and legal change urgent. As active citizens, they translated their needs into sophisticated lobbying, voting, and legal work.

The earliest efforts to change the nation's criminal abortion laws came not out of sexual liberation but out of the anxieties and responsibilities felt by married mothers. Women themselves quickly turned to the questions of privacy and sexual freedom, however. German measles provided a wedge for opening up discussion and a spark for physicians to act in defense of their own interests, but it soon became much less important than the general problem that women could not control their reproductive capacity, that they needed abortions, and that the law did not permit women to make these moral decisions for themselves. Indeed, when women's groups first heard of abortion law reform efforts, they saw that abortion reform should be broader than the expansion of therapeutic abortion on the grounds of the health of the woman or fetus and quickly embraced the legalization of abortion for reasons beyond health.[135]

Widmyer and the other mothers who sought abortions because of probable birth defects were joined by thousands of other women in the late 1960s and early 1970s who spoke out in public at rallies and to journalists, who signed their names to petitions and in letters to politicians and editors, who challenged the law by breaking it and by writing briefs, who declared that they too had had abortions and had the moral and legal right to make decisions about pregnancy and motherhood. Furthermore, they spoke clearly of female sexuality and women's rights to control their own bodies as well as their rights as (potential) mothers. By the time of Widmyer's abortion in 1970, a mass movement of women publicly declared their need for and right to abortion, demanded the dismantling of the paternalistic therapeutic abortion system, and insisted upon the legalization of abortion.

It is apparent too that fathers—"family men," as the Jaycees described themselves—joined in the difficult, heartrending conversations with their wives. They imagined themselves as fathers, scrutinized their own values, and concluded with women that these were decisions that in a democracy of people "of many faiths" could not be made by law or by religion for everyone but had to be left to individual citizens.[136] The movement to make abortions legal was rooted in motherhood and family. Middle-class family culture of the early 1960s—which mass media tended to represent as homogenous and white and which radical activists and feminists later tended to represent as conformist and simpleminded—was more complex, nuanced, and politically active than is sometimes now recalled or presumed.[137] The pearls and hats, the dark suits and portraits of respectability should not confuse us now—that respectability and the real felt needs of mothers began the groundswell toward radical transformations in patients' rights, reproductive rights, and women's sexual freedom.

"Unborn babies" were the victims of maternal rubella and the objects of protection. In this period the term *unborn babies* and the desire to protect them were not claimed exclusively by the antiabortion movement but instead represented a desire of mothers—and with them, fathers, physicians, health organizations, the federal government, and the general public. The desire to prevent birth defects and protect future children from the hazards of congenital rubella did not preclude abortion but went together with it hand in hand. The unborn was a being on a continuum, a possibility that was not yet a child. The unborn had not been detached from their mothers, who nurtured them in their bodies during pregnancy and then nurtured them later as children; they were understood to be the responsibility of their mothers. Mothers acted to protect their unborn children through prenatal care and through support of scientific research, and they made decisions about the future of their children, their families, and themselves. At times, that responsibility for the future made mothers decide upon abortion.

# FIVE

# "If Unborn Babies Are Going to Be Protected"

NEITHER THE MEDIA NOR HEALTH authorities linked abortion to the development, licensing, and distribution of the German measles vaccine and the campaign to immunize the nation's children. Yet they had been related in the medical and scientific imaginary of the disease from the time that the effects of maternal rubella were first understood in the 1940s. German measles was widely publicized and understood in the media through coverage of abortion law. Furthermore, the rubella vaccine was licensed in 1969, and a national vaccination campaign began precisely when the struggle over abortion law was reaching a peak in the streets, in state legislatures, and in the courts. With a vaccine, health experts hoped, the damaging effects of German measles during early pregnancy might be eliminated. Tens of thousands of children might be spared the heart problems, cataracts, blindness, deafness, and intellectual impairment caused by maternal rubella as well as the associated social costs of disabilities. Furthermore, as vaccine proponents explained, a vaccine could prevent the thousands of miscarriages, stillbirths, and early infant deaths produced by an epidemic. It should be noted, however, that prior to the campaign to vaccinate against rubella, pregnancy loss and infant deaths had never been highlighted as major concerns in warnings about the disease. By eradicating disease, the vaccine promised to prevent the damaging effects of maternal rubella as well as to provide other social solutions. The vaccine would take care of the "agony" of women and the dilemma of abortion decisions for women and doctors both, as well as the stigmatized practice of therapeutic abortion.

The worldwide thalidomide disaster had eroded public trust in the pharmaceutical industry, but because the FDA had successfully prevented the thalidomide tragedy in the United States, it had also bolstered Americans' trust in their government's protective role. The specter of tragedy on a massive scale presented by German measles drove scientific research, public health, and politics. Knowing that German measles epidemics arose every six to nine years, researchers around the world raced to produce a vaccine and prevent the next epidemic, which was predicted to occur circa 1970. In the U.S. government-supported push to develop a vaccine, we can see faith in the power of American science and pharmaceuticals and the state's commitment to protecting the health of mothers and children through science. The United States acted confidently in the belief that permanent eradication of disease could be achieved. Immunization of children had become standard practice; smallpox, diphtheria, and polio all appeared to have been virtually eliminated in the United States.[1] The United States was a world superpower; it had built and used the most devastating weapon in the world; it could change global politics, change nature, and change the world. It could conquer this virus too. Furthermore, a successful vaccine that prevented birth defects would implicitly help redeem the pharmaceutical industry that had produced the thalidomide disaster. The pressure to research, develop, and produce an effective and safe vaccine like the polio vaccine—and to do it before the next German measles epidemic—was intense. A looming epidemic and its consequences concentrated the energies and minds of scientists in much the same way that it concentrated the minds of expectant mothers.

Immunization against rubella was unique in the history of public health because the beneficiaries of the vaccine were not those who received the shots. All previous vaccines had directly benefited the immunized individual who could be harmed by the virus and at the same time had benefited the general public health by preventing the spread of disease and epidemics. As a general rule, we accept medical treatments—including vaccination—in order to protect our own health. But for the children now scheduled to receive immunization against rubella, the disease would be minor and protection against it unnecessary. This vaccination was for other people, for expecting mothers and for babies. The purpose of this vaccine was to protect other, future, potential children—indeed, to protect the nation's future citizens. The rubella vaccine represented a historic transformation in the expectations surrounding a vaccine.

For massive immunization to succeed, parents had to agree and children had to submit to vaccination when this treatment would not directly protect them or improve their health. The rapid achievement of this objective rested not only on enormous state and private monies for scientific research and a coordinated public health effort, but also on complicated cultural work embodied in the vaccination educational campaign. Health education materials provide an opportunity to analyze how the art of health persuasion worked. The 1969–70 immunization campaign continued to treat the disease as a family crisis, spotlighting children as both the victims and the source of danger. The racial picture, however, shifted. Whereas the media represented German measles and abortion as a white family crisis, vaccine educational materials represented the disease as a threat to black and brown children as well as white children in a new effort to ensure the immunization of the entire population, including the poor. This health effort, like others at the time, attempted to respond to black, Puerto Rican, and Chicano freedom movements by newly focusing on health inequalities.[2] Equally important, the vaccination campaign used fear of infant death and disability to motivate parents to immunize their children.

The campaign did not use fear alone, however. It also called upon hopes for the future and a desire that the future be freed from the ambiguities, pain, deaths, and disability that German measles represented. In protecting "unborn babies," mass immunization promised healthy bodies and normal lives. Children were recruited as responsible good citizens. In asking children, boys and girls both, to accept vaccination on behalf of future mothers and future babies, this public health campaign took an entirely new path in the history of prenatal care and reworked the standard relationship between gender and reproductive health. The campaign called upon civic responsibility, family duty, and gendered interests to garner support. Mass immunization was a complex scientific, social, and cultural achievement.

The earliest medical researchers in the 1940s in Australia had imagined that a vaccine could solve the problem of birth defects caused by rubella. Scientists in Australia, Japan, and the United States had immediately set to work, and in 1948, Sir Macfarlane Burnet and his colleagues in Australia showed that passive immunity to rubella could be achieved.[3] An effective vaccine would also simultaneously solve the problem of abortion by eliminating the risks of serious birth defects and thus the perceived need for abortion. Therapeutic abortion for German measles was "entirely justified," declared the Australian expert Dr. Charles Swan. "It is to be hoped, however," he continued, "that the elaboration in the near future of methods of immunization against the disease will render such drastic procedures as the termination of gestation unnecessary."[4] A vaccine, Swan hoped, would let women and their doctors escape the "drastic procedure" of abortion.

A vaccine seemed almost magical in medical thinking. It not only would prevent disease; it also would eliminate social problems, emotional devastation, stigmatized medical procedures, and legal and moral questions. This was a dream, of course, since many women turned to abortion every day, almost all for reasons unrelated to German measles. A vaccine would not eliminate abortion, though it might take away the specific uncertainty and controversy about what to do in individual cases when a woman had been exposed to German measles during pregnancy. Similarly, a vaccine might prevent future epidemics during which almost every women of childbearing age in the country who thought she might be(come) pregnant worried about the disease and during which tens of thousands of women experienced pregnancy loss and infant deaths and gave birth to children with serious physical and intellectual impairments. A vaccine would not, however, eliminate birth defects, disability, or the inequities faced by people with disabilities.

Abortion and the vaccine were also connected through narratives of family crisis and through the concurrent political struggle to legalize abortion. Debates and votes on vaccine research and distribution and on abortion law occurred simultaneously in state legislatures, in Congress, and in the media. As planning for universal immunization began in 1969, ABC-TV ran a special on abortion and the reform and repeal bills then being debated in the New York state legislature and elsewhere; the program included a section on German measles.[5] The documentary began with women's agonizing stories and discussion of the class differences in access to and safety of illegal abortion. It then moved to Dr. Lewis Cooper's clinic at Bellevue Hospital and filmed "the victims of congenital rubella," the multiply handicapped children. Two mothers—both married, white, and educated—spoke to the camera about their situations when they had learned they had rubella during pregnancy. The Reverend and Mrs. Baum talked about their "joy" when they had realized she was pregnant and then their "concern" about rubella. "We wanted to have a family that could grow as a normal family," recalled Mrs. Baum. "We had one child, whose happiness we got quite concerned about. And we thought we had a responsibility to any unborn child to insure its normalcy to whatever extent we could do this." Mrs. Baum outlined her thought processes, her own and her husband's worry for the family, and their sense of responsibility.

She eventually decided to have a therapeutic abortion. "A decision like this one," she continued, "is one you make as wisely as you can at the time, weighing all the factors to the best of your ability. You go forward from there." The documentary then showed the mother with two girls in the kitchen. "We have two children, and we're very happy about it." Mrs. Baum was a happy, responsible mother who had made a decision for abortion for herself and her family.

The contrast to this happy outcome was the situation of Air Force Captain and Mrs. Kent, who also had two children. Television viewers saw them with their oldest child, Kevin, at the Bellevue Hospital's rubella center, where children received intensive training. Four or five years old, Kevin lay in his crib disengaged and unaware as his mother talked and the camera filmed. Near tears throughout the interview, she described his condition. Knowing she had caught German measles from her students and knowing the consequences of having the disease during pregnancy, she had tried to get an abortion. Seven doctors had refused her. Feeling hopeless and defeated, she worried every night. "In Kevin," she reported learning at his birth, "there are five major malformations in his body." She described the nurses' confusion in determining his sex at birth, the cataracts and multiple operations, his hearing loss, the "hole in his heart," and his mental retardation. His doctors told the Kents that Kevin would have to be institutionalized.[6] This television interview, as one reviewer described it, was "absolutely shattering."[7] Abortion law reform, the news documentary made clear, not only would make access fair and abortions safe but also could alleviate distress by letting mothers and families choose to avoid having a severely disabled child if the mother had contracted this terrible disease.

Awareness of the agony of mothers in the early 1960s German measles epidemic spurred on researchers in the federal government, in university and industry labs, and in clinics. Dr. Paul Parkman, a virologist at Walter Reed Army Institute of Research in Washington, DC, who had codiscovered the virus in 1962 and later had gone to the NIH, was quite aware of the epidemic in progress and knew what it meant for women and doctors. "A mother had to decide," he later recalled. If she had a rash in the first trimester, she and her doctor had to weigh the risks and make a decision. He noted, "It was a wrenching decision for a mother to have to make, really bad."[8] Dr. Thomas H. Weller, part of the polio virus research team, a Nobel laureate, and the Harvard virologist who had simultaneously identified the rubella virus in 1962, described the need for a vaccine as "all too apparent." "The overwhelming personal tragedy, the extent of fetal wastage, and the expense . . . of the recent rubella epidemic," Weller remarked, "indict rubella as a major medical and social problem."[9] The devastating consequences of this disease drove virologists across the United States to develop a vaccine. Leading scientists like Parkman and Weller knew that their discoveries and inventions could make a real difference to women as well as to children.

Although it proved impossible to produce a vaccine before the 1964 epidemic reached the United States, scientists did make rapid progress. Once the virus had been identified in 1962 by scientists at Walter Reed and at Harvard School of Public Health, biomedical researchers went to work on developing tests and vaccines.[10] At the same time, physicians continued to learn more about the clinical manifestations of what came to be called *congenital rubella syndrome,* or *CRS,* to describe the multiple and varied effects of maternal rubella on the infected fetus. Medical research in all areas pushed forward, and researchers shared their clinical, epidemiological, and virological findings at major meetings in 1965 and 1969.[11] Scientists at the NIH pursued rubella with vigor and, once they had developed an attenuated live virus vaccine in 1966, offered the virus strain to other scientists who wanted to use it with the proviso that the vaccine could not be patented. At least eight pharmaceutical companies jumped at the opportunity. The U.S. government also helped pay for the research of nine pharmaceutical companies through grants made by the National Institute of Allergy and Infectious Diseases.[12]

"Every young married woman in the land can rejoice today," declared one medical columnist. "Our great laboratory research [has] removed from her and her sisters a number of great threats," including measles and, soon, German measles.[13] Medical advisers strongly advocated vaccination for German measles as a needed measure. After years of intensive research supported primarily by the U.S. federal government through the NIH but also by the March of Dimes (MOD),[14] pharmaceutical companies, and university researchers worldwide, NIH researchers announced an effective vaccine in 1969.[15] NIH scientists and private U.S., European, and Soviet pharmaceutical companies tested three different vaccines on tens of thousands of children worldwide in the United States, Canada, Europe, Africa, the USSR, Taiwan, and the Caribbean. In June 1969, HEW-USPHS licensed the live vaccine. The United States expected to need fifty to seventy million doses of vaccine over the next five years as federal, state, and local health departments geared up for massive vaccination. The federal government's plan to vaccinate nationwide, business observers noted, promised "a tidy profit" for companies that had won contracts.[16] A massive simultaneous nationwide vaccination campaign could not be immediately pursued, however, because of limited quantities of the vaccine. Although the Surgeon General and the American Academy of Pediatrics recommended vaccination of all boys and girls between the ages of one year and puberty, vaccination would focus first on the kindergarten to second-grade group.[17]

Given that German measles threatened pregnant women, not men and not children, one might have expected adult women and adolescent girls to be the focus of vaccination efforts. Initially health workers had assumed this would be the case,[18] but this plan posed problems. First, pregnant teenagers and women might inadvertently be vaccinated, thus exposing the exact population whom public health experts were trying to protect. Second, field trials had shown that adult women suffered side effects of swollen lymph glands and transient (temporary) arthritis from the vaccine while children rarely had rashes or joint pain.[19] Furthermore, a campaign directed at teens and adult women would have to emphatically publicize the necessity of avoiding pregnancy because it was not yet known whether the vaccines might cause birth defects. That scenario would mean talking about and insisting on the use of contraception or offering abortion as a backup. In a nation fighting over birth control, the Pill, abortion, and sex outside of marriage, a public discussion centering on the sexuality of teenagers or unmarried women and the government's or medical community's urging of contraceptive use might destroy the immunization campaign. Privately, physicians and clinics would talk to women, check their immune status, and then provide vaccinations when they knew that the woman planned to avoid pregnancy. Adult women, the USPHS advised, might receive vaccination "only when the possibility of pregnancy in the following two months is essentially nil, and each case must be considered individually." "Essentially nil" would have to mean either using the Pill or complete abstinence from vaginal intercourse.[20] Scientists and planners read the political climate and avoided a highly publicized discussion about birth control. Finally, public health authorities could also predict another devastating scenario: knowing that there was a baseline number of unpredicted anomalies in newborns, they knew that as soon as a woman who had been vaccinated gave birth to such a child, the vaccine would be blamed.[21]

Health authorities worldwide debated the question, and different countries pursued different strategies in the effort to eliminate congenital rubella syndrome (CRS). To eliminate congenital rubella through the vaccination of adult women or adolescent girls would require that every single one of these groups be immunized because the disease would still continue to appear regularly in the population, exposing pregnant women. Although concentrated effort in one small town in Wisconsin achieved the vaccination of every adolescent girl,[22] locating and immunizing 100 percent of female teens or women of childbearing age could not perpetually be achieved nationwide in the United States, particularly without a national health-care system. Britain, Australia, and Israel followed the policy of vaccinating schoolgirls. Canada vaccinated infants and preschool girls.[23] The United States would rely upon mass vaccination of the population where the disease concentrated (among young children) and upon herd immunity to prevent the development of epidemics among the population as a whole. (*Herd immunity* is the idea that if a large proportion of a population is immune to a disease, infectious disease will not be able to spread, and the susceptible will be protected as well.) Planners aimed to vaccinate forty to fifty million children.[24] The plan was to start in the fall of 1969 in most states and major cities; government immunization programs would focus on poor schools and Head Start programs.[25]

As an advertisement in *Life* magazine declared, "If unborn babies are going to be protected, it will have to be by inoculating the kids who infect the mothers who in turn infect the fetuses."[26] In one sentence, this advertisement placed responsibility on children and used two competing terms for a developing pregnancy. The pregnant woman carried an *unborn baby* and/or a *fetus.* By 1970, the terms were beginning to be associated with opposing perspectives on abortion and its legal and moral status. However, the political meaning of an "unborn" baby was not yet fixed or clearly associated with the antiabortion movement. As Mrs. Baum had remarked, she and her minister-husband "thought we had a responsibility to any unborn child to insure its normalcy."[27] She had a therapeutic abortion after learning that she had contracted rubella in early pregnancy. Women themselves—including those who had abortions or supported their legalization—wanted to protect pregnancies that they hoped to carry to term. As mothers-to-be, they may have thought of their pregnancies as "unborn babies," as children on the way.[28] At the same time, Catholic priests in Washington State formed the "Voice of the Unborn" in 1970 to oppose a statewide referendum to legalize abortion. This use of the term *the unborn* made a political argument for the belief that all pregnancies already were and would become children, that a pregnancy equaled an individual person separate from the pregnant woman.[29] Similarly, *fetus* and *embryo,* medical terms that had not been part of everyday language, became vocabulary for talking about pregnancy without equating it with a living child. This magazine advertisement incorporated the words' multiple meanings when it urged "protect[ion] of unborn babies" and "fetuses." It referred to both antiabortion and abortion rights agendas simultaneously and promised that use of the vaccine would protect pregnant women from the dangers of rubella and would safeguard the health of their future babies.

Inevitably, some proponents of the vaccine not only pointed to the harm caused by the disease; they also pointed to the price tag attached to caring for and educating the children hurt by rubella. In keeping with eugenic thinking since the beginning of the twentieth century and economic cost-benefit analysis, advocates of immunization compared the cost of the vaccine with the expense of caring for those harmed by the disease. Immunization cost less. Implicitly and explicitly, some argued that it would be better to avoid producing disabled children than to provide for their needs. As Jeannette Rockefeller, wife of Arkansas governor Winthrop Rockefeller, remarked, "It is much cheaper for a state to pay for shots or tests for the indigent than it is for the government to pay for care of mentally retarded or physically crippled babies." *Today's Health* pointed to the "dollar cost . . . as some 30,000 rubella-damaged children are ready for school."[30] These remarks drew upon and fed into growing antiwelfare and antitax sentiment that undercut social responsibility for the needs of all members of the society.[31] Taxpayers, these remarks suggested, would prefer the cheaper option of paying to vaccinate children instead of educating all children, including the "handicapped."

Volunteer Tricia Nixon swabbed children's arms before they received shots at an elementary school in Washington, DC, in the fall of 1969. It was a great photo-op—the president's daughter reassuring a young black girl and contributing to the effort to protect the nation's children, all of them, whatever their color.[32] As his daughter helped vaccinate African American children, President Richard Nixon tried to stop racial integration, cut budgets, and refused to support a national immunization campaign. The irony was great, as was the frustration and anger in Congress and among public health workers. "How can the administration," asked Senator Allen, "announce in one breath that it lacks the resources to save thousands of lives through health and medical programs, and in another breath signal the go-ahead for a supersonic transport airplane?" Billions of dollars, he charged, were being spent on a single airplane while millions for health were cut.[33] Although the federal government had spent $19.2 million on immunization by the end of 1969, public funds now were instead being poured into the Vietnam War as President Nixon cut social welfare programs. Nixon knew how to get credit for tackling racial injustice through health programs while simultaneously pursuing conservative economic policies and producing racial divides in the electorate. Federal funding would pay for immunizing at most 20 percent of the target group of children.[34]

Tricia Nixon was one volunteer among thousands. Without the essential work of unpaid volunteers—many of them housewives as well as health care professionals—mass vaccination would have failed because of the insufficient funding of public health at federal and local levels.[35] The rubella vaccination campaign was a public and private effort to reach the masses of Americans in order to prevent another epidemic of "defective babies." The CDC of the USPHS collaborated with city and state health agencies along with voluntary health organizations such as the National Foundation–March of Dimes (NF-MOD), Easter Seal Society, PTA, Jaycees, National Council of Catholic Women, and numerous other voluntary civic groups. Taylor Residents United, a group of African American women from a public housing development on Chicago's South Side, for instance, worked with Provident Hospital and the city health department to encourage "black youngsters" to get all of their immunizations, including rubella. Advocates for the deaf and the mentally retarded also supported the immunization campaign.[36] (See figure 12.)

Voluntary organizations played an indispensable role in running public vaccination clinics in schools, churches, fire stations, and other large venues capable of serving four thousand children per day in cities or through mobile clinics in rural areas. *Voluntary Action to Stop Rubella!*—a USPHS booklet—showed how to participate. It described in detail the type of space needed, including parking space; the importance of avoiding long lines; and the numbers of volunteers needed for specific jobs and provided a diagram of the clinic setup and flow of people. The government expected volunteers to provide two-thirds of the staff—twenty to thirty people at each site—to collect permission forms from parents, direct the flow of people, swab arms, immunize children, make phone calls, collect donations, and set up and take down the clinics. Volunteers would also pass out the badges and candy used to gain the cooperation of children.[37]

In its text, the USPHS pamphlet recruited volunteers by representing German measles as an aggressive assailant of babies; in its photos, it

Figure 12. These respectable women from Chicago public housing volunteered on behalf of their community, children, and public health. They are identified as (standing, from left) Mrs. Ora Reasoner, Mrs. Margaret Bolden, and (seated) Mrs. Shirley Collins and Mrs. Ora Ferguson. Their efforts in this health fair exemplify both the mobilization to immunize African American and low-income children and the women's welfare rights movement. Their portraits and activism remade the predominant media portrait of German measles as a concern of married white women and white families. Newspapers and magazines produced by and for African Americans offered such images. Majority newspapers that most whites read rarely ran such photos. Taylor Residents United in "Provident Hospital to Sponsor Health Carnival," *Chicago Defender,* weekend edition, October 17, 1970, p. 23.

suggested that children of all races needed protection and that all groups should join the voluntary effort. "Rubella has maimed and destroyed many thousands of unborn and newborn babies in the United States, some 50,000 in the epidemic of 1964 alone. A disease of this dimension," the booklet declared, "calls for equally determined opposition . . . to STOP RUBELLA before additional numbers of unborn babies are attacked." The booklet's photos show black babies, white babies, and white, black, and Asian youngsters all receiving shots; black and white nurses and white male doctors give them. The racial diversity of the photographs indicates a conscious effort to create and suggest a racially inclusive health project. The pamphlet's glossy cover spotlighted the modern technology of vaccination—the jet injector. The child receiving a shot from a pair of white medical hands is one of three Asian children. Of all the photos in this pamphlet, this one is the clearest and most compelling picture of the actual practice of vaccination and was presumably selected for that reason. I suspect that this photo came from the vaccine trials in Taiwan and want to think about what other meanings might be embedded within it. Perhaps health educators hoped to persuade Asians in Hawaii and on the West Coast to join the vaccination campaign. Perhaps the photo should also be read as a portrait of medical missionary work, with the exotic yet compliant Asian and the white helping hands as important as the display of technology's promise. Inside the pamphlet, photos showed campaigns and vaccinations in process: female volunteers vaccinating a line of white and black schoolchildren; a billboard that urged "Save a child in '70! . . . Rub Out Rubella," with a picture of a white Gerber baby; and men and women making phone calls on behalf of the campaign. (See figures 13 and 14.) Everyone, the pamphlet urged, could do his or her part to save babies of all colors.

The National Foundation–March of Dimes played a central role in promoting a nationwide rubella vaccination program modeled on its own earlier campaign to eradicate polio. The March of Dimes had produced and distributed millions of pieces of educational literature, was expert at winning publicity, and as important, had an "army" of women ready to volunteer their time, labor, smarts, and organizational expertise.[38] The campaign built upon the public's fear of "crippling" disease, its admiration for scientists, and its enthusiastic embrace of mass vaccination of children in the 1956 polio vaccine "trial." As in the polio campaign, scientists and health experts told the public that this was a dangerous disease that could be beat. "As a killer or crippler of unborn children," one science writer reported, "rubella probably claims more victims than polio, 'red' measles,

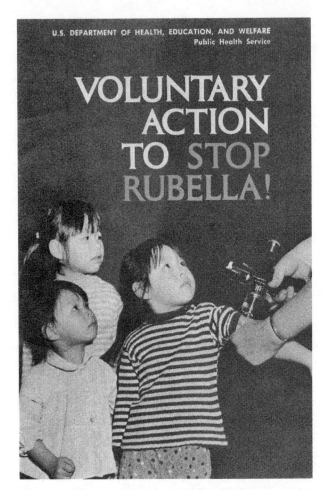

**VOLUNTARY
ACTION
TO STOP
RUBELLA!**

Figure 13. Through photos and detailed descriptions, this booklet from the Public Health Service showed how to run a vaccination clinic with volunteers to immunize thousands. The cover showed the new jet injector and calm Asian children receiving their rubella vaccines. There is no crying or balking. This photo spotlights the new, less painful technology for immunization. U.S. Department of Health, Education, and Welfare, Public Health Service, *Voluntary Action to Stop Rubella* [circa 1970], folder Birth Defects Rubella Printed Literature and Posters, 1970–71, box 3, series 3 Birth Defects, Medical Program Records, March of Dimes Archives. Reproduced with permission of the March of Dimes Foundation.

Figure 14. "Save a Child in '70!" This billboard advertised the drive to immunize all targeted children in order to save babies' lives. In keeping with the longtime visual emphasis on white families and children and commitment to their protection, this billboard showed a white Gerber baby as the one to be saved. White parents would surely have thought that the image on this sign applied to them; people of color might not have. Within a few years, this type of advertisement would be read as a right-to-life, antiabortion message, not one promoting a vaccine. Where this billboard appeared is not indicated. U.S. Department of Health, Education, and Welfare, Public Health Service, *Voluntary Action to Stop Rubella,* photo on inside page. Reprinted with the permission of the March of Dimes Foundation.

mumps, chicken pox, and scarlet fever put together." Mass vaccination, maintained Dr. Parkman, the lead NIH scientist who had developed the vaccine, would make rubella, "like smallpox and polio, . . . a rare disease."[39] "Birth Defects," Dr. Virginia Apgar remarked, "are 10 times the problem polio was. . . . If people could see the defect[ive] children, they would know how important mass immunization is." Dr. Apgar added, "With the polio vaccine, you could see the direct results."[40]

Quite unlike the earlier polio experience, though, Dr. Apgar and other proponents of immunization worried that too many people did not know that rubella threatened birth defects and might not grasp the need for the vaccine.[41] The effort to vaccinate against rubella had begun five years after the peak of the German measles epidemic, and despite the intense media coverage of maternal rubella at the time of the epidemic, health experts feared that class and ethnicity still kept many ignorant of the danger of German measles to pregnant women. In contrast, at the time of the polio vaccine trials, Americans knew polio well because it frightened them every summer. They had seen children paralyzed due to polio and knew that President Franklin D. Roosevelt had been struck by it (though many did not realize that he had been permanently paralyzed), and the country had rallied around raising dimes for research and for iron lungs for the afflicted.[42] Furthermore, the recent introduction of another new vaccine for a common childhood disease—measles—added to the confusion. As a result, the German measles vaccine campaign had to differentiate between "regular" measles and German measles (thus the new emphasis on using the "medical" name *rubella*). Furthermore, mothers (and interested fathers) could easily find the proliferation of recommended immunizations confusing. The growing list of vaccines now included rubella, measles, diphtheria, whooping cough, mumps, poliomyelitis, and smallpox. The recommendation: follow your doctor's advice and keep a record.[43]

Interest in and knowledge of rubella was shaped by gender, age, ethnicity, and class. The immunization of children was a mother's job; mothers had to bring their children in and be convinced of the necessity of immunization. Photographs of men and women together coordinating the rubella immunization campaign distorted the underlying gender assumption and reality that child immunization was a mother's business and duty.[44] Expectant mothers who were determined to learn all they could about how best to care for their pregnancies and who read magazines and advice literature would know of the disease while other pregnant women—particularly low-income and non-English-speaking women who could not afford or read English-language materials—as well as many men might know little about it. Health-care workers had learned from the earlier epidemic that many Spanish-speaking families did not know about the implications of rubella.[45] Public health workers knew they had to teach Americans about the dangers of maternal rubella for the immunization campaign to succeed. The United States Public Health Service (USPHS) targeted low-income mothers to receive educational materials in the form of pamphlets, lectures, and television and radio spots. Middle-class families would also receive educational materials, but the USPHS counted on them to seek out vaccinations from their private doctors and to pay for them privately. In fact, the USPHS planned on 75 percent of the targeted preschool population being covered privately. The federal government, with state and local governments contributing, expected to immunize only disadvantaged populations.[46]

Apgar and health authorities may have been particularly worried about low-income, black, and Latino communities because recent experience with the new measles vaccine had shown that they were slower to immunize against measles. Whether because of "indifference," "resist[ance]," or a lack of time and money, children in poor "ghetto" areas in major cities were, health experts observed, not getting shots and were still getting measles.[47] It would hardly be surprising if African Americans and Latinas and Latinos doubted the need for this government-sponsored health program given the coercive and humiliating treatment they often received from government and health officials. Furthermore, from personal experience, local knowledge, and news reports, these communities also knew of forced sterilizations and legislative attempts to mandate contraception, sterilization, and abortion for women who received welfare.[48] Avoiding programs that appeared to be sponsored by the government or white authorities could make much sense.

HEALTH EDUCATION'S MESSAGES

The representation of the child as a dangerous threat to its mother persisted throughout vaccine promotional materials. The rubella vaccine would keep "kids from becoming mother's worst enemy," proclaimed one pharmaceutical company's advertisement. Thanks to North American Philips, the very-pregnant mother pictured in a rocking chair could hug her toddler son without fear. "Rubella–German measles," the advertisement intoned, can make a child his "mother's worst enemy if she happens to be pregnant and catches it from him." The disease was personified, the child made an "enemy." Rubella vaccine would protect the mother-child bond. North American Philips advertised the vaccine and the company to potential shareholders.[49] Vaccine was good for babies, mothers, and business.

Health educational materials not only taught the public about disease and vaccines; they also taught the public about disability. Many mothers would receive a small red-and-white booklet with a portrait of a bright-eyed, long-haired woman in a curlicued frame and with the title *The Real Life Story of RUBY (a Tragedy)*.[50] This "true story without a happy ending"

# the Real Life Story
# of RUBY

## ( a Tragedy )

Figure 15. Mothers received this cute 3×5-inch informational pamphlet from doctors and health advocates who urged rubella immunization. Its red and white colors and title, *The Real Life Story of Ruby*, both played on the red spots that signaled German measles. The subtitle (*a Tragedy*) also taught mothers (and children who may have been intrigued by the pamphlet's appearance as a fairy tale) that a child who wore heavy glasses or hearing aids was a terrible outcome, a tragedy. U.S. Department of Health, Education, and Welfare, Public Health Service, *The Real Life Story of RUBY (a Tragedy)*, pamphlet, 1971, cover, folder Birth Defects Rubella Printed Literature and Posters, 1970–71, box 3, series 3 Birth Defects, Medical Program Records, March of Dimes Archives. Reprinted with the permission of the March of Dimes Foundation.

equated the birth of a disabled child with "tragedy." The story, as the booklet told its readers, "begins with a boy and girl falling in love and marrying—as they do in love stories. They were very happy for about a year." It then told of the boy next door who, when he borrowed flour, brought with him German measles, which Ruby caught. Although Ruby only felt like she had a bad cold, "the baby growing inside the mother wasn't as lucky," and when it was born seven months later, "it didn't act right." The discovery that the new baby had cataracts, was "partly deaf," and would need operations, "thick glasses," and "a hearing aid" was the abrupt ending to what had been a happy, romantic tale. (See figure 15.)

Equating congenital impairments and disabilities with "tragedy" was automatic, yet it is nonetheless striking to see the birth of a disabled child represented as "the end."[51] The ending in this pamphlet was a beginning for other families as they learned to care for and fight for the rights and needs of their children. CDC educational materials presented a future of thick glasses and hearing aids as a tragic future and a tragic ending. Yet these technologies helped many children gain an education and participate in the world. Others, however, found the hearing boxes useless and frustrating. Deaf children learned Sign language and entered schools and a community.[52] Materials designed to persuade parents to vaccinate their children were not designed to show the potential of the disabled or to inspire hope among their parents—there were other pamphlets for this.[53] Nonetheless, people learned about the meanings of disabilities and the expected futures for the disabled from these materials. They learned, first and foremost, that disability was "tragic." The CDC information office saw the booklet as a "compelling story of an average woman who contracts rubella during early pregnancy and subsequently gives birth to a defective baby." To avert this "tragedy," at its conclusion the booklet warned parents, "Immunize your children against rubella now!" It added that, unlike Ruby's, "Your true life story can have a happy ending." That happy ending was represented by a mother with a swaddled infant in her arms, a thrilled father who celebrated by tossing cigars in the air, and a smiling little girl.[54] (See figure 16.)

If the mother got the message of Ruby's tale, the little girl would be receiving a rubella vaccine shot at a clinic or her doctor's office soon. Some mothers may have remembered being taken as young girls by their mothers to German measles parties or exposed to other kids with the hope of their catching the disease. As a result, they may have understood the importance of immunizing their daughters in order to protect their (presumed) futures

Your true life story
can have a happy ending.

IMMUNIZE
YOUR CHILDREN
AGAINST RUBELLA
NOW!

Figure 16. In this illustration from the informational pamphlet *The Real Life Story of Ruby,* the family celebrates its new healthy and normal baby. Immunizing children, it appears, ensured the safety of babies like this one and the happiness of their families. U.S. Department of Health, Education, and Welfare, Public Health Service, *The Real Life Story of RUBY (a Tragedy),* pamphlet, 1971, back cover, folder Birth Defects Rubella Printed Literature and Posters, 1970–71, box 3, series 3 Birth Defects, Medical Program Records, March of Dimes Archives. Reprinted with the permission of the March of Dimes Foundation.

as heterosexuals and mothers. Furthermore, taking their daughters to the doctor for a shot was easier than trying to arrange German measles parties, which often did not work. Health authorities could safely assume that mothers would ensure the immunization of their daughters.

Boys too, however, needed to be vaccinated. The rubella campaign was the first public health campaign for maternal and infant health aimed at boys. As the rubella vaccination campaign reversed standard gender expectations by challenging boys to take action in order to protect future maternity, it rewrote the formulas of maternal and infant health campaigns. The rubella vaccination campaign would either have to degender and neutralize the maternal and infant health campaign or remake and re-gender it as male. Boys, like girls, had to be recruited for the future health and well-being of babies. The campaign asked boys to accept a vaccine shot to their bodies—something that all children feared—for the health of future babies. Parents and boys would have to be convinced of the necessity—personal and social—of having boys vaccinated. If boys or their parents refused, or simply neglected, to go along with immunization, the effort to prevent the next rubella epidemic through mass vaccination would fail. The campaign aimed to preempt any notion among boys and men that preventing German measles and the threat to "unborn babies" was "girl stuff" and not about them.[55]

The colorful comic book *Rubella Robs the Cradle,* produced by the March of Dimes, is a fine example of this gender trick, one that needed to succeed if the vaccination campaign itself was to succeed. The comic book for kids pointed the finger directly at children—specifically boys—for their potential role in causing family grief, tragedy, and death. Whereas Mummy in an earlier *Good Housekeeping* account of the tragedy of German measles had tried to keep secret her daughter's role in having harmed her mother's pregnancy, the rubella comic book did the opposite. It made it plain to children that they could spread disease, infect mothers, and cause the destruction of other children. "Rubella robs the cradle," declares the doctor on the cover while the scene behind his shoulder shows a baby's room with a grieving husband and wife leaning over a child in a crib. As boys and girls opened the pages of what looked to be both fun—a colorful cartoon—and serious with its depiction of grief on the cover, they would learn more about rubella, now personified as "Red-haired Stevie."[56] (See figure 17.)

More than 250,000 of these comic books and parental consent forms went home with New York City schoolchildren. The national NF-MOD office gave March of Dimes chapters the comic book and encouraged them to offer

# RUBELLA ROBS THE CRADLE

Figure 17. A doctor warns that "rubella robs the cradle" as the viewer of this educational pamphlet peers through a doorway to see a distraught couple and the tragic scene inside. By having the doctor's face take up half of the space on the pamphlet's front page, the artwork emphasized the authority of medicine and the obligation to listen to doctors' advice. *Rubella Robs the Cradle,* pamphlet, [March of Dimes, 1970], cover, folder Birth Defects Rubella Printed Literature and Posters, 1970–71, box 3, series 3 Birth Defects, Medical Program Records, March of Dimes Archives. Reprinted with the permission of March of Dimes Foundation.

it to their local health departments. Since the campaign intended to vaccinate virtually every child in the country, the MOD understood that it needed to reach varied groups in myriad places. To that end, national leaders suggested working with every possible organization and, more specifically, with "leaders of minority communities—black, Mexican, Puerto Rican, Chinese, Indian. As you no doubt know, health problems in these groups are substantially greater than in more affluent white communities." The comics could be used for school-based vaccination programs as they had been in New York City or could be distributed through churches, clubs, welfare offices, military bases, and day-care centers and door-to-door.[57] Minneapolis, Minnesota, and Charlottesville, Virginia, volunteers used the comic book and vaccinated nearly all of the targeted group of children.[58]

In the comic, the dangerous disease becomes the dangerous "red-haired Stevie," a good white boy who does his schoolwork and behaves well throughout the story. He is the exact opposite of the child historically identified as dangerous: he is a youngster, white, presumably native-born (though the red hair might suggest Irish or English heritage), middle-class, friendly, and good. He is not a teenager, not a boy of color, not an immigrant, not threatening in any way. Yet he is dangerous because he has rubella, and, whether he knows it or not, he is contagious and can "spread it like wildfire." Stevie is spreading the deadly disease to the young potential mothers who enjoy his company all day long—his teacher, his mother, his aunt, his neighbors, his friends, and strangers. The cartoon shows little Stevie reading quietly on the bus next to mothers with young children, helping his mother in the grocery store among other mothers and female clerks, and kissing his Aunt Katie, who tells him that he will soon "have a new baby cousin!" Months later, the doctor holds the newborn and tells the new parents, "I'm terribly sorry. . . . The baby has cataracts. He's blind . . . and may also have a heart defect." Now the reader realizes that the cradle "robbed" by rubella and the child shown harmed at the start of the story is Stevie's new cousin. Just in case the story isn't completely clear to little boys (and girls and parents), the doctor tells the stricken parents, "I'm afraid you caught Rubella months ago from little Stevie." When children learned from the rubella vaccination campaign that they could cause "tragedy" and death, good children got the message and gladly submitted to shots.

In contrast to the whiteness of the representations of German measles victims in most media, the people depicted in educational materials to promote vaccination were more racially mixed. Health educators expected that the middle-class white population would be fairly easily recruited to vaccination but that people of color would need to be convinced. For African Americans, seeing danger represented as a white boy may have been a refreshing change. Or the depiction may still have appeared to be a health message about and for white people. Americans' racialized view of the world made it difficult to produce any type of public health message that was entirely neutral and spoke effectively to people of every race, gender, ethnicity, and class.[59] This comic book clearly attempted to speak to a broader array of Americans. The ambiguous ethnicity of the comic book's doomed parents played more than one way. The parents' skin color is light, but their hair is dark, and the father has a mustache. The couple's ambiguous ethnicity might speak to multiple white ethnicities—Greeks or Italians, perhaps— while the mustache simultaneously could signal a Latino man. (See figure 17.) The rubella comic book also appeared in a Spanish-language version for New York's large Puerto Rican and Dominican populations. In the Spanish-language version, little Stevie is "Carlitos," and his hair color goes unnamed; Aunt Katie becomes tia Luisa, and Mrs. (and Mr.) Greyson are now "Sra. [and Sr.] Martinez."[60] (See figure 18.)

The doctor in the comic book then looks the reader in the eye to give an important message. Here we see physician communication: serious, expert, and authoritative. "*Parents! Don't let this happen again.*" It is up to the parents to read, listen, and do what the doctor advises: vaccinate their children in order to "eliminate the threat of Rubella to unborn babies." The doctor answers the parents' questions before they ask them. The vaccine, he explains, is safe, is approved by the government, and "immunizes the child so he can't catch, carry, or spread Rubella. Vaccinated boys and girls can't infect other people, including pregnant women." The strong advice continues on the last page as the doctor, still looking the reader in the eye, urges, "Unless you do your part, another Rubella epidemic may come within the next year." The unspecific "you" works for any and all readers—boys, girls, children, and parents all have a responsibility either to be vaccinated or to permit and support vaccination. "For everyone's sake, have your children vaccinated against Rubella," the doctor continues, but now the message is to mothers, the ones who make health decisions for the family, who bring their children to the doctor or the clinic, who sign school forms, and who may be threatened by rubella. The doctor adds, "Who knows? One of the unborn babies you save may be your own!" In the next frame, as kids leave school with the comic book in their hands, two boys declare their commitment to the program: they "want" to get vaccinated and say they plan to "show this to our mothers!"

Figure 18. Designed for New York's Puerto Rican and Dominican populations, this version of *Rubella Robs the Cradle,* retitled as *Sarampion Aleman . . . Tragedia Que Acecha La Cuna,* was received by thousands of Spanish-speaking children and their parents. In it, Carlitos (*Stevie* in the English version) bounces through streets and grocery stores with his mother, saying "Hola" and spreading German measles everywhere. The pamphlet also names the disease *rubella. Sarampion Aleman,* pamphlet, [March of Dimes, 1970], folder Birth Defects Rubella Printed Literature and Posters, 1970–71, box 3, series 3 Birth Defects, Medical Program Records, March of Dimes Archives. Reprinted with the permission of the March of Dimes Foundation.

This comic book was directed at boys: it is a boy who poses a threat and boys who express their wish to be vaccinated. The new father appears grief stricken alongside his wife; the newborn harmed by cousin Stevie/Carlitos is a baby boy. Boys spread disease and are hurt by it. Depending on how boys read and identified with the characters in the comic book, they might want to protect other boys and men or themselves as future fathers. Or they might imagine protecting the girls, women, and mothers in their lives. The comic book's last frame depicts girls walking out the doors of their public school, but it is the boys walking behind them who say, "I want to help. I'm getting vaccinated right away" and "Let's go show this to our mothers!" Implicitly, the comic book suggests that being vaccinated is something done *for* girls—for mothers, aunts, and teachers as well as peers, friends, and sisters. (One man remembers being told when he was ten-year-old Danny that he had gotten a shot "for" his friend's older sister, Becky.)[61]

Although the comic book was not directed at girls, it may have been effective for them as well. First, girls and their mothers learned from many other sources about the importance of vaccination against German measles. Furthermore, this comic book would have been no different than most schoolbooks or films that overlooked girls and focused on a boy as the main character and told the story of his travels, adventures, education, and emotional development. Girls had long been trained to learn from male-dominated materials and to take their own messages from them. No doubt advocates of vaccination assumed that girls too would realize the importance of being vaccinated both to protect babies now and to protect themselves as future mothers. Girls (and mothers) might learn too that the boy who did not raise alarm bells in any way—not through his behavior, race, or class—could nonetheless be dangerous for them and their children. They needed to be suspicious of and careful about boys. This message fit with earlier health warnings to women who might be pregnant to avoid small children (as well as with messages to girls that boys represented sexual danger). Finally, girls might join in lobbying their mothers to make sure that brothers and boys in the neighborhood were vaccinated.

The March of Dimes comic book presented a sophisticated argument for older kids. The exceptional artwork, the racial ambiguity, and the text's urgent message all made it a convincing health pamphlet. The New York City public health department produced a playful one-minute television message for little children watching their favorite cartoons that told them "that they needed a rubella umbrella." The spot showed a white-and-red polka-dotted umbrella "'walking' down a city street" and told viewers that "'kids—especially 4-year-olds and 5- and 6- and 7-year-olds'—should get rubella vaccine." The announcement had impressive success. Kids bothered their parents to call for the "umbrella," and more than 17,000 parents called. The health department understood that an amusing image and a big word could recruit kids to push their parents for the vaccine. As Dr. Vincent Guineé smartly observed, "Kids love to teach their parents new words."[62] One wonders what those kids thought when they got a shot and a lollipop instead of an umbrella. Surely some learned that advertising and adults could deliberately deceive.

Girls and boys both—and especially black kids—might also have gotten the message through a special film featuring stars Diahann Carroll and Marc Copage from the popular television show *Julia*. In *Julia*, Carroll played a (widowed) nurse with a young son; as a nurse, she represented a black professional woman who historically had great respect and responsibility in her community. As a nurse, and as a popular and beautiful actress, Julia/Carroll's support for immunization may have been a reassuring message to some parts of the black community. The fact that her (TV) son received a shot reinforced the message that boys as well as girls needed to be immunized. *Julia* did not speak to black audiences alone, however. Other school-age girls—white and Japanese American—also watched this show religiously and admired her. This 13½-minute film may well have worked across gender, racial, and class categories.[63] (See figure 19.)

Through film, comic books, billboards, pamphlets, and news stories, the immunization campaign worked to attract the attention and support of people of color. Japanese-language and Spanish-language materials encouraged parents to immunize their children.[64] A March of Dimes news release spotlighted "New Yorkers" Carmen Perdomo and her five-year-old son, Luisito, who wore hearing aids. In the 1940s and 1950s, the March of Dimes had produced posters to raise money for polio research that featured photographs of attractive and hard-working boys and girls who were polio victims. These poster children displayed the terrible effects of the disease while the organization simultaneously honored their heroic efforts to walk and to overcome their personal tragedies. The rubella immunization campaign built on this successful polio formula of using charming photographs of disabled children. The depiction of disabilities, the hard work to overcome them, and the respectability of the victims were now represented, however, by a Latino boy whose dedicated mother sat by his side as she participated in his education. With the intensive work of Luisito's mother and the specialized teaching and therapies given him at

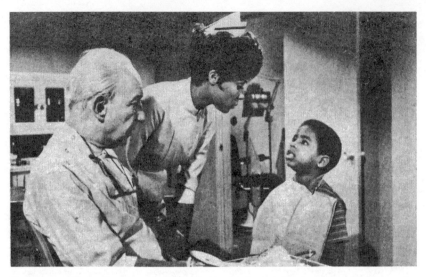

Figure 19. The endorsement of rubella immunization by the stars of the popular TV show *Julia* would encourage many children to accept the shot. At the same time, as can be seen in this still photo, the film showed children and parents what to expect: pleasant and informative physicians and nurses. No one needed to be afraid of the vaccine; children should see their doctors and get vaccinated. Promotional photo from *Stop Rubella* (educational film), *Children Limited* 18, no. 10 (December 1969): 3. Reprinted with the permission of the March of Dimes Foundation.

an experimental school for rubella-damaged children at Bellevue Hospital, his mother and doctor were "optimistic" that Luisito would soon be in school and able to talk and play with other children. The painful story of the boy's illness and many hospital visits and his mother's anxiety "need never be repeated," the March of Dimes declared, if children around the country received the rubella vaccine.[65] One could empathize with Mrs. Perdomo and Luisito, these news items suggested, and act to ensure that other mothers and children avoided their unfortunate experiences.

As we can see through these comic books and television spots, it was not only politicians, public health officials, the medical profession, and parents who had to be convinced of the value and necessity of vaccination; the subjects scheduled to receive the shots—children—needed convincing too. The promoters of vaccination understood that children could not simply be physically forced by adults to be vaccinated. Public health authorities in the nineteenth and early twentieth century had learned from attempts to vaccinate the population against smallpox that relying on coercion promised resistance, riots, legal challenges, and failure. Although many states and cities had passed laws in the mid-1960s requiring that children be immunized before beginning public school, this was not the primary method of achieving mass rubella immunization. Many parents did not even know of the laws.[66] Instead, authorities emphasized persuasion. Public health educators deliberately set out to get the cooperation of kids through favorite children's media like television shows and comic books and rewards like badges and candy. One child posed for a newspaper photographer and displayed his button that read, "I helped stop German measles and prevent birth defects."[67]

Educators used more than treats, however. They also aimed at children's sense of themselves as good and altruistic citizens. Treating kids with respect, as caring individuals, health educators sought the cooperation of school-age children by appealing to their senses of pride, heroism, civic duty, and guilt. Vaccination against rubella became a gendered civic responsibility in which children could take pride. Since infancy, girls were reared and recruited for motherhood while boys were raised to become workers and/or soldiers who provided for and protected mothers and children. Getting a vaccination for the good of future mothers and babies was a new responsibility for boys, but it fit with the model of men as protectors and with the postwar idealization of the child-centered dad. Boys would become responsible family men; girls would become mothers. The vaccination effort also created and called upon new gender responsibilities. Women and girls had long been expected to take responsibility for the health of babies—through prenatal care and Little Mothers' Clubs—but boys had always been exempted from this expectation.[68] In keeping with evolving gender expectations for adults by 1970, this new campaign made girls and boys equally responsible for child health. Both would accept shots in order to protect future mothers and babies. Like the "polio pioneers" who today still feel pride for their participation as children in the 1954 polio vaccine trials, these children also could embrace their own good citizenship and bravery in facing a shot.[69]

For children, shots were frightening. The rubella immunization campaign included silencing and denying those feelings of fear and pain while simultaneously sweetening the experience. The photos of children receiving immunizations in the U.S. HEW pamphlet showed no crying—only quiet, compliant children. The modern method of immunization was named the *jet gun injector* or *compressed air gun*—a large gunlike metal piece of technology that "shot" each child. If we think for a moment about commonplace terminology and the appearance of this medical instrument, we can imagine what some children must have thought. The entire experience of getting shots—lining up in school auditoriums, churches, or the local hospital for polio, measles, and rubella shots—was strange, scary, and memorable. One woman still remembers being lined up in her new school's gym and approaching a "big machine" for the vaccine.[70] Giving children lollipops after a shot was literally providing a sweet reward in exchange for their being good citizen-patients. Additionally, the suckers quieted cries and whimpers, thus helping to reduce the possibility of mass panic and to move lines of children steadily along toward their shots. Materials designed to encourage immunization never included pictures of crying children, but newspapers did run photos showing fearful kids. Children "wail[ed]," "scream[ed]," cringed, and cried.[71] As frightening as this new instrument and the entire process could be, the jet injection system was less painful than the old syringe and needle had been.[72]

To encourage vaccination, the campaign used exaggerated language to emphasize rubella's role as a killer. The more deadly the disease—and in this disease's drama, the more threatening to the family—the more likely that parents and children would acquiesce en masse. Obtaining mass agreement on the value of child vaccination against rubella rested on understanding the disease as being particularly deadly for babies. The comic book and other educational materials cited large, definitive numbers of deaths and birth defects, but these were all estimates. Given the fact that rubella had not been a reported disease in at least half of the states, the ambiguity of diagnosis, and the delay in identifying many of the affected children's health problems, no accurate accounting of the impact of German measles was possible.

By the time of the 1970 vaccination campaign, the figure of 50,000 affected pregnancies was commonly cited. (Note that the 50,000 pregnancies became 50,000 "families" in the comic book—a leap that evaded sex and equated pregnancy with children and family.) "When America's Stevies and their sisters spread Rubella in 1964," the comic-book doctor intoned, "tragedy followed for 50,000 families! There were 20,000 babies born dead. Another 30,000 came into the world seriously handicapped." It is not clear where these numbers come from. Other reports tallied an even higher toll, reporting 30,000 babies with "tragic defects" and another "30,000 babies [that] never had a chance at life" due to stillbirths and miscarriages.[73] Later CDC estimates were lower, but without an accurate reporting system, the CDC figures had to be an undercount.[74]

The number of deaths appear to represent estimated miscarriages, still-births, (therapeutic) abortions, and early infant deaths all collapsed into one category labeled "deaths." These events were not the same, however, from the point of view of the pregnant woman or her family. While each of these events provokes complicated feelings, a miscarriage may well have been regarded as sad but also as good luck or a blessing that averted the potential difficulties of caring for a disabled child and removed the dilemma of having to decide whether to abort.[75] Therapeutic abortions, though difficult and painful for the previously happily expecting woman, nonetheless resulted from decisions made with the sense that they were best for the family. A child who died soon after birth represented the devastating event that many parents actively worked to avoid by having abortions. Even if a woman who miscarried or aborted felt that she had lost a child, few would equate a miscarriage or a therapeutic abortion with the actual death of a child. Considering miscarriages, stillbirths, and therapeutic abortions as "babies" and "deaths" made German measles appear more threatening.

The vaccine promised not only to save babies' lives but also to make babies normal. "Babies who could otherwise be born blind or incurably deaf will be born healthy," proclaimed one medical writer. "Babies who might be born mentally retarded because of rubella will," she continued, "instead, be normal." *Normality*—meaning a "normal" body and a "normal life"—was what the society and individual parents and families sought.[76] The normal body promised a normal life with normal social expectations and experiences. As everyone knew, an "abnormal" life in a society that did little to accommodate people who were different in bodies or behaviors, who did not conform to social norms, was a hard one.

Finally, vaccine advocates used photographs of the bodies of actual children affected by rubella to depict the danger of rubella, the threat of disability, and the necessity of vaccination. A small, sad-looking child with enormous glasses and hearing equipment attached to his head and chest looked out from a full-page advertisement about the disease and the vaccine that appeared in *Life* magazine in 1970. "The mother got over her rubella in three days. Unfortunately, her unborn child didn't," read the headline. If the child's body, literally wrapped in technology, prompted sympathy— or perhaps panic—in pregnant women and potential parents, they would read on. (See figure 20.) Below the nearly full-page photo, the text explained the disease and its impact and urged parents to vaccinate their children. "If unborn babies are going to be protected," the text warned, "it will have to be by inoculating the kids who infect the mothers who in turn infect

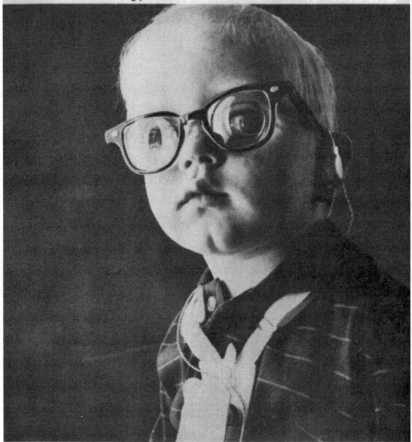

The mother got over her rubella in three
Unfortunately, her unborn child didn't.

Figure 20.  A child affected by rubella appears here in a rare media image as a representation of the danger of rubella. The advertisement uses his condition to urge parents to immunize their children. The technologies that aid this boy and allow him to interact with the world—glasses and hearing aids—represent disability. If he were normal, this young white boy in a carefully pressed shirt would typically be an image of playfulness, noisiness, and joy; instead, he appears sad and quiet. Metropolitan Life Insurance Advertisement in *Life* 69, no. 20 (November 13, 1970): 30.

the fetuses." This Metropolitan Life Insurance advertisement alerted magazine readers to rubella and the imperative to inoculate. In demonstrating
that it cared about babies and families, Metropolitan Life also sold itself to
customers as a caring and trustworthy company.[77]

A similar photo of a boy with hearing aids appeared below the slogan
"Vaccinate now. . . . One more rubella child is one too many" in a Cendevax
advertisement.[78] This ad was blunt: rubella children were not people who
needed medical and social services like everyone else but instead were unwanted and undesirable and should be prevented. There were already "too
many" rubella children. Thoughtless and cruel advertisements like this one
are precisely what makes many people with disabilities feel hated and anxious about the meaning of campaigns to prevent congenital anomalies. This
advertising slogan exposed the dislike of people with disabilities, the fear of
them, and the comfort with eugenic thinking among some promoters of immunization.

These advertisements and public health materials used children with
disabilities to simultaneously market a new medical practice and sell a new
medical product. Although not intended to teach the public about disabilities, these representations nonetheless were one source of popular "knowledge" about people with disabilities. All of these photographic representations used what disabilities scholar Rosemarie Garland Thomson calls the
predominant "sentimental mode," which taught benevolent pity and encouraged both sympathy (for people with disabilities) and consumption (of
vaccine, in this case). As disability activists and scholars have shown, the
use of "poster children" and telethons by voluntary health organizations
constructed disabled people as pitiful and dependent victims.[79] The German measles vaccination campaign used the bodies of disabled children to
convince parents and children to accept shots. As these pictures pushed
vaccination forward, they also represented disability as hopeless. The
threat of polio had been represented in educational materials and advertising campaigns through wheelchairs and braces; rubella's threat was represented through heavy glasses and hearing aids. Parents' greatest fear for
their future children—mental retardation—was not easily depicted. Because of the association of blindness and deafness with retardation, however, these children may well have been read as retarded. None of these
materials questioned the social circumstances that made vision or hearing
loss socially damaging. Nor did they suggest that the world in which the
children lived might be remade to incorporate them all. A fundamental rethinking about disabilities and about the need to make society hospitable to

all of its members was an emerging vision among parent organizations and people with disabilities, but public awareness of disability rights movements was in the future.

The children photographed with their headphones and glasses were also performing a civic health duty whether they knew it or not. Through their parents and teachers, they urged other children and other parents to accept rubella vaccination. At the same time, they performed the function of demonstrating their capacities and their ability to participate in the "normal" world. As in the earlier efforts against polio and measles, disabled children and their parents joined in the rubella vaccine campaign as responsible citizens. Deaf and vision-impaired children provided the tragic representations that encouraged immunization in order to avoid similar tragedies. Rubella children, as they were called, also appeared in a ten-minute film, *The Case Against Rubella,* which "vividly and alarmingly portrayed" the effects of rubella during pregnancy. In offering free copies of the film for viewing, pharmaceutical company Smith Kline and French Laboratories educated the public about disabilities and about the need for the vaccine in order to avoid them. The National Association for Retarded Children (NARC) advertised the film.[80]

Indeed, several of the disability organizations of the period—composed of parents, teachers, and other advocates for the disabled—supported research and immunization against rubella. As NARC explained in 1959, it supported research for the "elimination of the causes of mental retardation in children yet unborn."[81] The organization had supported research into PKU and universal testing as well as research and promotion of the vaccine to eliminate measles, which also caused mental retardation in some children.[82] The Easter Seal Society, NARC, and the Kennedy Foundation all joined in planning for and promoting rubella vaccination.[83] As a militant disabilities rights movement led by people with disabilities themselves developed, it criticized these earlier organizations for focusing on prevention and for perpetuating pitying attitudes toward people with disabilities. More militant adult self-advocates who sought social transformations and protested in their wheelchairs en masse, however, were just beginning to make their own demands at the University of California at Berkeley.[84] The earlier voluntary organizations and parents had contributed funds, helped organize mass immunizations, and loaned their children both to scientific research and to publicity campaigns against the disease.

In fact, a group of retarded children and teens in Arkansas had served as the first research subjects in NIH vaccine trials in 1965. The National

Association for Retarded Children had applauded this collaborative effort. After receiving letters explaining the proposed clinical trials, many parents granted permission for their children to be given the rubella vaccine in order to test whether the vaccine produced immunity and whether the inoculation made them contagious to others. The Arkansas Children's Colony at Conway offered a "perfect environment for closely controlled clinical trials of the vaccine" because children lived in separate cottages and could continue their normal daily routine while being completely isolated from others. In the study's first phase, NIH scientists Drs. Harry M. Meyer Jr. and Paul D. Parkman began with a group of sixteen girls, eight inoculated and eight serving as controls, and showed—after intensive tracking through physical exams, throat cultures, and blood tests over seven weeks—that the eight who had received the vaccine developed immunity to the disease and that none of the others had caught the virus. In the next phase, twenty-six children were vaccinated, and twenty-two were not. To test the vaccine and determine whether the virus could spread to the unvaccinated controls, the group played and "had a ball" together. Scientific research in this report read as a social benefit for its subjects. Again, those who had received shots gained immunity, and those who had not received shots did not catch the disease from their inoculated peers. The tests demonstrated that the vaccine did not produce the disease in nonimmune subjects. The scientists and colony staff were pleased with the collaboration. "The manner in which this project was designed and performed, with completely informed parental consent," Dr. Theodore Panos of the University of Arkansas Medical School observed, "may become a model for other scientists conducting clinical trials."[85] No doubt this assertion was carefully included in the wake of the recent exposé by Dr. Henry Beecher of the commonplace abuse of experimental subjects.[86]

This lengthy and proud report appeared in NARC's journal, *Children Limited*.[87] NARC encouraged this type of research at residential institutions, reported that Meyer and Parkman had received the United Cerebral Palsy–Max Weinstein Award, and supported the nationwide rubella vaccination campaign.[88] The CDC commended NARC's support of the vaccination campaign. At least one parent, however, objected to the emphasis on prevention of retardation. Although it was "laudable," he felt that research on prevention should be left to the March of Dimes. Parents of the retarded should be concerned with the "children who are already here."[89]

Using institutionalized and intellectually impaired children as research subjects had a long tradition in vaccine research. Hospitals and schools had helped eighteenth- and nineteenth-century physicians see diseases through autopsies and in live individuals. Similarly, twentieth-century scientists regarded these institutions as ideal research sites for biomedical experimentation with human subjects. Institutionalized populations served as a resource for science. Institutions offered a group of people isolated from the larger public, people whose lives followed highly structured routines and who could be monitored constantly during the testing of a new vaccine. Scientists tested influenza, measles, and polio vaccines on institutionalized children, many of them disabled physically and/or intellectually. Individual researchers may not have consciously found it more acceptable to risk the health or lives of the intellectually or physically disabled. Nonetheless, in using these particular populations who could not consent because they were institutionalized and/or unable to comprehend the risk of experimentation, researchers clearly assumed that their lives were of lesser value. Others believed that as dependents and recipients of assistance and service, this group owed society something in return and proved themselves socially useful by serving as research subjects. Although scientists looked automatically to these institutions for subjects and the institutions themselves welcomed research, funding organizations, other scientists, legal authorities, or outraged citizens periodically challenged experimental research.[90] Beecher's 1966 report on "Ethics and Clinical Research" exposed commonplace experimental practices that placed people at risk and that took advantage of vulnerable people, including children and mentally retarded people who could not consent. In response to congressional and public outrage about these and other incidents, the federal government instituted new controls and required institutional ethical reviews of human subject research.[91]

## THE EDUCATION OF "RUBELLA CHILDREN"

As the production of a vaccine and planning for its mass distribution moved forward, the problem of poor planning and limited educational opportunities for the children born as a result of the early 1960s epidemic became apparent. German measles mobilized parents to act collectively. As fathers, mothers, and citizens, they fought to secure a basic expectation of the state's responsibility to American children: the right to schooling. Rubella Parents of California, formed in 1967, sought, as did other groups of parents of disabled children, better medical and educational services for their own children and others like them.[92] German measles presented a unique problem, however, because the children did not all have the same disability and often had multiple disabilities. As a result, they did not flow easily into preexisting programs. Based in Los Angeles, Rubella Parents of California identified 140 "multi-handicapped" children in the Los Angeles area but knew there were more. The group hoped to alert other parents of potential health problems, identify children, and win state programs for children with multiple disabilities. Parents, physicians, and educators all realized that rubella children varied and did not fit into the preexisting programs designed to serve children with one type of disability, such as the deaf, blind, or retarded. Dr. Edgar Lowell, administrator of the John Tracy Clinic for deaf children, reported that parents had pressed the clinic to accept multihandicapped children and, being "soft-hearted," administrators had done so. He worried, however, that the children were not getting what they needed. "If multi-handicapped children are bounced from one place to another," Dr. Lowell warned, "there will be a great tendency for them to end up in one of our custodial facilities. . . . Inevitably [they] will develop emotional problems."[93]

German measles had exposed the limitations of the school system as well as the limitations of an educational system that segregated teacher training and disabled people by type. Teachers of blind children knew that they did not know how to teach deaf-blind children.[94] The California School for the Deaf in Berkeley had experience educating children who were both deaf and blind, but it accepted only a few students out of the many who needed school programs. A San Francisco Preschool Program for Hearing Handicapped Children, which usually had twelve to fifteen children, had more than one hundred children in 1967.[95] The school system could see the unusually large group of blind, deaf, and multihandicapped children coming and knew that the number of existing spaces in classrooms and the number of teachers were inadequate. Private charities raised money to fund schools and camps; parents privately shouldered the cost of education and privately trained their children at home through correspondence courses. Many could not find any school placements.[96]

"What we are most worried about," explained one mother of Rubella Parents of California, "is the future. We have a law that all children can have an education, and that's all we're asking [for]. We'll take care of the medical."[97] Mothers described their financial situation as "miserable" as they covered the costs of specialists, physical therapy, hearing aids, ear molds, and babysitters for their other children since they had to drive hours across town to take their handicapped children to special programs.

Education, however, more than money, was the foremost worry of parents. They worried that the state would not provide programs and that in the midst of state budget cutting under Governor Ronald Reagan, their children—who needed intensive educational programs and one-on-one teaching—would lose out. Parents of Rubella Children shared their lives and children with reporters in an effort to secure state educational funding. One doctor had seen Christina Robles as a "little vegetable" and had advised her parents to institutionalize her, Camelia Robles recalled, but now, a few years later, he could see a personality. Her daughter had been hospitalized eighteen times and was getting physical therapy.[98] At the same time that college students in wheelchairs were challenging the University of California to make college education and the university campus physically accessible to them, the parents of young disabled children fought for their public preschool and elementary school education.[99]

Parents and teachers pushed for local, state, and federal funding to educate teachers of deaf and blind students and for regional deaf-blind centers to provide specialized services. After eight years of work in Congress, President Lyndon B. Johnson—previously recognized for his support for education of Deaf and disabled children—had signed a funding bill in 1968. However, coverage remained insufficient; school officials from east to west worried about young children who would soon be entering school districts that lacked special education programs. "The response," Congressman Roman C. Pucinski of Illinois declared, "has been callously inadequate." Fewer than one-third of the affected children had access to special education, and fewer than half of the school districts even offered any special education programs. One federal official estimated that only 100 of 1,600 children who were both deaf and blind—fewer than 10 percent— were in the right types of educational programs. The number of children born of the rubella epidemic and about to enter school would soon make the squeeze worse. Enrollments in schools for the deaf were doubling, schools were crowded, and waiting lists were long. There were neither enough schools nor enough teachers.[100]

Even as Congress voted to support educational and medical services for the deaf and disabled children of rubella, the funds appropriated could not be sufficient. Congress appropriated $1 million for preschool education and $1 million for centers for deaf-blind children up to age twenty-one. Care and education cost $9,000 to $13,000 per year for each child. Experts estimated that costs for providing for all of the children harmed in the mid-1960s epidemic would approach $2.8 billion. "If the children were to miss out on this special care and become custodial or welfare cases for the rest of their lives," observed one educator, "the cost would triple."[101]

The German measles epidemic had produced a unique baby boom and, like the larger and well-known baby boom, it made itself heard. It also had produced a cohort of parents who—as they discovered their children's needs, the lack of services, inequity, and discrimination—became a force to be reckoned with. Parents made phone calls and demands; school principals avoided them; parents brought lawsuits or threatened to do so. In recounting the "hassles" of obtaining educational services for her son, one mother wrote, "For many years now I have felt that I was making more enemies than friends; everyone in education hated to hear our name."[102] But she and many other parents persisted on behalf of their children. Through their individual and organized efforts, the German measles epidemic contributed to pushing forward the major federal policy initiatives that emerged in the 1970s to improve the services for and rights of the disabled. The epidemic had produced a cohort of children and parents who first overwhelmed the existing meager system for caring for and teaching disabled children and then collectively demanded more from the state. The dramatic increase in the number of multiply handicapped children whose parents sought help rearing and educating them produced pressures on underfunded and unprepared schools.

That pressure created an opportunity: the need was obvious, and the ones seeking help deserving. German measles again energized law making as parents, mothers in particular, pushed schools to educate their children. *Deserving* is a key requirement in the American social welfare system.[103] That these children and their parents could be seen as deserving, good, and innocent people who had done nothing immoral or irresponsible to bring on their conditions helped the movement of parents and professionals win services and rights. The fact that this disease cut across social categories also helped create an image of the deserving. The disease and its effects were not confined to the destitute or to people of color. Instead, many of these children came from white middle-class families—families presumed to be trustworthy and able to frame their demands in acceptable middle-class terms. The activist parents of disabled children focused on education—a core middle-class value as well as a primary focus of black and Latino civil rights organizing in the 1950s and 1960s.

In the early 1970s, children born with congenital rubella syndrome, along with other disabled children, won major educational victories, and the campaign for mass vaccination to protect "unborn babies" from the dangers of rubella succeeded as well. Parents of rubella children joined with other parents, advocates, and disabled people to win federal legislation and the passage of the Education for All Handicapped Children Act of 1974 (now IDEA), which recognized the rights of people with disabilities to public education.[104] By the spring of 1972, 75 percent of all schoolchildren and more than half of all children between one and four years old had been immunized against rubella. This rate of immunization, the U.S. Public Health Service reported, "represent[ed] the highest level of protection ever achieved so quickly after licensure of a new vaccine."[105] Despite the funding failures and worries about poor populations, this vaccine had the greatest and quickest success ever.

Immunization not to protect one's own health but solely to protect others was an entirely new idea. This transformation in the purpose of vaccination and the national push for rubella immunization on a mass scale provoked little commentary or objection, however. The long history of hostility toward vaccination makes this outcome surprising. Furthermore, the state had passed a series of laws in the 1960s making vaccination mandatory when children entered school. Yet these too went practically unnoticed. Although several individuals brought lawsuits against these statutes, the suits neither overturned the laws mandating immunization nor produced a movement.[106] Considering the history of resistance to compulsory vaccination and to state intervention in parents' rights, one might have expected similarly strong resistance to this unprecedented program. Instead, masses of children received their immunizations at a very quick pace. That phenomenon has to be explained.

First, by 1970 vaccination had become routinized and bureaucratized at children's medical checkups and in school. A vaccination habit and the habit of child examination both developed over the twentieth century and accelerated in the 1950s and 1960s, thanks to expanded insurance coverage and American enthusiasm for the polio vaccine. Free and inexpensive vaccination clinics that were aimed at those who might otherwise skip immunization also helped. Neither laws nor routines nor free shots alone, however, were responsible for the massive uptake of rubella vaccination, something that had not occurred with the measles vaccine.

Parents and children had to believe in the need for this vaccine and accept their new responsibility for future children. Convincing children and their mothers to vaccinate for the health and protection of other, potential future babies took a great deal of real labor and cultural work. Health materials intended to be simple and persuasive contained historical echoes and a multiplicity of messages. Pamphlets, comic books, popular media, and films recalled other dread diseases and tragedies, told of gendered danger and responsibility, and simultaneously taught that disability meant disaster. Educational materials did not attempt to represent an accurate picture of the lives of people with disabilities presented from their own perspectives. Although the vaccination campaign did not challenge reigning ideas about disabilities—in fact, it reinforced them—it did remake gender expectations about boyhood and responsibility for future reproduction. The publicity materials that targeted mothers and children across gender, race, and class lines also appealed to their altruism and civic duty as they explained the need for the vaccine in order to protect other children. In the 1970s, masses of children and parents embraced immunization against rubella as a familial, gendered, public health, and civic responsibility.

Abortion had been vividly connected with German measles for years in public and private thinking through medicine, popular media, and politics. Abortion decriminalization and the rubella vaccine occurred simultaneously and were related, but there was public silence about that connection. The rubella immunization campaign did not need to make any explicit links to abortion to remind (potential) parents that it was part of the danger of German measles during pregnancy. Nor did pharmaceutical companies remind the public of the damages of thalidomide—the images of birth defects and tragedy most vivid in the media and in the minds of many women and men. The vaccination campaign could rely on implicit arguments for the need to eliminate German measles without explicitly naming abortion or the prominent "tragedy" of thalidomide. Furthermore, rubella vaccine advertising was another thread in the pharmaceutical industry's work to teach the American public of the virtues and benefits brought to them by the pharmaceutical industry.[107] Indeed, the success of the German measles vaccine redeemed the very industry that had created the thalidomide disaster. The immunization campaign focused on reminding parents of the dangers to babies and children, representing the sadness and difficulty of living with disabilities, and teaching parents and children alike of a new civic responsibility.

Most important, this disease uniquely threatened pregnant women and babies, and that truth energized scientific, public health, and personal commitment to this vaccination campaign. The fact that it was the developing fetus, a future imagined child carried by expectant mothers, who would be hurt by German measles surely propelled mothers to bring their sons and daughters in for shots. Many mothers recalled the recent epidemic and remembered polio and thalidomide as well. The threats of crippling disease and disastrous birth defects were real for them. They embraced the vaccine. In so doing, they sought to protect a class of women like themselves—expectant mothers, mothers, and women who would become pregnant and wanted healthy babies. They acted to protect their own children as future parents, their own future grandchildren, and children in general. Through vaccination, they hoped to help others avoid the hazards of German measles during pregnancy: pregnancy loss, newborn and early childhood deaths, and the disabling and sometimes terribly devastating consequences to children.

In adopting rubella immunization for their children, mothers, parents, and the general public also aimed to protect women and families from the extreme anxiety of knowing what German measles might mean and having to make decisions about the future of a desired pregnancy. Successful mass immunization promised that the terrible worry, the weighing of ambiguous knowledge about the disease's effects, the consideration of abortion, and the pursuit of a therapeutic abortion that could be impossible to obtain could all be eliminated. People would not have to make difficult decisions about whether to accept a pregnancy and a likely future of caring for a disabled child or whether to avoid that future through an abortion. If the disease disappeared, expectant mothers, along with their husbands or partners and families, would not have to ponder whether their pregnancies may have been harmed by this disease; they would not have to think about abortion.

The hope of avoiding both the ambiguity produced by rubella during pregnancy and abortions, the fear of disabilities, the belief in disease prevention, and the commitment of mothers and children to health, future reproduction, and civic responsibility all had made widespread immunization possible. The acceptance of rubella vaccine was a complicated cultural process rooted in history, fear, anxiety, and the hopes and dreams of mothers, in particular. As the consequences and meanings of rubella were forgotten by new generations, the vaccine became known as MMR, and its use became a standard expectation of pediatricians, schools, and health officials. By the 1980s, the rubella vaccine had become simply another required shot rather than a new idea.

# From Anxiety to Rights

GERMAN MEASLES, THE EPIDEMIC, its effects on bodies, the anxieties it provoked, and the victory of a vaccine have all practically been forgotten. Yet the issues and dilemmas, struggles and hopes that arose with German measles and the damage it caused to developing fetuses are still with us, still animating private lives and popular and political cultures. The changes that this disease helped initiate continue to shape laws, medical practices, schools, social services, and social movements. From the time that physicians first understood the teratogenic effects of German measles in the 1940s, they envisioned a vaccine to solve the problems caused by the disease. Scientists quickly produced a vaccine, and its mass distribution in the United States was a singular success. But it neither solved the problems and discrimination faced by people born with CRS or others with disabilities nor eliminated the quandaries of pregnant women who had to consider scientific knowledge about the health of their developing fetuses. A single vaccine, or any other technological fix, could not fix personal dilemmas, discrimination, or social and legal problems.

While some hoped that the rubella vaccine would eliminate the difficulty of weighing frightening and often ambiguous information about a specific pregnancy and dealing with the related question of whether to have an abortion when birth defects were likely, others specifically fought for the legal, moral, and medical right of women to make these difficult decisions. In fighting to make abortion legal and available, they ensured that this type of moral decision-making would continue—but under different conditions. Abortion and reproductive rights activists may not have foreseen that the legality of abortion and the growth of genetic testing, along with large social changes in family and gender in the late twentieth century, would expand this technologized, medicalized decision-making about pregnancy. They did aim, however, to place the information and the decision itself—no matter how difficult or painful and regardless of what decision any individual woman eventually made—firmly into the hands of pregnant women.

## POSSIBLE BIRTH DEFECTS AND ABORTION

The uncomfortable truth is that the fear of disabilities opened up the first respectful public conversation about abortion in the United States that listened to women telling why they believed they needed an abortion. Another truth is that when the women threatened by German measles appeared to be married, middle-class white mothers—the portrait of the respectable woman—it helped to win respectful attention from the media and politicians. It helped too that the perspectives of these trustworthy mothers were backed up, first, by leaders of the medical profession and soon enough by clergymembers as well. Why an abortion appeared essential to so many Americans in the case of German measles is not explained completely by the cultural fear of giving birth to children with physical and intellectual impairments. Expected medical challenges, the imagined future of a disabled child, the impact of a child with special needs on the family as a whole, and finally, the demanding labor required of parents—especially the mother-work required in caring for a child with disabilities—all conditioned individual and popular responses to the possibility of "tragedy."[1] To understand why the thought of a pregnancy that would possibly result in the birth of a "deformed" or disabled child made many women regard abortion as necessary, we must examine not only general attitudes toward the disabled but also the material realities of motherhood and childrearing—and, as men are increasingly deeply and equally involved in parenting, the realities of fatherhood as well.

The rubella vaccine did not eliminate the dilemmas arising out of scientific information about pregnancy nor did it eliminate decision making about carrying pregnancies with known or suspected fetal anomalies. Instead, the dilemmas inherent in making decisions after receiving information about the status of a pregnancy and the associated anxiety, angst, and moral decision-making persisted with the development of new monitoring technologies. As German measles and worry about its consequences disappeared, the number of other situations to consider and instances in which women had to decide multiplied. Indeed, the very availability of amniocentesis and legal abortion in the United States today is part of the legacy of German measles. By the beginning of the twenty-first century, almost all pregnant women in the United States had to make decisions about testing and about the consequences of new scientific knowledge about their fetuses.[2] Whether they were advised to have amniocentesis and whether they did or not, few pregnant women in modern America escaped the push to consider the health status of their pregnancies, the possibility of giving birth to a child with disabling conditions, and the possibility of abortion—however remote—as part of their thinking about pregnancy, childbearing, family making, and motherhood. Even those who lived by strict religious teachings that prohibited abortion could think about carrying a pregnancy to term as a choice and as a decision that was theirs to make.[3]

These potential children and potential abortions raise hard questions for people with disabilities and their families, advocates, and supporters. Yet there is no uniform view regarding abortion among people with disabilities or their political movements.[4] Since Down syndrome is the number one anomaly detected through genetic testing, and 90 percent of those who receive this diagnosis terminate their pregnancies, some parents of children with Down syndrome fear that expanding the use of genetic testing will mean fewer friends and fewer services for their own children. They hope to convince other parents to decide to have a child with Down. To give potential parents receiving this test result a realistic picture of what a future with a child with Down syndrome might look like, parents of children with the condition offer to meet with them. A child with Down syndrome, these families testify, is not as terrifying as might be imagined: they maintain that their children are healthy, communicative, and a pleasure. Parents in this group are not unanimous in their views on abortion; while some oppose amniocentesis and abortion, others pointedly declare that they are "pro-choice."[5] Some parents of children with disabling conditions keenly support genetic research in the hope of preventing those conditions in the future as they simultaneously work to create a better world for people with disabilities. A handful of people bridge the apparent divide between reproductive rights and disability rights, actively supporting both as part of a larger struggle to secure care, respect, individual rights, and social justice for all people.[6]

In the early 1960s, many American women—along with their supporters among husbands, physicians, clergy, lawyers, and others—fought for the right to think about these difficult and heart-wrenching issues and for the recognition of their moral authority to do so. As mothers, as the ones carrying the pregnancy in their bodies and the ones who gave birth to and nurtured their children, women insisted that they had the moral authority and unique responsibility to consider their situation and make these decisions. They insisted upon the right to honest information and the right to safe, legal abortion procedures. They did not seek to avoid the moral dilemmas but instead insisted that those moral dilemmas were theirs to consider and act upon. Rather than allowing others—whether religious mentors, doctors, judicial authorities, counselors, or ethics committees—to make difficult decisions for them, they left these decisions for individual women to face. No matter how well meaning or thoughtful such committees or counselors might sometimes be, many women already knew from their previous experiences with hospital abortion review committees that they could also be arbitrary and cruel.

Allowing legal and safe abortion is a sign of respect for women's morality and judgment and at the same time undergirds women's sexual freedom and their ability to craft their own lives. It is not simply symbolic, however, for the right to abortion—even if never actually used—has real consequences for the lives of women and men. Women realize that motherhood and maternity cannot be forced upon them but are life choices that they may select; girls and boys too learn that their lives are theirs to shape. The right to make these decisions has been labeled "choice," but as reproductive rights activists and the reproductive justice movement built by women of color have pointed out, choice is not enough. Choices might be made, but they are made within constraints. The means to carry out true reproductive choices—the finances needed to rear children, the basics of food and housing, medical care, social and emotional support, child care, and much more—were not guaranteed by winning the legalization of abortion or the right to make a choice.

Nor was the availability of safe abortions within a respectful atmosphere guaranteed. Indeed, the antiabortion movement dedicated itself to creating an atmosphere of disrespect, to ostracizing providers and women who had abortions, and to forcing women and providers to walk through gauntlets of hatred. Terrorist tactics not only terrified people and produced shame, stigma, and silence, but the threat of violence succeeded in reducing women's access to abortion and other reproductive health services. [7]

In the wake of first thalidomide and then German measles in the early 1960s, public health authorities and federal agencies implemented new protocols in order to protect women's developing pregnancies and future children. There was a downside, however, to this heightened awareness of pregnant women's need for protection from environmental hazards. The original demand for protection of "unborn babies" that came from expectant mothers themselves was changed in a new political atmosphere into blaming mothers and treating pregnant women as suspect. As the political and cultural power of the antiabortion movement increased throughout the 1980s and 1990s, it strengthened a culture of distrust and disrespect of pregnant women. That distrust permeated the media, health educational materials, law, medical attitudes, and the thinking of ordinary women and men at the end of the twentieth century.[8]

The shift from assuming that expectant mothers had their children's best interests in mind to regarding them as untrustworthy can be seen in the visual materials that accompanied the German measles story and later campaigns for prenatal care. As *Dangerous Pregnancies* has shown, early 1960s magazine stories on German measles portrayed the agony of white mothers *with* their children. Mother and child were connected, a pair. The mother faced the dilemmas of German measles; she made hard decisions on behalf of herself and her existing and future children. The pamphlets and media promoting the vaccine to the public continued to represent German measles as a family drama and a disease that threatened mothers and their children both physically and in their relationships. A 1970 U.S. government pamphlet on rubella, however, began to move the focus to the fetus alone. It represented the threat of the disease in a stark graphic that showed an arrow bearing down upon its target: a fetus within the outline of a uterus. The mother was no longer there. At most, she was a vessel, a line through which a virus passes and harms the fetus.[9] (See figure 21.)

By the time of a 1986 March of Dimes campaign for prenatal care, the mother herself had become the threat, and the fetus talked to her, warning, "Mommy, don't." This March of Dimes campaign represented the danger as the pregnant woman, the expectant mother herself who needed advice from the talking fetus. In "Mommy . . . don't," the mother-to-be threatens her baby on the way; she cannot be trusted; she needs a talking-to from her own future child. The campaign taught pregnant women of

Figure 21. This red-and-white detailed informational pamphlet was distributed by the U.S. Public Health Service to explain the dangers that rubella posed to a fetus and to promote the new rubella vaccine. U.S. Department of Health, Education, and Welfare, *Rubella,* pamphlet, prepared by Jane S. Lin-Fu (Washington, DC: GPO, 1970).

the dangers of drugs, smoking, and alcohol. Lost was the early-twentieth-century U.S. Children's Bureau's belief in the expectant mother's good sense and its trust in her ability and intention to do what was best for herself, her children, and her family.

Twenty- and thirty-second television spots showed a pregnant woman with pills in her hand; then a "fetal voice" implored, "Mommy, . . . don't." The fetus inside had knowledge and a point of view—it cried out for protection. Pregnant women, the MOD hoped, would get the message. As television audiences of men, women, and children heard this fetal voice warning women,[10] they too learned that pregnant women threatened their babies. If mothers could not be trusted, perhaps it was everyone's responsibility to watch the pregnant woman and warn her against drugs, drinks, and cigarettes. Indeed, in the 1980s bartenders, relatives, and strangers regularly stepped in to supervise visibly pregnant women (and still do today) while ignoring the drinks and cigarettes in the hands of men, whose health was also hurt by these habits. At the start of the twenty-first century, when smokers had become a distinct minority in the United States, new laws banned smoking in public spaces in order to protect the public's health and, most especially, to protect the health of children and fetuses.[11]

The March of Dimes educational videos and printed materials implicated white and black women alike as dangerous, yet the campaign's artwork and its focus on crack cocaine subtly suggested that the most dangerous mothers were black women. "Crack" had a specific and well-understood social identity at the time: the destitute black woman in the city. When the March of Dimes chose to focus its prenatal educational campaign first on the "drug use. . . . epidemic," it reflected President Ronald Reagan's war on drugs and the unprecedented incarceration of women, especially African American women, for illegal drugs.[12] The "Mommy . . . don't" campaign emphasized the danger to "unborn children" of taking both "hard drugs" and unprescribed medication. "Babies," it taught, may "suffer mental retardation, stunted growth, [or] physical or learning disabilities" as a result of a mother's drug use.[13]

Two women talking with drinks in one hand, cigarettes in the other appear on the cover of a related pamphlet. (See figure 22.) Their pregnant bellies protrude. One woman is black; the other, white. The talking fetus interrupts the party in capital letters: "MOMMY, . . . DON'T." White and black women both appear to threaten their babies. Upon opening the folded pamphlet, one sees three photographs of hands depicting the rules that these

Figure 22. The women pictured on the cover of this educational pamphlet have taken care with their lipstick, their nails, and their clothing but are being careless about the developing fetus within. As they drink and smoke, the babies inside cry out, "Mommy . . . don't." Designed to attract attention and to teach, the image belittled women by depicting them as careless and shallow. *Mommy . . . Don't,* pamphlet, 1986–87, folder Mommy . . . Don't Campaign Materials, 1986, box 11, series 13: Perinatal Health, Medical Program Records, March of Dimes Archives. Reprinted with the permission of the March of Dimes Foundation.

"mommies" are breaking, thus harming their own developing fetuses. Two of the three photos are of the black woman's hand; the white woman's hand appears in one. Most prominently displayed—on the top right side of the leaflet—is the command "Don't take drugs" next to a black woman's hand. Her hand pours capsules out of a plastic pill bottle.[14] (See figure 23.) The pamphlet most closely linked black women with illicit drug use. Women of color and their children—Latinas, African Americans, and most prominently, Native Americans—similarly became identified with fetal alcohol syndrome (FAS) in the mid-1980s. FAS, like crack, became racialized and came to be seen as both a result of and a source of crime.[15]

Representations like these erased history. They erased the clamoring of women for information about birth defects and potential dangers to their developing pregnancies, their efforts to protect their own health and that of their babies, and their practice of sharing worries and information with each other, whether over the kitchen table; through the U.S. Children's Bureau, newspaper columns, advice books, or visits to doctors; or by speaking to journalists to warn and protect other women, as Sherri Finkbine had done. Representations that equated black bodies with illegal drug use and belittled all women as potential threats to the babies they carried replaced active women dedicated to protecting their pregnancies. The use of images of pharmaceuticals to send the message that drugs should be avoided harkened back to 1962 and the time of thalidomide, when experts beginning with Dr. Helen Taussig newly taught women *and* doctors that all medicines and pills, both prescribed and over-the-counter medications, should be avoided during pregnancy because of their possible effects on the developing fetus. In its 1986 brochure, the MOD now equated pharmaceuticals taken without a prescription with illegal drugs and advised women to rely upon their doctors. The history of thalidomide, the pharmaceutical companies' inadequate research, the drug's availability over the counter in Europe, and its irresponsible distribution through physicians in Canada and the United States all became invisible in this advice.

As this campaign and many others like it highlighted women's poor behavior as the problem, they neglected and excused the contributions of industrial pollution, environmental toxins, poverty, lack of health insurance and health services, poor nutrition, and discrimination to poor prenatal care, premature births, and high infant mortality. Mainstream American health education materials focused on individuals, teaching them to change their behavior, while failing to teach the public about the value of tax-supported social programs for improving health and mortality. No doubt

When you're pregnant, every drug you take reaches your baby. Some drugs can cause severe birth defects. Cocaine or "crack" use during pregnancy can cause stroke and death of the unborn baby.

You wouldn't give your baby drugs after it is born. Don't take drugs while you're pregnant unless your doctor, who knows you're pregnant, prescribes them.

Don't Take Drugs

MOMMY...DO

Do Get Prenatal Care

There's no puzzle to giving your baby the best chance for health. While you're pregnant:

- Visit your doctor or clinic early and often
- Eat the right foods
- Get plenty of rest and exercise

Figure 23. An African American woman pours prescribed pills into her hand. Prescription medicine—and the black woman who pours it—were here implicitly equated with illegal drugs, cocaine, and the highly stigmatized "crack." This picture appears inside the *Mommy . . . Don't* pamphlet. Pamphlet, 1986–87, folder Mommy . . . Don't Campaign Materials, 1986, box 11, series 13: Perinatal Health, Medical Program Records, March of Dimes Archives. Reprinted with the permission of the March of Dimes Foundation.

the MOD's use of a racially integrated photo depicting an unlikely pair partying together was designed to show that all women needed to hear these messages. The March of Dimes may have been trying to reach black women in particular because infant mortality and prematurity were higher among African Americans (twice as high as the national rate).[16] The information is useful, and the goals of reducing infant mortality and improving child health are good, but health education often blames mothers rather than working to change the other contributors to poor health. Health pamphlets presented as straightforward information, however, have always also been filled with historical and cultural meanings, erasures, and assumptions about race, gender, responsibility, and history.

## CRIMINALIZING PREGNANT WOMEN

Prenatal advice became criminal law for some women. In the 1980s, some innovative doctors and prosecutors forged new ground by reporting and prosecuting women for their behaviors during pregnancy. Pregnant women who used alcohol and illegal drugs have been prosecuted for "delivery" of narcotics to a "child." These laws and prosecutions demand perfection of women *because* of pregnancy. Women themselves expect and try to live to a higher standard of behavior during their pregnancies, but to make that goal into criminal law is to criminalize women. Medical testing of patients is being used as evidence of crime in the legal system. These practices raise serious questions both about the privacy and rights of patients and about the rights of suspects under law. After she gave birth to a stillborn daughter, Regina McKnight of South Carolina was convicted of homicide by child abuse for having used cocaine while pregnant and sentenced to twenty years in prison. In 2004, when Melissa Ann Rowland of Utah refused a recommended cesarean section for her pregnancy of twins and one was stillborn, she was jailed and charged with murder. In 2007–08 in rural Alabama, one prosecutor brought eight cases against women found to have methamphetamine or cocaine in their bloodstreams. New mothers have been handcuffed, forced to leave their newborn babies behind, and made to spend a year in jail. California, Hawaii, Illinois, Maryland, New York, and other states have brought similar cases against pregnant women and new mothers. In 2008, the South Carolina Supreme Court reversed McKnight's conviction after eight years of imprisonment, finding no scientific evidence to support the allegation that cocaine had caused the stillbirth. Furthermore, when addicted (pregnant) women seek programs for help, there are rarely any to be found, and these programs are quickly cut when state budgets fall.[17]

When these types of arrests began, virtually every single one of the women prosecuted were women of color, but that fact is changing. Prosecutors initially targeted crack, and thus black women. As methamphetamine, or "meth," has become the new target of the drug wars, the demographics are changing. This drug's social address is poor, unemployed, rural white America. Low-income, uneducated, rural white women are being prosecuted and imprisoned for meth use during pregnancy.[18] The privileges of whiteness have not engendered sympathy or transformed the political landscape. The prosecution of meth-using pregnant women in Alabama underscores that class matters as much as gender and race.

Miscarriage has also become a marker for treating women as suspects and for police to make arrests just as it was during the century when abortion was a crime in the United States. Abortion law has changed, but the suspicion of pregnant women has been revived in a different form. When abortion was against the law, hospital staff and police automatically regarded women who entered emergency rooms bleeding and scared about miscarriages as suspects and questioned them about illegitimate abortions.[19] Recent laws written in order to restrict abortions by recognizing the fetus as a person have resulted in court-ordered c-sections, arrests, and prosecution of women during childbirth. Women already regarded as irresponsible or dangerous—whether because of poverty, race, drug or alcohol use, or resistance to doctors' recommendations—are most likely to be reported, investigated, arrested, and prosecuted for their pregnancy losses. Several strongly pro-life mothers who were arrested under these new measures to protect the fetus now oppose legislation to restrict abortion because they have learned firsthand that any woman—no matter what her beliefs, intentions, or efforts are—may become a victim of these punitive laws.[20]

The present-day pregnancy loss movement is rooted in very different experiences with and expectations of medicine and the state. The movement not only spotlights and honors the grief felt by many women about their miscarriages, stillbirths, and infertility but also actively challenges and seeks to change the dismissive attitudes of some medical staff and family members to their losses. Some demand that the state issue birth and death certificates for miscarriages and stillbirths to serve as official markers of births, losses, and their own motherhood. Members of this largely white and middle-class movement do not dream that doctors might turn them over to police or consider that they might be prosecuted in the event of a miscarriage or stillbirth.[21] However, this result is precisely what has happened to some women who have violated medical orders and social norms. For them, the unfortunate outcome of a miscarriage or stillbirth is not termed a *loss* or *perinatal death* but is renamed *manslaughter* or *homicide*. A miscarriage or stillbirth in this punitive system becomes murder, and mothers become murderers.

All of these prosecutions are predicated on the assumption that women need to be told, ordered, and even physically forced, if need be, to protect the health of the pregnancies they carry and need to be punished if they do not follow advice. Health advisories become medical orders become laws in this formulation; if a medical advisory is broken, then—in the eyes of some medical and state authorities—pregnant women deserve to be punished. The idea that pregnant women are uninterested in their own health and in the health of their developing fetuses and future children is wrongheaded. The only reason that prenatal advice could have been produced, disseminated, read, listened to, watched, and put into practice in the past (and in the present) is that expectant mothers have for centuries shown themselves to be eager for information and advice, willing to listen, and wanting and working to do their best for their children. Women have brought themselves to midwives and doctors for exams, have shared information about their bodies and their suspicions, and have done what they could to protect their pregnancies. Without an active, intellectually engaged, invested, and willing audience of expectant mothers, none of these health education materials would have had any effect. Instead, women ardently seek out knowledge and best practices. Perhaps as a result of the eager interest expressed by most women and their willingness to change their behavior, women receive a great deal of health advice. The desire for advice and the production of it then reinforce the messages; women learn from their mothers, sisters, and friends that they need to seek out and pay attention to health education and most especially to information and advice about reproduction.

The habit of prioritizing, observing, and caring for the bodies and health of the children around them and their own pregnancies has been instilled in and embraced by women throughout the twentieth and early twenty-first centuries and much earlier. Indeed, that commitment made by women—as mothers and as caretakers for the health of children, family, and community—has produced new science and new discoveries. This gendered awareness of and dedication to the health and needs of babies and children are often popularly labeled "maternal instinct," as though they are biological imperatives that come naturally to girls and women. In truth, gendered awareness and skills are knowledge that is produced, shared, handed down across generations, cultivated, taught, encouraged, applauded, and embraced. This gendered awareness of and dedication to child health are experienced by women and girls as a duty, as responsibility, as expertise, and as love. They may be all of those things. They are also deeply embedded in female gender identity.

The historical protectors of the unborn have always been the expectant women who worried about what to eat and what to avoid; who followed advice about rest, medicine, food, and medical exams; and who sought information, tests, and abortions. They also include the women who tried to protect each other from German measles by disinfecting voting booths and by vaccinating their children, and the women who collectively created and participated in movements for maternal and child health, reproductive justice, child education, and disability rights. The concerns, the observations, the commitment, the ideas, and the work of women to convince other women to follow good health practices on behalf of their future children as well as the knowledge, the science, and the voluntary and government programs activated out of mothers' anxieties, expectations, demands, and observations are too easily not only forgotten but also misrepresented.

## THE RUBELLA VACCINE

In 1970, the United States focused on vaccinating children to combat the damaging effects of rubella during pregnancy, but by the middle of the decade, it had become clear that herd immunity and targeting children were inadequate measures. As had been true historically, German measles continued to break out among military men and spread to others.[22] Within only a few years of the vaccine's introduction, health officials had targeted susceptible adult women and the traditional places where epidemics developed—among soldiers and college students—for immunization.[23] That combination brought results. After falling from the estimated 20,000 children born with CRS in the United States as a result of the mid-1960s epidemic to about 106 CRS cases per year in the 1970s, the number dropped to 20 per year in the 1980s. When German measles epidemics broke out among unimmunized immigrants, U.S. health authorities stepped up their immunization efforts.[24] Cuba announced first its success in eliminating the disease in the 1990s. The fact that this economically poor island nation achieved elimination of rubella first indicates that elimination of disease is not a product of wealth or superpower status alone but rather requires commitment and an effective public health infrastructure. In 2005, the Centers for Disease Control "celebrated" the elimination of rubella in the United States.[25]

As fear of the disease's effects faded from personal and public memory, new fears arose. In the 1980s, some critics argued that the MMR (combined measles, mumps, and rubella) vaccine caused autism, and frightened parents began asking more questions and avoiding this and other vaccines. Ironically, the very vaccine embraced by mothers in 1970 in order to protect their children from disabilities is now feared by some as the cause of another frightening disabling condition. Like earlier parents who had faced German measles, these twenty-first-century parents feared a condition that could be severely intellectually disabling, was highly stigmatized, and could be highly disruptive for the entire family. Autism requires intensive intervention from a very young age; social and educational support both at home and through outside services; parental work with schools that may be ill-prepared to teach these children; and coping with misunderstanding, discrimination, and rejection by schools, neighbors, relatives, and friends. This intense work tends to fall most heavily on mothers.[26] As in the past, many parents of children with autism and other cognitive and physical disabilities devote themselves to obtaining the best information, medical care, therapy, and education possible for their children. Parents and guardians of children with autism and other disabilities today can seek 504 plans and IEPs (individual educational plans) for their children and insist that schools make accommodations to ensure that their children learn.[27] These forms and plans are the concrete objects and methods by which parents implement and insist on the right to public education for their children with disabilities. This right was won in the 1970s and 1980s by people with disabilities and their advocates, including the parents of children born with congenital rubella syndrome. Today's parents of children with disabilities are the beneficiaries of previous struggles. They also continue the fight, for the right to education is only made in practice and through regular consultation and intervention in the school system.[28]

At the turn of the twenty-first century, a small but highly publicized segment of the population resisted immunization in order to protect their own children from suspected dangers.[29] Parents who avoided MMR included educated families who had researched the issues and doubted both orthodox medicine and the government. Despite the visibility of the challenge to vaccines in the media and the corresponding anxiety of health authorities, immunization rates in the United States are high. More than 93 percent of children under three years old have been vaccinated against rubella, and in

2008 the CDC reported that approximately 90 percent of infants and toddlers had had five of the six vaccines.[30] The routines of checkups and immunization, along with better provision of child health care, doctors' confidence in vaccines, and mandatory vaccine requirements for school, had won out over doubt.

Commitment to public health as a civic responsibility for the health of the entire public—an important part of the platform upon which rubella immunization was built—is less visible in public conversations about vaccines, however. Vaccine critics come from across the political spectrum, yet the turn to individualized considerations parallels the transformation of the political culture and the decline of the welfare state.[31] At the same time, ensuring the safety of children and adults requires extensive research and careful regulation of pharmaceuticals, both of which require active federal involvement and oversight of industry and medical practices.

### PEOPLE WITH CRS

Although immunization is now nearly universal in the United States, neither rubella nor rubella babies have disappeared. Rubella is endemic in poor and underprivileged parts of the world, particularly in South Asia and Africa; babies with CRS are still occasionally born in the United States;[32] and the disease continues to haunt former "rubella babies" in unforeseen ways as they reach middle age. Congenital rubella, researchers have found, has late-appearing and long-term effects. Infants first diagnosed as normal at birth despite their mothers having contracted rubella during pregnancy have shown evidence of rubella infection several years later.[33] Glaucoma, late-developing deafness, diabetes, gastrointestinal problems, hormone imbalances, and early menopause have all been found among people with CRS. On the social front, however, studies of some of the original children identified by Gregg in the 1940s found that they had done better than predicted by Gregg and early researchers. Most had jobs, relationships, and families.[34]

Dr. Lewis Cooper found a more worrisome record when he followed up on young adults born with CRS after the early-1960s epidemic in the United States. "About one-third," Cooper reported, were "leading relatively normal lives, a third still live with their parents, and . . . the remaining third are profoundly handicapped and require institutional care." Many had trouble with social skills. In addition, the hard-won system for funding and providing educational, training, medical, and support services for disabled children had created a later structural problem. As the children with CRS grew up and as adults had to leave the special education programs and the people who had long supported them, they were left in the lurch—sometimes with tragic results. Cooper found that "suicide attempts are not uncommon and most deaths are due to trauma."[35]

The loss of ongoing connections to doctors familiar with the disease had ramifications decades later for people with CRS. Healthy, independent Deaf adults in their forties developed glaucoma. Neither they nor their current optometrists and doctors realized that these were late-appearing effects of the CRS they had been born with. Some now describe these late-appearing effects as *post-rubella syndrome* (PRS). Like *post-polio-syndrome* (PPS), only recently identified by aging former polio patients who discovered their collective experience of muscle weakness, pain, fatigue, and respiratory problems, PRS is now being identified as a condition affecting the generation of rubella babies born in the 1950s and 1960s and now reaching middle age. Realizing that a disease from infancy might later disable them in an entirely new way has devastated CRS survivors. Former "rubella babies" may now be developing a collective identity that emerges around their shared medical history of rubella as well as around their shared experiences as people with a range of disabilities.[36]

Advertisements for the new rubella vaccine in 1970 had represented "rubella children" with CRS as pathetic and strange, a tragedy to be avoided; forty years later the affected child was now pictured as a man, a citizen, and a worker. "Help fight the 1964 rubella epidemic," a blue-and-white poster urges. A plastic employee photo-ID tag appears as though clipped to the slogan. Here is a new picture of a person born with CRS: Stephen Wenzler. The poster informs that he is "one of the thousands of Americans . . . left deaf and blind" by the 1964 epidemic. Wenzler is clean-cut and wears glasses, a mustache, and a sharply pressed dress shirt. He is ready to work. (See figure 24. Compare with figure 20.) Unlike the pharmaceutical advertisements of 1970 that featured the anonymous, pitiful child, this poster features a white man who has a name and is identified as an American citizen. He is not depicted as dependent, strange, or sad but instead as a capable worker. He appears in this educational campaign on behalf of himself and the thousands like him who are "college-educated, independent, and talented individuals highly qualified for the workplace." "Forty years ago the future looked bleak," the poster reminds, but, contrary to expectations, children born of the rubella epidemic have been successful—and desirable—employees.[37]

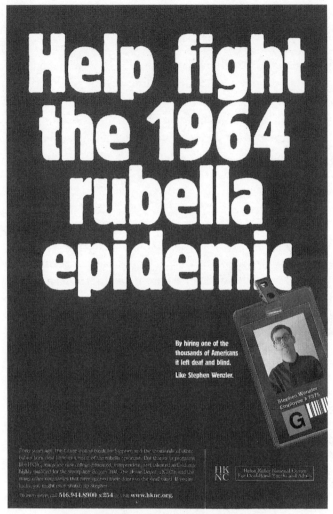

# Help fight the 1964 rubella epidemic

By hiring one of the thousands of Americans it left deaf and blind.

Like Stephen Wenzler.

Forty years ago, the future looked bleak for Stephen and the thousands of other babies born deaf-blind as a result of the rubella epidemic. But thanks to programs like HKNC, many are now college educated, independent, and talented individuals highly qualified for the workplace. So join IBM, The Home Depot, LECO/S, and the many other companies that have opened their doors to the deaf-blind. If you're lucky, you might even snatch up Stephen.

To learn more, call **516.944.8900 x254** or visit **www.hknc.org**.

HK NC    Helen Keller National Center
For Deaf-Blind Youths and Adults

Helen Keller Deaf-Blind Awareness Week: June 27 to July 3, 2004

Figure 24. This blue-and-white poster reminded people of the rubella (German measles) epidemic of the early 1960s. It portrays a deaf-blind man as an individual, not a victim. The poster announced Helen Keller Deaf-Blind Awareness Week: June 27 to July 3, 2004. Poster produced by the Helen Keller National Center for Deaf-Blind Youths and Adults (HKNC). Reprinted by the permission of the Helen Keller Center for Deaf-Blind Youths and Adults.

Three decades earlier, rubella children had performed a civic service by urging rubella vaccination; this poster reversed the equation by suggesting that employers had a civic duty to hire deaf-blind workers. Disabled men and women deserved the same opportunities and employment that were available to other American citizens. Other major corporations, such as IBM, Home Depot, and PETCO, the poster reports, had already hired them. "If you're lucky, you might even snatch up Stephen," it ends. Although the poster has a heroic undercurrent typical of disabilities representations that seek tolerance, it neither underscores heroic achievement nor evokes pity or surprise at the accomplishments of people with CRS. Nor does it ask for sympathy. Instead, it asks for recognition, equality, and fairness in the job market for citizens, arguing that people like Wenzler are exactly the kind of workers that companies want to hire. They'd be "lucky" to get them. The poster does not demand or point to law, but equal consideration of applications, as employers know, is required under the Americans with Disabilities Act. The Helen Keller National Center for Deaf-Blind Youths and Adults (HKNC), which produced this poster, was founded in 1967 by Congress to serve the educational needs of children handicapped by the German measles epidemic and today continues its work with people with CRS.

German measles energized new meanings of citizenship. Facing the fears and effects of this infectious disease, (potential) mothers—along with fathers, teachers, doctors, scientists, people with disabilities, and other allies—in the 1950s, 1960s, and 1970s mobilized for special schools, social inclusion, and the right to an education for children with disabilities; for legal abortion, informed consent, and patients' rights; and for scientific research and vaccination. They lobbied, petitioned, and testified in state legislatures, courtrooms, and Congress; broke the law and rewrote it; sued school districts and hospitals; volunteered in vaccination clinics; and brought their children to be immunized. In true American style and in keeping with the times, they framed the changes they wanted in the language of rights and turned to the law for equality and change.[38] German measles built upon and contributed to both an expanding welfare state and expanding individual civil rights.

German measles was contagious. More contagious than the disease itself or the anxiety about it, however, was the movement toward collective activism, social responsibility for individuals and communities, and the advancement of both legal rights of individuals and state responsibility for the social welfare of its diverse citizens. The activism that arose around German measles was one instigator among many forces for social change. It drew upon U.S. political culture and changed it. It both contributed to building social movements and drew upon the postwar cultures of parental action and responsibility, the civil rights movements' work for integration and education, and the women's movements' struggles for equality and reproductive rights. Western medical culture identified the problems of German measles and defined several ways to tackle, ameliorate, and prevent them—from surgeries to therapies to blood tests and vaccines. Parents and educators identified and named other problems, won the right to public education, and built institutions. Rubella children themselves grew up, and some entered Deaf schools. As college students at Gallaudet, these "rubella children"—the objects of so much political and cultural activism—became political actors themselves in the late 1980s. As they collectively demanded respect, autonomy, and rights as part of a Deaf community and energized the disability rights movement,[39] they created yet another facet in the history of political mobilization associated with German measles.

In another time or place, German measles could have produced the same physical effects but not the same social and political effects. Bodies might have still displayed rashes and fevers—or they might never have been seen, felt, or noticed; women might have suffered miscarriages and stillbirths; babies might have died; children might have been discovered to be blind, deaf, and intellectually impaired. The meanings given to these events and people would have been different, however, and the social services provided different. The push for a scientific solution; the battles to change law and to create a more just society for all of its members; and the mobilization of parents, professionals, and people born with CRS might never have happened. For rubella's effects to be noticed and acted upon required the preconditions found in Australia, North America, and western Europe at midcentury: low maternal, child, and infant mortality; control of childhood infectious diseases; and the assumption that most children would be born healthy and normal, and would survive. This history of German measles has shown how disease marked bodies and then marked the society. Even more, it shows that it is the culture and people who mark and make meanings of diseases and bodies.

In the early 1960s, at a time when the United States had broken through historic religious and ethnic divides to elect a Catholic president; when African Americans south and north pressed on for freedom, equality, and dignity in a land of segregation, discrimination, and danger; when an embryonic women's movement identified discrimination in education, hiring, and wages, German measles exposed other areas of American life and law that U.S. citizens identified as unfair and in need of change. The demand for changes grew out of the material conditions that they had experienced: the unfairness felt by pregnant women and married couples who had been prevented from making decisions based on their own moral compasses about their procreation, families, and futures; the unfairness felt by doctors not able to act on medical knowledge and advice; the unfairness that a deaf-blind child, a retarded child, a child in a wheelchair, or a child whose behavior did not conform to classroom convention could be abandoned by the public school system; the unfairness and pain of social rejection. The sense that routine and unquestioned policies and practices, behaviors, and remarks were unfair pushed many to insist that things should be different, to join groups and speak collectively as citizens, and to make demands and form coalitions for change. The changes sought initially may look conservative in retrospect, but they broadened in unexpected ways into movements that sought fundamental changes in people's thinking and radical reorganization of society.

German measles had acted as a crucible for change. German measles had inspired fear, and ultimately, it inspired hope that the world could be different. With hope and the ability to imagine how it could be better, people made the United States a different place. What began in fear of dangerous pregnancies and "deformed" children—the demand for legal abortion and the development of a vaccine—ultimately became a source of changes that moved toward greater recognition and respect as well as legal rights in a diverse society of people with different bodies, different dreams and plans, and diverse religions and beliefs. In fear and frustration, and with hope and imagination, people turned this disease into a source of personal insight, social movements, and change. The changes that were made are incomplete, as projects for equality and justice must always be. The United States today continues to grapple with the questions that arose and to live with the benefits and quandaries made out of this epidemic of anxiety.

# NOTES

1. National Foundation–March of Dimes estimate made in May 1964, "Rubella (German Measles) and Birth Defects," National Foundation, *March of Dimes Science News Backgrounder,* updated May 12, 1965, p. 6, folder Birth Defects and Epidemics, box 3, Series 3 Birth Defects, Medical Program Records, March of Dimes Archives, White Plains, NY.

2. Paula Treichler focuses on the production of language and discourses, in particular in Paula A. Treichler, *How to Have Theory in an Epidemic: Cultural Chronicles of AIDS* (Durham, NC: Duke University Press, 1999). There are many excellent social and cultural histories of disease. See, for example, Allan M. Brandt, *No Magic Bullet: A Social History of Venereal Disease in the United States since 1880* (New York: Oxford University Press, 1987); Judith Walzer Leavitt, *Typhoid Mary: Captive to the Public's Health* (Boston: Beacon Press, 1996); Nayan Shah, *Contagious Divides: Epidemics and Race in San Francisco's Chinatown* (Berkeley: University of California Press, 2001).

3. Stanley A. Plotkin, "Rubella Vaccine," in *Vaccines,* ed. Stanley A. Plotkin and Edward A. Mortimer Jr., 2nd ed. (Philadelphia: W.B. Saunders, 1998), 303–36; Allan Chase, *Magic Shots: A Human and Scientific Account of the Long and Continuing Struggle to Eradicate Infectious Diseases by Vaccination* (New York: William Morrow, 1982); Louis Galambos, with Jane Eliot Sewell, *Networks of Innovation: Vaccine Development at Merck, Sharp & Dohme, and Mulford, 1895–1995* (Cambridge: Cambridge University Press, 1995), 103–21; Harry F. Dowling, *Fighting Infection: Conquests of the Twentieth Century* (Cambridge, MA: Harvard University Press, 1977), 220–21; James Colgrove, *State of Immunity: The*

*Politics of Vaccination in Twentieth-Century America* (Berkeley: University of California Press, 2006), 179–80, 216–17; Joseph P. Shapiro, *No Pity: People with Disabilities Forging a New Civil Rights Movement* (New York: Random House, 1994), 85; Kristin Luker, *Abortion and the Politics of Motherhood* (Berkeley: University of California Press, 1985), 80–81, 86–87, 90; David J. Garrow, *Liberty and Sexuality: The Right to Privacy and the Making of Roe v. Wade* (New York: Macmillan, 1994), 300–307; Leslie J. Reagan, *When Abortion Was a Crime: Women, Medicine, and Law in the United States, 1867–1973* (Berkeley: University of California Press, 1997), 203–4. For German measles as a source of new torts, see Barry R. Furrow et al., *Health Law,* 2nd ed., vol. 2, Practitioner Treatise Series (St. Paul, MN: West Group, 2000), chap. 17, 361–73.

4. Rachel Adams, *Sideshow U.S.A.: Freaks and the American Cultural Imagination* (Chicago: University of Chicago Press, 2001); Susan Burch, *Signs of Resistance: American Deaf Cultural History, 1900 to World War II* (New York: New York University Press, 2002); Lennard Davis, *Enforcing Normalcy: Disability, Deafness, and the Body* (New York: Verso Press, 1995); Robert Buchanan, *Illusions of Equality: Deaf Americans in School and Factory, 1850–1950* (Washington, DC: Gallaudet University Press, 1999); James W. Trent Jr., *Inventing the Feeble Mind: A History of Mental Retardation in the United States* (Berkeley: University of California Press, 1994); Paul K. Longmore, and Lauri Umansky, eds., *The New Disability History: American Perspectives* (New York: New York University Press, 2001); Joseph P. Shapiro, *No Pity: People With Disabilities Forging a New Civil Rights Movement* (New York: Random House, 1994); Catherine J. Kudlick, "Disability History: Why We Need Another 'Other,'" *American Historical Review* 1083 (June 2003): 763–93.

5. My research included *Children Limited* (published by the National Association for Retarded Children), *The Volta Review* (Alexander Graham Bell Association for the Deaf), and *NF News* (published by the National Foundation–March of Dimes) along with other publications by and about organizations of parents and educators of disabled children.

6. For exceptions, see Janice Brockley, "Rearing the Child Who Never Grew: Ideologies of Parenting and Intellectual Disability in American History," in *Mental Retardation in America: A Historical Perspective,* ed. Steven Noll and James W. Trent Jr. (New York: New York University Press, 2004), 130–64; Katherine Castles, "'Nice, Average Americans': Postwar Parents' Groups and the Defense of the Normal Family," ibid., 322–50; Janice A. Brockley, "Martyred Mothers and Merciful Fathers: Exploring Disability and Motherhood in the Lives of Jerome Greenfield and Raymond Repouille," in *The New Disability History,* ed. Longmore and Umansky, chap. 11; Trent, *Inventing the Feeble Mind,* chap. 7.

7. The field of reproductive history is vast and cited throughout this book. For an overview, see Leslie J. Reagan, "Medicine, Law, and the State: The History of Reproduction," *Companion to American Women's History,* ed. Nancy A.

Hewitt (New York: Blackwell Publishers, 2002), 348–65. Important historical scholarship on birth defects and congenital conditions includes Martin S. Pernick, *The Black Stork: Eugenics and the Death of 'Defective' Babies in American Medicine and Motion Pictures Since 1915* (New York: Oxford University Press, 1996); Janet Golden, *Message in a Bottle: The Making of Fetal Alcohol Syndrome* (Cambridge, MA: Harvard University Press, 2005); Janet Golden, "An Argument That Goes Back to the Womb: The Demedicalization of Fetal Alcohol Syndrome, 1973–1992," *Journal of Social History* 33 (1999): 269–98; Molly Ladd-Taylor, "Who is Defective and Who Decides? Minnesota's Feebleminded and the Courts" (paper presented at the annual meeting of the American Association of the History of Medicine, Boston, May 2, 2003; in author's possession); Susan Lindee, *Moments of Truth in Genetic Medicine* (Baltimore: Johns Hopkins University Press, 2005); Keith Wailoo, *Dying in the City of Blues: Sickle Cell Anemia and the Politics of Race and Health* (Chapel Hill: University of North Carolina Press, 2001); Keith Wailoo and Stephen Pemberton, *The Troubled Dream of Genetic Medicine: Ethnicity and Innovation in Tay-Sachs, Cystic Fibrosis, and Sickle Cell Disease* (Baltimore: Johns Hopkins University Press, 2006); Barbara Clow, "An Illness of Nine Months' Duration: Pregnancy and Thalidomide Use in Canada and the United States," in *Women, Health and Nation: Canada and the United States since 1945,* ed. Georgina Feldberg et al., (Montreal: McGill; Kingston, ON: Queen's University Press, 2003), 45–66; Alice Wexler, *Mapping Fate: A Memoir of Family, Risk, and Genetic Research* (Berkeley: University of California Press, 1996); Alice Wexler, *The Woman Who Walked into the Sea: Huntington's and the Making of a Genetic Disease,* with a foreword by Nancy S. Wexler, (New Haven, CT: Yale University Press, 2008).

8. Barbara Katz Rothman, *The Tentative Pregnancy: How Amniocentesis Changes the Experience of Motherhood* (W. W. Norton, 1993); Rayna Rapp, *Testing Women, Testing the Fetus: The Social Impact of Amniocentesis in America* (New York : Routledge, 1999), 3, 130–36, and passim.

9. For a transcript of Dr. George Tiller's speech before the Feminist Majority Foundation, March 9, 2008, see www.democracynow.org/2009/6/3/tiller_speech (accessed June 5, 2009). See also Carole Joffe, "The Legacy of George Tiller," June 4, 2009, www.beaconbroadside.com/broadside/2009/06/carole-joffe-the-legacy-of-george-tiller.html (accessed June 5, 2009).

10. Charles E. Rosenberg, *The Cholera Years: The United States in 1832, 1849, and 1866* (Chicago: University of Chicago Press, 1962).

11. Much of the history of disease reveals this phenomenon. See Howard Markel, *Quarantine! East European Jewish Immigrants and the New York City Epidemics of 1892* (Baltimore: Johns Hopkins University Press, 1997); Alan M. Kraut, *Silent Travelers: Germs, Genes, and the "Immigrant Menace"* (Baltimore: Johns Hopkins University Press, 1995); Leavitt, *Typhoid Mary;* Barron H. Lerner,

*Contagion and Confinement: Controlling Tuberculosis Along the Skid Road* (Baltimore: Johns Hopkins University Press, 1998); Barbara Bates, *Bargaining for Life: A Social History of Tuberculosis, 1876–1938* (Philadelphia: University of Pennsylvania Press, 1992); Tera W. Hunter, *To 'Joy My Freedom: Southern Black Women's Lives and Labors After the Civil War* (Cambridge, MA: Harvard University Press, 1997); Susan M. Reverby, ed. *Tuskegee's Truths: Rethinking the Tuskegee Syphilis Study* (Chapel Hill: University of North Carolina Press, 2000); Elizabeth Fee and Daniel M. Fox, eds., *AIDS: The Burdens of History* (Berkeley: University of California Press, 1988); Treichler, *How to Have Theory in an Epidemic*; Alexandra Minna Stern, *Eugenic Nation: Faults and Frontiers of Better Breeding in Modern America* (Berkeley: University of California Press, 2005), chap. 2; Michelle T. Moran, *Colonizing Leprosy: Imperialism and the Politics of Public Health in the United States* (Chapel Hill: University of North Carolina Press, 2007).

12. A growing number of historians are now investigating the ways in which whiteness has been historically constructed as a race, its political uses, and the advantages that have accrued to people identified as "white." In the post–World War II era, white ethnic working-class families increasingly came to be seen as one race, as "white," and as middle class. The expansion of home ownership and suburbanization was subsidized by the government, and most benefited white families. For examples, see David R. Roediger, *How Race Survived U.S. History: From the American Revolution to the Present* (New York: Verso, 2008); David R. Roediger, *The Wages of Whiteness: Race and the Making of the American Working Class,* rev. and exp. (New York: Verso, 2007); George Lipsitz, *The Possessive Investment in Whiteness: How White People Profit from Identity Politics* (Philadelphia: Temple University Press, 1998); Linda Gordon, *The Great Arizona Orphan Abduction* (Cambridge, MA: Harvard University Press, 2001).

13. Chris Bell, "Introducing White Disability Studies: A Modest Proposal," in *The Disability Studies Reader,* ed. Lennard J. Davis, 2nd ed. (New York: Routledge, 2006), chap. 22.

14. In the 1960s, Dr. Virginia Apgar (medical director of the National Foundation, later named the March of Dimes), lectured and led an effort to educate the public about birth defects and their prevention. By the early 1970s, this advice had become a book. *Is My Baby All Right?* was the title of a popular paperback on pregnancy, prenatal care, and birth defects. See Virginia Apgar and Joan Beck, *Is My Baby All Right?* (New York: Simon and Schuster, 1972). This book provided information about birth defects and included lists of organizations for parents who had discovered that their babies were not "all right," but it was highly advertised to prospective parents so that they could avoid birth defects. See also David B. Pitt, "Congenital Malformations and Maternal Rubella," *Medical Journal of Australia* I: 8 (February 23, 1957): 223.

15. Judith Walzer Leavitt, *Brought to Bed: Childbearing in America, 1750–1950* (New York: Oxford University Press, 1986); Molly Ladd-Taylor, *Mother-Work:*

*Women, Child Welfare, and the State, 1890–1930* (Urbana: University of Illinois Press, 1994); Molly Ladd-Taylor, *Raising a Baby the Government Way: Mothers' Letters to the Children's Bureau, 1915–1932* (New Brunswick, NJ: Rutgers University Press, 1986), 32–60; Michele Mitchell, *Righteous Propagation: African Americans and the Politics of Racial Destiny After Reconstruction* (Chapel Hill: University of North Carolina Press, 2005), chap. 3; Susan L. Smith, *Sick and Tired of Being Sick and Tired: Black Women's Public Health Activism in America, 1890–1950* (Philadelphia: University of Pennsylvania Press, 1995); Richard A. Meckel, *Save the Babies: American Public Health Reform and the Prevention of Infant Mortality* (Baltimore: Johns Hopkins University Press, 1990).

16. Molly Ladd-Taylor reports that *Prenatal Care* (1913) and *Infant Care* (1914) "quickly became best-sellers. Between 1914 and 1921, almost 1,500,000 copies of *Infant Care* were distributed. By 1929, the Children's Bureau estimated that one-half of U.S. babies had benefited from the government's child-rearing information." Ladd-Taylor, *Raising a Baby the Government Way,* 2. On the Children's Bureau, see Ladd-Taylor, *Mother-Work;* Alisa Klaus, *Every Child a Lion: The Origins of Maternal and Infant Health Policy in the United States and France, 1890–1920* (Ithaca, NY: Cornell University Press, 1993).

17. Margaret Sanger, *Motherhood in Bondage* (New York: Brentano's Publishers, 1928); Sarah Stage, *Female Complaints: Lydia Pinkham and the Business of Women's Medicine* (New York: W. W. Norton, 1979); letters to the president may be found in the U.S. Children's Bureau files. For examples of letters to the Children's Bureau, see Ladd-Taylor, *Raising a Baby the Government Way.* On the ways that popular media informed mid-twentieth-century women's letter writing, see Regina G. Kunzel, "Pulp Fictions and Problem Girls: Reading and Rewriting Single Pregnancy in the Postwar United States," *American Historical Review* 100, no. 5 (December 1995): 1465–87.

18. Menominee, WI, to Katharine Lenroot, 19 May 1940, folder 4–5–7–6, box 741, Children's Bureau Records, Central Files, 1914–1940, Record Group 102, National Archives, College Park, MD (hereafter cited as CB). Ethel C. Dunham to Mrs. Norman W. Goercke, 8 June 1940, ibid. For earlier examples, see the letters sent in 1918 and 1921 in Ladd-Taylor, *Raising a Baby the Government Way,* 61–63. Because I want to preserve the style and sense of the original sources and also keep this book readable, I have occasionally silently corrected punctuation and spelling rather than fill quotations with bracketed corrections and insertions.

19. We know that today women in the most industrialized, scientific, technologized nation in the world still worry when they miscarry or find health problems in their children that they somehow caused the problem through their own bad thoughts or actions. These letters offer something like what an anthropologist or sociologist might hear today through participant observation or in focus groups, methods unavailable to the historian. On current belief in maternal

marking among white, Dominican, Chinese, and African American women and men, see Rapp, *Testing Women, Testing the Fetus,* 88–89, 275. Anecdotally, acquaintances have reported feeling that the water or wine they had drunk or strenuous exertion caused a miscarriage or developmental delays in their children.

20. Mrs. R. W. Bennet, Hartford, CT, to Dr. Meigs, 26 February 1916, folder 4–2–1–4–3, box 25, CB.

21. Mrs. W. L. Hester, McCalla, AL, to Children's Bureau, 2 November 1926, folder 4–4–2–3, box 268 (but should be box 270), CB.

22. Viola Russell Anderson, MD, to Mrs. W. L. Hester, 6 November 1926, ibid.

23. Ibid.

24. Ibid. Emphasis added.

25. Leavitt, *Brought to Bed.*

26. Viola Russell Anderson, MD, to Mrs. Clifford Webster, 25 July 1927, folder 4–4–2–2, box 269, CB.

27. Leslie J. Reagan, "From Hazard to Blessing to Tragedy: Representations of Miscarriage in Twentieth-Century America," *Feminist Studies* 29, no. 2 (Summer 2003): 361–62.

28. Mrs. H. Heppel (North Bergen, NJ) to Dear Sirs, 23 February 1928, folder 4–4–2–3, box 268, CB.

29. The last phrase of four quotations was second in the original. Mrs. E. E. Goley, Eckerty, IN, to Sir, 18 June 1918, folder 4–2–1–5, box 25, CB.

30. Anna E. Rude, MD, to Mrs. E. E. Goley, 9 July 1918, folder 4–2–1–5, box 25, CB.

31. Mrs. Clifford Webster, Forestburg, SD, to Florence E. Walker, 13 July 1927, folder 4–4–2–2, box 269, CB; Viola Russell Anderson, MD, to Mrs. Clifford Webster, 25 July 1927, ibid.

32. Mrs. J. H. Atwater, Jamestown, NY, to Miss Lathrop, 27 January 1925, folder 4–4–2–3, box unknown, RG 102; Katherine F. Lenroot to Mrs. J. H. Atwater, 26 January 1925, ibid.

33. Linda Gordon, *Woman's Body, Woman's Right: Birth Control in America,* rev. and updated ed. (New York: Penguin Books, 1999), 63–65, 313–14; Andrea Tone, "Contraceptive Consumers: Gender and the Political Economy of Birth Control in the 1930s," in *Women and Health in America: Historical Readings,* ed. Judith Walzer Leavitt, 2nd ed. (Madison: University of Wisconsin Press, 1999), 306–26.

34. Mrs. L. H. McKenzie of NY to Dr. Meigs, 15 November 1920, folder 4–2–1–2, box 25, CB.

35. Anna E. Rude, MD, to Mrs. L. H. McKenzie, 17 November 1920, folder 4–2–1–2, box 25, CB.

36. Mrs. F. M. Smith, New Haven, CT, to Miss Lathrop, 12 October 1920, folder 4–2–1–5, box 25, CB; Anna E. Rude, MD, to Mrs. F. M. Smith, 14 October 1920, ibid.

37. George J. Benecke to Gentlemen, 23 October 1918, folder 4–2–1–2, box 25, CB.

38. Anna E. Rude, MD, to Mr. George J. Benecke (Brooklyn, NY), 25 October 1918, folder 4–2–1–2, box 25, CB. This adviser did not enter the family and intervene but, like early-twentieth-century social workers, was brought in because of a difference of opinion within a family. In other instances wives or parents called in social workers and agents of the state to try to make their husbands change or to gain control over disobedient children. See Linda Gordon, *Heroes of Their Own Lives: The Politics and History of Family Violence—Boston, 1880–1960* (New York: Viking, 1988); Mary E. Odem, *Delinquent Daughters: Protecting and Policing Adolescent Female Sexuality in the United States, 1885–1920* (Chapel Hill: University of North Carolina Press, 1995).

39. Mrs. W. S. Strong, Watertown, CT, to Miss Julia C. Lathrop, 30 July 1916, folder 4–2–1–5, box 25, CB.

40. Mrs. Max West to Mrs. W. S. Strong, 2 August 1916, ibid.

41. Ibid.

42. Women addicted to alcohol or drugs often try to limit their substance abuse during pregnancy and as mothers. See Cynthia R. Daniels, "Fathers, Mothers, and Fetal Harm: Rethinking Gender Difference and Reproductive Responsibility," in *Fetal Subjects, Feminist Positions,* ed. Lynn M. Morgan and Meredith W. Michaels (Philadelphia: University of Pennsylvania Press, 1999), 93–96; Lynn M. Paltrow and Robert Newman, "Treatment, Not Sterilization," *Houston Chronicle,* January 30, 2000, p. C4, available at http://advocatesforpregnantwomen.org/main/publications/articles (accessed May 17, 2009).

43. Mrs. A. M. Solomon, Ft. Holley, GA, to Chief of the Children's Bureau, 12 June 1915, folder 4–2–1–2, box 25, RG 102.

44. Mary E. Fissell, *Vernacular Bodies: The Politics of Reproduction in Early Modern England* (New York: Oxford University Press, 2004), 207–9; Mary E. Fissell, "Hairy Women and Naked Truths: Gender and the Politics of Knowledge in *Aristotle's Masterpiece," William and Mary Quarterly* 60 (2003): 43–74.

45. Wm. L. Crawford, Long Island, to Better Babies Bureau, 24 April 1919, folder 4–2–1–5, box 25, CB. See Stern, *Eugenic Nation,* on the strength of hereditarian thinking through the twentieth century. On better babies contests among African Americans and maternal and infant health work, see Mitchell, *Righteous Propagation,* 95–100; and Smith, *Sick and Tired of Being Sick and Tired.* On these campaigns in rural areas, see Lynne Curry, *Modern Mothers in the Heartland: Gender, Health and Progress in Illinois, 1900–1930* (Columbus: Ohio State University Press, 1999).

46. Anna E. Rude, MD, to Mr. Wm. L. Crawford, 26 April 1919, folder 4–2–1–5, box 25, CB.

47. Brandt, *No Magic Bullet;* David J. Pivar, *Purity and Hygiene: Women, Prostitution, and the "American Plan," 1900–1930* (Westport, CT: Greenwood

Press, 2002); Mitchell, *Righteous Propagation,* 100–103; Robin E. Jensen, "The Birth of Public Sexual Education in the United States: Women, Rhetoric, and the Progressive Era" (PhD diss., University of Illinois, Urbana-Champaign, 2007), fig. 4 on p. 194, 178–79, 195; Elizabeth Fee, "Sin Versus Science: Venereal Disease in Twentieth-Century Baltimore," in *AIDS,* 124–36; Reverby, *Tuskegee's Truths.*

48. See the World War II films *Pick-Up* and *Personal Hygiene for Women;* prints held at the National Library of Medicine, Washington, DC.

49. Mrs. R. H. Odell, Williamsport, PA, to Julia C. Lathrop, 16 September 1915, folder 4–2–1–2, box 25, CB.

50. Mrs. E. E. Goley, Eckerty, IN, to Sir, 18 June 1918, folder 4–2–1–5, box 25, CB.

51. Anna E. Rude, MD, to Mrs. E. E. Goley, 9 July 1918, folder 4–2–1–5, box 25, CB.

52. Quotation in Viola Russell Anderson to Mrs. G. C. Gibbens, 5 December 1927, folder 4–4–2–2, box 269, CB. Compare with the earlier advice given in MD to Mrs. Odell, 21 September 1915, folder 4–2–1–2, box 25, CB. *Prenatal Care* by Mrs. Max West (U.S. Children's Bureau [Washington, DC: GPO, 1915]) did not discuss sexual intercourse as did later editions and as did bureau advisers in their correspondence. It did discuss miscarriage and other causes, such as "heavy work," exercise, and "imperfect development of the embryo." Discussion of miscarriage on pp. 18–19. Later publications warned of the danger of "marital relations." See, for example, U.S. Children's Bureau, *The Expectant Mother,* (Washington, DC: GPO, 1943), pp. 5–6; and U.S. Children's Bureau, *Prenatal Care,* (Washington, DC: GPO, 1942), p. 15, on avoiding sexual intercourse; on the dangers of heavy lifting, driving cars, and exercise as causes of miscarriage, see *Prenatal Care,* p. 27. The 1962 publication no longer insisted on the importance of avoiding intercourse during the early months and last two months of pregnancy but still considered practicing abstinence good advice. U.S. Children's Bureau, *Prenatal Care* (Washington, DC: GPO, 1962), pp. 6, 54–55.

53. Gordon, *Woman's Body, Woman's Right,* 121–24; Sanger, *Motherhood in Bondage.*

54. Mrs. A. J. Toft, Oakland, CA, to Dr. Lathroppe, 2 March 1920, folder 4–2–1–2, box 25, CB.

55. Anna E. Rude, MD, to Mrs. Grant Swisher, 1 April 1920, folder 4–2–1–2, box 25, CB. Emphasis in original.

56. Molly Ladd-Taylor also saw that "by the end of the 1920s, 'consult a physician' was the almost exclusive recommendation Bureau staff made to the mothers who wrote them." Ladd-Taylor, *Raising a Baby the Government Way,* 23. On the Sheppard-Towner Act, see Ladd-Taylor, *Mother-Work;* J. Stanley Lemons, *The Woman Citizen: Social Feminism in the 1920s* (Urbana: University of Illinois Press, 1973).

57. See Allan M. Brandt, *No Magic Bullet: A Social History of Venereal Disease in the United States Since 1880,* expanded ed. (New York: Oxford University Press, 1987), 148–50.

58. There is a large literature on the expectations of motherhood, maternalism, and welfare among different populations and on how ideas and policies were created and made into official requirements. This note provides a sampling. On the imperative that mothers specifically and consciously protect the health and ensure the survival of their children, see Nancy Schrom Dye and Daniel Blake Smith, "Mother Love and Infant Death, 1750–1920," *Journal of American History* 73 (September 1986): 329–53; Ladd-Taylor, *Raising a Baby the Government Way,* chap. 2; Ladd-Taylor, *Mother-Work*; Emily K. Abel, *Hearts of Wisdom: American Women Caring for Kin, 1850–1940* (Cambridge, MA: Harvard University Press, 2000); Mitchell, *Righteous Propagation,* chaps. 3 and 8; Rima D. Apple, *Mothers and Medicine: A Social History of Infant Feeding, 1890–1950* (Madison: University of Wisconsin Press, 1987); Rima D. Apple, *Perfect Motherhood: Science and Childrearing in America* (New Brunswick, NJ: Rutgers University Press, 2006); Leslie J. Reagan, "Engendering the Dread Disease: Women, Men, and Cancer," *American Journal of Public Health* 87, no. 11 (November 1997): 1779–87; Smith, *Sick and Tired of Being Sick and Tired*; Linda Gordon, *Pitied But Not Entitled: Single Mothers and the History of Welfare, 1890–1935* (New York: Free Press, 1994); Jacqueline H. Wolf, *Don't Kill Your Baby: Public Health and the Decline of Breastfeeding in the Nineteenth and Twentieth Centuries* (Columbus: Ohio State University Press, 2001); Ellen Ross, *Love and Toil: Motherhood in Outcast London, 1870–1918* (New York: Oxford University Press, 1993); Jane Lewis, *The Politics of Motherhood: Child and Maternal Welfare in England, 1900–1939* (London: Croom Helm, 1980); Curry, *Modern Mothers in the Heartland.*

59. Dr. Steven Cochi, Acting Director, CDC National Immunization Program, "CDC Announces Rubella, Once a Major Cause of Birth Defects, Is No Longer a Health Threat in the U.S.," *Telebriefing Transcript* (March 21, 2005), www.cdc.gov/od/oc/media/transcripts/t050321.htm (accessed June 13, 2009).

60. *TORCH* refers to a set of teratogens: Toxoplasmosis (from cat feces); Other (measles, syphilis, and more); Rubella; Cytomegalovirus; and Herpes simplex (genital herpes). www.medicineonline.com/articles/t/2/TORCH-Infections.html (accessed November 20, 2008); Vandana Mehta, C. Balachandran, and Vrushali Lonikar, "Blueberry Muffin Baby: A Pictorial Differential Diagnosis," *Dermatology Online Journal* 14, no. 2 (2008), http://dermatology.cdlib.org/142/case_reports/blueberry/mehta.html (accessed October 28, 2008); Agatha Christie, *The Mirror Crack'd from Side to Side* (New York: HarperCollins, 2002), first published in Great Britain by Collins, 1962.

61. I am grateful to Dr. Lewis Leavitt for sharing this insight.

62. Mrs. Robert Bliss, Cleveland, OH, to Miss Lathrop, 2 September 1920, folder 4–2–1–2, box 25, CB.

1. See Michel Foucault, *The Birth of the Clinic: An Archaeology of Medical Perception* (1963; trans. 1973; repr., New York: Random House, 1994), and Barbara Duden, *The Woman Beneath the Skin: A Doctor's Patients in Eighteenth-Century Germany,* trans. Thomas Dunlap (Cambridge, MA: Harvard University Press, 1991).

2. In her excellent book, Susan Lindee makes a similar argument about scientific knowledge as a "community project" and shows how "folk or social knowledge" is part of genetics specifically. As she remarks, "biomedical knowledge more generally expresses community knowledge in ways we have barely considered in our theorizing in science studies." In *Moments of Truth in Genetic Medicine* (Baltimore: Johns Hopkins University Press, 2005), 3, 4, 6. This community knowledge is also shaped by gender, race, class, family, and histories.

3. Henry Veale, "History of an Epidemic of Rotheln, with Observations on Its Pathology," *Edinburgh Medical Journal* 12 (November 1866): 404–14.

4. Ibid.; William Squire, "Remarks on Epidemic Roseola; Rosella, Rosalia, or Rubeola," *British Medical Journal* 1 (January 29, 1870): 99–100. For consistency, the spelling of *rotheln* is used in the text. Variant spellings of the disease have been retained in quotations and references.

5. T. Morley Rooke, "Clinical Memoranda. The Diagnosis of Rotheln," *British Medical Journal* 2 (July 24, 1880): 126.

6. B. E. Cotting, "Roetheln—German Measles," *Boston Medical and Surgical Journal* 88, no. 20 (May 15, 1873): 486.

7. J. H. Etheridge, "Diagnostic Syllabus of Roetheln (German Measles), Scarlet Fever and Measles," *Chicago Medical Journal and Examiner* 38 (April 1876): 312.

8. Squire, "Remarks on Epidemic Roseola; Rosella, Rosalia, or Rubeola," 100.

9. Dr. Fergus of Marlborough, Dr. Martin Oxley of Liverpool on p. 31; Dr. A. Jacobi of New York on p. 32; Dr. Shuttleworth of Lancaster, on p. 33, in discussion of papers on Rotheln in *Transactions of the International Medical Congress* 4 (August 1881).

10. C. A. Earle, Des Plaines, IL, in discussion of H. M. McClanahan, "Differential Diagnosis Between Measles and Rubella," *Journal of the American Medical Association* (hereafter cited as *JAMA*) 49, no. 2 (December 7, 1907): 1917. See also J. P. Crozer Griffith, "Rubella (Rotheln: German Measles) With a Report of One Hundred and Fifty Cases," *Medical Record* 32, no. 1 (July 2, 1887): 1.

11. Veale, "History of an Epidemic of Rotheln."

12. Ibid., 405–9, table on 413.

13. Shuttleworth in discussion of rotheln.

14. May Michael, "Rubella: A Report of an Epidemic of Eighty Cases," *Archives of Pediatrics* 25 (1908): 601.

15. F. Forchheimer, "The Enanthem of German Measles," *Archives of Pediatrics* 15, no. 10 (October 1898): 725; G. Floystrup, "Rubella Without a Rash (Rubella Sine Exanthemate), *British Journal of Children's Diseases* 20 (1923): 20–23. On the emerging field of developmental psychology and parents' use of their own children as universal examples of child development, see Amanda M. Brian, "A *Kinderland* in the Fatherland: Growing Children in Imperial Berlin," (PhD diss., University of Illinois, Urbana-Champaign, 2009), chap. 2.

16. Squire, "Remarks on Epidemic Roseola," 100.

17. John Harley Warner, "From Specificity to Universalism in Medical Therapeutics: Transformation in the 19th-Century United States," in *Sickness and Health in America: Readings in the History of Medicine and Public Health,* ed. Judith Walzer Leavitt and Ron Numbers, 3rd rev. ed. (Madison: University of Wisconsin Press, 1997), 87–101; Charles E. Rosenberg, "The Therapeutic Revolution: Medicine, Meaning, and Social Change in 19th-Century America" in *The Therapeutic Revolution: Essays in the Social History of American Medicine,* ed. Morris J. Vogel and Charles E. Rosenberg (Philadelphia: University of Pennsylvania Press, 1979), 3–25.

18. I have not been able to learn who these children were—whether Indian or British—whose bodies were being observed and used to understand a disease found in Britain and on the Continent. The assumptions that bodies were different and that climate, food, culture, gender, and race produced different diseases in different bodies continued to be reigning ideas in nineteenth-century America. Indeed, these ideas were central to the development of regional and racialized medicine.

19. Nancy Tomes, *The Gospel of Germs: Men, Women, and the Microbe in American Life, 1870–1930* (Cambridge, MA: Harvard University Press, 1997); Gerald L. Geison, *The Private Science of Louis Pasteur* (Princeton, NJ: Princeton University Press, 1995); Phyllis Allen Richmond, "American Attitudes Toward the Germ Theory of Disease," *Journal of the History of Medicine and the Allied Sciences* 9 (October 1954): 428–54.

20. Veale, "History of an Epidemic of Rotheln," 414.

21. Ibid.

22. None of the following used *rubella*: Squire, "Remarks on Epidemic Roseola" (1870); Cotting, "Roetheln—German Measles" (1873); Smith, "Rotheln" (1874); Dyce Duckworth, "A Case of Rubeola (Rotheln)," *Lancet* 115 (March 13, 1880): 395–96; James Robinson, "The Diagnosis of Rotheln," *British Medical Journal* 1 (June 19, 1880): 922.

23. Cotting, "Roetheln—German Measles," 485.

24. Smith, "Rotheln," 1–13.

25. Ibid., quotation on p. 2. By 1881, when Smith presented a revised version of this paper at the International Medical Congress, he knew of Cutting and the earlier epidemics in the United States. See J. Lewis Smith, "Contributions to the

Study of Rotheln," *Transactions of the International Medical Congress* 4 (1881): 14–15. The sixty-one volume U.S. Army, *Index-Catalogue of the Library of the Surgeon-General's Office*, 1880–1961, is an essential research tool. It is also now available online at the National Library of Medicine website. The digitized name is IndexCat, available at http://indexcat.nlm.nih.gov (accessed May 9, 2009).

26. Dr. Mulheron in discussion of William Brodie, "German Measles," *Michigan Medical News* 4, no. 13 (July 11, 1881): 201.

27. Dr. Klein in ibid., 201.

28. Charles Warrington Earle, "The Prevailing Epidemic—Rotheln," *Transactions of the Illinois State Medical Society* 31 (1881): 297.

29. Ibid., 292, 296.

30. The American Dermatological Association proposed the name *rubella* for the disease, and the International Medical Congress followed this suggestion. In William Squire, "Rubella; Rubeoloa sine Catarrho; Rotheln, or German Measles," *Transactions of the International Medical Congress* 3 (1881): 31.

31. I. E. Atkinson, "Rubella (Rotheln)," *Archives of Pediatrics* [vol. no. missing] (1886): 679.

32. Michael, "Rubella," 599; Smith, "Rotheln," 13; Duckworth, "A Case of Rubeola (Rotheln)," 395; Floystrup, "Rubella Without a Rash," 23.

33. J. P. Crozer Griffith, "Rubella (Rotheln: German Measles), With a Report of One Hundred and Fifty Cases," *Medical Record* 32, no. 1 (July 2, 1887): 1.

34. Brodie, "German Measles," 201.

35. On the range of available practitioners, see William G. Rothstein, *American Physicians in the 19th Century: From Sects to Science* (Baltimore: Johns Hopkins University Press, 1972). On patient comparison and selection of doctors, see Regina Morantz-Sanchez, *Conduct Unbecoming a Woman: Medicine on Trial in Turn-of-the-Century Brooklyn* (New York: Oxford University Press, 1999), and Leslie J. Reagan, *When Abortion Was a Crime.*

36. Earle, "The Prevailing Epidemic—Rotheln," 292.

37. Nayan Shah, *Contagious Divides: Epidemics and Race in San Francisco's Chinatown* (Berkeley: University of California, 2001); Judith Walzer Leavitt, "Politics and Public Health: Smallpox in Milwaukee, 1894–1895," *Bulletin of the History of Medicine* 50 (1976): 553–68; Judith Walzer Leavitt, *Typhoid Mary: Captive to the Public's Health* (Boston: Beacon Press, 1996); Tera W. Hunter, *To 'Joy My Freedom: Southern Black Women's Lives and Labors After the Civil War* (Cambridge, MA: Harvard University Press, 1997), chap. 9; Michelle T. Moran, *Colonizing Leprosy: The Politics of Public Health in the United States* (Chapel Hill: University of North Carolina Press, 2007).

38. "Measles in Senators' Camp?" *Chicago Tribune* (hereafter cited as *CT*), April 14, 1914, p. 13.

39. Track: "Meredith Has Measles," *New York Times* (hereafter cited as *NYT*), April 24, 1914, p. 11; basketball: "Enlists to Battle 'Teuts,' German Measles Get

Him," *CT,* April 16, 1917, p. 16; rowing: "Cornell Oarsman Has Measles," *NYT,* May 5, 1914, p. 9; "Five More Yale Oarsmen Are Ill of Measles," *CT,* May 5, 1926, p. 25; "Measles Hit Yale Crew," *Los Angeles Times* (hereafter cited as *LAT*), May 7, 1926, p. B2; opera singer: "On the Aisle," *CT,* May 2, 1945, p. 13.

40. Colleges: reference to "Rich college boys" in "Measles Epidemic at Harvard," *CT,* April 2, 1911, p. 1; "Cornell Has Measles," *NYT,* March 25, 1914, p. 1; on "modified quarantine" of students at the University of Illinois, see "How to Keep Well," *CT,* April 8, 1928, p. 10; "Measles at Colgate," *NYT,* Feb. 27, 1935, p. 4. For elementary schools, see "Measles in the Schools," *CT,* Jan. 16, 1896, p. 1; Dr. W. A. Evans, "How to Keep Well," *CT,* Oct. 10, 1913, p. 4; "Close Lake Forest Schools Due to Measles Epidemic," *CT,* April 8, 1935, p. 5.

41. Remark by Dr. W. B. Drummond, medical superintendent of the Baldovan Institution for the Feebleminded, reported in "Cinnamon Stops Measles," *NYT,* Aug. 12, 1917, p. 15.

42. J. G. McNaught, "Notes on an Epidemic of German Measles," *Journal of Royal Army Medical Corps* 21 (1913): 439, 442.

43. J. C. Geiger, "Epidemic of German Measles in a City Adjacent to an Army Cantonment and Its Probable Relation Thereto," *JAMA* 70, no. 24 (June 15, 1918): 1818–20.

44. Maj. Henry C. Michie, MC, "German Measles," chap. 14 in United States, *Communicable and Other Diseases,* ed. Joseph F. Siler, vol. 9, *The Medical Department of the United States Army in the World War* (Washington, DC: GPO, 1928), 463–72. Note that this official report calls the disease *German measles,* not *rubella.* Note 17,378 primary admissions on p. 463, number of days lost on p. 464; acute arthritis as a complication noted on p. 470. The chapter also discusses the difficulty of differential diagnosis, which would explain why the disease appeared to be epidemic in some camps and nonexistent in others. It also explains that although deaths are listed to German measles, it was known to be a mild disease, and death was unlikely to be the result of a patient's having had it. Instead, the listing of deaths by disease was due to a practice of recording a death by noting the initial reason for the patient's hospital admission. Some deaths listed under *German measles* might have been due to another cause, such as influenza.

For comparison: Influenza was the top killer among diseases during the war, but venereal diseases claimed second place in the number of admissions and service days lost. The venereal diseases accounted for more than three hundred thousand hospital admissions, representing more than 10 percent of the total of the war's three million hospital admissions and a loss of more than six million days from duty. Michie, "The Venereal Diseases: Statistical Considerations," ibid., 263.

45. Geiger, "Epidemic of German Measles," 1818–20.

46. "Enlists to Battle 'Teuts.'"

47. Dr. Emerson is quoted in "German Measles Invades Navy Yard," *NYT,* June 1, 1917, p. 5.

48. "Bright Sayings of Children," *CT,* Feb. 3, 1918, p. B4.

49. "Women in Wartime," *CT,* May 20, 1918, p. 14.

50. Reference to "the Liberty itch" in "Senator Soaper Says," *LAT,* May 9, 1939, p. A4. "But They Are Still Measles," *NYT,* March 17, 1944, p. 19.

51. W. E. Hill, "These Troubled Times," *LAT,* Aug. 4, 1940, p. 14.

52. June Provines, "Front Views and Profiles," *CT,* April 12, 1941, p. 11. See also *NYT,* July 30, 1944, p. E9.

53. "German Measles Delays New Zealand Mobilizing," *NYT,* Sept. 9, 1940, p. 2; "Measles Quarantines 62d Artillery," *NYT,* May 13, 1941, p. 12. The latter tiny report began with the usual joke, "A strong 'German force' is holding the 1,050 officers and men."

54. "Chanute Field Quarantined by Measles Wave," *CT,* Jan. 26, 1941, p. 10.

55. N. McAlister Gregg, "Congenital Cataract Following German Measles in the Mother," *Transactions of the Ophthalmological Society of Australia* 3 (1941): 40–43.

56. "Communicable Disease Toll Nearly Doubled for State," *LAT,* May 21, 1942, p. 26.

57. "Chicago Births Rise 2.6 Per Cent in First 6 Months," *CT,* July 15, 1942, p. 16.

58. Gregg, "Congenital Cataract Following German Measles in the Mother," 35–46, quotation on p. 37. Australian women had long learned to bring their concerns to doctors. On the medicalization of pregnancy and infant care in Australia at the turn of the twentieth century, much like the American experience, see Lisa Featherstone, "Surveying the Mother: The Rise of Antenatal Care in Early Twentieth-Century Australia," *Limina* 10 (2004): 16–31.

59. This is from a later series of cases, babies born in 1943 and 1944. N. McAlister Gregg, "Further Observations on Congenital Defects in Infants Following Maternal Rubella," *Transactions of the Ophthalmological Society of Australia* 4 (1944): quotation on p. 127.

60. Gregg, "Congenital Cataract Following German Measles in the Mother," 35, 36.

61. The story about the women's conversation and a "clue" are from Margaret A. Burgess, "Gregg's Rubella Legacy 1941–1991," *Medical Journal of Australia* (hereafter cited as *MJA*) 155, no. 6 (September 16, 1991): 355; *Australian Dictionary of Biography,* vol. 14, s.v. "Gregg, Sir Norman McAlister (1892–1966)" (by Paul A. L. Lancaster), 325–27, in the *Australian Dictionary of Biography Online Edition,* www.adb.online.anu.edu.au (accessed June 7, 2008).

62. Gregg, "Congenital Cataract Following German Measles in the Mother"; Charles Swan and A. L. Tostevin, "Congenital Abnormalities in Infants Following Infectious Diseases During Pregnancy, with Special References to Rubella: A Third Series of Cases," *MJA* 1, no.19 (May 11, 1946), table IV, 652–54.

63. Gregg, "Congenital Cataract Following German Measles in the Mother."

64. Sir Lorimer Dods, "Obituary of Norman McAlister Gregg," *MJA* 2, no. 24 (December 10, 1966): 1168. Gregg presented his paper at a specialist society meeting; the *Medical Journal of Australia* gave Gregg's findings great prominence by making a review of his paper the lead article, "Congenital Cataract Following Rubella," *MJA* 3 (December 6, 1941). Gregg remarked on the newspaper coverage and the phone calls from three mothers in N. McAlister Gregg, "Rubella During Pregnancy of the Mother, with its Sequelae of Congenital Defects in the Child," *MJA* 3 (March 31, 1945): 314.

65. Gregg noted, "Dr. Erick Blashki kindly saw these patients for me, and he said . . . they appeared to be deaf. In the course of the succeeding two years, 1942 and 1943, more and more of these cases of 'deaf-mutism' appeared. Their appearance at a later stage than cases with ocular complications is natural, because deafness would not be suspected even by the mothers until a much later date than blindness." Gregg, "Rubella During Pregnancy of the Mother," 314.

66. Experts in embryology, however, had known that diseases could cross the placenta.

67. Sir Macfarlane Burnet, *Changing Patterns: An Atypical Autobiography* (Melbourne: Heinemann, 1968), 78.

68. Gregg, "Congenital Cataract Following German Measles in the Mother," 42.

69. On the work of mothers in matters of health, see Molly Ladd-Taylor, *Mother-Work: Women, Child Welfare, and the State, 1890–1930* (Urbana: University of Illinois Press, 1994); Rima Apple, *Mothers and Medicine: A Social History of Infant Feeding* (Madison: University of Wisconsin Press, 1987); Lynn Curry, *Modern Mothers in the Heartland: Gender, Health, and Progress in Illinois, 1900–1930* (Columbus: Ohio University Press, 1999); Leslie J. Reagan, "Engendering the Dread Disease: Women, Men, and Cancer," *American Journal of Public Health* 87, no. 11 (November 1997): 1779–87; Ellen Ross, *Love and Toil: Motherhood in Outcast London, 1870–1918* (New York: Oxford University Press, 1993).

70. Gregg, "Congenital Cataract Following German Measles in the Mother," 37.

71. Ibid., 40.

72. D. G. Carruthers, "Congenital Deaf-Mutism as a Sequela of a Rubella-Like Maternal Infection During Pregnancy," *MJA* 1, no. 13 (March 31, 1945): 316.

73. Charles Swan and A. L. Tostevin, "Congenital Abnormalities in Infants Following Infectious Diseases During Pregnancy, with Special References to Rubella: A Third Series of Cases," *MJA* 1, no. 19 (May 11, 1946), Table IV; case 78, p. 652; case 104, p. 653. Last quotation from case 81, p. 652.

74. Mark M. Smith, *Listening to Nineteenth-Century America* (Chapel Hill: University of North Carolina Press, 2000); Lisa Cartwright, "*Mandy* (1952): On Voice and Listening in the (Deaf) Maternal Melodrama," in *Medicine's Moving*

*Pictures: Medicine, Health, and Bodies in American Film and Television,* ed. Leslie J. Reagan, Nancy Tomes, and Paula A. Treichler (Rochester, NY: Rochester University Press, 2007), chap. 5.

75. Personal communication from Dr. Donald Vickery, reprinted in N. McAlister Gregg, "Further Observations," 122.

76. Gregg, "Rubella During Pregnancy of the Mother," 315.

77. Gregg, "Congenital Cataract following German Measles in the Mother," 44.

78. Gregg, "Further Observations," 121–22, 123.

79. Carruthers, "Congenital Deaf-Mutism as a Sequela of a Rubella-Like Maternal Infection During Pregnancy," 316.

80. Gregg, "Further Observations," 123–24. For an example of the distress that mothers felt as they cared for infants born with congenital rubella syndrome, see Mary Jean Beaton, *The Road to Autonomy* (Enumclaw, WA: WinePress Publishing, 2003), chaps. 1–2. On the expectations of mothers of children with intellectual impairments in this period, see Janice Brockley, "Rearing the Child Who Never Grew: Ideologies of Parenting and Intellectual Disability in American History," in *Mental Retardation in America: A Historical Reader,* ed. Steven Noll and James W. Trent Jr. (New York: New York University Press, 2004), 130, 143–44.

81. Katherine Castles, "'Nice, Average Americans': Postwar Parents' Groups and the Defense of the Normal Family," in *Mental Retardation in America,* 362–63; Brockley, "Rearing the Child Who Never Grew."

82. Congratulations offered at the meeting where Gregg presented his findings. See the Discussion of Gregg, "Congenital Cataract Following German Measles in the Mother," 45.

83. "Annotations. Rubella and Congenital Malformations," *Lancet* 246 (March 4, 1944): 316. Note that the author is anonymous; considering that this was the 1940s, I am assuming here that the author is male. In response to the critique that there needed to be investigation of cases in which malformation had not occurred, Gregg had reported that for five months he had queried every mother of a healthy baby about whether she had had German measles and had not found one who had. These remarks were buried in the discussion of his original paper. See Gregg, "Congenital Cataract Following German Measles in the Mother," 46. On changing research protocols in the 1940s, see Harry Marks, *The Progress of Experiment: Science and Therapeutic Reform in the United States, 1900–1990* (Baltimore: Johns Hopkins University, 2000).

84. "Annotations. Rubella and Congenital Malformations."

85. Ibid. Emphasis added.

86. John R. Paul makes a similar remark about the attitude toward Australia and Australian researchers in his discussion of Macfarlane Burnet's 1931 findings in virology on poliovirus. John R. Paul, *A History of Poliomyelitis* (New Haven: Yale University Press, 1971), 227.

87. "Annotations. Rubella and Congenital Malformations."

88. Ida Mann, "Some Embryological Observations on Congenital Cataract Associated with Rubella in the Mother," *Transactions of the Ophthalmological Society of Australia* 4 (1944): 115–18, quotation on 115. Ida Mann, surgeon at Moorfields, Westminster, and at Central Eye Hospital, who later moved to Australia, was well known for her detailed study, *The Development of the Human Eye* (1928; 3rd ed., British Medical Association, 1964). Gregg consulted with Ida Mann and quoted her in his first report: "Ida Mann has stated that the exanthemata, measles, mumps, smallpox, chickenpox, scarlet fever et cetera, are all known to be transmissible transplacentally." Gregg, "Congenital Cataract Following German Measles in the Mother," p. 41. Gregg again quoted Ida Mann in "Further Observations," p. 120. In another follow-up article, Gregg pointed to the "embryologist," Miss Ida Mann, who "expressed the opinion that it had been proved beyond question that there was a causative relationship between a virus infection early in pregnancy and the appearance of certain congenital defects in the infant." Gregg, "Rubella During Pregnancy of the Mother," p. 314.

Edith L. Potter, MD, PhD, of the Department of Obstetrics and Gynecology at the University of Chicago and the Chicago Lying-In Hospital, began her 1946 report on Gregg's findings with the observation that "The fact that viruses are easily propagated in embryonic tissue has been known for many years, but not until Gregg in 194[1] found an association between rubella in early pregnancy and congenital defects of the eyes and heart, was it recognized that virus diseases might be the cause of certain human malformations." In Edith L. Potter, "The Rh Factor, Vitamin K and Rubella Virus in Relation to Infant Mortality and Morbidity," *American Journal of Public Health* 36, no. 2 (February 1946): 107. See also Edith L. Potter, *Pathology of the Fetus and Infant* (1953; repr., Chicago: Year Book Medical Publishers, 1961), 116–18.

89. Algernon B. Reese, "Congenital Cataract and Other Anomalies Following German Measles in the Mother," *American Journal of Ophthalmology* 27, no. 5 (May 1944): 487.

90. John J. Prendergast, "Congenital Cataract and Other Anomalies Following Rubella in Mother During Pregnancy: A California Survey," *Archives of Ophthalmology* 35 (January 1946): 39–41, quotation on 41.

91. Reese, "Congenital Cataract and Other Anomalies," 483. Gregg in his first article, "Congenital Cataract Following German Measles in the Mother," pointed to epidemics of German measles and sore throat originating in the military "camps and spread[ing] to the civilian population." See also "The Occurrence of Congenital Defects in Children Following Maternal Rubella in Pregnancy," 123.

92. Prendergast, "Congenital Cataract and Other Anomalies," 39.

93. Burnet, *Changing Patterns*, 78. *JAMA* summarized Swan's research and Gregg's findings in a small report that could easily be overlooked. "Current Medical Literature, Medical Journal of Australia, Sydney," *JAMA* 123, no. 17

(December 25, 1943): 1144–45; Potter, "The Rh Factor, Vitamin K and Rubella Virus," 107–8; Conrad Wesselhoeft, "Medical Progress: Rubella (German Measles)," *New England Journal of Medicine* 236, no. 25 (June 19, 1947): 943–50, and "Medical Progress: Rubella (German Measles) (Concluded)," *New England Journal of Medicine* 236, no. 26 (June 26, 1947): 978–88. Burnet identified Wesselhoeft's article in the *New England Journal of Medicine,* but Potter's was the earlier (and shorter) report. It was also likely to reach a different audience. On Burnet, see Paul, *History of Poliomyelitis,* 225–30.

94. "German Measles in Pregnancy May Give Cataracts to Baby," *Newsweek* 24 (August 28, 1944): 74, 76; "German Measles Menace," *Time* 45 (March 5, 1945): 57. Dr. Theodore R. Van Dellen, "How to Keep Well. Defects Following German Measles," *CT,* July 15, 1947, p. 12.

95. Charles Swan, "Rubella in Pregnancy as an Aetiological Factor in Congenital Malformations, Stillbirth, Miscarriage, and Abortion," Pts. 1 and 2, *Journal of Obstetrics and Gynaecology of the British Empire* (1949): 341–63, 591–604. Swan cited ninety-one publications related to the effects of maternal rubella.

96. Ibid., 348–61. Subheading "Miscellaneous Abnormalities" on p. 360.

97. Ibid., 600.

98. For a medical study that found that the general background risk for "abnormal" babies was 1.6 percent, see Victoria P. Coffey and W. J. E. Jessop, "Rubella and the Incidence of Congenital Abnormalities," *Irish Journal of Medical Science,* 6th ser., 397 (January 1959): 11. A chapter titled "Malformations of the Fetus" in *Williams Obstetrics* illustrates the complexity of estimating the usual incidence of congenital malformations, for the number varied depending on what was being counted or considered—whether it included all variations, including "trivial defects" or "grave deformities incompatible with life"; whether it included pregnancy losses; and the way in which one interpreted whether something was significant. This source notes: "If deformities of clinical significance only be considered, their incidence is probably between 1 and 2 per cent. . . . Malformations in this category include such conditions as congenital heart disease, harelip, cleft palate, mongolism, pyloric stenosis, tracheo-esophagal fistula, imperforate anus, hyupospadias, [and] clubfoot." The authors also suggested a figure of 2 or 3 percent, but that figure includes stillbirths. Nicholson J. Eastman and Louis M. Hellman, *Williams Obstetrics,* 12th ed. (New York: Appleton-Century-Crofts, 1956), 1105.

99. Swan, "Rubella in Pregnancy as an Aetiological Factor," 362–63.

100. Ibid., 600. Swan and A. L. Tostevin had earlier called therapeutic abortion "entirely justifiable in the case of any woman who suffers from German measles in the first four months of pregnancy" in "Congenital Abnormalities in Infants Following Infectious Diseases During Pregnancy, with Special Reference to Rubella: A Third Series of Cases," *MJA* 1, no. 19 (May 11, 1946): 658.

101. Swan, "Rubella in Pregnancy as an Aetiological Factor," 601; Stimson to Albaugh in "Congenital Anomalies."

102. Charles Swan et al., "Further Observations on Congenital Defects in Infants Following Infectious Diseases During Pregnancy, With Special Reference to Rubella," *MJA* 1, no. 19 (May 6, 1944): 412.

103. Swan, "Rubella in Pregnancy as an Aetiological Factor," 601.

104. Ibid., 600.

105. On this idea in the early twentieth century and the deliberate efforts to bring about a "defective" newborn's death, see Martin S. Pernick, *The Black Stork: Eugenics and the Death of "Defective" Babies in American Medicine and Motion Pictures Since 1915* (New York: Oxford University Press, 1996).

106. Gregg, "Congenital Cataract Following German Measles in the Mother."

107. Charles Swan, A. L. Tostevin, and G. H. Barham Black, "Final Observations on Congenital Defects in Infants Following Infectious Diseases During Pregnancy, With Special Reference to Rubella," *MJA* 2, no. 26 (December 28, 1946): table 1, 891–94.

108. Gregg, "Further Observations," 128.

109. German measles was not a reportable disease, a situation that made it difficult to know the number of cases in a region or given year. The effects of epidemics could be seen in mortality data, however: "In 1941, deaths from congenital heart disease reached the highest figure so far recorded for Queensland" (at fifty-seven compared with forty the year before, which probably had been an epidemic year too) and "reached its highest point" in South Australia in 1943. See L. P. Winterbotham, "Congenital Cardiac Defects Associated with Maternal Rubella," *MJA* 2, no. 1 (July 6, 1946): 17.

110. Swan, "Rubella in Pregnancy as an Aetiological Factor," 601.

111. Ibid., 600. On Gregg's support for a vaccine and therapeutic abortion and Swan's "more conservative" view, see "German Measles in Pregnancy May Give Cataracts to Baby."

112. See Van Dellen, "How to Keep Well: Defects Following German Measles," *CT,* July 15, 1947, p. 12.

113. I have not been able to locate the newspaper article that Gregg mentioned.

114. Van Dellen, "How To Keep Well: Defects Following German Measles."

115. The newspaper reported on the research and the *JAMA* article in "Baby Often Affected by German Measles Early in Pregnancy," *CT,* August 13, 1949, p. 9. Stuart Abel and Theodore R. Van Dellen, "Congenital Defects Following Maternal Rubella," *JAMA* 140, no. 15 (August 13, 1944): quotation on 1212. Van Dellen and his colleague (both of Northwestern University) acknowledged that mothers whose children had various anomalies were more likely to search for a cause than those whose children were normal, thus making it likely that women who had had rubella in pregnancy but whose babies were normal would not

come to the surface. Yet they did also hear from mothers whose babies had not been affected. The authors concluded that the data confirmed a "significant . . . correlation between congenital defects and maternal rubella." Their analysis was based on eighty-two letters regarding eighty-four infants. They reported that ten letters had been thrown out. Thus, we know Van Dellen received ninety-two letters. See description of method on p. 1211.

116. Abel and Van Dellen, "Congenital Defects Following Maternal Rubella," 1211.

117. Ibid. I have not been able to locate the original research or the letters.

118. "German Measles in Pregnancy May Give Cataracts to Baby," 74. *Time* magazine also used the term *menace* to describe the disease in "German Measles Menace." *Newsweek's* emphasis on "Australia's most important contributions to medical knowledge" suggests that this assessment grew out of Burnet's tour since this was his description of Gregg's discovery.

119. "German Measles Menace." This *Time* account was one of fewer than a dozen articles on the disease published in popular periodicals between 1941 and 1950. There were only eight articles between 1951 and 1960, and none during 1958, an epidemic year. These counts are from the *Reader's Guide to Periodical Literature*. I did not count citations to the *American Journal of Public Health* as articles published in popular periodicals.

120. Dr. P. M. Stimson reported receiving only one letter against his view that "abortion would have to be considered seriously" from an Arizona lawyer. Personal communication from P. M. Stimson in C. H. Albaugh, "Congenital Anomalies Following Maternal Rubella in Early Weeks of Pregnancy," *JAMA* 129, no. 11 (November 10, 1945): 722–23.

121. Dr. Theodore Van Dellen, "How To Keep Well," *CT,* March 2, 1946, p. 10. The column included a drawing of a boy sick in bed.

122. "German Measles Menace." According to one medical observer at the time, the "relationship between maternal rubella and congenital defects in the offspring first entered the national consciousness early in 1945 with the remarks of Dr. P. M. Stimson of New York, whose discussion of the subject at the New York Academy of Medicine was reviewed (without Dr. Stimson's knowledge) by a *Time* magazine reporter." This remark makes one wonder whether some physicians believed that Gregg's finding should not have been shared with members of the public because it would frighten them or because they would want it confirmed by other researchers. The need to emphasize that Dr. Stimson was unaware of the reporter's presence would also be important for defending him against any charges of seeking publicity—conduct that would be considered unprofessional and unethical. Albaugh, "Congenital Anomalies," 720.

123. Nicholson J. Eastman, *Expectant Motherhood,* 2nd ed. (Boston: Little, Brown, 1947), v.

124. "Protection Thru [sic] Vaccines" in Theodore R. Van Dellen, "How to Keep Well," *CT,* August 26, 1949, p. 10.

125. U.S. Children's Bureau, *So You're Expecting a Baby* (Washington, DC: GPO, 1947), 2–3. Eastman's *Expectant Motherhood* did not mention German measles, either.

126. U.S. Children's Bureau, *So You're Expecting a Baby,* 14, 15. *So You're Expecting a Baby* told readers they need not fear maternal marking. The pamphlet framed its reassurance in such a way that made the fetus seem to be almost insulated from the pregnant woman: "Are you bothered by someone's gloomy prediction that your baby may be 'marked' by disagreeable things you chance to see or experience? Such old notions have absolutely no basis, for the fetus has no connection whatever with your nervous system through which any such shocks would have to be transmitted. Its only connection with your body is indirectly through your bloodstream." Quotation on p. 14. *The Expectant Mother* (by the U.S. Children's Bureau [Washington, DC: GPO, 1943]) did not mention German measles or diseases at all until it advised that for ten days after the baby's birth, there should be very few visitors because they might bring "a cold" with them and infect mother and child. "Of course," the pamphlet added, "no visitor should be allowed to pick up the baby." Quotation on p. 10.

127. U.S. Children's Bureau, *When Your Baby Is on the Way* (Washington, DC: GPO, 1961). This is a "picture leaflet." The lengthier *Prenatal Care* mentioned therapeutic abortions and their rarity, as well as various diseases, including syphilis and tuberculosis, but did not mention German measles. U.S. Children's Bureau, *Prenatal Care* (Washington, DC: GPO, 1962), 55, 58–59. One book mentioned that "German measles during early pregnancy can be a serious peril to your baby," but did not explain how. See Adeline Bullock, RN, *Parents Magazine Book for Expectant Mothers* (New York: McGraw-Hill, 1954), 159–60.

128. William Brady, "Here's to Health," *LAT,* April 4, 1951, p. B6. In an earlier column, Dr. Brady had suggested that the "best preventive" was to "stay away from those who have . . . a 'cold.'" William Brady, "Here's to Health," *LAT,* Dec. 27, 1949, p. B4.

129. "German Measles Handicapped My Child," as told to Mary Margaret Kern, *Today's Health* 32 (March 1954): 38–39, 44. The mother told of coming to realize that her daughter was deaf at age three and then learning from her neighbor that German measles was probably the cause. As she summarized medical knowledge, she remarked, "After reading all we could find about German measles, my husband and I believe we are lucky to have a child as little handicapped as Helen." Quotation on p. 39.

130. Theodore R. Van Dellen, "How to Keep Well," *CT,* June 22, 1951, p. 20.

1. "Spots All Over," *Newsweek* 73 (April 13, 1964): 90. See also "Worst Rash of Measles," *Business Week* (April 4, 1964): 98.

2. "Measles Threat to Unborn," *Science News Letter* 86 (September 26, 1964): 194. The ratio of 50–50 appears to have become the simple accepted description of the risk of damage. Theodore Van Dellen used this shorthand of a "50–50 chance" of the baby's being "born with defective vision, hearing, or heart" for the first trimester in "How To Keep Well," *Chicago Tribune* (hereafter cited as *CT*), May 5, 1956, p. 10.

3. *Malformed* and *dangerous* in "Dangerous Babies," *Time* 85 (February 26, 1965): 77; *hopelessly deformed* and *abnormal* in "Measles Threat to Unborn"; *defective* in "Defective Births Are on the Rise," *U.S. News and World Report* 58 (May 3, 1965): 11, and Harry Nelson, "Doctors Say 'Powerless' Against Expected Epidemic That Perils Infants," *Los Angeles Times* (hereafter cited as *LAT*), April 22, 1965, p. 3.

4. If a woman was infected early in pregnancy, the magazine article continued, "the chances are dangerously high that her child will be born dead, deformed or hopelessly retarded." "Spreading Across U.S.: German Measles," *U.S. News and World Report* 56 (May 11, 1964): 8. Like many other frightening diseases, German measles was represented as an enemy through the use of military metaphors. The language of war has also been used for tuberculosis, syphilis, and, especially, cancer. On the use of war metaphors for disease, see Susan Sontag, *Illness as Metaphor* (New York: Farrar, Straus, and Giroux, 1978), 98–99; Suzanne Poirier, *Chicago's War on Syphilis, 1937–1940* (Urbana: University of Illinois Press, 1995); Barron H. Lerner, *The Breast Cancer Wars: Hope, Fear, and the Pursuit of a Cure in Twentieth-Century America* (New York: Oxford University Press, 2001); James T. Patterson, *The Dread Disease: Cancer and Modern American Culture* (Cambridge, MA: Harvard University Press, 1987).

5. For examples, see "Vaccine Against German Measles," *Time* 87 (May 6, 1966): 60; "Spreading Across U.S." The *Saturday Evening Post* advertised a "report on German measles, crippler of unborn infants," in its March 13, 1965, issue; advertisement, *LAT,* March 2, 1965, p. 17.

6. Jane Smith, *Patenting the Sun: Polio and the Salk Vaccine* (New York: Anchor, 1991); David M. Oshinsky, *Polio: An American Story* (New York: Oxford University Press, 2005); Tony Gould, *Summer Plague: Polio and its Survivors* (New Haven, CT: Yale University Press, 1997); John R. Paul, *A History of Poliomyelitis* (New Haven, CT: Yale University Press, 1971); Naomi Rogers, *Dirt and Disease: Polio Before FDR* (New Brunswick, NJ: Rutgers University Press, 1992).

7. Henning Sjostrom and Robert Nilsson, *Thalidomide and the Power of the Drug Companies* (Middlesex, UK: Penguin Books, 1972); Insight Team of the (London) *Sunday Times, Suffer the Children: The Story of Thalidomide* (New York:

Viking Press, 1979); Trent Stephens and Rock Brynner, *Dark Remedy: The Impact of Thalidomide and Its Revival as a Vital Medicine* (Cambridge, MA: Perseus Publishing, 2001); Barbara Clow, "An Illness of Nine Months' Duration: Pregnancy and Thalidomide Use in Canada and the United States," in *Women, Health, and Nation: Canada and the United States since 1945,* ed. Georgina Feldberg et al. (Montreal and Kingston, ON: McGill–Queen's University Press, 2003), 45–66; Philip J. Hilts, *Protecting America's Health: The FDA, Business, and One Hundred Years of Regulation* (Chapel Hill: University of North Carolina Press, 2003), chap. 10.

8. *Child protection* became the watchword. As Michael Grossberg observes, the phrase neatly encapsulated both the fear *for* children and the fear *of* children, the desire to protect children and the desire to be protected from them. Michael Grossberg, "A Protected Childhood: The Emergence of Child Protection in America," in *American Public Life and the Historical Imagination,* ed. Wendy Gamber, Michael Grossberg, and Hendrik Hartog (Notre Dame, IN: Notre Dame Press, 2003).

9. Martin S. Pernick, *The Black Stork: Eugenics and the Death of "Defective" Babies in American Medicine and Motion Pictures Since 1915* (New York: Oxford University Press, 1996), 91–94.

10. Of a large literature demonstrating this, see Howard Markel, *Quarantine! East European Jewish Immigrants and the New York City Epidemics of 1892* (Baltimore: Johns Hopkins University Press, 1997); Alan M. Kraut, *Silent Travelers: Germs, Genes, and the "Immigrant Menace"* (Baltimore: Johns Hopkins University Press, 1995); Judith Walzer Leavitt, *Typhoid Mary: Captive to the Public's Health* (Boston: Beacon Press, 1996); Nayan Shah, *Contagious Divides: Epidemics and Race in San Francisco's Chinatown* (Berkeley and Los Angeles: University of California Press, 2001); Tera W. Hunter, *To 'Joy My Freedom: Southern Black Women's Lives and Labors After the Civil War* (Cambridge, MA: Harvard University Press, 1997); Susan M. Reverby, ed., *Tuskegee's Truths: Rethinking the Tuskegee Syphilis Study* (Chapel Hill: University of North Carolina Press, 2000); Elizabeth Fee and Daniel M. Fox, eds., *AIDS: The Burdens of History* (Berkeley: University of California Press, 1988); Michelle T. Moran, *Colonizing Leprosy: Imperialism and the Politics of Public Health in the United States* (Chapel Hill: University of North Carolina Press, 2007).

11. Figures reported from state public health records and public health surveys in Gabriel Stickle to Charles Massey, NF memo re Rubella epidemic, 4 June 1968, folder Birth Defects and Epidemics, box 3, series 3 Birth Defects, Medical Program Records (hereafter MPR), March of Dimes Archives (hereafter MODA), White Plains, NY. New York City figures in "German Measles Hits 200 Daily Here," *NYT,* March 31, 1964, p. 37. According to the U.S. Public Health Service, epidemics had begun in Puerto Rico and Hawaii by April 1965. As reported in John A. Osmundsen, "A Blood Test Is Devised for German Measles," *NYT,* April 21, 1965, p. 27.

12. "Measles Epidemic Here May be Diminishing," *LAT,* May 4, 1965, p. A1.

13. Dr. W. Lenz of West Germany and Dr. W. G. McBride of Australia both made the connection between phocomelia and thalidomide. Their conclusions, like Norman Gregg's twenty years earlier, again demonstrated the importance of specialization, clinical investigation, and a perceptive clinician in identifying teratogens. On the history of thalidomide, see Sjostrom and Nilsson, *Thalidomide;* Insight Team, *Suffer the Children;* Stephens and Brynner, *Dark Remedy;* Arthur Daemmrich, "A Tale of Two Experts: Thalidomide and Political Engagement in the United States and West Germany," *Social History of Medicine* 15, no. 1 (2002): 137–58; Hilts, *Protecting America's Health,* chap. 10; Clow, "An Illness of Nine Months' Duration"; Leslie J. Reagan, "'Monstrous' Babies in the News: Thalidomide, Birth Defects, and Public Policy in the U.S., 1962" (unpublished paper).

14. Trade names included Distaval in Britain, Australia, and New Zealand; Talimol in Canada; and Softenon in Finland. Countries and trade names in Sjostrom and Nilsson, *Thalidomide,* 37–41; "Trade Names," box 62, Helen B. Taussig Papers, Alan Mason Chesney Medical Archives, Johns Hopkins Medical Institutions, Baltimore, MD.

15. The FDA estimated that 3,760 women of childbearing age in the United States had taken the pills and that 207 were pregnant. At least eleven thalidomide babies were born in the United States. The number of affected pregnancies that ended in miscarriage or death in early childhood are unknown, but the original researcher estimated that 40 percent died in the first year of life. Stephens and Brynner, *Dark Remedy,* 56.

16. "U.S. Mother Seeks Aid From Sweden," *NYT,* August 5, 1962, p. 64; "Finkbine to Leave Sweden," *NYT,* August 26, 1962, p. 57; "Finkbines Return to U.S.," *NYT,* August 27, 1962, p. 18; "Vatican Sees 'Crime' in Finkbine Abortion," *NYT,* August 20, 1962, p. 9. These stories were filed through AP, UPI, and Reuters news services. Kristin Luker found that press coverage in California on Finkbine ranged from twenty-one articles in the *San Francisco Chronicle* to four in the *Los Angeles Times.* In *Abortion and the Politics of Motherhood* (Berkeley: University of California Press, 1984), 279, n. 16. Sherri Finkbine reported receiving "thousands of pieces of hate mail" that called her a murderer and threatened the lives of her entire family. The deluge of criticism created self-doubt and pain in her years later. See Sherri Finkbine, "The Lesser of Two Evils," in *The Case for Legalized Abortion Now,* ed. Alan F. Guttmacher (Berkeley: Diablo Press, 1967), 20–22. Chapter 3 of this text will discuss the medical practice of therapeutic abortion.

17. Hilts, *Protecting America's Health,* chap. 13; Stephens and Brynner, *Dark Remedy,* chap. 3; Reagan, "'Monstrous' Babies in the News." On Finkbine, see also Rickie Solinger, "Sherri Finkbine and the Origins of *Roe v. Wade,*" in *True Stories from the American Past, Vol. II: Since 1865,* ed. William Graebner, 3rd ed.

(New York: McGraw-Hill, 2002), chap. 13, 226–245; and Luker, *Abortion and the Politics of Motherhood*, 62–65, 78–20.

18. On the Pill, see Lara V. Marks, *Sexual Chemistry: A History of the Contraceptive Pill* (New Haven, CT: Yale University Press, 2001); Elizabeth Siegel Watkins, *On the Pill: A Social History of Contraceptives, 1950–1970* (Baltimore: John Hopkins University Press, 2001). On vaccines, see James Colgrove, *State of Immunity: The Politics of Vaccination in Twentieth-Century America* (Berkeley: University of California Press, 2006), chaps. 3–4; Allan Chase, *Magic Shots: A Human and Scientific Account of the Long and Continuing Struggle to Eradicate Infectious Diseases by Vaccination* (New York: William Morrow, 1982). On the use of medications during pregnancy, see Clow, "An Illness of Nine Months' Duration," 50–57; on DES to prevent miscarriage, see Sheryl Burt Ruzek, *The Women's Health Movement: Feminist Alternatives to Medical Control* (New York: Praeger, 1978), 38–42; Adele E. Clarke, *Disciplining Reproduction: Modernity, American Life Sciences, and "The Problem of Sex"* (Berkeley: University of California Press, 1998), 160, 244–45.

19. Rachel Carson, *Silent Spring* (New York: Houghton Mifflin, 1962). *Silent Spring* was first serialized in the *New Yorker* in June 1962. Janet Golden, *Message in a Bottle: The Making of Fetal Alcohol Syndrome* (Cambridge, MA: Harvard University Press, 2005), 40–41; Ann Oakley, *The Captured Womb: A History of the Medical Care of Pregnant Women* (New York: Basil Blackwell, 1984), 102–5.

20. For the contemporaneous change in advice, see Dr. Helen Taussig of Johns Hopkins University, who was the first American physician to investigate thalidomide in Europe and broadcast the danger. Dr. Taussig published articles and editorials in the leading medical and science journals in the country, including the *Journal of the American Medical Association, Science,* the *New England Medical Journal,* and *Scientific American,* which popular media then excerpted for general readers. Taussig sought to educate her colleagues and the country about the "terrible" effects of thalidomide. "Young women," she warned repeatedly, "must learn to be cautious about new drugs." Meanwhile, "physicians," she urged, "must bear in mind that sleeping tablets, tranquilizers, and other apparently innocent drugs may do terrible harm to the rapidly growing embryo and the unborn child." Quotation in Helen B. Taussig, MD, "Dangerous Tranquility," editorial, *Science* 136, no. 3517 (May 25, 1962): 683; Taussig's report on thalidomide and advice to women excerpted from Helen B. Taussig, "A Study of the German Outbreak of Phocomelia," *JAMA* 180, no. 13 (June 30, 1962), in "A Firsthand Report on What Happened in Europe," *U.S. News and World Report* 53 (August 13, 1962): 54–56.

21. For an example of a lack of awareness in the late 1950s, see Nancy D. Price, *Living With Robbie* (Bloomington, IN: First Books Library, 2003), 8.

22. Susan Gardner, personal communication.

23. *National Enquirer* 36, no. 48 (August 12, 1962), 1, 14–15.

24. "Sleeping Pill Nightmare," *Time* 79 (February 23, 1962): 86, 88.

25. Quoted in Robert K. Plumb, "Deformed Babies Traced to a Drug," *NYT,* April 12, 1962, p. 58.

26. The description of "seal limbs" comes from the medical term *phocomelia,* given to the rare malformation of shortened limbs. "Sleeping Pill Nightmare," 88; "flipper-like arms" in "The Doctor and the Drug," *Newsweek* 60 (July 30, 1962): 70; "The Drug That Left a Trail of Heartbreak," *Life* 53, no. 6 (August 10, 1962), 26.

27. John Lear, "The Unfinished Story of Thalidomide," *Saturday Review* 45 (September 1, 1962): 37.

28. "The Drug That Left a Trail of Heartbreak."

29. "Orthopedics: Help for Thalidomide Victims," *Time* 81 (April 26, 1963): 63.

30. "The Drug That Left a Trail of Heartbreak." For the perspective of adult thalidomiders, see *Frontline Reports: Extraordinary People* (one-hour television news show), PBS, May 2, 1989.

31. Using the *Readers' Guide to Periodical Literature* as a gauge of media attention, I found that no articles had appeared in 1941, the year that congenital defects were first associated with rubella, and over the next few years there were only one or two. During the 1958 epidemic in the United States, when one might have expected more coverage, there were no articles. In 1962, there were two articles. In contrast, for 1963–65, there were sixteen articles on thalidomide and ten on German measles.

32. Scholars offer different estimates. Stephens and Brynner, *Dark Remedy,* 63, report that an estimated 5,000 survived infancy and another estimated 10,000 died at a young age. Hilts, *Protecting America's Health,* 158, 361, reports current "conservative" estimates of about 8,000 "grossly deformed babies born because of thalidomide treatment" mostly in Europe, about 40 cases in the United States, about 100 in Canada, and another 5,000 to 7,000 that ended in miscarriage or died in infancy; Arthur Daemmrich, *Pharmacopolitics: Drug Regulation in the United States and Germany* (Chapel Hill: University of North Carolina Press, 2002), 61, reports 10,000 "deformed children born," 4,000 to 5,000 in Germany and seventeen in the United States.

33. See, for example, "I Pray They'll Hurry" and "Rubbing Out Rubella," *Newsweek* 60 (August 6, 1962): 52.

34. Price, *Living with Robbie,* 8, 13.

35. National Foundation–March of Dimes estimate made in "Rubella (German Measles) and Birth Defects," *March of Dimes Science News Backgrounder,* May 1965, p. 6, folder Birth Defects and Epidemics, series 3 Birth Defects, box 3, MPR-MODA. The CDC estimated that the 1964–65 epidemic resulted in 2,100 excess neonatal deaths, 6,500 excess fetal wastage, 20,000 total children born with congenital rubella syndrome, and 5,000 therapeutic abortions (all

terms used in original). From U.S. Center for Disease Control, *Rubella Surveillance,* 1 (June 1969), as cited and shown in table 11–5 in Plotkin, "Rubella Vaccine," 308.

36. On the changing representation of children hurt by thalidomide, see Reagan, "Monsters in the News." On the March of Dimes and the heroism of "cripples" in general and polios (as people with polio call themselves) in particular, see Oshinsky, *Polio;* Shapiro, *No Pity: People with Disabilities Forging a New Civil Rights Movement* (New York: Random House, 1994), chap. 1; and Daniel J. Wilson, *Living with Polio: The Epidemic and Its Survivors* (Chicago: University of Chicago Press, 2005). Americans were both aware that President Roosevelt had had polio and kept ignorant of his permanent paralysis. See Hugh Gregory Gallagher, *FDR's Splendid Deception* (New York: Dodd, Mead, 1985). For quotation and a clip of the National Foundation film known as *The Crippler* and for informants' stories of the social ramifications of polio and the "cruel[ty]" of other children, see *A Paralyzing Fear: The Story of Polio in America,* VHS and DVD, directed by Nina Gilden Seavey (Washington, DC: George Washington University, 1998), distributed by PBS. On poster children and telethons, see Fred Pelka, *The ABC-CLIO Companion to The Disability Rights Movement* (Santa Barbara, CA: ABC-CLIO, 1997), 301–2.

37. Theodore R. Van Dellen, "How To Keep Well: Harelip Can Be Corrected," *CT,* January 4, 1951, p. 18.

38. Gladys Priddy, "Seek Answers to Tragedies of Pregnancy," *CT,* July 12, 1951, p. W4. On eugenic thought, see Stern, *Eugenic Nation;* on the role of families and communities in the development of genetics, see Susan Lindee, *Moments of Truth in Genetic Medicine* (Baltimore: Johns Hopkins University Press, 2005).

39. Van Dellen, "How To Keep Well: Harelip Can Be Corrected." The doctor also reassured that "heredity is not always responsible for defects" in Theodore R. Van Dellen, "How to Keep Well: Heredity and Disease," *CT,* May 26, 1951, p. 10. Both of these columns pointed out the effects of German measles. Although doing this was not the primary point of the columns, such mention means that regular readers of this type of health column would have known about the danger of the disease during pregnancy. See also E. M. D. Watson, "How to Have a Perfect Baby," *Cosmopolitan* 147 (December 1959): 74, 77; "Will the Baby be Normal?" *Time* 76 (August 1, 1960): 40.

40. Lester David, "New Miracles of Baby Surgery," *Good Housekeeping* 156 (April 1963): 76. See also Bernard Seeman, "New Hope for Perfect Babies," *Coronet* 50 (August 1961): 30–35; Faye Marley, "We Are Not Created Equal," *Science News Letter* 84 (July 27, 1963): 55, 63.

41. Paul K. Longmore and Lauri Umansky, eds., *The New Disability History: American Perspectives* (New York: New York University Press, 2001), 7–9, 19–20, and *passim;* Gary L. Albrecht, ed. *Encyclopedia of Disability* (Thousand Oaks, CA: Sage, 2006).

42. Pernick, *The Black Stork;* James W. Trent, *Inventing the Feeble Mind: A History of Mental Retardation in the United States* (Berkeley and Los Angeles: University of California Press, 1994). On venereal disease films, see Stacie Colwell, "The End of the Road: Gender, the Dissemination of Knowledge, and the American Campaign Against Venereal Disease During World War I," in *The Visible Woman: Imaging Technology, Science, and Gender,* ed. Paula A. Treichler, Lisa Cartwright, and Constance Penley (New York: New York University Press, 1998), 44–82; and John Parascandola, "Syphilis at the Cinema: Medicine and Morals in VD Films of the U.S. Public Health Service in World War II," in *Medicine's Moving Pictures: Medicine, Health, and Bodies in American Film and Television,* ed. Leslie J. Reagan, Nancy Tomes, and Paula A. Treichler (Rochester, NY: Rochester University Press, 2007), 71–92. For World War II films by and for the military with this message, see *Pick-Up* and *Personal Hygiene for Women,* both available at the National Library of Medicine, Washington, DC. The novel is *The Day Is Ours* by Hilda Lewis (1947), as described in Lisa Cartwright, "*Mandy* (1952): On Voice and Listening in the (Deaf) Maternal Melodrama," in *Medicine's Moving Pictures,* chap. 5.

43. Susan Burch, *Signs of Resistance: American Deaf Cultural History, 1900 to World War II* (New York: New York University Press, 2002), 134–37; Pauline M. Moor, "Blind Children with Developmental Problems," *Children* 18, no. 1 (January–February 1961): 9–13; Wendy Kline, *Building a Better Race: Gender, Sexuality, and Eugenics from the Turn of the Century to the Baby Boom* (Berkeley: University of California Press, 2001).

44. Leontyne Hunt, "Keep Your Family the Right Size," *Chicago Defender,* October 26, 1968, p. 11.

45. These accounts are frank reports from parents speaking to other parents, offering moral support and encouragement, and advocating on behalf of parents and people with sensory disabilities. They are rightly proud of their own and their children's achievements. Mary Jean Beaton, *The Road to Autonomy* (Enumclaw, WA: Winepress Publishing, Pleasant Word, 2003); Price, *Living with Robbie;* Marilyn Frederick, "One Mother's Story of Her Daughter with CRS" (paper presented at the National Conference on Deaf-Blindness, Washington, DC, 1997), rubella files, Library, Helen Keller National Center, Sands Point, NY [hereafter cited as HKNC]), also available online at http://hknc.org/Rubella_One_Mothers_Story .htm (accessed January 16, 2008); *Our Deaf-Blind Children Are Whole Persons, Too: Parents Tell Their Story,* comp. Harry C. Anderson, pub. series no. 3 (Office of Demographic and Vocational Potential for the Deaf-Blind, August 1979), HKNC. On the privatized and highly gendered work of caring for children done primarily by women as well as the high divorce rates among couples with disabled children, see Rayna Rapp and Faye Ginsburg, "Enabling Disability: Rewriting Kinship, Reimagining Citizenship," *Public Culture* 13, no. 3 (2001): 542, 551.

46. Theodore R. Van Dellen, "How to Keep Well: Incomplete Mental Development," *CT,* October 8, 1954, p. 16. Van Dellen estimated that 1 percent of the population of the United States was "mentally retarded" and that one-tenth required institutionalization.

47. Moor, "Blind Children with Developmental Problems," quotations on 10, 11, 12, and 9.

48. Thelma Hunt Shirley, "Confetti," *Chicago Defender,* April 25, 1966, p. 12; Trent, *Inventing the Feeble Mind,* 242.

49. Robert B. Kugel et al., "An Analysis of Reasons for Institutionalizing Children with Mongolism," *Journal of Pediatrics* 64, no. 1 (January 1964): 68–74; Brad Byram, "A Pupil and a Patient: Hospital Schools in Progressive America," in *The New Disability History,* 133–156; Michael Bérubé, *Life As We Know It: A Father, A Family, and an Exceptional Child* (New York: Random House, Vintage Books, 1996), 27–33.

50. Trent, *Inventing the Feeble Mind,* 236–42, 250–54.

51. Beaton, *The Road to Autonomy,* 24, 27.

52. Stern, "Take Them Off the Human Scrap Heap," 32. Emphasis in original. The idea that the retarded remained children into their adulthood was new, fostered institutionalization, and would be challenged in the 1970s and 1980s by the movement for independent living. Trent, *Inventing the Feeble Mind,* 230–50.

53. Stern, "Take Them Off the Human Scrap Heap," 32, 62–64. Photos of lost adults and children and "Jail-like discipline—a little girl chained in bed" on p. 32.

54. Trent, *Inventing the Feeble Mind,* 248–56. The mid-1960s exposés included Robert F. Kennedy's attack on Willowbrook State School in 1965 and Burton Blatta and Fred Kaplan's *Christmas in Purgatory* (1966), which *Look* magazine reprinted in 1967.

55. Eunice Kennedy Shriver, "Hope for Retarded Children," *Saturday Evening Post* 235, no. 33 (September 22, 1962): 72. On the Kennedy family, Trent, *Inventing the Feeble Mind,* 246–50; Edward Shorter, *The Kennedy Family and the Story of Mental Retardation* (Philadelphia: Temple University Press, 2000).

56. The author used pseudonyms. Marcia Winn, "Family Has Usual Problems and One That Never Ends," *CT,* September 3, 1956, pp. B7–B8.

57. Ibid., B7.

58. Ibid.

59. Ibid.

60. Ibid.

61. Richard K. Scotch, *From Good Will to Civil Rights: Transforming Federal Disability Policy* (Philadelphia: Temple University Press, 1984).

62. "Rex Morgan, M.D.," *LAT,* October 3, 1965, p. 5. First created in 1948, "Rex Morgan, M.D.," was a popular nationally syndicated comic strip that earned great praise from the medical profession and health organizations. "Rex

Morgan Revealed," *Time,* January 25, 1954, www.time.com/time/magazine/article/0,9171,823238,00.html (accessed June 26, 2009).

63. "Rex Morgan Revealed"; Kathleen W. Jones, "Mother Made Me Do It: Mother-Blaming and the Women of Child Guidance," in Molly Ladd-Taylor and Lauri Umansky, eds. *"Bad" Mothers: The Politics of Blame in Twentieth-Century America* (New York: New York University Press, 1998), 99–134; Paula J. Caplan, "Mother-Blaming," ibid., 127–44.

64. Trent, *Inventing the Feeble Mind,* 230–37; Cartwright, *"Mandy* (1952)," 136.

65. Steven M. Spencer, "Attack on the Unborn," *Saturday Evening Post* 238 (March 13, 1965): 83. See also a photo of an African American boy identified as mentally retarded because his mother had had German measles. "Will It Help, Doc?" *Chicago Defender,* January 9, 1965, p. 9.

66. Spencer, "Attack on the Unborn." Six months later U.S. Senator Robert F. Kennedy assailed the conditions at Willowbrook and other state institutions for the retarded. In 1972, Geraldo Rivera produced an ABC-TV special news report on Willowbrook and other New York Institutions. Trent, *Inventing the Feeble Mind,* 254; Geraldo Rivera, *Willowbrook: A Report on How It Is and Why It Doesn't Have to Be That Way* (New York: Random House, 1972).

67. "Has Problem with Glasses," *CT,* September 2, 1965, p. C10; "Sporting Her Specs," entry posted August 24, 2006, at www.theohreally.com/?p = 1447 (accessed March 27, 2007). Original photo cited to *Clarion-Ledger,* September 1, 1965.

68. Milt Bourhard, "Lenses Brighten Baby's World," *LAT,* March 31, 1966, p. OC1.

69. "Sporting Her Specs." Quotations from original AP wire photo caption and from Sally, online commentator at www.theohreally.com. For another column emphasizing the benefits of modern science and glasses on babies, see T. R. Van Dellen, "How to Keep Your Child Well: Tiniest Specs Wearer," *CT,* February 13, 1966, F6. On freaks, see Rosemarie Garland Thomson, "Seeing the Disabled: Visual Rhetorics of Disability in Popular Photography," in *The New Disability History,* 335–75; Rachel Adams, *Sideshow U.S.A.: Freaks and the American Cultural Imagination* (Chicago: University of Chicago Press, 2001).

70. Personal communication, Chris Tarr.

71. This is a moving account of Eugene Beaton's childhood and Mary Jean's mothering. Beaton, *The Road to Autonomy,* 29–32.

72. "The Boy Who Tuned Out," *Newsweek* 73 (April 13, 1964): 90.

73. See Lynn Lilliston, "Variety of Handicaps Hurts Rubella Children," *LAT,* Feb. 12, 1968, p. C1. One example comes from a later lawsuit. This family, whose daughter was identified as a "rubella baby" in 1977, moved from rural Kamiah, Idaho, to an urban area of Ohio "in order to have access to the type of special education and medical attention that Dessie requires, as well as to be able to earn enough money to be able to pay for her extraordinary needs. At the time the

Blakes made the move, the only special education for the deaf available in Idaho was a residential school in southern Idaho, and Mr. and Mrs. Blake did not want to send their daughter away from home at age three for the duration of her schooling." *Blake v. Cruz* 698 P2d 315 (Idaho 1984), p. 317.

74. "Spots All Over." See also "Worst Rash of Measles."

75. On baby books, personal communication from Janet Golden, 23 March 2008. See Dorothy Barclay, "Medical Records Vital Throughout Child's Life," *NYT,* June 11, 1957, p. 38, for discussion of the difficulty of keeping track of health information. An African American newspaper urged its readers that for New Year's they "resolve to begin in 1962 keeping a family health record." It suggested recording immunizations and diseases, including German measles. "Urge Families to Keep Health Records in 1962," *Tri-State Defender* (Memphis, TN), January 13, 1962, p. 9. Located through the online collection *Ethnic Newswatch.*

76. Goodrich C. Schauffler, MD, "Tell Me, Doctor," *Ladies' Home Journal* 79 (March 1962): 12.

77. Ibid.

78. Ibid.

79. L. Emmett Holt, MD, "The German Measles Problem," *Good Housekeeping* 139 (September 1954): 102; quotation in Spencer, "Attack on the Unborn," 83.

80. For example, see "Worst Rash of Measles."

81. T. R. Van Dellen, "How to Keep Well: Blood Tests in German Measles," *CT,* December 28, 1964, p. 14.

82. The holding of Mary Mallon for typhoid was the complicated exception to the general rule that the sick are held in isolation, not the healthy. See Leavitt, *Typhoid Mary.*

83. Lundy Braun, personal communication, 15 November 2008.

84. Eight nurses and one physician at New York University Hospital contracted the disease from babies, Dr. Louis Z. Cooper reported. "Infectious Diseases: Dangerous Babies," *Time* 85 (February 26, 1965): 77. See also "Three on Hospital Staff Get Rubella From Babies," *Science News Letter* 88 (September 11, 1965): 169.

85. "Infectious Diseases"; "Rubella Vaccine Urgent," *Science News Letter* 88 (November 6, 1965): 293.

86. Leavitt, *Typhoid Mary.*

87. Charles Swan and A. L. Tostevin, "Congenital Abnormalities in Infants Following Infectious Diseases During Pregnancy, With Special Reference to Rubella: A Third Series of Cases," *Medical Journal of Australia* (hereafter cited as *MJA*) vol. I–33rd year, no. 19 (May 11, 1946): 658; Charles Swan, "Congenital Malformations Associated with Rubella and Other Virus Infections," *Modern Practice in Infectious Fevers* (New York: Harper, 1951).

88. According to *Newsweek,* Gregg "is firm in his recommendation of therapeutic abortion in all cases where rubella is contracted in the first or second

month of pregnancy. The Swan group in Adelaide is more conservative. . . . But in American laboratories, where researchers are digging into the question of the exact effect of rubella on the mother, and on the heart, mental condition and auditory system of her offspring, Gregg has solid support. Many New York City eye men who estimate that cataract complications occur in 90 per cent of the rubella cases, unquestionably advise an expectant mother with German measles to undergo an abortion." "German Measles in Pregnancy May Give Cataracts to Baby," *Newsweek* 24 (August 28, 1944): 75–76.

89. Gregg's remark also suggests an assumption that the doctor or man of the family would make these decisions. At the same time, physicians indicated the strength of their medical judgments when they asserted that they would follow specific therapies for their own wives, children, and family members. Gregg spoke at the annual meeting of the American Academy of Ophthalmology and Oto-laryngology (eye, ear, nose, and throat); quoted in John H. Thompson, "Urge Aborting Pregnancy in Measles Cases," *CT,* October 15, 1955, p. A11.

90. For summaries of the medical literature and opposing views on therapeutic abortion for maternal rubella by American and Swedish physicians, see Conrad Wesselhoeft, "Medical Progress: Rubella (German Measles) (Concluded)," *New England Journal of Medicine* 236, no. 26 (June 26, 1947): 985; and Rolf Lundstrom, *Rubella During Pregnancy: A Follow-Up Study of Children Born after an Epidemic of Rubella in Sweden, 1951, with Additional Investigations on Prophylaxis and Treatment of Maternal Rubella* (Uppsala, Sweden: Appelbergy Boktryckeri, 1962), 80–83. For a summary of reports in the medical literature on the percentage of therapeutic abortions performed for rubella, see Luker, *Abortion and the Politics of Motherhood,* 278 n. 11, 279 n. 18; and Nicholson J. Eastman, *Williams Obstetrics,* 10th ed., (New York: Appleton-Century- Crofts, 1950), 707. Dr. John Rendle-Short of the University of Queensland, Australia, observed that the decision to end a pregnancy due to rubella "is a matter for the parents to decide in the light of their religious beliefs." As reported in "Measles Threat to Unborn," *Science News Letter* 86 (September 26, 1964): 194. See also Lawrence Lader, *Abortion* (Boston: Beacon Press, 1966), 36–37, 181 nn. 6, 7.

91. Watson, "How to Have a Perfect Baby," 75.

92. Reagan, *When Abortion Was a Crime;* Lader, *Abortion,* chaps. 2–3; Rickie Solinger, " 'A Complete Disaster': Abortion and the Politics of Hospital Abortion Committees, 1950–1970," *Feminist Studies* 19, no. 2 (Summer 1993): 241–68.

93. On abortion and birth control in the 1930s, see Reagan, *When Abortion Was a Crime,* chap. 5; Gordon, *Woman's Body, Woman's Right,* chaps. 11–12; Andrea Tone, *Devices and Desires: A History of Contraceptives in America* (New York: Hill and Wang, 2001).

94. Quotation in Robert E. Hall, "Abortion in American Hospitals," *American Journal of Public Health* (hereafter cited as *AJPH*) 57, no. 1 (November 1967): 1934–35. See also Robert E. Hall, "Therapeutic Abortion, Sterilization, and

Contraception," *American Journal of Obstetrics and Gynecology* (hereafter cited as *AJOG*) 91, no. 4 (February 15, 1965): 523. Hall found that for rubella, as for therapeutic abortion generally, more therapeutic abortions were performed for private patients than for ward patients, a ratio of 9–1.

95. Reagan, *When Abortion Was a Crime,* chap. 6; Rickie Solinger, *The Abortionist: A Woman Against the Law* (New York: Free Press, 1994).

96. "The Abortion Menace," *Ebony* 6 (January 1951), quotation on 21, photo and caption on 22.

97. John Bartlow Martin, "Abortion," Part 1, *Saturday Evening Post* 234 (May 20, 1961): 19, photos on 20–21. "Abortion," Part 2, *Saturday Evening Post* 234 (May 27, 1961): 20–21, 49, 52, 55; "Abortion," Part 3, *Saturday Evening Post* 234 (June 3, 1961): 25; "The Abortion Menace," 22, 24, 25. See also Reagan, *When Abortion Was a Crime;* and Solinger, *The Abortionist.*

98. Reagan, *When Abortion Was a Crime,* chap. 2.

99. On labeling women as psychologically immature, see Reagan, "From Hazard to Blessing to Tragedy," 362–63; Jane Taylor McDonnell, "On Being the 'Bad' Mother of an Autistic Child," in *"Bad" Mothers: The Politics of Blame in Twentieth-Century America,* ed. Molly Ladd-Taylor and Lauri Umansky (New York: New York University Press, 1998), 220–29; Regina G. Kunzel, "White Neurosis, Black Pathology: Constructing Out-of-Wedlock Pregnancy in the Wartime and Postwar United States" in *Not June Cleaver: Women and Gender in Postwar America, 1945–1960,* ed. Joanne Meyerowitz (Philadelphia: Temple University Press, 1994), 304–31; Rickie Solinger, *Wake Up Little Susie: Single Pregnancy and Race Before Roe v. Wade* (New York: Routledge, 1992); Ruth Feldstein, "Antiracism and Maternal Failure in the 1940s and 1950s," in *"Bad" Mothers,* 145–90; Margaret Marsh and Wanda Ronner, *The Empty Cradle: Infertility in America from Colonial Times to the Present* (Baltimore: Johns Hopkins University Press, 1996); Lillian Faderman, *Odd Girls and Twilight Lovers: A History of Lesbian Life in Twentieth-Century America* (New York: Columbia University Press, 1991).

100. Martin, "Abortion," Part 1, 72.

101. Ibid., 72, 74. In my previous research, white men and women told me repeatedly of the black abortionist that "everyone" went to or referred to going into black neighborhoods for illegal abortions. To some extent, black practitioners did provide abortions to white women as well as to black women, but by no means were African Americans the majority of abortion specialists.

102. For an example, see James McBride, *The Color of Water: A Black Man's Tribute to His White Mother* (New York: Penguin Putnam, Riverhead Books, 1996).

103. Peggy Pascoe, "Miscegenation Law, Court Cases, and Ideologies of 'Race' in Twentieth-Century America," *Journal of American History* 83, no. 1 (June 1996): 44–69; *Loving v. Virginia,* 388 U.S. 1 (1967); Elizabeth Pleck, "The Stigma

of Cohabitation in the United States, 1960–1990," forthcoming; Johanna Schoen, *Choice and Coercion: Birth Control, Sterilization, and Abortion in Public Health and Welfare* (Chapel Hill: University of North Carolina Press, 2005), 95; Linda Gordon, *Heroes of Their Own Lives: The Politics and History of Family Violence—Boston, 1880–1960* (New York: Viking, 1988); Solinger, *Wake Up Little Susie,* chaps. 1, 2, and 6.

104. The Nashville physician and baseball team owner was Dr. Reuben Jackson. "The Abortion Menace," *Ebony* 6 (January 1951): photo and caption on p. 25.

105. Ed Keemer, *Confessions of a Pro-Life Abortionist* (Detroit: Vinco Press, 1980), 171–72; Ida B. Wells, *Crusade for Justice: The Autobiography of Ida B. Wells,* ed. Alfreda M. Duster (Chicago: University of Chicago Press, 1991); Darlene Clark Hine, "Rape and the Inner Lives of Black Women in the Middle West," *Signs* 14, no. 4 (Summer 1989): 919–20. On twentieth-century rape trials and race, see Dawn Flood, " 'They Didn't Treat Me Good': African American Rape Victims and Chicago Courtroom Strategies during the 1950s," *Journal of Women's History* 17, no. 1 (Spring 2005): 38–61. On the linking of rape and abortion in legal thought, see Leslie J. Reagan, "Victim or Accomplice?: Crime, Medical Malpractice, and the Construction of the Aborting Woman in American Case Law, 1860s–1970," *Columbia Journal of Gender and Law* 10, no. 2 (2001): 311–32.

106. Reagan, *When Abortion Was a Crime,* especially chap. 1.

107. Winfield Best and Frederick S. Jaffee, "Should Abortion Laws Be Liberalized?" *Parents Magazine* 40 (June 1965): 50.

108. Solinger, *Wake Up Little Susie;* Ruth Feldstein, *Motherhood in Black and White: Race and Sex in American Liberalism, 1930–1965* (Ithaca, NY: Cornell University Press, 2000); Elena R. Gutierrez, "Policing 'Pregnant Pilgrims': Sterilization Abuse of Mexican-Origin Women in Los Angeles County," in *Women, Health, and Nation: Canada and the United States Since 1945* (Montreal: McGill; Kingston, ON: Queen's University Press, 2003), chap. 19.

109. Schauffler, "Tell Me, Doctor," 12, 14.

110. Ibid.

111. The likelihood of having a child with malformations was generally put at 1 percent or between 1 and 2 percent. See Van Dellen, "How to Keep Well: Heredity and Disease"; Victoria P. Coffey and W. J. E. Jessop, "Rubella and the Incidence of Congenital Abnormalities," *Irish Medical Journal of Medical Science* 6, no. 397 (January 1959): 11. Many doctors would have considered this one's estimate of the 10 percent risk following maternal contractions of rubella low. This topic will be discussed further in chapter 3.

112. Schauffler, "Tell Me, Doctor," 14.

113. Ibid., 12, 14.

114. Marcia Winn, "You and Your Child: Problem of Childhood Contagious Ailments," *CT,* June 12, 1951, p. A1.

115. Schauffler, "Tell Me, Doctor," 14.

116. On advising parents to expose their daughters to the disease, see "Rubella and the Unborn," *Newsweek* 31 (March 29, 1948): 48; "Catch German Measles"; and "Catch It If You Can."

117. Barbara Goodheart, "Exit German Measles?" *Today's Health* 47 (June 1969): 28. By the early 1960s, responsible mothers were urged to keep their sick children away from other (potentially pregnant) women. Compare U.S. Children's Bureau, *Infant Care* (Washington, DC: GPO, 1955), 85; and U.S. Children's Bureau, *Infant Care* (Washington, DC: GPO, 1963), 80.

118. "Infectious Diseases: German Measles Epidemic," *Time* 83 (April 24, 1964): 42.

119. "Pre-Natal Care Life Saving, Should Begin in Childhood," April 16, 1964, Colorado Medical Society, folder American Baby, box 1, series 1: Correspondence, Apgar Papers, MODA (hereafter cited as AP-MODA). See also Virginia Apgar, "Preparing for Motherhood Can Avoid Birth Defects," *(Vallejo, CA) Times-Herald,* January 12, 1968, folder 11, box 11, series 6, Virginia Apgar Papers, Mt. Holyoke College Archives and Special Collections (hereafter cited as VAP-MHCA), South Hadley, MA; and Virginia Apgar, "The ABC's of Motherhood," *St. Louis Globe-Democrat,* January 23, 1969, ibid.

120. T. R. Van Dellen, "How to Keep Well: Have Your Rubella Before Marriage," *CT,* April 25, 1957, p. 14.

121. Schauffler, "Tell Me, Doctor," 14.

122. Bill Becker, "Abortion to Bar Defective Birth Is Facing Legal Snag in Arizona," *NYT,* July 25, 1962, p. 22.

123. "Abortion—With the Future Dim, Should the Unborn Die?" *Life* 53 (August 1962): 33.

124. A local newspaper named the Finkbines' religious affiliation with the Unitarian Church; her husband's parents were Jewish-Protestant. Gene McLain, "Court Decision Delay Couple's Big Concern," *(Phoenix) Arizona Republic,* July 26, 1962, 16, folder 520. T15, General Subject File 1938–1974, Division of General Services, RG88, FDA Records, National Archives, College Park, MD.

125. "The Drug That Left a Trail of Heartbreak," photos on 31–33.

126. Finkbine, "The Lesser of Two Evils," 20–22.

127. Sherri Finkbine, as told to Joseph Stocker, "The Baby We Didn't Dare to Have," *Redbook* 120 (January 1963): quotations on 99, 100, 104.

128. Gallup Poll no. 662, for August 23–28, 1962. Gallup Brain, http: institution.gallup.com/documents/questionnaire.aspx?study=AIP00662 (accessed May 7, 2009).

129. Finkbine, "The Lesser of Two Evils," 19.

130. *CBS Reports: Abortion and the Law,* broadcast April 5, 1965, now distributed as *Before Roe v. Wade: Abortion and the Law, 1965,* Films for the Humanities and Sciences, print held at the University of Illinois, Urbana-Champaign Media Center, Undergraduate Library. Produced by David Lowe, *CBS Reports: Abortion*

*and the Law* was originally broadcast the evening of April 5, 1965, when it competed with the Academy Awards, and then rebroadcast May 17, 1965. It received positive reviews; CBS reported receiving many letters from viewers saying "thank you." Though condemned by some, the station advertised its commitment to investigation and to an open airing of "the facts." Newspaper advertisements showed a young woman in profile with this headline above: "I'm going out to have an abortion if you don't do it. It'll probably be done badly. I may die." Advertisement for *CBS Reports: Abortion and the Law, NYT,* May 17, 1965, p. 70. The advertisement also appeared in the *Washington Post* and the *Chicago Tribune.* The show received a highly positive review from Jack Gould, "T.V. Documentary Views Abortion," *NYT,* April 6, 1965, p. 79. The columnist for the (African American) *Chicago Defender* used the show as an opportunity to discuss birth control. Louise P. Dumetz, "Keeping Pace," *Chicago Daily Defender,* April 7, 1965, p. 18. There are no numbers available to indicate the size of the viewing audience.

131. The German measles epidemic was not yet over at the time of this show, for it was then hitting the West Coast and Hawaii.

132. "Question of Emphasis," *America* 112 (April 17, 1965): 513. A search of popular periodicals did not uncover other discussions of this show.

133. See chapter 4 of this text.

134. *Life* 58, no. 22 (June 4, 1965), cover.

135. "The Agony of Mothers about Their Unborn," *Life* 58, no. 22 (June 4, 1965): 29.

136. Betty Friedan, *The Feminine Mystique* (New York: W. W. Norton, 1963); Daniel Horowitz, *Betty Friedan and the Making of* The Feminine Mystique: *The American Left, the Cold War, and Modern Feminism* (Amherst: University of Massachusetts Press, 1998).

137. T. R. Van Dellen, "How to Keep Well: Blood Tests in German Measles," *CT,* December 28, 1964, p. 14.

138. Roy Gibbons, "Reveal Test Finds Measles in Pregnancy," *CT,* October 23, 1964, p. B11.

139. Spencer, "Attack on the Unborn," 83; "Test Reassures Women Exposed to Rubella," *Science News* 90 ( November 12, 1966): 401; Gibbons, "Reveal Test." For a description of the older tests and the later, quicker tests (the HI test), see U.S. Department of Health, Education, and Welfare, *Rubella,* PHS pamphlet no. 2041, prepared by Jane S. Lin-Fu (Washington, DC: GPO, 1970), pp. 5, 3, folder Birth Defects Rubella Printed Literature and Posters, 1970–71, series 3 Birth Defects, box 3, MPR–MODA. Dr. D. Paul Parkman, oral history by Sarah Leavitt, June 7, 2005, p. 13, Office of NIH History, National Institutes of Health, Bethesda, MD.

140. Ronald Kotulak, "See German Measles Vaccine in 5 Years," *CT,* October 28, 1966, p. 14. NIH's Dr. Harry M. Meyer Jr. and Dr. Paul D. Parkman re-

ported their successes at the annual meeting of the American Academy of Pediatrics in October.

141. Harry Nelson, "Quick Measles Immunity Test for Pregnant Women Due Soon," *LAT*, November 17, 1966, p. B1.

142. "The Agony of Mothers About Their Unborn," photos on 24–25, quotation on 24.

143. The legal status of therapeutic abortions will be discussed further in the next chapter.

144. "The Agony of Mothers About Their Unborn," 26–27.

145. See Leslie Woodcock Tentler, *Catholics and Contraception: An American History* (Ithaca, NY: Cornell University Press, 2004), chaps. 5 and 6; on Rock and media interest in Catholic dissent and disagreement on these issues specifically, see pp. 210–216; Lara V. Marks, *Sexual Chemistry: A History of the Contraceptive Pill* (New Haven, CT: Yale University Press, 2001), chap. 9; Margaret Marsh and Wanda Rommer, *The Fertility Doctor: John Rock and the Reproductive Revolution* (Baltimore: Johns Hopkins University Press, 2008). Margaret Sanger, raised in the Catholic Church, had always vehemently attacked the church herself. See David M. Kennedy, *Birth Control in America: The Career of Margaret Sanger* (New Haven, CT: Yale University Press, 1970), chap. 6; Ellen Chesler, *Woman of Valor: Margaret Sanger and the Birth Control Movement in America* (New York: Simon and Schuster, 1992).

146. Each of these conversations invokes two unequal partners; each includes a parental/paternalistic figure: the mother to child, doctor to female patient, priest to female communicant. The magazine also reported that her parish priest was "a member of a committee opposing legislation that would liberalize the California abortion law," but when Mrs. Stonebreaker was deciding what to do, he had told her, "You should not use religion as an excuse for not making a decision." "The Agony of Mothers about Their Unborn," 27.

147. The magazine and the two Los Angeles correspondents singled out the doctor for his bravery. Mothers, an editor's note began, made the shattering decision to have therapeutic abortions. It is a tragic story, but the mothers themselves wanted it told because, as they put it, "it might help other women as terribly caught up as we are." The doctor, "a brave man," was found after sixty fruitless phone calls to physicians and then a conversation with Dr. Keith Russell, head of the California Obstetricians Society, who believed the abortion law should be "updated" and gave them a name of another doctor friend. After "deliberating," the unnamed doctor "decided that such an important moral and medical issue should be brought into the open." George P. Hunt, "Editor's Note: Two Mothers and a Brave Doctor," *Life* 58, no. 22 (June 4, 1965): 3.

148. "Five Priests Sue Magazine for $5 Million," *LAT*, June 10, 1965, p. B5; "Merced Priests to Drop Suit," *LAT*, September 1, 1965, p. 23.

149. "Current Comment: Catholic Abortions," *America* 113 (September 18, 1965): 273. See "A Correction," *Life* (September 3, 1965).

150. Tentler finds much distress among priests about their role in enforcing church teachings on contraception and some relief when they could avoid the issue or express more liberal and forgiving views to confessors. In this period of high expectation that the church would change its views on contraception and of turmoil among priests as well as the laity, it is likely that some priests did express forgiving and reassuring attitudes concerning abortion. Indeed, some Catholic priests, nuns, theologians, and laity advocated legalization of abortion and compassion. Priests and nuns could also be punished for expressing more liberal attitudes. On priests and contraception, see Tentler, *Catholics and Contraception,* 144–53, 232–63. On Catholic advocates for legal abortion, see Barbara Ferraro and Patricia Hussey, with Jane O'Reilly, *Turning Back: Two Nuns' Battle with the Vatican over Women's Right to Choose* (New York: Ivy Books, 1990); and publications and statements from Catholics for Free Choice, available at www .catholicsforchoice.org. On Catholic women opposed to the feminism they find in their church and their organizing in the 1980s, see Helen Hull Hitchock, "Women for Faith and Family: Catholic Women Affirming Catholic Teaching," in *Being Right: Conservative Catholics in America,* ed. Mary Jo Weaver and R. Scott Appleby (Bloomington: Indiana University Press, 1995), chap. 7.

151. On the emerging antiabortion movement in California, see chapter 4 of this book and also Luker, *Abortion and the Politics of Motherhood;* and Carol Mason, *Killing for Life: The Apocalyptic Narrative of Pro-Life Politics* (Ithaca, NY: Cornell University Press, 2002), chap. 5.

152. "The Agony of Mothers About Their Unborn," 29.

153. Rubella Symposium, *American Journal of Diseases of Children* 110, no. 4 (October 1965).

154. The provision of therapeutic abortion for German measles increased with the epidemic. For instance, one study of two Buffalo hospitals found that German measles accounted for over one third of the therapeutic abortions performed in 1964; "Indications for Therapeutic Abortions Change," *JAMA* 193, no. 1 (July 5, 1965): 45.

155. Marilyn Frederick, "One Mother's Story of Her Daughter with CRS"; Price, *Living With Robbie,* 6–9; Beaton, *The Road to Autonomy.* All of these accounts are about the women's own experiences as mothers of "rubella babies," about their work to care and advocate for their children, and about their children. They do not focus on pregnancy and decisions but rather on the next thirty or forty years.

156. "The Agony of Mothers about Their Unborn," 30–31.

157. Photo of infant at New York University Medical Center, ibid., 31.

158. "Tragic Pregnancy," *Good Housekeeping* 162 (January 1966): 12–26.

159. Ibid., quotations on 12.

160. Ibid., 22.

161. Reagan, *When Abortion Was a Crime;* Solinger, "A Complete Disaster." See the documentary *Voices of Choice* (25 min., produced by Physicians for Reproductive Choice and Health and Fly on the Wall Productions, 2003) for a discussion of these committees. See http://prch.org/physicians-voices-voices-choice. On the nineteenth-century criminalization of abortion, see James Mohr, *Abortion in America: The Origins and Evolution of National Policy, 1800–1900* (New York: Oxford University Press, 1978); Gordon, *Woman's Body, Woman's Right;* Janet Farrell Brodie, *Contraception and Abortion in Nineteenth-Century America* (Ithaca, NY: Cornell University Press, 1994).

162. "Tragic Pregnancy," 22. Note that this sentence is the only place where the husband, Joel, is named, and the structure of the question "What about Joel, and the other children?" almost places him as one of the children. "Mummy" is never named.

163. Ibid., 22, 26.

164. On the formulaic pronatalist ending of popular articles at the time, see Reagan, "From Hazard to Blessing to Tragedy," 361.

165. Reagan, *When Abortion Was a Crime.*

166. "Tragic Pregnancy," photo (which I assume is staged) and quotations on 15.

167. When people are ignorant about the realities of disability, however, they may imagine their worst fears. See Bérubé, *Life As We Know It;* Rayna Rapp, *Testing Women, Testing the Fetus: The Social Impact of Amniocentesis in America* (New York: Routledge, 1999), chaps. 5–6.

168. Gordon, *Woman's Body, Woman's Right.*

169. Working-class women and couples tended to be ready for children at a younger age than middle-class, college-educated women and couples, for example. Wealthier families judged that they needed more money to have a child than the poor or working-class mother or couple did. During the baby boom, however, the age of marriage fell, family size rose, and families grouped births together rather than spacing them. On the idea of family planning and the commitment to planning in general during this period, see Gordon, *Woman's Body, Woman's Right,* 340–43; Rose Holz, "The Birth Control Clinic in America: Life Within, Life Without, 1923–1973" (PhD diss., University of Illinois, Urbana-Champaign, 2002).

170. On the prevention of inherited conditions, see Stern, *Eugenic Nation;* Keith Wailoo, *Dying in the City of Blues: Sickle Cell Anemia and the Politics of Race and Health* (Chapel Hill: University of North Carolina Press, 2001); Keith Wailoo and Stephen Pemberton, *The Troubled Dream of Genetic Medicine: Ethnicity and Innovation in Tay-Sachs, Cystic Fibrosis, and Sickle Cell Disease* (Baltimore: Johns Hopkins University Press, 2006); M. Susan Lindee, *Moments of Truth in Genetic Medicine* (Baltimore: Johns Hopkins University Press, 2005). The March of Dimes was a leader in expanding genetic counseling and in counseling the

prevention of birth defects. For example, see Virginia Apgar, "Birth Defects . . . A National Concern," *Journal of Home Economics* 56, no. 1 (January 1964): 18–21, folder Professional Journals and Associations, 1951–1965, series 2: Publications, Box 2, AP-MODA.

171. Seeing pregnancy and children as products of *desire* in both senses of the term—sexual desire and desire for children—too narrowly describes the processes of pregnancy, childbearing, and family formation. In saying this, I do not mean that desire is bad nor that it should be the only basis for family.

172. Rapp, *Testing Women, Testing the Fetus*, 3, 306–11. See also Barbara Katz Rothman, *The Tentative Pregnancy: How Amniocentesis Changes the Experience of Motherhood* (New York: W. W. Norton, 1993).

### THREE. WRONGFUL INFORMATION

1. E. M. D. Watson, "How to Have a Perfect Baby," *Cosmopolitan* 147 (December 1959): 75. The 1950, 1956, and 1961 versions of *Williams Obstetrics* all had the same sentence. In Nicholson J. Eastman, *Williams Obstetrics*, 10th ed. (New York: Appleton-Century Crofts, 1950), 786; Nicholson J. Eastman and Louis M. Hellman, *Williams Obstetrics*, 11th ed. (New York: Appleton-Century Crofts, 1956), 786; Nicholson J. Eastman and Louis M. Hellman, *Williams Obstetrics*, 12th ed. (New York: Appleton-Century Crofts, 1961), 786.

2. *Gleitman v. Cosgrove*, 49 N.J. 22, 227 A.2d 689 (1967); *Stewart v. Long Island College Hospital*, 296 N.Y.S.2d 41, 58 Misc.2d 432 (1968); *Stewart v. Long Island College Hospital* 313 N.Y.S.2d 502, 35 A.D.2d 531 (1970); *Stewart v. Long Island College Hospital*, 30 N.Y.S.2d 695, 283 N.E.2d 616 (1972).

3. *Roe v. Wade*, 410 U.S. 479 (1973); *Doe v. Bolton*, 410 U.S. 179 (1973).

4. Most states now permit wrongful birth suits, though they remain subject to debate. Only three states permit wrongful life suits. These phrases are currently used in cases regarding amniocentesis and genetic testing, but they have also been used in suits regarding failed contraception or sterilization. The origin of these labels is not clear. *Gleitman* and *Stewart* were not referred to as "wrongful birth" or "wrongful life" suits at the time. The terms appear to be derived from torts for "wrongful death." *Gleitman* cited Tedeschi, "On Tort Liability for 'Wrongful Life,'" *Israel Law Review* 1 (1966): 513, 529. "Wrongful birth" did not appear in a similar appellate case regarding rubella and abortion until *Jacobs v. Theimer*, 519 S.W.2d 846, 18 Tex.Sup.J. 222 (1975). On this type of tort, see Wendy F. Hensel, "Disabling Impact of Wrongful Birth and Wrongful Life Actions," *Harvard Civil Rights and Civil Liberties Law Review* 40, no. 1 (Winter 2005): 141–96; Barry R. Furrow et al., *Health Law*, vol. 2, 2nd ed. (St. Paul, MN: West Group, 2000), chap. 17, 361–73; Elizabeth Weil, "A Wrongful Birth?" *New York Times Magazine*, March 12, 2006.

5. James C. Mohr, *Doctors and the Law: Medical Jurisprudence in Nineteenth-Century America* (New York: Oxford University Press, 1993); Kenneth Allen De Ville, *Medical Malpractice in Nineteenth-Century America* (New York: New York University Press, 1990); Barbara Young Welke, *Recasting American Liberty: Gender, Race, Law, and the Railroad Revolution, 1865–1920* (London: Cambridge University Press, 2001); Leslie J. Reagan, "Victim or Accomplice?: Crime, Medical Malpractice, and the Construction of the Aborting Woman in American Case Law, 1860s–1970," *Columbia Journal of Gender and Law* 10, no. 2 (2001): 311–31; Chester R. Burns, "Malpractice Suits in American Medicine Before the Civil War," *Bulletin of the History of Medicine* 43 (1969): 41–56. See also Leslie J. Reagan, "Law and Medicine," in *Cambridge History of Law in America*, vol. 3, ed. Christopher Tomlins and Michael Grossberg (London: Cambridge University Press, 2008), chap. 7.

6. Furrow, *Health Law*, 363. There is a large legal literature on these types of suits. I cite some examples. On the continuing significance of *Gleitman v. Cosgrove* as precedent and on early jurists' dismissal of these torts because of abortion, see Deana A. Pollard, "Wrongful Analysis in Wrongful Life Jurisprudence," *Alabama Law Review* 55 (Winter 2004): 327–75. For a discussion of the pro-life movement's use of tort against physicians who perform abortions in order to erode the legitimacy of wrongful birth cases, thus clearing the way for health care providers to mislead women about their pregnancies, see A. J. Stone, "Consti-tortion: Tort Law as an End-Run Around Abortion Rights After *Planned Parenthood v. Casey*," *American University Journal of Gender, Social Policy and the Law* 8 (2000): 472, 514. On disabilities, see Hensel, "The Disabling Impact of Wrongful Birth and Wrongful Life Actions," 141; Jennifer R. Granchi, "The Wrongful Birth Tort: A Policy Analysis and the Right to Sue for an Inconvenient Child," *South Texas Law Review* 43 (Fall 2002): 1261–87 (both were opposed to these types of suits); and Pilar N. Ossorio, "Prenatal Genetic Testing and the Courts," in *Prenatal Testing and Disability Rights,* ed. Erik Parens and Adrienne Asch (Washington, DC: Georgetown University Press, 2000), 308–33. For arguments that wrongful life suits should be permitted and treated as negligence and that they are advantageous to people with disabilities, see Pollard, "Wrongful Analysis," 369–74. For historical analysis of similar suits regarding FAS, see Janet Golden, *Message in a Bottle: The Making of Fetal Alcohol Syndrome* (Cambridge, MA: Harvard University Press, 2005), chap. 7.

7. For a helpful article analyzing the assertions of tort reformers in the 1990s and 2000s and a review of the research—including studies that begin by identifying medical errors through hospital medical records and then finding out how many patients complained or contacted attorneys, see David A. Hyman and Charles Silver, "Medical Malpractice Litigation and Tort Reform: It's the Incentives, Stupid," *Vanderbilt Law Review* 59 (May 2006): 1085–1136.

8. The Stewarts' attorney lost a similar case, as reported in Marion K. Sanders, "The Right Not to Be Born," *Harper's* 240 (April 1970): 92. There may have been other cases that never went anywhere in the legal system nor received public attention. I do not present the two cases in chronological order because the record is thinner for the earlier case, for which I do not have a transcript. How these patients found their attorneys is unknown. Nor do I know whether the Stewarts knew of the earlier suit brought by the Gleitmans. The news coverage of *Gleitman* appeared after the Stewarts had filed their complaint, but it seems likely that the two attorneys knew each other or knew of the suits.

9. Transcript of *Stewart v. Long Island College Hospital,* 35 AD2d 531 (1970), 132, 135, 138, 305–6; New York Supreme Court Appellate Division Cases and Briefs held at New York State Library, Albany, NY. Hereafter cited as Transcript of *Stewart.* For news reports, see "Worst Rash of Measles," *Business Week* (April 4, 1964): 98; quotation from "Spots All Over," *Newsweek* 73 (April 13, 1964): 90.

10. Transcript of *Stewart,* 284.

11. Rayna Rapp, *Testing Women, Testing the Fetus: The Social Impact of Amniocentesis in America* (New York: Routledge, 1999).

12. Transcript of *Stewart,* 204.

13. Ibid., 195; Robert E. Hall, "New York Abortion Law Survey," *AJOG* 93, no. 8 (December 15, 1965): 1182–83.

14. Dr. Louis Z. Cooper in Transcript of *Stewart,* 8–83.

15. Transcript of *Stewart,* 149, 150, quotation on 151.

16. Transcript of *Stewart,* 298, quotation on 306.

17. See Plaintiffs' Exhibit 4 in Transcript of *Stewart,* 693.

18. The complaint was first served on March 19, 1965. Brief of Plaintiff-Appellant, Rosalyn Stewart in *Rosalyn Stewart v. Long Island College Hospital,* 30 NY 2d 695 (1970), pp. 1–4, quotation on 4; New York Court of Appeals Cases and Briefs, New York State Library, Albany, NY.

19. Barbara Stewart in Transcript of *Stewart,* 156; "upset" and "irritable" on 157. See also Brief of Plaintiff-Appellant, Rosalyn Stewart, pp. 1–4.

20. Reagan, *When Abortion Was a Crime,* chap. 6; Rickie Solinger, "'A Complete Disaster': Abortion and the Politics of Hospital Abortion Committees, 1950–1970," *Feminist Studies* 19, no. 2 (Summer 1993): 241–68.

21. Dr. Robert Gordon in Transcript of *Stewart,* quotation on 369; on calling Dr. Cohen at Kings but not Dr. Domsky, 358–59.

22. Dr. Vincent Tricomi, Transcript of *Stewart,* 463, 467. Attorney Grutman's questions concerning whether some patients would be "rich enough" to have gone to a specialist for diagnosis on 474–75.

23. Analysis of 1950–1960 data found that therapeutic abortion rates fell after the creation of therapeutic abortion boards. Robert E. Hall, "Therapeutic Abortion, Sterilization, and Contraception," *AJOG* 91, no. 4 (February 15, 1965): 518–20. See also Christopher Tietze, "Therapeutic Abortions in New York City, 1943–

1947," *AJOG* 60, no. 1 (July 1950): 146, 147. Further analysis of New York City data for 1943–1962 showed decreasing numbers of therapeutic abortions overall and that the downward trend was greatest among Puerto Ricans and lowest among whites. Rates of (illegal) abortion-related deaths were much higher among Puerto Rican and nonwhite women. Edwin M. Gold et al., "Therapeutic Abortions in New York City: A 20-Year Review," *American Journal of Public Health* 55, no. 7 (July 1965): quotations on 966, 968–69, 971.

24. The staff at this hospital was willing to perform abortions for low-income women, an unusual situation. That such a large number considered and approved these cases may have been a politically prudent maneuver rather than a method of restricting access. Nonetheless, a private paying patient only needed the approval of one physician. Inter-Departmental Communication from Department of Professional and Vocational Standards, Division of Investigation to Board of Medical Examiners, 19 August 1965, p. 1, folder 822, Abortion Investigative Files, 1925–1969, State Board of Medical Examiner Records, Department of Consumer Affairs, California State Archives, Sacramento, CA.

25. Reagan, *When Abortion Was a Crime,* chaps. 3, 4, and 6.

26. Leslie J. Reagan, "Engendering the Dread Disease: Women, Men, and Cancer," *American Journal of Public Health* 87, no. 11 (November 1997): 1781–2; Lara Marks, *Sexual Chemistry: A History of the Contraceptive Pill* (New Haven, CT: Yale University Press, 2001), 196.

27. Dr. Robert A. MacKenzie, in discussion of Walter T. Dannreuther, "Therapeutic Abortion in a General Hospital," *AJOG* 52 (July 1946): 64; Reagan, *When Abortion Was a Crime,* 178.

28. Transcript of *Stewart,* 171, 172, 705. See also 478–79.

29. Ibid., 282, 155; Sanders, "The Right Not to Be Born," 92.

30. Transcript of *Stewart,* 487–504; Tietze, "Therapeutic Abortions in New York City," 147; Gold, "Therapeutic Abortions in New York City," 966.

31. Hall, "Therapeutic Abortion."

32. See Vanessa Northington Gamble, "Under the Shadow of Tuskegee: African Americans and Health Care," *American Journal of Public Health* 87, no. 11 (November 1997): 1774; Elizabeth Fee, "Sin Versus Science: Venereal Disease in Twentieth-Century Baltimore," in *AIDS: The Burdens of History,* ed. Elizabeth Fee and Daniel M. Fox (Berkeley: University of California Press, 1988), 125–28; Dorothy Roberts, *Killing the Black Body: Race, Reproduction, and the Meaning of Liberty* (New York: Random House, Vintage Books, 1997).

33. Transcript of *Stewart,* 436–37. The Stewarts were represented by Norman Roy Grutman, a personal injury attorney who became quite successful. David Margolick, "Roy Grutman is Dead at 63," *New York Times* (hereafter *NYT*), June 28, 1994.

34. Furthermore, this research was published in the nation's leading medical journal by New York physicians. "Rashless German Measles," *Science News Letter*

63, no. 44 (February 7, 1953), reported on research by Saul Krugman et al. in *JAMA* (January 24, 1953). See also G. B. Avery et al., "Rubella Syndrome After Inapparent Maternal Illness," in Rubella Symposium in *American Journal of Diseases of Children* 110, no. 4 (October 1965): 444–46.

35. Sanders, "The Right Not to Be Born," 92; Val Adams, "Hospital Loses Suit in Refusal to Perform Abortion," *NYT,* October 5, 1968, p. 32.

36. On intersectionality and the law's inability to see how racial and gender discrimination can operate simultaneously, see Kimberle Crenshaw, "Demarginalizing the Intersection of Race and Sex: A Black Feminist Critique of Antidiscrimination Doctrine, Feminist Theory and Antiracist Politics," *University of Chicago Legal Forum* 30 (1989): 139–67; Patricia J. Williams, *Alchemy of Race and Rights* (Cambridge, MA: Harvard University Press, 1992).

37. Sanders, "The Right Not to Be Born," 92.

38. Ibid., 99. The last quotation was taken from the appeals brief and N. J. Berrill's *The Person in the Womb.* On the "jungle," see Stuart Hall, "The Spectacle of the 'Other,'" in *Representation: Cultural Representations and Signifying Practices,* ed. Stuart Hall (London: Sage, 1997), 223–79; Jullilly Kohler-Hausman, "Militarizing the Police: Officer Jon Burge, the 'Vietnamese Treatment,' and Vigilantism in the 'Urban Jungle,'" in *Challenging the Prison-Industrial Complex: Activism, Arts, and Educational Alternatives,* ed. Stephen Hartnett (Urbana: University of Illinois Press, 2010).

39. *Gleitman v. Cosgrove.*

40. The 1958 controversy reported in Lawrence Lader, *Politics, Power, and the Church: The Catholic Crisis and Its Challenge to American Pluralism* (New York: Macmillan, 1987), 73–4.

41. Brief for Defendants-Respondents in *Gleitman v. Cosgrove,* Superior Court of New Jersey, Appellate Division, A-559–65 (1966), p. 6; New Jersey State Law Library, Law Division, Trenton, NJ.

42. Robert Gordon in Transcript of *Stewart,* 361.

43. Brief on Behalf of Plaintiffs-Appellants in *Gleitman v. Cosgrove,* 2–4, 6, 8; New Jersey State Law Library. Brief for Defendants-Respondents in *Gleitman v. Cosgrove,* 7.

44. Brief for Defendants-Respondents in *Gleitman v. Cosgrove,* 4–5.

45. Brief on Behalf of Plaintiffs-Appellants in *Gleitman v. Cosgrove,* 6.

46. For a summary of the international discussion, see Rolf Lundstrom, *Rubella During Pregnancy: A Follow-Up Study of Children Born after an Epidemic of Rubella in Sweden, 1951, with Additional Investigations on Prophylaxis and Treatment of Maternal Rubella* (Uppsala, Sweden: Appelbergy Boktryckeri, 1962), 80–83.

47. Morris Greenberg and Ottavio Pellitteri, "Frequency of Defects in Infants Whose Mothers had Rubella During Pregnancy," *JAMA* (October 12, 1957): 675.

48. Ibid., 678.

49. Ibid. On the idea of risk in medicine, see Thomas Schlich and Ulrich Trohler, eds., *The Risks of Medical Innovation: Risk Perception and Assessment in Historical Context* (London: Routledge, 2006).

50. David B. Pitt, "Congenital Malformations and Maternal Rubella," *MJA* I:8 (February 23, 1957): 233–39; "Rubella in Pregnancy," *MJA* II:17 (October 24, 1959): 609.

51. Victoria P. Coffey and W. J. E. Jessop, "Rubella and Incidence of Congenital Abnormalities," *Irish Journal of Medical Science* 6, no. 397 (January 1959): 5.

52. Ibid., table III on 4, 5, 9, 11. Quotation on 11.

53. Brief on Behalf of Plaintiffs-Appellants in *Gleitman v. Cosgrove,* 2–4, 8.

54. Brief for Defendants-Respondents in *Gleitman v. Cosgrove,* 8.

55. S. A. Cosgrove and Patricia A. Carter, "A Consideration of Therapeutic Abortion," *AJOG* 48 (September 1944): 299–305. First quotation on 304, "abortion-murder" on 305, reference to Russians on 308–9; table comparing abortion rates on 305. Emphasis in original. See Reagan, *When Abortion Was a Crime,* 173–81. Although it was a municipal hospital, Margaret Hague Hospital's hostile, Catholic-based stance toward abortion continued after *Roe v. Wade.* See Lader, *Politics, Power, and the Church,* 75. On the Catholic Church's interventions in medical practice around birth control, see Garrow, *Liberty and Sexuality,* chaps. 1–2; on Catholic and Protestant views in the early twentieth century, see David M. Kennedy, *Birth Control in America: The Career of Margaret Sanger* (New Haven, CT: Yale University Press, 1970), 144–71.

56. Cosgrove and Carter boasted that Margaret Hague had the lowest ratio of 1 therapeutic abortion to 16,750 deliveries, and Hopkins the highest with a ratio of 1 therapeutic abortion to 35 deliveries. Cosgrove and Carter, "A Consideration of Therapeutic Abortion," table 1, p. 305. In the eleven years since the publication of that article, Dr. S. A. Cosgrove reported, "no abortion has been performed in the [Margaret Hague] hospital which I until recently directed," in "Therapeutic Abortion," *Journal of the Michigan State Medical Society* 55 (July 1956): 798. In response to Robert Cosgrove Jr.'s remark during the trial, the Gleitmans' attorney pointed out that therapeutic abortions were in fact performed in New Jersey, that they were legal, and that Jersey City was in New Jersey. The doctors, he argued, had a duty to inform their patient of the consequences of German measles during pregnancy and to alert her to the availability of therapeutic abortion at other hospitals. Brief on Behalf of Plaintiffs-Appellants in *Gleitman v. Cosgrove,* Robert Cosgrove quotation on p. 18, argument concerning the duty of physicians to inform their patients on pp. 10–14.

57. Brief on Behalf of Plaintiffs-Appellants in *Gleitman v. Cosgrove,* 11, 4.

58. Mrs. Kent in *Abortion*, ABC News, June 5, 1969; print at Wisconsin State Historical Society, Madison, WI.

59. Gallup Poll no. 662, for August 23–28, 1962. Gallup Brain, http: institution .gallup.com/documents/questionnaire.aspx?study=AIP00662 (accessed May 7, 2009).

60. *Williams Obstetrics,* vol. 12, 786.

61. A 1967 nationwide survey of 40,000 physicians found that almost half of the Catholic physicians also agreed upon the need to liberalize the nation's abortion laws. 49.1 percent of Catholic doctors and 93.3 percent of non-Catholic doctors supported liberalizing the abortion law. April 1967 report in *Modern Medicine* cited in Phil Kerby, "Abortion: Laws and Attitudes," *Nation* 204 (June 12, 1967): 755; "Changing Morality: The Two Americas, A Time–Louis Harris Poll," *Time* 93 (June 6, 1969): 27; Petchesky, *Abortion and Woman's Choice,* chap. 3.

62. Transcript of *Stewart,* 99–100.

63. Ibid., 101.

64. I deliberately mention race here because the notion of who was "deserving"—as children, mothers, and citizens—was structured by race. Respectability and the respect that a person deserved were attributes also read through demeanor, dress, hairstyle, and cleanliness—all gendered, all classed, and all areas that were the responsibility of a mother to her daughter. At the moment of this case, African Americans were vocally demanding equal rights as citizens and the welfare rights movement was making demands for poor mothers of color, especially black single mothers. See Felicia Kornbluh, *The Battle for Welfare Rights: Politics and Poverty in Modern America* (Philadelphia: University of Pennsylvania Press, 2007); Rickie Solinger, *Beggars and Choosers: How the Politics of Choice Shapes Adoption, Abortion, and Welfare in the United States* (New York: Hill and Wang, 2001), chap. 5.

65. Dr. Louis Z. Cooper testimony and presentation of Rosalyn Stewart in Transcript of *Stewart,* 99–110, quotations on 107, 108–9; Trent, *Inventing the Feeble Mind,* 254–55. Report of Stewart's being on a waiting list in Sanders, "The Right Not to Be Born," 94. Robert F. Kennedy toured Willowbrook in 1965. See Geraldo Rivera, *Willowbrook: A Report on How It Is and Why It Doesn't Have to Be That Way* (New York: Random House, 1972); Museum of DisABILITY History, media timeline at www.museumofdisability.org (accessed July 25, 2007); "A Push to Preserve Willowbrook's Legacy," *Staten Island Advance,* March 19, 2006, http://csinews.net/IntheNews/March_06/19_Willowbrook.htm (accessed July 25, 2007); Sheila M. Rothman and David J. Rothman, *The Willowbrook Wars* (New York: Harper and Row, 1984).

66. For Exhibits, see Transcript of *Stewart,* iv, 587–710.

67. On looking at the disabled, see Rosemarie Garland Thomson, "Seeing the Disabled: Visual Rhetorics of Disability in Popular Photography," in *The New Disability History,* eds. Longmore and Umansky, 335–75; Rachel Adams, *Sideshow U.S.A.: Freaks and the American Cultural Imagination* (Chicago: University of Chicago Press, 2001); Shapiro, *No Pity,* 20–23.

68. Although there are far too many cases to cite here, there are many concerning blood tests, urine tests, and physical examinations. See Fred E. Inbau, "Self-Incrimination—What Can an Accused Person Be Compelled to Do?" *Journal of the American Institute of Criminal Law and Criminology* 28, no. 3 (1937–38): 261–92; Mason Ladd and Robert B. Gibson, "Legal-Medical Aspects of Blood Tests to Determine Intoxication," *Virginia Law Review* 29, no. 6 (April 1943): 749–70. See also Alan Hyde, *Bodies of Law* (Princeton, NJ: Princeton University Press, 1997).

69. The case began on September 28, 1968, and the jury reached its verdict on October 4, 1968.

70. Transcript of *Stewart,* 514, 515.

71. Ibid., 518, 520, 523; and see 525, 528.

72. Garrow, *Liberty and Sexuality,* 379.

73. Transcript of *Stewart,* 530.

74. Ibid., 533–34.

75. Ibid., 547–48.

76. Ibid., 544.

77. See Margaret Marsh and Wanda Ronner, *The Empty Cradle: Infertility in America from Colonial Times to the Present* (Baltimore: Johns Hopkins University Press, 1996); Elaine Tyler May, *Barren in the Promised Land: Childless Americans and the Pursuit of Happiness* (New York: Basic Books, 1995); Linda Layne, *Motherhood Lost: A Feminist Account of Pregnancy Loss in America* (New York: Routledge, 2002); Leslie J. Reagan, "From Hazard to Blessing to Tragedy: Representations of Miscarriage in Twentieth-Century America," *Feminist Studies* 29, no. 2 (Summer 2003): 356–78.

78. Shapiro, *No Pity.*

79. Transcript of *Stewart,* 535, 533, 548, 538. On toileting, Stella Chess, Sam J. Korn, and Paulina B. Fernandez, *Psychiatric Disorders of Children With Congenital Rubella* (New York: Brunner/Mazel; London: Butterworths, 1971), 141.

80. Transcript of *Stewart,* 550–51.

81. Ibid., 579–84. The jury met for almost three hours. Ibid., 551; Adams, "Hospital Loses Suit."

82. New York repealed its criminal abortion law in 1970. On polls, the political progress of reform, and repeal in New York and nationally in this period, see "Changing Morality"; Petchesky, *Abortion and Woman's Choice,* chap. 3; Garrow, *Liberty and Sexuality,* chaps. 6–7; Jennifer Nelson, *Women of Color and the Reproductive Rights Movement* (New York: New York University Press, 2003).

83. This report, like so many others, mentioned Catholics, assumed their opposition to abortion, and did not name the religious affiliations of the other jurors or attorneys. Sanders, "A Right Not to Be Born," 92.

84. Robert Stewart agreed that his marriage relationship had been hurt. Transcript of *Stewart,* 303. See also Chess, Korn, and Fernandez, *Psychiatric Disorders,*

136–37; Rayna Rapp and Faye Ginsburg, "Enabling Disability: Rewriting Kinship, Reimagining Citizenship," *Public Culture* 13, no. 3 (2001): 542.

85. Adams, "Hospital Loses Suit."

86. Gretchen Ritter, "Jury Service and Women's Citizenship before and after the Nineteenth Amendment," *Law and History Review* 20, no. 3 (Fall 2002), 479–516.

87. Adams, "Hospital Loses Suit."

88. *Stewart v. Long Island College Hospital* (1970); *Stewart v. Long Island College Hospital*, (1972).

89. First quotation from Transcript of *Stewart*, 37; second quotation from *Stewart v. Long Island College Hospital* (1968), 42.

90. *Gleitman v. Cosgrove*, 692, 693.

91. Judgment of the trial court dismissing the three counts of the complaint affirmed by Justices Francis, Proctor, Hall, and Haneman–4. For reversal in part, Chief Justice Weintraub–1; for reversal: Justices Jacobs and Schettino–2. *Gleitman v. Cosgrove*, 694.

92. Justice C. Weintraub, dissenting opinion on "spiritual supposition" in *Gleitman v. Cosgrove*, 709.

93. On the debate within the court about the legality of abortion in a case like Gleitman's, see *Gleitman v. Cosgrove*, 701–7.

94. *Gleitman v. Cosgrove*, Weintraub on 711–12; Jacobs on 703–4.

95. *Stewart v. Long Island College Hospital* (1970); *Stewart v. Long Island College Hospital* (1972).

96. *Stewart v. Long Island College Hospital* (1970), quotation at 503–4, citing *Gleitman*.

97. California, New Jersey, and Washington permit wrongful life cases. See Mark Strasser, "Yes, Virginia, There Can Be Wrongful Life: On Consistency, Public Policy, and the Birth-Related Torts," *Georgetown Journal of Gender and the Law* 4 (Summer 2003): 821; Pollard, "Wrongful Analysis," 327.

98. *Dumber v. St. Michael's Hospital*, 60 Wis.2d 766, 233 N.W.2d 372 (1975); *Berman v. Allan*, 80 N.J. 421, 404 A.2d 8 (1979); *Procanik v. Cillo*, 97 N.J. 339, 478 A.2d 755 (1984); Furrow, *Health Law*, 361–62; Rapp, *Testing Women, Testing the Fetus*, 40–41.

99. On abortion law reform and repeal movements, see Garrow, *Liberty and Sexuality;* Luker, *Abortion and the Politics of Motherhood;* Petchesky, *Abortion and Woman's Choice;* Laura Kaplan, *The Story of Jane: The Legendary Underground Feminist Abortion Service* (New York: Pantheon Books, 1995); Leslie J. Reagan, "Crossing the Border for Abortions: California Activists, Mexican Clinics, and the Creation of a Feminist Health Agency in the 1960s," *Feminist Studies* 26, no. 2 (Summer 2000): 323–48; Reagan, *When Abortion Was a Crime*.

100. Transcript of *Stewart*, quotations on 157.

101. Ibid., quotations on 300, 303, 304.

102. In my use of the term *suffering,* I am thinking of the numerous tests, surgeries, and therapies that some children born with rubella syndrome endured. Many at the time—and many still—equated blindness, deafness, retardation, and disability with suffering, assumptions that need to be challenged. The current disability rights movements have helped people to rethink those assumptions and to see the ways in which society creates disability and suffering.

103. Transcript of *Stewart,* 155–57.

104. Brief on Behalf of Plaintiffs-Appellants, *Gleitman v. Cosgrove,* by Leon A. Consales (May 2, 1966), 3.

105. Lynn Lilliston, "The Rubella Children—A Sad Picture Edged with Hope," *LAT,* February 11 1968, pp. K1, 20.

106. We cannot assume, however, that Latinas rejected abortion because of their Catholicism. Catholic women and Latinas also used abortion at the time, and we know that today Catholic women seek abortions when they receive "positive" amniocentesis tests to the same extent that non-Catholic women do so. They tend to express more guilt, however. Hall, "Therapeutic Abortion, Sterilization, and Contraception," 518; Gold et al., "Therapeutic Abortions in New York City"; Rapp, *Testing Women, Testing the Fetus,* 142–46, 155–59.

107. Chess, Korn, and Fernandez, *Psychiatric Disorders,* 142, 151. These authors did not suggest that Catholicism might explain their findings.

108. Richard K. Scotch, *From Good Will to Civil Rights: Transforming Federal Disability Policy* (Philadelphia: Temple University Press, 1984); Trent, *Inventing the Feeble Mind,* 238–43; Shapiro, *No Pity,* 144–45, 165–75. For examples of parents' efforts to educate children who were deaf due to German measles, see "The Parents Talk It Over," *Volta Review* (hereafter *VR*) 63, no. 7 (September 1961): 346–47; "The Parents Talk It Over," *VR* 63, no. 4 (April 1961): 192–97; "Problem of Deaf Children Discussed Through Roundabout Correspondence Group," *VR* 71, no. 4 (April 1969): 241–42.

109. Donald Kerr Grant, "Out of the Shadows" (editorial), *American Journal of Diseases of Children* 110, no. 1 (July 1965): 2.

110. The attorneys' remarks and briefs, however, conveyed their (widely shared) view that the children born with birth defects as a result of maternal rubella were themselves "tragedies" and their lives destined to be tragic and miserable. Brief on Behalf of Plaintiffs-Appellants in *Gleitman v. Cosgrove,* 22; Transcript of *Stewart,* 44–45, 55, 533.

111. Leon A. Consales argued in *Gleitman* that "the issue here is akin to what is known as 'informed consent.'" He cited *Salgo v. Leland Stanford Jr. University Bd. of Trust,* 154 Cal.App.2d 560, 317 P.2d 170, 181 (1953); and Louis J. Regan, *The Doctor and Patient and the Law,* 2nd ed. (1949), in Brief on Behalf of Plaintiffs-Appellants, *Gleitman v. Cosgrove,* 10–14. On informed consent, see John Harkness, Susan E. Lederer, and Daniel Wickler, "Public Health Classics: Laying Ethical Foundations for Research," *Bulletin of the World Health Organization* 79,

no. 4 (2001): 365–66; and Henry K. Beecher, "Ethics and Clinical Research," *New England Journal of Medicine* 274, no. 24 (June 6, 1966): 1354–60, reprinted ibid., 367–72; David J. Rothman, *Strangers at the Bedside: A History of How Law and Bioethics Transformed Medical Decision Making* (New York: Basic Books, 1991); Jonathan D. Moreno and Susan E. Lederer, "Revising the History of Cold War Research Ethics," *Kennedy Institute of Ethics Journal* 6, no. 3 (1996): 223–37.

## FOUR. LAW MAKING AND LAW BREAKING IN AN EPIDEMIC

1. "Measles Can't Keep Woman From Voting," *LAT*, June 3, 1964, p. E8. The article does not say that Boettner informed the precinct, but she must have done so. Nor does the newspaper explain how a reporter and photographer happened to be on the scene. For our purposes here, however, the incident remains a telling one even without this information.

2. German measles was a viral, not a bacterial, infection, but this distinction would not have been important in popular thinking and practices to prevent the spread of the disease. On the female responsibility for cleanliness and protection from germs and disease, see Nancy Tomes, *The Gospel of Germs: Men, Women, and the Microbe in American Life* (Cambridge, MA: Harvard University Press, 1998).

3. Cholera in the nineteenth century pushed the creation of state boards of health; typhoid in the early twentieth century strengthened the state's power to hold healthy individuals in order to protect the public. But official action during an epidemic could also so alienate sections of the public and politicians that the health department could lose its powers, as Leavitt demonstrated in her study of late-nineteenth-century Milwaukee. Charles Rosenberg, *The Cholera Years: The United States in 1832, 1849, and 1866* (Chicago: University of Chicago Press, 1962); Judith Walzer Leavitt, *Typhoid Mary: Captive to the Public's Health* (Boston: Beacon Press, 1996); Judith Walzer Leavitt, "Politics and Public Health: Smallpox in Milwaukee, 1894–1895" in *Sickness and Health in America: Readings in the History of Medicine and Public Health,* ed. Judith Walzer Leavitt and Ronald L. Numbers (Madison: University of Wisconsin Press, 1985), chap. 26; originally published in *Bulletin of the History of Medicine* 50 (1976): 553–68.

4. Since the disease was not reportable in California, the state could not even come up with good numbers on the epidemic. Harry Nelson, "Can't Block Measles, Doctors Say," *LAT,* April 22, 1965, p. 3.

5. If a woman contracted the disease, she could try gamma globulin—blood taken from "patients convalescent from German measles [whose] . . . antibody level is high." Thousands of women received gamma globulin shots during the epidemic, but health authorities were dubious about their value. As reported in Steven M. Spencer, "Attack on the Unborn," *Saturday Evening Post* 238 (March

13, 1965): 83. Gamma globulin appears to have been a panacea that made doctor and patient feel that they had done something. "German Measles Danger," *Science News Letter* 85 (March 7, 1964): 149. Stanley A. Plotkin, "Rubella Vaccine," in *Vaccines*, ed. Stanley A. Plotkin and Edward A. Mortimer Jr., 2nd ed. (Philadelphia: W. B. Saunders, 1998), 309.

6. Kristin Luker, *Abortion and the Politics of Motherhood* (Berkeley: University of California Press, 1985), chap. 4; Leslie J. Reagan, *When Abortion Was a Crime: Women, Medicine, and Law in the United States, 1867–1973* (Berkeley: University of California Press, 1997), 218–22.

7. Martin S. Pernick, "Politics, Parties, and Pestilence: Epidemic Yellow Fever in Philadelphia and the Rise of the First Party System," *William and Mary Quarterly* 29 (1972): 559–86, reprinted in *Sickness and Health,* 356–71; Rosenberg, *Cholera Years;* Michelle T. Moran, *Colonizing Leprosy: Imperialism and the Politics of Public Health in the United States* (Chapel Hill: University of North Carolina Press, 2007); Nayan Shah, *Contagious Divides: Epidemics and Race in San Francisco's Chinatown* (Berkeley: University of California Press, 2001); Leavitt, *Typhoid Mary.*

8. Winfield Best and Frederick S. Jaffee, "Should Abortion Laws Be Liberalized?" *Parents* 40 (June 1965): 50, 122.

9. McNulty called them "technically illegal." "State Reported Probing Abortion Law Evasions," *LAT,* March 22, 1966, p. 4.

10. "Doctors Urge More Liberal Abortion Laws," *CT,* October 12, 1960, p. C8; H. L. Packer and R. J. Gampell, "Therapeutic Abortion: A Problem in Law and Medicine," *Stanford Law Review* 11 (1959): 417.

11. The reporter referred to remarks by Dr. Robert Sack, chief attending obstetrician at John Wesley Hospital. "Changes in 'Archaic' Abortion Laws Urged," *LAT,* November 18, 1964, p. A2.

12. Physicians performed illegal abortions as well, but these were performed in private offices, hotels, and homes and had become highly clandestine by the 1960s. The distinction between legal and illegal abortion was largely defined by the status of therapeutic abortions performed in hospitals with medical approval versus those done without medically approved "indications." Police and prosecutors in this period raided safe practitioners and prosecuted physicians as well as other abortion providers. See Reagan, *When Abortion Was a Crime,* chaps. 6–7.

13. Luker, *Abortion and the Politics of Motherhood,* chap. 2. As Luker observes in her important book, for the reform movement, the board's actions were ultimately a gift, ibid., 87. See also David J. Garrow, *Liberty and Sexuality: The Right to Privacy and the Making of Roe v. Wade* (New York: Macmillan, 1995), 306.

14. On my argument that these events represented a shift away from an ecumenical political culture, I have been most helped by conversations with my colleague Mark Leff. After allowing the legalization of abortion in Hawaii in 1970, Governor John A. Burns remarked on his own views versus his job as governor

and on the personal attacks made against him by other Roman Catholics. He insisted on the importance of the "separate roles of State authority and Church authority." Quoted in Garrow, *Liberty and Sexuality,* 414. See also George Marsden, "Fundamentalism Yesterday and Today" (paper in progress, presented at the University of Illinois, Urbana-Champaign, April 2005). Although Marsden fails to recognize it, feminist scholars of abortion and sexuality have understood for quite a while that abortion played a central role in building the New Right. See Rosalind Pollack Petchesky, *Abortion and Woman's Choice: The State, Sexuality, and Reproductive Freedom* (Boston: Northeastern University Press, 1984); and Linda Gordon, *Woman's Body, Woman's Right: Birth Control in America,* rev. ed. (New York: Penguin Books, 1990).

15. Dick Doyle, "Former Chief of Staff Hits Abortion Policy at Hospital," *Garden Grove (CA) News,* March 26, 1965.

16. Remarks of Dr. Robert Helton, chief of obstetrics, in "Defend Therapeutic Abortions in Grove," *Garden Grove (CA) News,* March 26, 1964.

17. On the American Law Institute and reform, see Luker, *Abortion and the Politics of Motherhood,* chap. 4, on California; Petchesky, *Abortion and Woman's Choice,* chap. 2; Garrow, *Liberty and Sexuality,* chap. 5, p. 277; Reagan, *When Abortion Was a Crime,* 220–22.

18. Harry Nelson, "Therapeutic Abortions at 4 Leading Hospitals Revealed," *LAT,* May 13, 1965, pp. 3, 28.

19. The paper named UCLA Medical Center, Cedars of Lebanon, California, and Huntington Memorial Hospital in Los Angeles and UC Medical Center, Children's, and Presbyterian in San Francisco. Ibid.

20. Remarks of Dr. Henry V. Eastman in Harry Nelson, "Garden Grove Hospital Admits It Permits Therapeutic Abortions," *LAT,* May 15, 1965, p. 2.

21. Bill Farr, "Medico-Legal Dilemma Faces District Attorney," *Register* (n.p.), [n.d.–May ? 1965], in Memorandum, 9 July 1965 and 15 July 1965, file no. 07–11116C-664, folder 826, Abortion Investigative Files, 1925–1969, State Board of Medical Examiner Records, Department of Consumer Affairs, California State Archives, Sacramento, CA. Luker also discusses the importance of the term *reputable* in *Abortion and the Politics of Motherhood,* 85–87.

22. Harry Nelson, "Therapeutic Abortions Fall in Varying Pattern," *LAT,* May 17, 1965, p. A3.

23. Memorandum, 9 July 1965 and 15 July 1965, file no. 07–11116C-664, folder 826, Abortion Investigative Files, 1925–1969, State Board of Medical Examiner Records, Department of Consumer Affairs, California State Archives, Sacramento, CA. Orange County, it should be remembered, has long been known as the most conservative county in the state of California, settled by white Midwesterners, the home of Governor Ronald Reagan's supporters, and a birthplace of the New Right in the 1980s. Lisa McGirr, *Suburban Warriors: The Origins of the New Right* (Princeton, NJ: Princeton University Press, 2001).

24. "The Agony of Mothers about Their Unborn," *Life* 58 (June 4, 1965): 24–31, as discussed in chapter 2 of this text.

25. "The MD, The Law, and Abortions," [New Jersey medical journal, n.p.], (1966): p. 7, folder 10, box 10, CCTA. Dr. McNulty was known as "the most outspoken Roman Catholic foe of abortion" on the board. "Abortion Hearings Will Go On," *San Francisco Examiner,* June 20, 1967, p. 1, folder 10, box 10, CCTA. I do not know the religious backgrounds of the board members.

26. USC medical student forum in Nelson, "Changes in 'Archaic' Abortion Laws Urged"; Garrow, *Liberty and Sexuality,* 197.

27. Harry Nelson, "Therapeutic Abortions: No Action Expected," *LAT,* May 14, 1965, p. A1; Nelson, "Therapeutic Abortions Fall in Varying Pattern." Younger cited in both articles.

28. "Assembly Unit OKs Abortion Law Changes," *LAT,* May 27, 1965, p. 3. It was the Criminal Procedure Committee. The same committee killed the bill in 1961 and 1963. In 1965, two of nine committee members voted no after a hearing that lasted four and a half hours.

29. "The MD, The Law, and Abortions"; Garrow, *Liberty and Sexuality,* 306, 365.

30. Kristin Luker and David Garrow have looked at the aftermath of this surprising state investigation, but no one has previously analyzed the process of the investigation itself. Luker, *Abortion and the Politics of Motherhood,* 86–89; Garrow, *Liberty and Sexuality,* 306–10.

31. Abortion Investigative Files, 1925–1969, California State Board of Medical Examiner Records, Department of Consumer Affairs, California State Archives, Sacramento, CA (hereafter cited as AIF).

32. Investigators found hospitals that had ended their policy of permitting therapeutic abortions for German measles following news reports and investigations, and one administrator, whose hospital did not back down, told the investigator that he would continue to perform abortions for this reason. This hospital's policy had always been to permit abortions for rubella with proof and the approval of two consultants and the head of the ob-gyn department. Five abortions had been performed for this reason in July 1965, and eight had been performed in the previous six months. Investigation Report, case no. 07–9769A-365, 16 August 1965, pp. 2 and 3, folder 822, AIF.

33. Investigation Report, case no. 07–8844A-265, 13 August 1965, p. 2, folder 822, AIF. For similar remarks, see also the Inter-Departmental Communication from Department of Professional and Vocational Standards–Division of Investigation to Board of Medical Examiners, 19 August 1965, p. 2, folder 822, AIF.

34. Interview with Acting Chief of Ob-Gyn on 7 August 1965, Investigation Report, case no. 07–8844A-265, 18 August 1965, quotation on p. 4, folder 822, AIF.

35. Ibid. Another hospital administrator expressed similar feelings. "It was the feeling of the doctors on the staff, who represented all faiths," the investigator summarized in his own words, "that their moral obligation to prevent the birth of malformed children is of greater responsibility than any legal obligation." Investigation Report, case no. 07–9769A-365, 16 August 1965, pp. 2 and 3, folder 822, AIF.

36. On hereditarian thinking and sterilization practices in California in particular, see Alexandra Minna Stern, *Eugenic Nation: Faults and Frontiers of Better Breeding in Modern America* (Berkeley: University of California Press, 2005); and Wendy Kline, *Building a Better Race: Gender, Sexuality, and Eugenics from the Turn of the Century to the Baby Boom* (Berkeley: University of California Press, 2001). See also Johanna Schoen, *Choice and Coercion: Birth Control, Sterilization, and Abortion in Public Health and Welfare* (Chapel Hill: University of North Carolina Press, 2005), chaps. 2–3; Felicia Kornbluh, *The Battle for Welfare Rights: Politics and Poverty in Modern America* (Philadelphia: University of Pennsylvania Press, 2007); Dorothy Roberts, *Killing the Black Body: Race, Reproduction, and the Meaning of Liberty* (New York: Random House, Vintage Books, 1997); Rosalind Pollack Petchesky, "Reproduction, Ethics, and Public Policy: The Federal Sterilization Regulations," *Hastings Center Report* 9, no. 5 (October 1977): 29–42; Philip R. Reilly, *The Surgical Solution: A History of Involuntary Sterilization in the United States* (Baltimore: Johns Hopkins University Press, 1991); Robert G. Weisbord, *Genocide? Birth Control and the Black American* (Westport, CT: Greenwood Press; New York: Two Continents Publishing Group, 1975); Elena R. Gutierrez, "Policing 'Pregnant Pilgrims': Situating the Sterilization Abuse of Mexican-Origin Women in Los Angeles County," in *Women, Health, and Nation: Canada and the United States since 1945,* ed. Georgina Feldberg et al. (Montreal and Kingston, ON: McGill–Queen's University Press, 2003), 378–403; Molly Ladd-Taylor, "Who is 'Defective' and Who Decides? The 'Feebleminded' and the Courts" (unpublished paper presented at the annual meeting of the American Association of the History of Medicine, 2003); and Laura Briggs, *Reproducing Empire: Race, Sex, Science, and U.S. Imperialism in Puerto Rico* (Berkeley: University of California Press, 2002).

37. Interview with Acting Chief of Ob-Gyn on 7 August 1965; quotation on p. 4, figures reported on p. 3. For an interview with local prosecutors, see the Inter-Departmental Communication.

38. Quotation from Investigation Report, case no. 07–9769A-365, 16 August 1965, p. 3; and see also Investigation Report, case no. 07–9831A-265, 18 Aug. 1965, p. 2, both in folder 822, AIF.

39. Investigation Report, case no. 07–9833A-265, [1965], p. 2, folder 822, AIF. Therapeutic abortions for psychiatric reasons rose in the 1950s and 1960s and eventually became a well-known route for obtaining an abortion if one could find two psychiatrists who would sign off on suicidal tendencies.

40. Inter-Departmental Communication.

41. In the early years, the Los Angeles county grand jury supported Beilenson. By 1967, Kings, Shasta, Tulare, Yolo, Siskiyou, Orange, Los Angeles, Sacramento, San Diego, and Alameda counties supported state Senator Anthony C. Beilenson's Therapeutic Abortion Bill, *CCTA Newsletter* (March 1967): p. 3, folder 2, box 11, CCTA; Senator Anthony C. Beilenson Statement Made Before [state] Senate Judiciary Committee, 27 April 1967, p. 2, folder 10, box 184, Anthony C. Beilenson Papers (hereafter ACB), Department of Special Collections, Young Research Library, University of California–Los Angeles (hereafter UCLA).

42. Reagan, *When Abortion Was a Crime,* chap. 6.

43. Emphasis in original. Investigation Report, case no. 07–8844A-265, 16 July 1965, p. 2, folder 822, AIF.

44. George Dusheck, "German Measles–Scourge of the Unborn," *San Francisco Examiner,* July 24, 1966, p. 15, clip in folder 5, box 9, CCTA.

45. One pediatrician observed that "mental defects create a greater feeling of shame than do physical defects, even though the shame is unjustified." James L. Wilson, "The Effect on the Whole Family of a Child With a Severe Birth Defect," in *Birth Defects,* ed. Morris Fishbein (Philadelphia: J. B. Lippincott, 1963), 37; "The Better Way: Medical Help That Prevents Birth of Defective Children," *Good Housekeeping* 165 (October 1967): 193.

46. The obstetrician who had previously delivered her babies performed the abortion. Investigation Report, case no. 07–8681A-265, 20 August 1965, pp. 1 and 2, folder 822, 1925–1969, AIF. Catholic women used abortion in the past and still use it today to approximately the same degree that Protestant and Jewish women do. See Reagan, *When Abortion Was a Crime,* 137; Rayna Rapp, *Testing Women, Testing the Fetus: The Social Impact of Amniocentesis in America* (New York: Routledge, 1999), 143–59.

47. Investigation Report, case no. 07–8668A-265, 20 August 1965, p. 2, folder 822, AIF. Another patient whose interview appears in the same report was the "wife of a physician" and a mother of three. Ibid.

48. The first two doctors charged were John P. Shively, chief of obstetrics and gynecology, St. Luke's Hospital, San Francisco, and Seymour Smith. The seven additional were Dr. Ronald Smith, assistant professor at UCSF Medical Center and obstetrics staff member at St. Luke's Hospital; Dr. Maxwell V. Parker, resident at St. Luke's; Dr. Alan Moss, clinical assistant professor at the University of California–San Francisco; Dr. Antonio Franzi, St. Luke's staff; Dr. John A. Spencer and Dr. Gregory Smith, obstetrics and gynecology staff members at St. Francis Memorial Hospital; and Dr. Andrew Chilos, clinical instructor at UCSF Medical Center and obstetrical staff member at St. Luke's Hospital. "Pike Blasts State Law on Abortion," *LAT,* May 20, 1966, p. 30; [no article title], *LAT,* May 22, 1966, p. A [table of contents]; Caspar W. Weinberger, "Abortions and the Law," *LAT,* June 22, 1966, p. A5; Harry Nelson, "7 More Named in Abortion Test Case," *LAT,* June 24, 1966, p. 4.

49. Peter Bart, "California Faces Abortion Debate," *NYT,* June 19, 1966, p. 88; Patricia Maginnis to Dear Gentlemen, 12 June 1966, folder Society for Humane Abortion, box 1, CCTA.

50. "The MD, the Law, and Abortions," 9.

51. Dorothy C. Stolz to Norma Zarky, 14 July 1966, folder California Committee, box 7, CCTA; Harry Nelson, "Fund Set Up for 2 Doctors in Therapeutic Abortion Case," *LAT,* June 16, 1966, p. 3.

52. Timanus quoted in Mary Steichen Calderone, ed., *Abortion in the United States: A Conference Sponsored by the Planned Parenthood Federation of America, Inc., at Arden House and the New York Academy of Medicine* (New York: Harper Brothers, 1958), 63; Reagan, *When Abortion Was a Crime,* 181–91.

53. The California state legislature had already seen an ALI-like model law three times—in 1961, 1963, and 1965—but the Catholic Church had mobilized opposition and the bills had failed. The leadership of CCTA included Keith P. Russell, an obstetrician-gynecologist; Ruth Roemer, UCLA School of Public Heath professor; Herma Hill Kay, University of California–Berkeley law professor; and the Reverend Lester Kinsolving, Episcopal Church priest. Dorothy C. Stolz and Elizabeth K. Canfield were staff members and played major roles in CCTA's efforts. See Board of Directors on "The Truth about Abortion" pamphlet, CCTA, folder Various Leaflets, box 5, David S. Hall Papers, UCLA (hereafter cited as DSH). On the American Law Institute, CCTA, and reform efforts, see also Reagan, *When Abortion Was a Crime,* 216–22; Luker, *Abortion and the Politics of Motherhood,* chap. 4; Garrow, *Liberty and Sexuality,* chaps. 5–6.

54. Thirty-one petitions with twenty-five names on each were quickly collected in Los Angeles. The last paragraph of the petition read, "Please think of this bill as it would apply in your family if the circumstances defined in this bill should occur. We urge you to lend your support to passage of Assembly Bill No. 1305. It is a minimal and conservative step to safeguard maternal health and family well-being." May 18, 1965, petition, folder 7, box 511, ACB.

55. Ruth Roemer to Alan Charles, 24 May 1967, folder 7, box 11, ACB. Bernie Burton to Board Members, 15 June 1966, LA Press Club, folder CCTA, box 7, CCTA. The campaign won editorials in favor of abortion law reform from the state's major papers in San Francisco and Los Angeles and from state television and radio stations. "Statewide Support Mounts for Abortion Change," *CCTA Newsletter* (September 1966): p. 1, folder 2, box 11, CCTA; KXTV 10 Opinion, 19 March 1964, folder 1, box 510, ACB; Jim to Tony Beilenson (KACB Radio), 10 February 1967, folder 11, box 210, ACB.

56. CCTA "The Truth about Abortion" pamphlet, September 1966, folder Various Leaflets, box 5, DSH; Senator Anthony C. Beilenson Statement Made Before [state] Senate Judiciary Committee, 27 April 1967, p. 2, folder 10, box 184, ACB; William J. Cassel Jr., Chief of Maternal and Perinatal Health, Bureau of Maternal and Child Health, California State Department of Public Health, "Statement

to the Legislature on AB 1305," 20 May 1965, folder 8, box 510, ACB; "Young Republican Clubs," *CCTA Newsletter* (June 1967): p. 1, folder 2, box 11, CCTA; "Large L.A. Retail Clerks Union Newspaper Urged Adoption of Beilenson Abortion Bill," ibid., p. 3. In Orange County, where there had been earlier talk of prosecuting local physicians for performing therapeutic abortions, the grand jury supported legal reform. See Don Angel, "Liberalize Abortion Laws, Grand Jury Urges," *LAT,* August 25, 1966, p. OC1; Don Angel, "DA, Grand Jury to Study Abortions," *LAT,* March 23, 1966, p. OC8. By then too, the American Medical Association, the American Bar Association, and the American Academy of Pediatrics had also endorsed abortion law reform; Luker, *Abortion and the Politics of Motherhood,* 88.

57. The attorney was a former Los Angeles prosecutor and a member of the Women's Lawyers Club. Statement of Miss Terr T. Olender before the California State Assembly, Interim Committee on Criminal Procedure, *Abortion Hearing (Continued) AB2614 (*Dec. 17 and 18, 1962), San Diego, CA, p. 176. (Copy available at the University of California–Santa Cruz Library.)

58. Ellen Studhalter to Tony [Beilenson], 6 March [1967], folder 3, box 510, ACB. In an earlier letter to the editor, a Southern California leader announced the state AAUW's support for the reform law and declared, "We believe it is essential to the welfare of families in California for humane abortions to be allowed under carefully constituted medical control." The local president added a gender critique of the law, noting that the "present 100-year-old law [that] allows abortion only to 'preserve the life' of the mother . . . [was] passed many years before women had the vote." Mrs. Thad Wolinsky (president San Fernando Valley Branch, AAUW), "Women Demanding Action," letter to the editor, *LAT,* April 3, 1965, p. B4.

59. "Large L.A. Retail Clerks Union Newspaper Urged Adoption of Beilenson Abortion Bill," *CCTA Newsletter* (June 1967): p. 3, folio 2, box 11, CCTA.

60. Maginnis, along with the Humanist Association of San Francisco, opposed the Beilenson bill at a 1964 hearing. She testified: "The present law is anti-human, but at the same time we are against [the] proposals of the Beilenson bill. We feel that the Beilenson bill has been a courageous move, . . . [but] what the bill provides is that any woman wanting an abortion would have to appeal her case before at least seven physicians." Patricia Maginnis in California State Assembly, Interim Committee on Criminal Procedure, *San Francisco Hearing (July 20, 1964),* p. 53. (Copy available at the University of California–Santa Cruz Library.) Patricia Maginnis to Dear Gentlemen, 12 June 1966, folder Society for Humane Abortion, box 1, CCTA. See Leslie J. Reagan, "Crossing the Border for Abortions: California Activists, Mexican Clinics, and the Creation of a Feminist Health Agency in the 1960s," *Feminist Studies* 26, no. 2 (Summer 2000): 323–48; and Ninia Baehr, *Abortion Without Apology: A Radical History for the 1990s* (Boston: South End Press, 1990).

61. These groups are listed in the CCTA pamphlet *The Truth about Abortion,* September 1966, folder Various Leaflets, box 5, David S. Hall Papers; Florence Snyder to Anthony C. Beilenson, 16 March 1967, folder 3, box 510, ACB; Phil Kerby, "Abortion: Laws and Attitudes," *Nation* 204 (June 12, 1967): 755.

62. The Reverends James A. Pike and C. Julian Bartlett officiated, and the chaplain of St. Luke's Hospital and a physician and vestryman of All Saint's Church served as "lectors." Rev. Lester Kinsolving, "Honor a Physician—There Is a Time When in Their Very Hands Is the Issue for Good," sermon preached at Grace Cathedral, San Francisco, June 29, 1966, quotations on pp. 1 and 2, folder Kinsolving, Lester, box 1, CCTA. On the immediate support for the physicians and for abortion law reform from the Episcopal Church, see "Pike Blasts State Law on Abortion"; and "World Parish," *LAT,* July 3, 1966, p. A5. On the disagreement between Catholic and Episcopal bishops, see "Cardinal Chides Bishop Pike for Abortion View," *LAT,* Sept. 24, 1966, p. B5.

63. Reverend Howard Moody of the Judson Memorial Baptist Church in Manhattan founded CCS in 1967; after *Roe v. Wade,* it became the Religious Coalition for Abortion Rights. Garrow, *Liberty and Sexuality,* 333–34; Arlene Carmen and Howard Moody, *Abortion Counseling and Social Change from Illegal Act to Medical Practice: The Story of the Clergy Consultation Service on Abortion* (Valley Forge, PA: Judson Press, 1973); Reagan, "Crossing the Border for Abortions."

64. Rev. Lester Kinsolving to the Board of Directors, CCTA, 28 September 1966, quotations on p. 4, folder Kinsolving, Lester, box 1, CCTA.

65. Kinsolving, "Honor a Physician."

66. Garrow, *Liberty and Sexuality,* 228, 234–35, 256; Lara V. Marks, *Sexual Chemistry: A History of the Contraceptive Pill* (New Haven, CT: Yale University Press, 2001), chap. 9; David M. Kennedy, *Birth Control in America: The Career of Margaret Sanger* (New Haven, CT: Yale University Press, 1970); Leslie Woodcock Tentler, *Catholics and Contraception: An American History* (Ithaca, NY: Cornell University Press, 2004).

67. At state hearings in 1964, representatives of the Catholic Physicians' Guilds, the Catholic Parent-Teachers Groups, the Guild of Catholic Psychiatrists, and the California Conference of Catholic Hospitals testified against abortion reform. As listed in "Agenda of Therapeutic Abortion Legislation, 20 July 1964, California Legislature Assembly Committee on Criminal Procedure," folder 15, box 512, ACB; "Support for Change Grows in Sacramento," *CCTA Newsletter* (March 1967): p. 2, folder 2, box 11, CCTA. "The Opposition to Reform the State Abortion Law Is Revealed," *Pacific Churchman* (April 1967), box 229, ACB. For Catholic analysis of the reform movement, condemnation of the Episcopal Church's support for reform, and Catholic responses across the state to the sermons of Rev. Kinsolving, see "'Humane' (?) Abortion Is Still Murder," [no title] (January–February 1967), pp. 1, 3–4, folder 17, box 511, ACB. Luker points out that the early pro-life activists were nearly all Catholic professional men;

with but one exception, all had been raised in the Catholic Church "knowing" that an embryo equaled a person and were unaware of the widespread practice of abortion. Luker, *Abortion and the Politics of Motherhood*, 127–37. On Catholic leadership in opposition to birth control and abortion, see also Garrow, *Liberty and Sexuality*, 114–16, 118, 330–1, 369; Gordon, *Woman's Body, Woman's Right*, 406–9.

68. "Bishops Hit Abortion in Joint Letter," *NYT*, Feb. 13, 1967, p. 19.

69. In 1967, a national network of Catholic pro-life leaders was also formed by a priest, Father James McHugh of the Catholic Family Life Bureau. Michael W. Cuneo, "Life Battles: The Rise of Catholic Militancy within the American Pro-Life Movement," in Mary Jo Weaver and R. Scott Appleby, *Being Right: Conservative Catholics in America* (Bloomington: Indiana University Press, 1995), 273. The Catholic Church hierarchy played a central role in developing and supporting the antiabortion movement in the 1960s and 1970s, even if that role was hidden with ecumenical and nonreligious names. Petchesky, *Abortion and Woman's Choice*, 252–53. As Cuneo observes, "Indeed, without Catholics the movement might never have gotten started." Cuneo, "Life Battles," 273.

70. Miss Ruth M. Exley to Anthony C. Beilenson and Allen Sieroty, 1 May 1967, folder 3, box 517, ACB; Mrs. Fay DeHardt to Anthony C. Beilenson, 1 May 1967, folder 3, box 517, ACB (capitalized and with *murderer* underlined in original).

71. Father William Kenneally in California, Interim Committee, *Abortion Hearing (Continued)*, p. 213. Kenneally's 1962 and 1963 remarks reported in Jack Star, "The Growing Tragedy of Illegal Abortion," *Look* 29 (October 19, 1965): 156, 168.

72. Quoted in Betty Brenner, "Episcopal Priest Advocates Birth Control Steps," *Flint* [MI] *Journal*, March 8, 1968, folder 1, Post-Legislation CCTA Activities, box 5, CCTA; "The Opposition to Reform the State Abortion Law Is Revealed." Although some suggest that the Catholic hierarchy initially had a moderate response to the legalization of abortion and that this highly charged language developed in the 1970s and 1980s, the association of abortion with slavery and Nazis was, as shown here, already in circulation among Catholics in the early 1960s. Cuneo, "Life Battles," 270–71, 276; and Patrick Allitt, *Catholic Intellectuals and Conservative Politics in America, 1950–1985* (Ithaca, NY: Cornell University Press, 1993), 185, 189–90, place these metaphors in the 1970s. Carol Mason shows the importance of abortion in the early 1960s to the developing conservative movement and the Goldwater presidential campaign. For insightful analysis of the language, metaphors, and representations of the pro-life movement, particularly its racist underpinnings, see Carol Mason, *Killing for Life: The Apocalyptic Narrative of Pro-Life Politics* (Ithaca, NY: Cornell University Press, 2002); and Carol Mason, "Minority Unborn," in *Fetal Subjects, Feminist Positions,* ed. Lynn M. Morgan and Meredith W. Michaels (Philadelphia: University of Pennsylvania Press, 1999), 159–74.

73. Paula M. Kane, *Separatism and Subculture: Boston Catholicism, 1900–1920* (Chapel Hill: University of North Carolina Pres, 1994), 6; John Parascandola, "Syphilis at the Cinema: Medicine and Morals in VD Films of the U.S. Public Health Service in World War II," in *Medicine's Moving Pictures: Medicine, Health, and Bodies in American Film and Television,* ed. Leslie J. Reagan, Nancy Tomes, and Paula A. Treichler (Rochester, NY: University of Rochester Press, 2007), 83–85.

74. On this observation, see also Petchesky, *Abortion and Woman's Choice,* 120–21.

75. Intervention into state politics violated the principle taught to Catholic schoolchildren that religious life was separate from public and political life. Conversation with Jim Barrett, April 2005; Garrow, *Liberty and Sexuality,* 155. For a similar discussion and outrage over Catholic bishops' pronouncements on voting and abortion forty years later, see the letters to the editor in "Voice of the People," *Chicago Tribune,* November 24, 2007, p. 22. Quotation from Mrs. A. M. Breslin to Anthony C. Beilenson, 5 May 1967, folder 5, box 484, ACB.

76. Letter to Anthony C. Beilenson, Lewis Sherman, and Don Mulfor, 27 April 1967, folder 5, box 484, ACB.

77. Joyce Gerritsen to Senator A. C. Beilenson, [n.d., 1967], folder 5, box 484, ACB.

78. Marks, *Sexual Chemistry,* 229–30, chap. 9; Tentler, *Catholics and Contraception,* 136–203; Loretta McLaughlin, *The Pill, John Rock and the Catholic Church: The Biography of a Revolution* (New York: Little, Brown, 1982); Elizabeth Siegel Watkins, *On the Pill: A Social History of Contraceptives, 1950–1970* (Baltimore: John Hopkins University Press, 2001), 46–47.

79. Memo from Rev. Lester Kinsolving to Board of Directors, CCTA, 25 July 1966, folder 5, box 9, CCTA; Memo from Rev. Lester Kinsolving re Progress Report Northern California, 19 July–24 August 1966, folder 5, box 9, CCTA; Kinsolving to CCTA Board of Directors, 1 August 1966, folder CCTA, box 7, CCTA; Susan Berman, "The Abortion Crusader," *San Francisco Magazine* 12 (July 1970): 77.

80. Lester Kinsolving, "Abortion Battle Among Catholics," *San Francisco Chronicle,* July 15, 1967, n.p.; Homer Bigart, "RFK, Backing Abortion in Assault Cases, Is Challenged by Priest," *Sacramento Bee,* February 23, 1967, both clips in folder 17, box 511, ACB. Television station WFLD in Chicago taped the Illinois State Medical Society's Symposium on the Medical Implications of Illinois' Abortion Law and showed pieces of it in "Abortion: Old Laws—New Problems" on March 15, 1967. The show also polled its viewers on possible legal revisions. This was, of course, not a random survey. Of 1,013 viewers (75 percent of them women), 71 percent agreed that "abortions should be allowed when the unborn baby is expected to be deformed." In addition, 90 percent disagreed with the statement that "all abortions should be prohibited." "Questionnaire

Response: Illinois State Medical Society Symposium on Abortion–WFLD–March 15, 1967," *Illinois Medical Journal* 131, no. 5 (May 1967): 693–95.

81. April 1967 report in *Modern Medicine* cited in Phil Kerby, "Abortion: Laws and Attitudes," *Nation* 204 (June 12, 1967): 755.

82. "California Poll–July 1966," folder 6, box 10, CCTA; "Statewide Support Mounts for Abortion Change," *CCTA Newsletter* (September 1966): p. 1, folder 2, box 11, CCTA. "Of all persons having an opinion on the subject," Beilenson reported, "72.2 percent favor liberalization of our abortion laws." Senator Anthony C. Beilenson Statement Made Before Senate Judiciary Committee, April 27, 1967, folder 10, box 184, ACB.

83. The *Oakland Tribune* reported on Assemblyman Robert W. Crown's poll on February 9, 1967. "Support for Change Grows in Sacramento," *CCTA Newsletter* (March 1967): p. 2, folder 2, box 11, CCTA.

84. Alan S. Maremont, a San Francisco attorney, spoke for the state organization at the San Francisco hearing. California, State Assembly Interim Committee on Criminal Procedure (July 20, 1964), testimony 49–53; size of organization on 49; vote and "ordinary citizens and family men," "religious beliefs," and thalidomide on 50; "surprise" on 52; "layman's verdict" on 53.

85. Lynn Lupien to Senator B (from Pacifica), 21 April 1967, folder 1, box 517, ACB.

86. Betsey Warwick to Sen. Anthony Beilenson, 1 May 1967, folder 3, box 517, ACB. This was one of the many letters sent after the Easter antiabortion masses. On the developing discussions concerning disabilities and reproductive rights, see Judy Rohrer, "Toward a Full-Inclusion Feminism: A Feminist Deployment of Disability Analysis," *Feminist Studies* 31, no. 1 (Spring 2005): 54–58. For overviews of disability history, see Catherine J. Kudlick, "Disability History: Why We Need Another 'Other'" *American Historical Review* 1083 (June 2003) 763–93; Paul K. Longmore and Lauri Umansky, eds., *The New Disability History: American Perspectives* (New York: New York University Press, 2001); Joseph P. Shapiro, *No Pity: People with Disabilities Forging a New Civil Rights Movement* (New York: Random House, 1993).

87. The relationships among the Catholic Church, Catholic belief and culture, and the emerging disabilities movements are questions worthy of investigation.

88. Grace A. Rhoads in Letters to the Editor, *Wall Street Journal,* March 9, 1966, p. 18.

89. On miscarriages as a blessing during this period, see Reagan, "From Hazard to Blessing to Tragedy"; "Letters Bare Grief," *CCTA Newsletter* (September 1966): p. 2, folder 2, box 11, CCTA.

90. Elizabeth C. Morris, "Spare the Innocent?" *New York Times Magazine,* February 12, 1967, p. 12. *Mongoloid* was a common term since the nineteenth century for people with Down syndrome. The term suggested a devolution from Caucasian to Asian races. On Down syndrome, see Michael Bérubé, *Life*

*as We Know It: A Father, a Family, and an Exceptional Child* (New York: Pantheon, 1996); Rapp, *Testing Women, Testing the Fetus,* chap. 10.

91. *Children Limited,* the journal of the National Association for Retarded Children (NARC; now renamed ARC, Association of Retarded Citizens), reported on German measles and covered abortion now and again, but this was neither a central topic nor one on which the journal took an editorial position. Its pages were more devoted to medical research, employment, and education of the retarded as well as to presidential support of public policy initiatives on behalf of the retarded. For coverage of abortion, see "Abortions Pose Ethical Problems," *Children Limited* 16, no. 5 (October 1967): 2; Kenneth J. Ryan, MD, "Some Medical Indications for Therapeutic Abortion," ibid., 6; "Colorado Abortion Rise Since Law Liberalized," ibid., 5; "Abortion Refused, Couple Wins Suit," *Children Limited* 17, no. 8 (December 1968): 1. For letters from parents in support of abortion, see Anonymous (New York State), "Abortion News Needed," *Children Limited* 18, no. 3 (March 1969): 4; Mrs. Rose Lang (Shickshinny, PA), "Abortion for the MR," *Children Limited* 18, no. 5 (May 1969): 4. For an editorial against abortion, see Sister Andrea Curran, DSMS (Chicago), "One Person's Opinion: Drawing the Line," *Children Limited* 18, no. 6 (July 1969): 4.

92. Memo from Norma G. Zarky re Proposed Plaintiffs—California—Federal Case, 20 January 1970, folder 2, box 5, CCTA.

93. The men were William K. Coblentz and Dr. Chauncey D. Leake as cochairmen and Dr. George K. Herzog as secretary-treasurer for the Citizen's Defense Fund.

94. "Notables Spark Defense Fund for S.F. Doctors," *CCTA Newsletter* (March 1967): p. 3, folder 2, box 11, CCTA.

95. George K. Herzog Jr., MD, and Edmund W. Overstreet, MD, to specialists in obstetrics, n.d., 1967, folder 10, box 10, CCTA.

96. Contributions came from fourteen states, including a check from seven U.S. Air Force doctors stationed in Germany, *CCTA Newsletter* (June 1967): p. 2, folder 2, box 11, CCTA.

97. Amici Curiae Brief for Doctors in *Shively v. Stewart, Board of Medical Examiners of the State of California,* November 1966, by Zad Leavy and Herma Hill Kay, folder 10, box 10, CCTA. The first hearing of Dr. J. Paul Shively did not take place until January 1968. Daryl E. Lembke, "German Measles Case Abortion Defended by Accused Surgeon," *LAT,* January 23, 1968, p. 3.

98. Amici Curiae Brief for Doctors in *Shively v. Stewart,* quotations on pp. 14 and 33, folder 10, box 10, CCTA. "Additional Signers of the Brief," folder 10, box 10, CCTA; Lawrence Sherwin and Edmund Overstreet, "Therapeutic Abortion: Attitudes and Practices of California Physicians," *California Medicine* 105, no. 5 (November 1966): 338; Gampell and Packer, "Therapeutic Abortion," 417, 447. Zad Leavy declared the ten-page opinion written by Chief

Justice Traynor to be a "landmark." Zad Leavy to Harriet W. Pilpel, 23 December 1966, folder 10, box 10, CCTA. The court found that, as in criminal trials, defendants in administrative hearings had the right to due process. The Medical Board's power to investigate and the "punitive character" of the hearings through which "the agency can prohibit an accused from practicing his profession" made these like criminal trials. *Shively v. Stewart,* 65 Cal.2d 475; 421 P.2d 65 (1965) opinion of the Supreme Court of California, Dec. 16, 1966, pp. 5 and 8, copy in folder10, box 10, CCTA.

99. Statement by Senator Anthony C. Beilenson on Therapeutic Abortion Act made before Senate Judiciary Committee, April 27, 1967, pp. 1 and 3–4, folder 10, box 184, ACB.

100. Society for Humane Abortion flyer attached to "Abortion Program Given in Long Beach," January 14, 1967, Los Angeles County Health Department Bureau of Maternal and Child Health, folder Correspondence and Papers, box 1, DSH. For a constituent letter arguing along the lines of Maginnis and SHA/ARAL, see Nancy Simmons (SF) to Anthony C. Beilenson, 30 March 1967, folder 2, box 517, ACB.

101. "Reagan Reluctantly Signs Bill Easing Abortion," *NYT,* June 16, 1967, p. 24.

102. The Status of Women Commission reported receiving 756 letters from women about the bill: "608 *Support,* 156 not liberal enough, 2 opposed." M. Ash, Status of Women Commission to Tony [Beilenson], [1967], folder 5, box 484, ACB. Many Californians wrote critical letters arguing that the new law did not go far enough; see folder Support, Out of District; folders 1 and 2, box 517, ACB.

103. Tom Goff, "Doctors Disciplined for Abortion Roles," *LA Times,* Feb. 15, 1968, p. 3, folder 1, box 530, ACB; "2 MDs Reproved for Abortions in California," *Hospital Tribune Report,* n.d., folder 1, box 5, CCTA. Ten months later the other seven physicians received the same penalties. Robert S. Fairbanks, "State Board Finds 7 Doctors Guilty in Abortion Operations," *LA Times,* October 25, 1968, pp. 3 and 21, folder 1, box 5, CCTA.

104. Wallace Turner, "Two Coast Physicians Rebuked For Violating Law on Abortion," *NYT,* February 15, 1968, p. 14.

105. Keith Monroe, "How California's Abortion Law Isn't Working," *New York Times Magazine,* December 29, 1968. "Abortion Is Denied to Stockton Woman," *Sacramento Bee,* January 25, 1968, p. C4, folder 1, box 530, ACB. Nancy J. Adler, "New Abortion Law in Effect on Coast," *NYT,* December 17, 1967, p. 47.

106. "Press Conference Statement of Senator Anthony C. Beilenson," 15 April 1968, folder 17, box 184, ACB. The California Medical Association supported legalizing abortions of pregnancies that "probably will lead to the birth of a malformed child." See "Further Liberalization of Abortion Law Asked," *LAT,* Feb. 14, 1968, folder 1, box 530, ACB.

107. Notes on speech in Albany, NY, n.d., 1969, folder 20, box 184, ACB.

108. The decision was on August 2, 1968. "Judge Overrules Board in Dr. Shively Decision," *CCTA Newsletter* (August 1968): p. 2, quotations on p. 4; folder 2, box 11, CCTA. *Deformed child* is CCTA's term; the other remarks are the words of the judge.

109. Reform laws passed in Colorado, Arkansas, California, Delaware, Georgia, Kansas, Maryland, New Mexico, North Carolina, Oregon, South Carolina, and Virginia. Judith Hole and Ellen Levine, *Rebirth of Feminism* (New York: Quadrangle Books, 1971), 284; Garrow, *Liberty and Sexuality*, 412–14, 431–32, 466.

110. "Statement of Senator Anthony C. Beilenson on SB 544," 30 June 1970, folder 22, box 184, ACB, UCLA. On CCTA's efforts against the law they had won, see Ruth Roemer to Zad Leavy, 18 January 1970, and "Approaches to Attacking the Therapeutic Abortion Act of 1967 by Declaratory Relief Action," Memo from Norma G. Zarky, re Proposed Plaintiffs—California—Federal Case, 20 January 1970, both in folder 2, box 5, CCTA.

111. David Garrow reports that women reformers immediately wanted to support Belous, but moderate doctors were disinclined to do so. Although the doctors believed Belous had been doing abortions himself for years, they were most disturbed by their feeling that Belous had accepted kickbacks for referrals to the illegal abortionist. Garrow, *Liberty and Sexuality*, 354–56. "San Francisco Nine" in "Judge Overrules Board in Dr. Shively Decision," *CCTA Newsletter* (August 1968), p. 2 folder 2, box 11, CCTA. Amici Brief on Behalf of Medical School Deans and Others in Support of Appellant, *California vs. Leon Phillip Belous* (January 1969), quotation re "baby factory" on p. 21 and the physician/patient relationship on p. 45. In folder Belous Case, box 1, CCTA.

112. "High Court Weighs Law Challenge," *CCTA Newsletter*, April 1969, folder 6 Abortion–Calif, box 10, CCTA; Luker, *Abortion and the Politics of Motherhood*, 88–89; Garrow, *Liberty and Sexuality*, 354–56, 377–81; *People v. Belous*, 80 Cal. Rptr. 354, 458 P.2d 194 (1969).

113. "Dr. Russell Named Chief of American College of Ob-Gyn," *CCTA Newsletter*, April 1969, folder 6 Abortion-Calif, box 10, CCTA.

114. Amici Brief on Behalf of Medical School Deans and Others in Support of Appellant, *California vs. Leon Phillip Belous*. German measles mentioned in one paragraph on p. 17 out of 48 pages.

115. For medical support of reform in 1969, Lucinda Cisler cites *Modern Medicine* and the Ortho Pharmaceutical Company and offers a useful analysis of polling on abortion in Lucinda Cisler, "Unfinished Business: Birth Control and Women's Liberation," in *Sisterhood Is Powerful: An Anthology of Writings from the Women's Liberation Movement*, ed. Robin Morgan (New York: Random House, Vintage Books, 1970), 310–11. On earlier support among African American physicians, public health professionals, and psychiatrists for repeal, see Reagan, *When Abortion Was a Crime*, 234.

116. Laura Kaplan, *The Story of Jane: The Legendary Underground Feminist Abortion Service* (New York: Pantheon Books, 1995); Baehr, *Abortion without Apology;* Reagan, "Crossing the Border for Abortions"; Carmen and Moody, *Abortion Counseling.*

117. Keith P. Russell to the Signers of the Physicians' Brief in *People v. Belous,* 28 October 1969, folder Belous Case, box 1, CCTA.

118. The trial was held November 12–18, 1970. Seth S. King, "Minnesota Gynecologist, a Mother, Risks Her Career to Test State's Abortion Law," *NYT,* November 15, 1970, p. 75, folder Hodgson Case, box 2, CCTA. For an insightful biography, see Carole Joffee, *Doctors of Conscience: The Struggle to Provide Abortion before and after Roe v. Wade* (Beacon Press, 1996), 8–26. See also Garrow, *Liberty and Sexuality,* 428–30, 466–69, 580, 681–84; Peter Irons, *The Courage of Their Convictions* (New York: Free Press, 1988), 265–79.

119. King, "Minnesota Gynecologist." Similarly, a UPI article on Hodgson's case described her as "an attractive doctor." In William Fox, "Abortion Test Case in High Court," *Chicago Defender,* April 6, 1972, p. 8.

120. Garrow, *Liberty and Sexuality,* chaps. 7, 8; Irons, *Courage of Their Convictions,* 255–79.

121. *Hodgson v. Minnesota, Appellant's Brief* [1970], brief in folder Hodgson Case, box 2, CCTA; King, "Minnesota Gynecologist." Widmyer was twenty-four years old. Fox, "Abortion Test Case in High Court."

122. Drs. Edgar Bass Keemer, of Detroit, and George Loutrell Timanus, of Baltimore, had tried to suggest similar arguments in their trials for criminal abortion in the 1950s, but they had lacked open medical support and a movement to back them. The requirement that therapeutic abortions be performed in a hospital to be considered legitimate was being newly created at that time. Reagan, *When Abortion Was a Crime,* 181–92.

123. "Case Histories of Patients Denied Therapeutic Abortion by Defendant, Exhibits Nos. 37 and 38," in *Hodgson v. Minnesota,* 295 Minnesota 294 (1970), Appellant's Appendix, A 50–54, *Cases and Briefs, (Minnesota) Supreme Court,* Minnesota State Law Library, St. Paul, MN; Garrow, *Liberty and Sexuality,* 428–30. Irons, *Courage of Their Convictions,* 273–74.

124. Jane E. Hodgson, "Abortion: The Law and the Reality 1970," *Mayo Alumnus* 6, no. 4 (October 1970): 4.

125. 40A Minn. Statute. Ann. 617.19 at 286 (1964), as cited in *Hodgson v. Minnesota,* Appellant's Brief [1970], p. 3; in folder Hodgson Case, box 2, CCTA. The prosecution of Shirley Wheeler in Florida is one known, and highly politicized, exception; see Reagan, *When Abortion Was a Crime,* 243.

126. As quoted in Irons, *Courage of Their Convictions,* 259.

127. From the lack of remarks concerning Nancy Widmyer's race in news reports or later accounts, I conclude that Nancy Widmyer was white. The phrase "model mother" in Dr. Jane Hodgson's account in Irons, *Courage of Their*

*Convictions,* 271; "once in a lifetime" as quoted in Garrow, *Liberty and Sexuality,* 429. See also Joffee, *Doctors of Conscience,* 13.

128. Jo Ann Robinson, *Montgomery Bus Boycott and the Women Who Started it: The Memoir of Jo Ann Gibson Robinson,* ed. David J. Garrow (Knoxville: University of Tennessee Press, 1987); Elizabeth Pleck, "The Stigma of Cohabitation in the United States, 1960–1990," forthcoming; Garrow, *Liberty and Sexuality,* chap. 4. On the state's encouragement and reward for heterosexuality and marriage, see Margot Canaday, "Heterosexuality as a Legal Regime," in *The Cambridge History of Law in America,* vol. 3, *The Twentieth Century and After (1920-),* ed. Michael Grossberg and Christopher Tomlins (Cambridge: Cambridge University Press, 2008), chap. 13.

129. King, "Minnesota Gynecologist."

130. Quotation on the courtroom in J. C. Wolfe, "Abortion Law Isn't Moral—Dr. Hodgson," *St. Paul* (MN) *Pioneer Press,* November 18, 1970, p. 1, folder Hodgson Case, box 2, CCTA. On the sentencing, see *Hodgson v. Minnesota,* Appellant's Appendix, A36, A39.

131. While Dr. Hodgson waited on the appeal, she worked in Washington, DC, as the medical director of Preterm Clinic. Upon returning to Minnesota, she helped open abortion clinics and worked to ensure that abortions were legally available. Marcia D. Greenberger and Rachel K. Laser, "Human Rights Hero Jane Hodgson, M.D." *Human Rights* (April 2003), Section of Individual Rights and Responsibilities, American Bar Association, www.abanet.org/irr/hr/spring03/humanrightshero.html, April 1, 2003 (accessed July 2, 2008). See also Irons, *Courage of Their Convictions;* Joffe, *Doctors of Conscience;* and Carole Joffe, "The Unending Struggle for Legal Abortion: Conversations with Jane Hodgson," *Journal of the American Medical Women's Association* 49, no. 5 (September/October 1994): 160–164; Margalit Fox, "Jane Hodgson, 91, Supporter of Abortion Rights, Is Dead," *NYT,* Nov. 5, 2006, p. 46.

132. Eric Lichtblau, "Defending '03 Law, Justice Dept. Seeks Abortion Records," *NYT,* Feb. 12, 2004, p. 1; Eric Lichtblau, "Ashcroft Defends Subpoenas," *NYT,* Feb. 13, 2004, p. 5; Editorial, *NYT,* Feb. 14, 2004, p. 18; Robert Pear and Eric Lichtblau, "Administration Sets Forth a Limited View of Privacy," *NYT,* March 6, 2004, p. 8; William Safire, "Privacy in Retreat," editorial, *NYT,* March 10, 2004, p. 27; "ACOG Files Amicus Brief in *Gonzales v. Carhart* and *Gonzales v. PPFA,*" news release, September 22, 2006, http://www.acog.org/from_home/publications/press_releases/nr09–22–06.cfm (accessed June 28, 2009); *Carhart v. Gonzales,* 550 U.S. 124 (2007); Linda Greenhouse, "In Reversal of Course, Justices, 5–4, Back Ban on Abortion," *NYT,* April 19, 2007, p. 1; Linda Greenhouse, "Precedents Begin Falling for Roberts Court," *NYT,* June 21, 2007, p. 21. For current information on HIPAA, see the U.S. Department of Health and Human Services, www.hhs.gov/ocr/hipaa.

133. Carol Mason, "Guest Commentary: Killing for Life Returns," Political Research Associates website, June 3, 2009, www.publiceye.org/reproductive_rights/violence/mason.html (accessed June 7, 2009); Carole Joffe, "The Legacy of George Tiller," June 4, 2009, www.beaconbroadside.com/broadside/2009/06/carole-joffe-the-legacy-of-george-tiller.html (accessed June 7, 2009); Dr. Susan Robinson, "This Shouldn't Have Been Ignored," transcript, June 3, 2009, www.democracynow.org/2009/6/3/susan_robinson (accessed June 7, 2009); Joe Stumpe and Monica Davey, "Abortion Doctor [sic] Shot to Death in Kansas Church," *NYT,* May 31, 2009, www.nytimes.com/2009/06/01/us/01tiller.html?scp=1&sq=abortion%20doctor%20slain&st=cse (accessed June 7, 2009).

134. See Kornbluh, *The Battle for Welfare Rights*; Rickie Solinger, *Beggars and Choosers: How the Politics of Choice Shapes Adoption, Abortion, and Welfare in the United States* (New York: Hill and Wang, 2001), chap. 5; Jennifer Nelson, *Women of Color and the Reproductive Rights Movement* (New York: New York University Press, 2003); Jael Silliman, Marlene Gerber Fried, Loretta Ross, and Elena R. Gutierrez, *Undivided Rights: Women of Color Organize for Reproductive Justice* (Cambridge, MA: South End Press, 2004); Petchesky, *Abortion and Woman's Choice,* introduction, chap. 3. On parents of disabled children, see Rosemary F. Dybwad, *Perspectives on a Parent Movement: The Revolt of Parents of Children with Intellectual Limitations* (Brookline, MA: Brookline Books, 1990); Shapiro, *No Pity,* 42–45, 56–57; "Parents' Movement," in *The ACB-CLIO Companion to The Disability Rights Movement,* ed. Fred Pelka (Santa Barbara, CA: ACB-CLIO, 1997), 240–41; and chapter 5, this text.

135. CCTA Progress Report, September 28, 1966, in folder CCTA, box 7, CCTA. Conversation with Ruth Roemer, June 2005, Los Angeles.

136. As Jaycee spokesman Alan S. Maremont explained, "We do not intend to express an opinion on the merits of the questions or the differing moral views held by our members of many faiths. Rather, we take the view, whatever our faith, that each citizen should be allowed to take the course dictated by his own beliefs and judgment, rather than having the views of others thrust upon him." California State Assembly, Interim Committee, *San Francisco Hearing,* 51–52.

137. Joanne Meyerowitz makes a related argument in "Beyond the Feminine Mystique: A Reassessment of Postwar Mass Culture, 1946–1958," in *Not June Cleaver: Women and Gender in Postwar America, 1945–1960,* ed. Joanne Meyerowitz (Philadelphia: Temple University Press, 1994), 229–62. Suburban white women were also active in creating and sustaining the Old and the New Right. See Michelle Nickerson, "Women, Domesticity, and Postwar Conservatism," *OAH Magazine of History* 17 (January 2003); McGirr, *Suburban Warriors.*

1. For the schedule of immunizations advised by the American Academy of Pediatrics, see Judy Graves, *Right From the Start: The Importance of Early Immunization,* Public Affairs Pamphlet no. 350 (New York: Public Affairs Committee, 1963). The goal of disease eradication was new. James Colgrove, *State of Immunity: The Politics of Vaccination in Twentieth-Century America* (Berkeley: University of California Press, 2006).

2. James Colgrove observes, "As with most other aspects of health care in the United States, a strong socioeconomic gradient has characterized vaccination uptake; people of lower income and less formal education, and their children, have been much less likely to be vaccinated than those of higher income and more formal education. . . . As infectious disease became increasingly limited to poverty areas, the issue of immunization . . . was recast as a problem of inequality and social justice in the 1960s." Colgrove, *State of Immunity,* quotation on p. 13. On the racial identification of disease and its political uses, see Keith Wailoo, *Dying in the City of the Blues: Sickle Cell Anemia and the Politics of Race and Health* (Chapel Hill: University of North Carolina Press, 2001), chaps. 6–7.

3. Charles Swan et al., "Congenital Defects in Infants Following Infectious Diseases During Pregnancy," *Medical Journal of Australia* (hereafter cited as *MJA*) II–30th year, no. 11 (September 11, 1943): 210. See also the Report of the Committee appointed by the Director-General of Public Health of New South Wales, N. McA. Gregg, chairman, "The Occurrence of Congenital Defects in Children Following Maternal Rubella During Pregnancy," *MJA* II–30th year, no. 4 (July 28, 1945): 126; Allan Chase, *Magic Shots: A Human and Scientific Account of the Long and Continuing Struggle to Eradicate Infectious Diseases by Vaccination* (New York: William Morrow, 1982), 314–15.

4. Charles Swan, "Rubella in Pregnancy as an Aetiological Factor in Congenital Malformations, Stillbirth, Miscarriage, and Abortion," *Journal of Obstetrics and Gynaecology of the British Empire* 56, no. 3 (June 1949): 600. In an earlier report, Swan et al. had declared therapeutic abortion unjustified. In 1943, the coauthors had declared that "there are no legal grounds" for abortion, but Swan's later articles supported abortion for rubella. Swan et al., "Congenital Defects in Infants," 210.

5. *Abortion,* ABC-TV News, June 5, 1969; print viewed at the Wisconsin State Historical Society, Madison, WI. All quotations are from this print.

6. Ibid.

7. Myra MacPherson, "Abortion Documentary: Primer," *Washington Post* (June 5, 1969), p. C10.

8. Dr. Paul D. Parkman, oral history by Sarah Leavitt, June 7, 2005, Office of NIH History, National Institutes of Health, Bethesda, MD, p. 24.

9. Thomas H. Weller made these introductory remarks to the proceedings of the 1965 "Rubella Symposium," *American Journal of Diseases of Children* (hereafter cited as *AJDC*) 110, no. 4 (October 1965): 347. The entire October 1965 issue of the *American Journal of Diseases of Children* was devoted to rubella, edited by Dr. Saul Krugman, and attested to the driving laboratory and clinical interest in the disease. The special issue arose out of the realization by the presidents of the Society for Pediatric Research and the American Pediatric Society that much research was being conducted and duplicated across the country. As reported by Hattie E. Alexander, MD, president, American Pediatric Society, on pp. 345–46. On Weller, see also Chase, *Magic Shots,* 315–16.

10. Researchers at Harvard (Dr. Thomas H. Weller of the Department of Tropical Public Health) and at Walter Reed (Paul Parkman, E. L. Buescher, and Malcolm S. Artenstein) isolated the virus in 1962. T. H. Weller and F. A. Neva, "Propagation in Tissue Culture of Cytopathic Agents from Patients with Rubella-like Illness," *Proceedings of the Society for Experimental Biology and Medicine* 8 (1962): 215–25; P. D. Parkman, E. L. Buescher, and M. S. Artenstein, "Recovery of a Rubella Virus from Army Recruits," ibid., 225–30. The scientific progress against the disease was reported to the general public. See "Rubbing Out Rubella," *Newsweek* 60 (August 6, 1962): 52, which appeared on the same page with an article on and photo of Sherri Finkbine, "I Pray They'll Hurry," ibid. See also "Find Viruses That Attack Unborn Baby," *CT,* June 14, 1962, p. W6; "Two Doctors Find German Measles Virus," *CT,* July 27, 1962, p. 17; John A. Osmundsen, "Doctors Find Virus of German Measles," *NYT,* 27 July 27, 1962, pp. 1, 21; Louis Galambos, with Jane Eliot Sewell, *Networks of Innovation: Vaccine Development at Merck, Sharp & Dohme, and Mulford, 1895–1995* (Cambridge: Cambridge University Press, 1995), 105–6.

11. "Rubella Symposium." The National Institutes of Health and the Department of Pediatrics at New York University School of Medicine cosponsored an International Conference on Rubella Immunization February 18–20, 1969, with participants from twenty-seven countries. Saul Krugman again served as guest editor in publishing the proceedings in two issues of the *AJDC* 118, nos. 1 and 2 (July and August 1969). For a review of the vaccine research, see Stanley A. Plotkin, "Rubella Vaccine," in *Vaccines,* ed. Stanley A. Plotkin and Edward A. Mortimer Jr., 2nd ed. (Philadelphia: W. B. Saunders, 1998), 303–36.

12. In April 1966, NIH scientists Paul D. Parkman and Harry M. Meyer Jr. of the Division of Biologics Standards of the National Institutes of Health announced that they had developed an attenuated live rubella vaccine that did not spread to susceptible monkeys. "Infectious Diseases: Vaccine Against German Measles," *Time* 87 (May 6, 1966): 87; "Rubella Vaccine Needs Several Year's Study," *Science News* 89 (May 7, 1966): 349; Louis Z. Cooper, "German Measles," *Scientific American* 215 (July 1966): 37; "Rubella: Vaccine Still in Future," *Science*

*News* 90 (November 19, 1966): 423. On U.S. government funding of pharmaceutical company research, see "U.S. Girds for War on German Measles," *Business Week* (March 22, 1969): 57; "Rubella: Vaccine Still in Future," 423.

13. Dr. Walter Alvarez (syndicated column), "Measles Vaccine Reason to Rejoice," *LAT,* May 23, 1966, p. C20.

14. On federal expenditures for basic science and biomedical research, see Roswell Quinn, "Broader Spectrum: A History of Antibiotic R&D" (PhD diss., University of Illinois, Urbana-Champaign, 2008), chap. 3. Quinn reports that federal funding increased ten times between 1947 and 1957, and then jumped even further in the 1960s, up to about fifty times between 1947 and 1967. Pharmaceutical industry spending on research, in contrast, increased about twelve times. Basil O'Connor reported that NF-MOD had invested $600,000 in rubella research and supported 107 Birth Defects Centers in Basil O'Connor, "Draft Statement Concerning the Rubella Virus Vaccine Licensed June 9, 1969," 10 June 1969, folder Rubella Apgar, Virginia, Statements and Correspondence, 1969, Birth Defects, box 3, series 3, Medical Program Records, March of Dimes Archives, White Plains, NY (hereafter MPR-MODA). For a detailed history of MOD's rubella research and medical program, see "Rubella (German Measles) and Birth Defects," *March of Dimes Science News Backgrounder,* May 12, 1965, folder Birth Defects and Epidemics, series 3 Birth Defects, box 3, MPR-MODA.

15. H. M. Meyer, P. D. Parkman, T. E. Hobbins, H. E. Larson et al., "Attenuated Rubella Viruses: Laboratory and Clinical Characteristics," *AJDC* 118 (1969) 155–65; Sarah Leavitt, "'Something to Think About When I Can't Sleep': The Development of Rubella Vaccine" (unpublished paper presented at the American Association for the History of Medicine Annual Meeting, Halifax, Nova Scotia, May 2006). There were other vaccines produced as well and a debate about which ones should be licensed and used. See Victor Cohn, "Priority Held Problem on Measles Vaccines," *Washington Post,* Feb. 21, 1969, p. 26; Stuart Auerbach, "Battle Looms on Vaccines for Measles," *Washington Post,* Feb. 15, 1969, pp. A1, 7.

16. "Vaccines May Be Licensed by Fall," *Science News* 95 (March 1, 1969): 209; Stanley L. Englebardt, "Now: A Vaccine to Conquer Another Crippler," *Reader's Digest* 94 (April 1969): 126.

17. Virginia Apgar, MD, "Priorities for Progress," speech to medical advisors of NF-MOD, April 1969, pp. 5–6, Apgar Papers, MODA. See also U.S. Department of Health, Education, and Welfare, Public Health Service, *Rubella* (pamphlet), prepared by Jane S. Lin-Fu (Washington, DC: GPO, 1970), p. 6, folder Birth Defects Rubella Printed Literature and Posters, 1970–71, box 3, series 3 Birth Defects, MPR-MODA.

18. See, for example, "Rubella (German Measles) and Birth Defects."

19. U.S. HEW press release, April 18, 1969, folder Rubella Apgar, Virginia, Statements and Correspondence, 1969, box 3, series 3 Birth Defects, MPR-MODA; O'Connor, "Draft Statement Concerning the Rubella Virus Vaccine";

"Recommendation of the Public Health Service Advisory Committee on Immunization Practices," *AJDC* 118, no. 2 (August 1969): 398; U.S. Dept. of HEW, *Rubella.*

20. U.S. Dept. of HEW, *Rubella.*

21. "Recommendation of the Public Health Service Advisory Committee on Immunization Practices," 398.

22. On efforts to target adolescent girls, which succeeded in a small town in Wisconsin but were less successful in the United Kingdom, where many refused vaccination, see Plotkin, "Rubella Vaccine," 319, 323–24.

23. Harold M. Schmeck Jr., "Scientists Split Over Who Gets Rubella Vaccine," *NYT,* Feb. 21, 1969, p. 24. The papers of the NIH International Conference on Rubella Immunization, where these debates occurred, were published in two issues of the *American Journal of Disease of Children,* vol. 118, nos. 1 and 2 (July and August 1969). In his later study, Plotkin pointed out that "vaccination of all infants will probably eradicate CRS in 30 to 40 years, vaccination of all schoolgirls will presumably eradicate CRS in 10 to 20 years, and vaccination of adult women will eradicate CRS immediately." He advised strategies depending on the "local circumstances," including willingness to vaccinate and what the nation or individual could afford. Plotkin recommended infant vaccination (with MMR, if acceptance rates were high and if the nation could afford the expense), but he found "schoolgirl vaccination [an] excellent alternative strategy if high acceptance rates cannot be guaranteed, and it has the advantage of ensuring that girls are immune before bearing children without requiring tedious checks of old vaccination records or serological determinations." Plotkin, "Rubella Vaccine," 325.

24. Mr. Michel, "Inoculation Against Rubella," *Congressional Record–House* (November 6, 1969): 33323. In 1969, the United States had approximately 56 million children age one to fourteen. Statement by Virginia Apgar, MD, to Subcommittee on Health, Senate Committee on Labor and Public Welfare, on June 30, 1969, p. 3, folder 1, box 21, series 8, Virginia Apgar Papers, Mt. Holyoke College Archives and Special Collections, South Hadley, MA (hereafter cited as AP-MHCA).

25. HEW called for $26 million for rubella immunization, which would cover only low-income children. See Jonathan Spivak, "Vaccination Attack Against German Measles Aimed at Eradicating Disease in 5 Years," *Wall Street Journal,* July 1, 1969, in "Federal Vaccination Campaign to Eradicate German Measles," *Congressional Record–Senate* (July 2, 1969): 18247–48.

26. Metropolitan Life Insurance Co. advertisement in *Life* (November 13, 1970): 30.

27. ABC-TV, *Abortion.*

28. For a discussion of maternal thinking during pregnancy, see Barbara Katz Rothman, *The Tentative Pregnancy: How Amniocentesis Changes the Experience of Motherhood* (New York: W. W. Norton, 1993).

29. The referendum to legalize abortion in Washington won. David Garrow, *Liberty and Sexuality,* 466. By the late 1970s, "the unborn" had been thoroughly claimed by the right-wing antiabortion movement. The antiabortion movement developed "The Human Rights for the Unborn" in 1977 in reaction to President Jimmy Carter's work on human rights and arms disarmament. Personal communication from Carol Mason, 6–7 August 2008. See also Barbara Duden, "The Fetus on the 'Farther Shore': Toward a History of the Unborn," in *Fetal Subjects, Feminist Positions,* ed. Lynn M. Morgan and Meredith W. Michaels (Philadelphia: University of Pennsylvania Press, 1999), 13–25. On the language and world views of "pro-life" and "pro-choice" groups, see Carol Mason, *Killing for Life: The Apocalyptic Narrative of Pro-Life Politics* (Ithaca, NY: Cornell University Press, 2002); Kristin Luker, *Abortion and the Politics of Motherhood* (Berkeley: University of California Press, 1985); Faye D. Ginsburg, *Contested Lives: The Abortion Debate in an American Community* (Berkeley: University of California Press, 1998); Rickie Solinger, *Beggars and Choosers: How the Politics of Choice Shapes Adoption, Abortion, and Welfare in the United States* (New York: Hill and Wang, 2001); Monica J. Casper, *The Making of the Unborn Patient: A Social Anatomy of Fetal Surgery* (New Brunswick, NJ: Rutgers University Press, 1999).

30. Rockefeller quoted in Charlotte Slater, "German Measles Vaccine," *Detroit News,* October 23, 1968, clipping in folder 4, box 19, series 8, AP-MHCA; "Aftermath of an Epidemic: Tragic and Costly," sidebar with Barbara Goodheart, "Exit German Measles?" *Today's Health* 17 (June 1969): 27. At an early planning meeting, Dr. Mason observed of the 1964 epidemic, "This is not only a problem for the child, the family, relatives, etc. It is, in addition, a serious economic problem. Thirty million dollars has been spent in Washington, D.C., alone for rehabilitation and custodial care for these children." "Proceedings," National Foundation, Rubella Vaccination Planning Meeting, September 29, 1969, quotation on p. 1, folder 4, box 21, series 8, AP-MHCA.

31. Robert O. Self, "Prelude to the Tax Revolt: The Politics of the 'Tax Dollar' in Post-War California," in *New Suburban History,* ed. Kevin M. Kruse and Thomas J. Sugrue (Chicago: University of Chicago Press, 2006), chap. 7.

32. About 80,000 children in Washington, DC, were expected to be immunized by six "teams" through the schools by the end of the month. The *Washington Post* reported that an estimated five hundred babies had been harmed in the recent German measles epidemic. Marie Smith, "Tricia Is Aide at Measles Clinic," *Washington Post,* Nov. 4, 1969, p. B2, photo on p. A1; "Measles Shot," *CD,* Nov. 4, 1969, p. 1.

33. Senator Allen continued, "The administration can find $1.2 billion for the SST. But it cannot find just $9 million for five important research programs," including the rubella immunization campaign, which was "being forced into stagnation." In "Cutback in Health and Medical Research Funds," *Congressional Record–Senate* (November 6, 1969): 33368. See also " 'Pound Foolish' Cutbacks

in Federal Programs Threaten Nation with Growing Health Crisis," *Congressional Record–House* (December 4, 1969): 36907.

34. Michel, "Inoculation Against Rubella"; "The Lonely Medical Runner," *Nation* 209 (November 10, 1969): 493–94; Spivak, "Vaccination Attack Against German Measles." On Nixon, see Wailoo, *Dying in the City of the Blues,* 165–74.

35. "The Lonely Medical Runner"; "Chapter Guidelines for Assisting Rubella Programs," NF-MOD, [1970–71], quotation from unnumbered preface, folder Birth Defects Rubella Chapter Guidelines for Assisting Rubella Programs 1970, box 3, series 3 Birth Defects, MPR-MODA. For an example of one of many private financing efforts, the Arlington (Virginia) County Medical Society paid for 5,000 doses of vaccine while the county covered the cost for 4,000. Report in "Flag Salute Proposed in Schools," *Washington Post,* November 12, 1969, p. B12. At many clinics, parents were asked to donate $2 to cover the cost of vaccine; see "Around the Beltway," *Washington Post,* January 29, 1970, p. F2.

36. U.S. Department of Health, Education, and Welfare, Public Health Service, *Voluntary Action to Stop Rubella,* [circa 1970], folder Birth Defects Rubella Printed Literature and Posters, 1970–71, box 3, series 3 Birth Defects, MPR-MODA. For national organizations tapped by the March of Dimes, see "Proceedings." Taylor Residents United in "Provident Hospital to Sponsor Health Carnival," *CD,* October 17, 1970, weekend edition, p. 23. For support for immunization from advocates for deaf people, see the report of private funding for rubella vaccination by members of the Louisville, Kentucky, A. G. Bell Association in "Kentucky's Rubella Inoculation Program," *Volta Review* 72, no. 5 (May 1970): 288; Letter from Martha M. Mills, "On Prevention of Rubella," *Volta Review* 73, no. 4 (April 1971): 200. For support from National Advocates for Retarded Children, see Joan Orth, "National Effort to Support Rubella Vaccination Drive," *Children Limited* 18, no. 5 (May 1969): 1, 3; "Vaccine Can Prevent Rubella," *Children Limited* 18, no. 8 (November 1969): 5.

37. U.S. Dept. of HEW, *Voluntary Action to Stop Rubella.*

38. The National Foundation began educating its membership and the public about rubella in 1968 and called a national meeting in September 1969 with other organizations to coordinate efforts. See "Proceedings"; Statement by Virginia Apgar, MD, to Subcommittee on Health, Senate Committee on Labor and Public Welfare, June 30, 1969, p. 3. On the National Foundation, see Tony Gould, *A Summer Plague: Polio and Its Survivors* (New Haven, CT: Yale University Press, 1995), chap. 2, 141–43; Allan M. Brandt, "Polio, Politics, Publicity, and Duplicity: Ethical Aspects in the Development of the Salk Vaccine," *International Journal of Health Services* 8, no. 2 (1978): 257–70. Elaine Whitelaw made the connections to women's clubs and built up the volunteer component that made the NF so successful. See Elaine Whitelaw, interview by Gabriel Stickle, June 8, 1984, transcript, Oral History Records, MODA; Melvin A. Glasser, conversation with Gabriel Stickle, September 12, 1983, transcript, Oral

History Records, MODA; Richard Carter, *The Gentle Legions* (Garden City, NY: Doubleday, 1961); Leslie J. Reagan, "Engendering the Dread Disease: Women, Men, and Cancer," 150th anniversary issue, *American Journal of Public Health* (hereafter cited as *AJPH*) 87, no. 11 (November 1997): 1780–81.

39. Stanley L. Englebardt, "Now: A Vaccine to Conquer Another Crippler," *Reader's Digest* 94 (April 1969): 123.

40. Dorothy Stockbridge, "Doctor's Goal is Prevention of Birth Defects," *Tribune* [n.p.], November 15, 1969, clipping in AP-MHCA.

41. Apgar, "Priorities for Progress"; Harry Nelson, "Reports Cite Dangers in New Measles Shot," *LAT*, Feb. 20, 1969, p. 10.

42. Hugh Gregory Gallagher, *FDR's Splendid Deception* (New York: Dodd, Mead, 1985); David M. Oshinsky, *Polio: An American Story* (New York: Oxford University Press, 2005); Jane S. Smith, *Patenting the Sun: Polio and the Salk Vaccine* (New York: William and Morrow, 1990); Gould, *Summer Plague.*

43. With the exceptions of rubella and measles, this was the list of immunizations advised in 1963. The schedule of immunizations, as advised by the American Academy of Pediatrics, began in infancy and continued through age eight with revaccination. See Graves, *Right From the Start.* On differentiating between the two diseases and vaccines, see Frank Falkner, "The Measles," *Washington Post,* Feb. 4, 1969, p. D3; Frank Falkner, "The Implications of Immunization Histories," *Washington Post,* Nov. 15, 1969, p. C4.

44. For a standard health pamphlet that showed a mother and her baby with a doctor at the time of immunization (with a white mother and infant on the cover and a black mother and infant with a black male physician pictured inside), see Graves, *Right From the Start,* illustrations on cover and p. 4. The responsibility of mothers to immunize (and their implicitly being the ones who needed to be convinced of the necessity) can also be seen in current materials on global immunization campaigns. See World Health Organization, *Immunization in Practice: A Guide for Health Workers Who Give Vaccines* (Oxford: Oxford University Press, 1989), 208–15, and illustrations of mothers and children in "villages" on 201, 205, and 215. Fathers too, then and now, might also take children to doctors' appointments, but their performance of this activity was unusual, putting them in the position of "mothering" and acting as "mothers," as Barbara Katz Rothman explains in *Weaving a Family: Untangling Race and Adoption* (Boston: Beacon Press, 2005), 97–100.

45. Stella Chess, Sam J. Korn, and Paulina B. Fernandez, *Psychiatric Disorders of Children with Congenital Rubella* (New York: Brunner/Mazel, 1971), 142, 151.

46. U.S. Department of HEW, *Rubella;* Michel, "Inoculation Against Rubella."

47. "Ghetto indifference to immunization is hindering the national effort to eradicate measles, according to J. Lyle Conrad, MD, of the National Communicable Disease Center." Quoted in "Slums Resist Measles Shots," *Children*

*Limited* 17, no. 7 (November 1968): 2. On health authorities' ideas about a "hard-to-reach" population, see Colgrove, *State of Immunity,* 168–70.

48. Johanna Schoen, *Choice and Coercion: Birth Control, Sterilization, and Abortion in Public Health and Welfare* (Chapel Hill: University of North Carolina Press, 2005).

49. PEPI, Inc., touted its rubella vaccine and then went on to advertise vaccines for lions and leopards at the zoo and its successful corporate philosophy. Advertisement, *Wall Street Journal,* February 10, 1970, p. 11.

50. U.S. Dept. of HEW, Public Health Service, *The Real Life Story of RUBY,* 1971, folder Birth Defects Rubella Printed Literature and Posters, 1970–71, box 3, series 3 Birth Defects, MPR-MODA. All quotations are from this pamphlet.

51. It is true that in all marriages and families a new baby "ends" in a metaphoric and emotional way the form and dynamics of the family because a new person has entered the story, but it is also the beginning of a new relationship and a new person.

52. The emphasis on orality, lipreading, and hearing aids, however, was often difficult, did not always work, and made many children extremely frustrated. See Angelique N. Wahlstedt, "An Oral Failure from Oklahoma," 1995, updated November 30, 2005, on Deaf-Info, Omer Zak's website, www.zak.co.il/deaf-info/old/oral_failure_oklahoma.html (accessed June 23, 2006). On Deaf schools, community culture, and identity, see Douglas C. Baynton, *Forbidden Signs: American Culture and the Campaign Against Sign Language* (Chicago: University of Chicago Press, 1998); Susan Burch, *Signs of Resistance: American Deaf Cultural History, 1900-World War II* (New York: New York University Press, 2004); Robert Buchanan, *Illusions of Equality: Deaf Americans in School and Factory, 1850–1950* (Washington, DC: Gallaudet University Press, 1999).

53. National Foundation–March of Dimes, *Birth Defects: The Tragedy and the Hope* (pamphlet) (New York: National Foundation–March of Dimes, 1964), folder Birth Defects Literature, Media Records, series 2 Birth Defects, Media Records, MODA.

54. U.S. Department of HEW, *The Real Life Story of RUBY.* Last quotation from the pamphlet is reversed in the original, and "immunize . . . now" is capitalized in the original. The pamphlet and proofs for reprinting were made available to health departments and to (private) voluntary agencies, including the March of Dimes, for mass distribution. Cost was estimated to be one penny per copy. James J. Cox (Assistant Information Officer, Center for Disease Control) to Rubella Project Coordinators, 15 March 1971, folder Birth Defects Rubella Printed Literature and Posters, 1970–71, box 3, series 3 Birth Defects, MPR-MODA. Another pamphlet produced by the USPHS more graphically depicted the potential results of maternal rubella through a drawing that named and indicated where specific birth defects occurred by pointing to the areas on a baby's body: "brain damage" with a line to the baby's head, "deafness" with a line to the ear, and lines to

respective locations for "cataracts," "heart defects," "enlarged liver," and "bone malformations." The cover made clear who had caused the rubella as it declared, "Rubella[—] Stop the Spread from child to mother." U.S. Dept. of HEW, Public Health Service, *Rubella[—]Stop the Spread From Child to Mother,* circa 1970, folder Birth Defects Rubella Printed Literature and Posters, 1970–71, box 3, series 3 Birth Defects, MPR-MODA.

55. I have not found evidence suggesting that men or boys expressed skepticism about their need for rubella vaccination, but the emphasis on boys in the public health materials indicates the concern of health educators. For one example of the work to convince parents of the need to vaccinate boys, see Virginia Apgar, "Questions and Answers on German Measles," *PTA Magazine* 63 (May 1969): 12–13, which included the questions "Why should my son be vaccinated against German measles? He's never going to get pregnant," and "Why not vaccinate women since they're the only ones in whom the infection can be dangerous?"

56. March of Dimes, *Rubella Robs the Cradle,* comic book, [1970], folder Birth Defects Rubella Printed Literature and Posters, 1970–71, box 3, series 3 Birth Defects, MPR-MODA. All quotations are from this comic book.

57. "Chapter Guidelines for Assisting Rubella Programs," NF-MOD, 7, 16–17, quotation on 4, folder Birth Defects Rubella Chapter Guidelines for Assisting Rubella Programs 1970, box 3, series 3 Birth Defects, box 3, MPR-MODA.

58. Minneapolis reported immunizing over 80 percent of the targeted group; Charlottesville reported that 11,637 of the city's estimated 12,000 children between the ages of one and twelve received shots. Minneapolis in "Chapter Guidelines for Assisting Rubella Programs," 7, 16–17; "Charlottesville 'Rubs Out Rubella' in Community Campaign," *National Foundation News* (hereafter cited as *NF News*) (April 1970): 2.

59. On this point, see Reagan, "Engendering the Dread Disease."

60. *Sarampion Aleman . . . Tragedia Que Achecha La Cuna,* comic book, [1970], folder Birth Defects Rubella Printed Literature and Posters, 1970–71, box 3, series 3 Birth Defects, MPR-MODA.

61. Personal communication.

62. Jane Brody, "City's Rubella Drive on TV 'Sells' Children on Need for Shots," *NYT,* June 14, 1970, p. 60.

63. Photo in "Stop Rubella," *Children Limited* 18, no. 10 (December 1969): 3. Stars from NBC-TV's *Julia* appeared in an NIH, 16 mm, 13½-minute film available from the National Medical Audiovisual Center. I have not (yet) been able to locate the film. *Julia* began in September 1968 and quickly became one of the top ten shows. On the television show, see Aniko Bodroghkozy, "Julia: U.S. Domestic Comedy," Museum of Broadcast Communications, www.museum.tv/archives/etv/J/htmlJ/julia/julia.htm (accessed July 9, 2008). On the young audience, this is purely anecdotal. My friend Elaine Kihara and I both remember avidly watching this show.

64. Japanese- and Spanish-language materials mentioned in "3,000 from 50 Groups Work Rubella Project," *NF News* (January 1971): 2. More than 15,000 children received rubella shots in one day in Long Beach, California, as a result of this effort.

65. Mrs. Perdomo was originally from Santo Domingo. Rubella press kit/feature story (with photo) by Helen Hickey, 1970, folder Birth Defects Rubella, box 3, series 3 Birth Defects, MPR-MODA.

66. On resistance to vaccination and the move toward advertising and persuasion, see Judith Walzer Leavitt, "Politics and Public Health: Smallpox in Milwaukee, 1894–1895," *Bulletin of the History of Medicine* 50 (1976): 553–68; Judith Walzer Leavitt, " 'Be Safe. Be Sure.' New York City's Experience with Epidemic Smallpox," in *Sickness and Health in America: Readings in the History of Medicine and Public Health,* ed. Judith Walzer Leavitt and Ronald L. Numbers, 3rd ed. rev. (Madison: University of Wisconsin Press, 1997), chap. 25; Colgrove, *State of Immunity,* 9–11, chap. 1. Colgrove's important study shows that the compulsory immunization laws were passed in the mid-1960s with little debate during the measles eradication effort. Colgrove reports that "a CDC survey in the late 1970s suggested that many people were not aware of their state's laws: about one-quarter of respondents said that their state did not require vaccination of children prior to school entry, even though virtually all Americans by this time lived in areas covered by such laws. More than nine out of ten respondents said that even if their state did not have such a law, they would have their child vaccinated anyway." Opinion Research Corporation, *Public Attitudes toward Immunization: August 1977 and February 1978* (Princeton, NJ: Opinion Research Corporation, 1978), 84–85, as cited in Colgrove, *State of Immunity,* 136n, 297, quotation on 178. On the passage of these laws, 174–78.

67. Photo, *Washington Post,* Dec. 19, 1969, p. B1.

68. Robert L. Griswold, *Fatherhood in America: A History* (New York: Basic Books, 1994); Jacqueline H. Wolf, *Don't Kill Your Baby: Public Health and the Decline of Breastfeeding in the Nineteenth and Twentieth Centuries* (Columbus: Ohio State University Press, 2001), 21–22, 120–22; Rima D. Apple, *Perfect Motherhood: Science and Childrearing in America* (New Brunswick, NJ: Rutgers University Press, 2006), 45–46.

69. Smith, *Patenting the Sun,* 265, 273.

70. Personal communication from Christina Tarr.

71. Smith, "Tricia Is Aide at Measles Clinic." In the tried and true manner of adults denying the fear and pain of children, "to one little girl who screamed from fear as she approached the injector, Tricia Nixon said, 'There, that didn't hurt at all.' " Ibid. See also "Anticipation," in *Pittsburgh Post-Gazette,* November 22, 1966, folder Birth Defects Rubella (German Measles) Stop Measles Sunday Dec 7 1966, series 3 Birth Defects, box 3, MPR-MODA.

72. Henry Rosenberg, "Robert Andrew Hingson, MD: OB Analgesia Pioneer," *ASA Newsletter* 63, no. 9 (1999), online at the American Society of Anesthesiologists, www.asahq.org (accessed May 2, 2009).

73. *Rubella Robs the Cradle. Voluntary Action to Stop Rubella* also used the number 50,000. A 1965 *March of Dimes Science News Backgrounder* clarified how the organization came up with what it believed to be conservative estimates. It estimated that between 10 and 36 percent of pregnancies ended in "fetal death"—meaning miscarriage or stillbirths—(approximately 8,000 to 30,000) and that 28 percent (or 15,000 to 20,000) of liveborn deliveries would have birth defects. "Rubella (German Measles) and Birth Defects," 6. By 1968, however, Virginia Apgar and rubella researchers believed previous estimates to be too low. Higher estimates in Goodheart, "Exit German Measles?" 26. These numbers also appeared in Shirley Motter Linde, "An End to the German Measles Menace?" *Woman's Day* (October 1968), as reprinted with the testimony of Senator Ralph Yarborough of Texas, *Congressional Record. Extension of Remarks* (October 14, 1968): 31394.

74. In June 1969, the National Communicable Disease Center offered these estimates of the results of the 1964–65 rubella epidemic: 12,500,000 cases, 2,160 deaths (stillbirths, neonatal, child), 6,250 "fetal wastage" (miscarriages), 20,000 children with CRS, and 5,000 therapeutic abortions. Plotkin, "Rubella Vaccine," table 11–5, 308.

75. In the postwar period, women were taught that a miscarriage was a "blessing" because it meant that there had been something wrong with the embryo, and Nature had taken its course. Leslie J. Reagan, "From Hazard to Blessing to Tragedy: Representations of Miscarriage in Twentieth-Century America," *Feminist Studies* 29, no. 2 (Summer 2003): 356–78. One anonymous informant tells me that when she received an ambiguous diagnosis following amniocentesis, she often wished for a miscarriage to take away the stress and suffering of deciding. See also Rayna Rapp, *Testing Women, Testing the Fetus: The Social Impact of Amniocentesis in America* (New York: Routledge, 1999).

76. Quotation and "normal life" in Goodheart, "Exit German Measles?"

77. Advertisement in *Life* 69, no. 20 (November 13, 1970): 30. Omer Zak remembers being at the Tracy Clinic and having a grand time playing with kids "all wearing those box things with cords and ear plug just like myself!" but says he never learned to lip-read. Omer Zak, [humor] "An Oral Failure from Oklahoma," updated November 30, 2005, www.zak.co.il/deaf- info/old/oral_failure_oklahoma.html (accessed June 23, 2006).

78. Cendevax advertisement with the slogan above it: "vaccinate now . . . one more rubella child is one too many," *AJPH* 60 (May 1970): 22–23.

79. Rosemarie Garland Thomson, "Seeing the Disabled: Visual Rhetorics of Disability in Popular Photography," in *The New Disability History: American Perspectives,* ed. Paul K. Longmore and Lauri Umansky (New York: New York

University Press, 2001), chap. 13; "Telethons," in *The ABC-CLIO Companion to The Disability Rights Movement,* ed. Fred Pelka (Santa Barbara, CA: ABC-CLIO, 1997), 301–2; Joseph P. Shapiro, *No Pity: People with Disabilities Forging a New Civil Rights Movement* (New York: Three Rivers Press, 1994), 12–24.

80. The children were filmed at a school for the blind and in a children's hospital. "'Case Against Rubella' Film Is Available," *Mental Retardation News* 19, no. 5 (May 1970): 2. Lucy Helen Dunn, review of *A Case Against Rubella* (produced by Aegis Productions, Inc., New York), *American Journal of Nursing* 70, no. 5 (May 1970): 110.

81. National Association for Retarded Children, *Research in Mental Retardation: Why and How* (New York: NARC, 1959), folder National Association for Retarded Children, box 12, Leonard Mayo Papers, Social Welfare Archives, University of Minnesota Libraries, Minneapolis, MN.

82. On PKU, Lindee, *Moments of Truth in Genetic Medicine,* 45–46. On measles, see "Shy Poster Girl Missed Measles Shot," *Pittsburgh Press,* December 1, 1966; and "Measles Vaccine for County Urged by Mother of Stricken Girl, 3," *(Monongahela, PA) Daily Republican,* December 1, 1966, both clippings in folder Measles, box 3, series 3 Birth Defects, MPR-MODA.

83. "Proceedings, National Foundation, Rubella Vaccination Planning Meeting." On the Kennedy Foundation, see Edward Shorter, *The Kennedy Family and the Story of Mental Retardation* (Philadelphia: Temple University Press, 2000).

84. Shapiro, *No Pity,* 45–53.

85. "That Other Kind—German Measles," *Children Limited* 15, no. 3 (June–July 1966): 7. The clinical trial is also reported in Englebardt, "Now: A Vaccine to Conquer Another Crippler," 125–26. This article reported that because the scientists wanted to ensure that no "infected volunteer passed [rubella] along to a pregnant woman," they needed a "closed population environment" to test the vaccine. It also highlighted the research protocols: "In October 1965, with the written consent of the parents of each child, the first clinical trial began." Quotations on p. 125.

86. Henry K. Beecher, "Ethics and Clinical Research," *New England Journal of Medicine* 274, no. 24 (June 6, 1966): 1354–60.

87. "That Other Kind—German Measles."

88. See inset, which reported on the NARC-sponsored conference in May 1964 on "The Role of the Residential Institution in Mental Retardation Research" in "That Other Kind—German Measles"; "Scientists Honored for Rubella Research," *Children Limited* 18, no. 4 (April 1969): 2; Joan Orth, "National Effort to Support Rubella Vaccination Drive," *Children Limited* 18, no. 5 (May 1969): 1, 3; "Vaccine Can Prevent Rubella," *Children Limited* 18, no. 8 (November 1969): 5. NARC also supported the earlier anti-measles efforts. "NARC Spurs Measles Campaign," *Children Limited* 15, no. 3 (June–July 1966): 1, 3.

89. See letters from James J. Cox, National Communicable Disease Center, and Thomas F. McNulty, Baltimore, MD, in Letters to the Editor, *Children Limited* 18, no. 7 (September 1969): 4.

90. On the tradition of experimentation on the "feeble-minded," vaccine research (smallpox and scarlet fever) on institutionalized children (foundlings and orphans) and associated scandals in late-nineteenth- and early-twentieth-century Europe and the United States, see Susan E. Lederer, *Subjected to Science: Human Experimentation in America before the Second World War* (Baltimore: Johns Hopkins University Press, 1995), 7–9, 51, 107–8; Sydney Halpern, *Lesser Harms: The Morality of Risk in Medical Research* (Chicago: University of Chicago Press, 2004), 76–79, 99, 114. On the use of intellectually impaired children in polio research and the National Foundation for Infantile Paralysis's insistence on consents, see Oshinsky, *Polio,* 134–37, 157–60, 245–46.

91. John Harkness, Susan E. Lederer, and Daniel Wickler, "Public Health Classics: Laying Ethical Foundations for Research," *Bulletin of the World Health Organization* 79, no. 4 (2001): 365–66; and Beecher, "Ethics and Clinical Research," reprinted ibid., 367–72; David J. Rothman, *Strangers at the Bedside: A History of How Law and Bioethics Transformed Medical Decision Making* (New York: Basic Books, 1991), chap. 4.

92. Sheldon J. Kaplan announced the group's first meeting in "Birth Defect Group to Meet," *LAT,* May 28, 1967, p. 7 (Sheldon J. Kaplan, cochairman [Santa Monica], meeting held at the John Tracy Clinic). See also "Rubella Parents to Meet Sunday," *LAT,* Jan. 30, 1968, p. C2 (Mrs. Camellia Robles [Whittier], meeting held at Sacred Heart of Mary High School). For examples of collective and individual parent activism, see Katherine Castles, " 'Nice, Average Americans': Postwar Parents' Groups and the Defense of the Normal Family," in *Mental Retardation in America: A Historical Reader,* ed. Steven Noll and James W. Trent Jr. (New York: New York University Press, 2004), 353; Shapiro, *No Pity,* 42–45, 56–57; "Parents' Movement," in *The ABC-CLIO Companion,* 240–41. On the importance of education to people with disabilities, see Catherine J. Kudlick, "The Outlook of *The Problem* and the Problem with the *Outlook:* Two Advocacy Journals Reinvent Blind People in Turn-of-the-Century America," in *The New Disability History,* ed. Longmore and Umansky, chap. 7.

93. Lynn Lilliston, "Variety of Handicaps Hurts Rubella Children," *LAT,* Feb. 12, 1968, p. C1. The Tracy Clinic was the powerful proponent of *oralism,* an emphasis that the Deaf movement of the 1980s—enlarged because of rubella—actively opposed. On oralism, Sign, and Deaf education, see Baynton, *Forbidden Signs*; R. A. R. Edwards, "Speech Has an Extraordinary Humanizing Power: Horace Mann and the Problem of Nineteenth-Century American Deaf Education," in *The New Disability History,* ed. Longmore and Umansky, chap. 2; Shapiro, *No Pity,* 86–99.

94. Kathryn Kinman in "Education Problems Loom in Near Future," *LAT,* Feb. 13, 1968, p. C14.

95. Lilliston, "Variety of Handicaps Hurts Rubella Children"; Donald R. Calvert, *Rubella and Deaf Children in California* (San Francisco: San Francisco Hearing and Speech Center, 1967), 10.

96. For charitable schools and camps, see Jean Murphy, "SOS From Foundation for Junior Blind," *LAT,* April 20, 1969, p. E10; Richard D. Lyons, "German Measles Victims Tax Special Schools," *NYT,* Feb. 12, 1969, in Roman C. Pucinski, "The Coming Crisis in Education for the Handicapped," *Congressional Record. Extensions of Remarks* (Feb. 18, 1969): 3657; Mrs. Claud Wynn in Letters to the Editor, *Children Limited* 18, no. 3 (March 1969): 4.

97. Lynn Lilliston, "The Rubella Children—A Sad Picture Edged With Hope," *LAT,* Feb. 11, 1968, p. 20.

98. Ibid., p. K1. See the entire series on Rubella Children in the *LAT,* Feb. 11, 12, and 13, 1968.

99. Shapiro, *No Pity,* 41–53.

100. Yarborough in *Congressional Record*; Public Law 90–538, Sept. 30, 1968; "The 1967 Bell Award Given to President Johnson at the White House," *Volta Review* 69, no. 4 (April 1967): 244–47; Pucinski, "The Coming Crisis in Education for the Handicapped." Dr. Donald Calvert of the Federal Bureau of Education for the Handicapped had provided the estimates cited in Lyons, "German Measles Victims Tax Special Schools." "Aftermath of an Epidemic."

101. "Aftermath of an Epidemic."

102. Mary Jean Beaton, *The Road to Autonomy* (Enumclaw, WA: Winepress Publishing, Pleasant Word, 2003), 56.

103. Nancy Fraser and Linda Gordon, "A Genealogy of Dependency: Tracing a Keyword of the U.S. Welfare State," *Signs* 19, no. 2 (Winter 1994): 309–36.

104. Title V of the Rehabilitation Act of 1973 and the Education for All Handicapped Children Act of 1974 (later renamed the Individuals with Disabilities Education Act [IDEA]). Richard K. Scotch, "American Disability Policy in the Twentieth Century," in *The New Disability History,* ed. Longmore and Umansky, chap. 14; Richard K. Scotch, *From Good Will to Civil Rights: Transforming Federal Disability Policy* (Philadelphia: Temple University Press, 1984); Paul K. Longmore, *Why I Burned My Book and Other Essays on Disability* (Philadelphia: Temple University Press, 2003), chap. 5.

105. The figures were through the end of April 1972. U.S. Department of Health, Education, and Welfare, *Report on Promoting the Health of Mothers and Children* (Washington, DC: GPO, 1972), 101–2; quotation on 102. The CDC reported more than 45.8 million doses distributed by December 31, 1972. Center for Disease Control, *Rubella Surveillance* (Washington, DC: GPO, November 1973), 8.

106. See Colgrove's excellent book *State of Immunity.* On resistance, persuasion versus compulsion, see passim. On school requirements, see 174–84. The

strong objections to vaccination in order to enter public schools and to the MMR specifically developed later, in the 1980s and 1990s. See also Robert D. Johnston, "Contemporary Anti-Vaccination Movements in Historical Perspective," in *The Politics of Healing: Histories of Alternative Medicine in Twentieth-Century North America,* ed. Robert D. Johnston (New York: Routledge, 2004), 259–86.

107. Roswell Quinn argues that the pharmaceutical industry produced a cultural campaign in the 1950s and 1960s to deflect government regulation and attention to profits and to claim that longer life—as well as democracy and efficiency—existed thanks to an unregulated pharmaceutical industry. See Quinn, "Broader Spectrum," chap. 3.

EPILOGUE: FROM ANXIETY TO RIGHTS

1. "Mother-work" is Molly Ladd-Taylor's apt phrase for succinctly describing the work involved in mothering. Molly Ladd-Taylor, *Mother-Work: Women, Child Welfare, and the State, 1890–1930* (Urbana: University of Illinois Press, 1994). See also Ellen Ross, *Love and Toil: Motherhood in Outcast London, 1870–1918* (New York: Oxford University Press, 1993). For an in-depth study of the reactions of parents, see Milton Seligman and Rosalyn Benjamin Darling, *Ordinary Families, Special Children: A Systems Approach to Childhood Disability,* (New York: Guilford Press, 1989).

2. Roni Rabin, "Screen All Pregnancies for Down Syndrome," *NYT,* Jan. 9, 2007, p. 5; Rayna Rapp, *Testing Women, Testing the Fetus: The Social Impact of Amniocentesis in America* (New York: Routledge, 1999); Susan Lindee, *Moments of Truth in Genetic Medicine* (Baltimore: Johns Hopkins University Press, 2005).

3. During the 2008 presidential campaign, many noticed when Governor Sarah Palin of Alaska, remarking about her son with Down syndrome, said that she had "decided" to have him (and implicitly had decided against an abortion). While opponents of legal abortion applauded Palin for her decision, supporters of legal abortion and privacy rights pointed out Palin's hypocrisy: she had decided, she had made a choice, but she wanted to make that decision for every other woman in the country by overturning *Roe v. Wade.* The point is that in this culture women like Palin are encouraged to think of carrying their pregnancies as a "choice" too.

4. For examples of differing views, see Jackie Leach Scully, "Genetics" in *Encyclopedia of Disability,* ed. Gary L. Albrecht (Thousand Oaks, CA: Sage Publications, 2006), 780–81; Adrienne Asch, "Reproductive Rights," ibid., 1399–1401; Trent Stephens and Rock Brynner, *Dark Remedy: The Impact of Thalidomide and Its Revival as a Vital Medicine* (Cambridge, MA: Perseus Publishing, 2001),

151–58; Faye Ginsburg and Rayna Rapp, "Fetal Reflections: Confessions of Two Feminist Anthropologists as Mutual Informants," in *Fetal Subjects, Feminist Positions*, ed. Lynn M. Morgan and Meredith W. Michaels (Philadelphia: University of Pennsylvania Press, 1999), chap. 14, especially 9n295; Michael Bérubé, *Life As We Know It: A Father, A Family, and an Exceptional Child* (New York: Random House, Vintage Books, 1996).

5. Rabin, "Screen All Pregnancies for Down Syndrome"; Amy Harmon and Kassie Bracken, "Reporter's Notebook: An Unusual Campaign: Difficult Diagnosis: A Positive Perspective," *NYT* video, photography and videography by Jack Manning and Jigar Mehta, May 2007, nytimes.com/video/2207/05/03/health/11948/7102668/difficult-diagnosis.html (accessed May 3, 2007); Rapp, *Testing Women, Testing the Fetus,* chap. 10; Janet Lyon and Michael Bérubé, "Living on Disability: Language and Social Policy in the Wake of the ADA," in *The Visible Woman: Imaging Technologies, Gender, and Science,* ed. Paula A. Treichler, Lisa Cartwright, and Constance Penley (New York: New York University Press, 1998), chap. 9.

6. Ginsburg and Rapp, "Fetal Reflections," 291, 294.

7. Carole Joffe, *Doctors of Conscience: The Struggle to Provide Abortion before and after Roe v. Wade* (Boston: Beacon Press, 1995), chap. 6; Carol Mason, *Killing for Life: The Apocalyptic Narrative of Pro-Life Politics* (Ithaca, NY: Cornell University Press, 2002).

8. Mason, *Killing for Life;* Janet Golden, *Message in a Bottle: The Making of Fetal Alcohol Syndrome* (Cambridge, MA: Harvard University Press, 2005), chaps. 6–7; Petchesky, *Abortion and Woman's Choice,* part 3.

9. U.S. Department of Health, Education, and Welfare, Public Health Service, *Rubella* (pamphlet), prepared by Jane S. Lin-Fu, publication no. 2041 (Washington, DC: GPO, 1970). An earlier pamphlet on rubella used a photo of the virus on its cover. See U.S. Department of Health, Education, and Welfare, Public Health Service, *Rubella Vaccine* (Washington, DC: GPO, 1969).

10. 1986–1987 March of Dimes Prenatal Care Campaign, folder Mommy . . . Don't Campaign Materials, 1986, box 11, series 13: Perinatal Health, Medical Program Records, MPR-MODA.

11. Golden, *Message in a Bottle,* chap. 7, 169–70;

12. Dorothy Roberts, *Killing the Black Body: Race, Reproduction, and the Meaning of Liberty* (New York: Random House, Vintage Books, 1997); Cynthia R. Daniels, *At Women's Expense: State Power and the Politics of Fetal Rights* (Cambridge, MA: Harvard University Press, 1993); Golden, *Message in a Bottle.*

13. Susan Eisner, Director of Communications, to General Manager, 25 September 1986. Cocaine and crack named in the *Mommy . . . Don't* pamphlet, March of Dimes Prenatal Care Campaign.

14. *Mommy . . . Don't* pamphlet.

15. Janet Golden finds that television representations of drinking mothers and FAS changed from a white woman in 1977 to a Latina woman in 1984. Golden, *Message in a Bottle,* 102–17.

16. For an excellent account of women's concerns today about the effects of environmental pollution on the fetus and the child and of the scientific research, see Sandra Steingraber, *Having Faith: An Ecologist's Journey to Motherhood* (Cambridge, MA: Perseus Publishing, 2001). On black infant mortality, see Roberts, *Killing the Black Body,* 183–84.

17. Adam Nossiter, "Rural Alabama County Cracks Down on Pregnant Drug Users," *NYT,* March 15, 2008, p. A9; Kirsten Scharnberg, "Pregnant Addicts Face Rise in Prosecutions," *CT,* Dec. 23, 2003, p. 11; Daniels, *At Women's Expense,* chap. 4; J. A. Talvi, "Criminalizing Motherhood," *Nation,* December 3, 2003, www .thenation.com (accessed May 4, 2009); "South Carolina Supreme Court Reverses 20-Year Homicide Conviction of Regina McKnight," *Drug Policy News,* May 12, 2008, www.drugpolicy.org/news/pressroom/pressrelease (accessed May 4, 2009).

18. Nossiter, "Rural Alabama County Cracks Down on Pregnant Drug Users."

19. Reagan, *When Abortion Was a Crime,* chap 4.

20. See the spot produced by the National Advocates for Pregnant Women (NAPW) on the state antiabortion referendum that includes footage and quotations from (white) pro-life women who have been prosecuted and who now oppose these types of laws. "Anti-Abortion Measures Can Hurt All Pregnant Women," www.youtube.com/watch?v = YuC4gGSZ-yU (accessed October 30, 2008); see also www.nationaladvocatesforpregnantwomen.org.

21. Leslie J. Reagan, "From Hazard to Blessing to Tragedy: Representations of Miscarriage in Twentieth-Century America," *Feminist Studies* 29, no. 2 (Summer 2003): 361–62; Linda Layne, *Motherhood Lost: A Feminist Account of Pregnancy Loss in America* (New York: Routledge, 2002).

22. At best, herd immunity appeared to offer about 50 percent protection against rubella to the nonimmune population. For instance, a soldier on leave from Fort Ord in California went to Kauai and spread rubella to fifteen people who had not been immunized. This epidemic and others brought to Hawaii by the military resulted in a mandatory rubella immunization policy for all soldiers before entering the state. U.S. Center for Disease Control, *Rubella Surveillance* (Atlanta, GA: CDC, 1971), 16; Daniel E. Lehane et al., "Evaluation of Rubella Herd Immunity During an Epidemic," *JAMA* 213, no. 13 (September 28, 1970): 2239; Stanley A. Plotkin, "Rubella Vaccine," in *Vaccines,* ed. Stanley A. Plotkin and Edward A. Mortimer Jr., 2nd ed. (Philadelphia: W. B. Saunders, 1998), 316, 323.

23. In addition to premarital and prenatal testing for immunity and immunizations, the U.S. Public Health Service advised testing for immunity at colleges, military bases, hospitals, and clinics and recommended "rigorous attempts to vaccinate susceptible women in the postpartum period." Center for

Disease Control, *Rubella Surveillance,* summary January 1976–December 1978 (Atlanta, GA: CDC, 1980), p. 13; and see "Recommendations of the Public Health Service Advisory Committee on Immunization Practices," January 1979, in the appendix, pp. 29–32.

24. Plotkin, "Rubella Vaccine," 323. Between 2001 and 2004, four children born with CRS were reported to the CDC; see "Elimination of Rubella and Congenital Rubella Syndrome–United States, 1969–2004," *MMWR* 54, no. 11 (March 25, 2005): 281.

25. There were still individual cases that had originated outside the United States, but there had been no outbreaks in the country since 2000. See Dr. Steven Cochi, Acting Director, CDC National Immunization Program, "CDC Announces Rubella, Once a Major Cause of Birth Defects, Is No Longer a Health Threat in the U.S.," *Telebriefing Transcript,* March 21, 2005, www.cdc .gov/od/oc/media/pressrel (accessed May 5, 2009); David Brown, "Rubella Virus Eliminated in the United States," *Washington Post,* March 21, 2005.

26. Rayna Rapp and Faye Ginsburg, "Enabling Disability: Rewriting Kinship, Reimagining Citizenship," *Public Culture* 13, no. 3 (2001): 533–56.

27. Autism is frequently covered in the news. A search of the *New York Times* online will yield thousands of articles (at www.nytimes.com). For examples, see Diana Jean Schemo and Jennifer Medina, "Disabilities Fight Grows as Taxes Pay for Tuition," *NYT,* Oct. 27, 2007.

28. Janet Lyon and Michael Bérubé, "Living on Disability: Language and Social Policy in the Wake of the ADA," in *The Visible Woman: Imaging Technologies, Gender, and Science,* ed. Paula A. Treichler, Lisa Cartwright, and Constance Penley (New York: New York University Press, 1998), chap. 9; Rapp and Ginsburg, "Enabling Disability."

29. Robert D. Johnston, "Contemporary Anti-Vaccination Movements in Historical Perspective," in *The Politics of Healing: Histories of Alternative Medicine in Twentieth-Century North America,* ed. Robert D. Johnston (New York: Routledge, 2004), 266–82; Donald G. McNeil Jr., "Sharp Drop Seen in Deaths From Ills Fought by Vaccine," *NYT,* Nov. 14, 2007; Jennifer Steinhauer, "Public Health Risk Seen as Parents Reject Vaccines," *NYT,* March 21, 2008, and comments posted online at http://community.nytimes.com/article/comments/ 2008/03/21/us/21vaccine.html.

30. Brown, "Rubella Virus Eliminated." The 2008 report found that 90 percent or more were vaccinated with all but one vaccine (most missing four doses of DTP), 77 percent had received all six of the recommended vaccines, and fewer that 1 percent had received none. Immunization rates varied by state and area; children living below the poverty level had somewhat lower rates. "National State and Local Area Vaccination Coverage Among Children Aged 19–35 Months–United States, 2007," *MMWR* 87, no. 35 (September, 5, 2008): 961–66, and online at www.cdc.gov/mmwr/preview/mmwrhtml/mm5735a1.html; Will Dunham,

"Child Vaccination Rates Hit Record Levels," September 5, 2008, www.reuters
.com/article/healthNews/idUSCOL4718522008090 5?feedType=RSS&feedName=
healthNews, September 5, 2008 (accessed June 30, 2009).

31. On vaccine critics, see Johnson, "Contemporary Anti-Vaccination Movements." Interestingly, the idea of a community responsibility to vaccinate for the
health of others has come up in the discussions about the new vaccine against the
sexually transmitted infectious disease HPV, Gardasil, which has been targeted
exclusively at girls in order to prevent cervical cancer. Some parents and physicians began to ask why boys had not also been included to protect their own
health as well as to protect their future sexual partners, who could transmit the
infection. Rubella occasionally arises in comments as a vaccine that is already
routinely used to protect others. See Jan Hoffman, "Vaccinating Boys for Girls'
Sake?" *NYT,* February 24, 2008; and comments posted on Tara Parker-Pope's
Well blog, "A Vaccine for Boys to Help Girls?" February 25, 2008, well.blogs
.nytimes.com/2008/02/25 (accessed May 4, 2009); Laurie Tarkan, "Vaccinations
Battling Disease; People Battling Vaccines," *NYT,* March 28, 2008, http://health
.nytimes.com/ref/health/healthguide/esn-vaccinations-expert (accessed May 9,
2009). On the political turn, see Robert O. Self, "Prelude to the Tax Revolt: The
Politics of the 'Tax Dollar' in Post-War California," in *New Suburban History,*
ed. Kevin M. Kruse and Thomas J. Sugrue (Chicago: University of Chicago
Press, 2006), chap. 7; Lisa McGirr, *Suburban Warriors: The Origins of the New
Right* (Princeton, NJ: Princeton University Press, 2001).

32. "Elimination of Rubella and Congenital Rubella Syndrome–United
States, 1969–2004," 279–82; C. P. Muller et al., "Reducing Global Disease Bur-
den of Measles and Rubella: Report of the WHO Steering Committee on Research Related to Measles and Rubella Vaccines and Vaccination," *Vaccine* 25,
no. 1 (January 2, 2007): 1–9; Plotkin, "Rubella Vaccine," 321–25.

33. For a summary of the research on this issue, see Jan van Dijk, with the cooperation of Ruth Carlin and Heather Hewitt, *Persons Handicapped by Rubella:
Victors and Victims—A Follow-Up Study* (Amsterdam: Swets and Zeitlinger,
1991), 17–18.

34. Margaret A. Burgess, "Gregg's Rubella Legacy 1941–1991," *MJA,* 155, no.
6 (September 16, 1991): 355–57; Jill M. Forrest et al., "Gregg's Congenital
Rubella Patients 60 Years Later," *MJA* 177 (2002): 664–67. Forrest summarizes
related findings as well: Nancy O'Donnell's study at the Helen Keller National
Center and a Canadian study found "higher than expected rates of glaucoma
and diabetes, hypo- and hyperthyroidism, hormone imbalances, premature age-
ing, and oesogphageal and gastrointestinal problems." A UK study found that
"10 percent of affected subjects born since 1965 had died, most as infants with
heart defects." The Australian researchers suspected that of the original subjects
identified by Gregg, those who had been most severely affected had died when
cardiac surgery was not yet available. Thus, the survivors of the earlier epidemic

had "probably [been] less severely affected than survivors of rubella epidemics in the 1960s and 1970s." See Forrest et al., discussion. See also Nancy O'Donnell, "History of Congenital Rubella Syndrome," *Journal of Vocational Rehabilitation* 6 (1996): 149–97. As Lewis Cooper reported, congenital rubella is a progressive disease, "some who did not have cataracts in infancy manifest glaucoma in their late teens or early 20s, and patients with initially little or no hearing loss can become deaf." In "Congenital Rubella—50 Years On," *Lancet,*

35. Nancy O'Donnell discussed the history of the system created for people with CRS and deaf-blind people and the problems it later created. Personal communication, June 2008. As in the Australian studies, Lewis Cooper found about 15 percent of the patients in their twenties had insulin-dependent diabetes. Cooper, "Congenital Rubella—50 Years On." For a historical overview of rubella and the failure to organize services to fit the needs of people with CRS, see Ed Hammer, "Programmatic Considerations Taken into Account When Developing Educational Programs for Persons with Congenital Rubella Syndrome" (paper presented at the Helen Keller National Center International Symposium on Rubella, March 15, 2005, HKNC International Symposium Binder, HKNC). Hammer emphatically pointed out, "It is the system that is disabled, not the person with Congenital Rubella Syndrome. . . . The budget drove the service delivery system, not the needs of the client." On the problem of aging out for the disabled, see Marc Santora, "For the Disabled, Age 18 Brings Difficult Choices," *NYT,* Metro. desk., May 14, 2008, p. 1.

36. Personal communications at HKNC. On PPR, see Daniel J. Wilson, *Living with Polio: The Epidemic and Its Survivors* (Chicago: University of Chicago Press, 2005), chap. 9. See also "Desperately Seeking . . . Rubella Babies" on Deafness Blog by Jamie Berke, http://deafness.about.com/b/2006/05/28/desperately-seekingrubella-babies.htm (accessed October 1, 2008).

37. Helen Keller Deaf-Blind Awareness Week: June 27 to July 3, 2004, HKNC poster. In author's possession. Approximately one-sixth of those with CRS are deaf-blind, according to Jan van Dijk, *Persons Handicapped by Rubella,* 14.

38. Mark Tushnet, "The Rights Revolution in the Twentieth Century," in *The Cambridge History of Law in America,* vol. 3, *The Twentieth Century and After (1920-),* ed. Michael Grossberg and Christopher Tomlins (Cambridge: Cambridge University Press, 2008), chap. 11. See also Gwendolyn Mink, with Samantha Ann Majic and Leandra Zarnow, "Poverty Law and Income Support: From the Progressive Era to the War on Welfare," ibid., chap. 10.

39. Joseph P. Shapiro, *No Pity: People with Disabilities Forging a New Civil Rights Movement* (New York: Three Rivers Press, 1994), 74–85. Jamie Berke, born deaf as a result of the rubella epidemic, describes her own education and activism and her work for closed captioning in the late 1980s and early 1990s in "Caption Action." She is now an About.com guide on deafness. See Jamie Berke, http://deafness.about.com/mbiopage.htm (accessed October 10, 2008).

# BIBLIOGRAPHY

PRIMARY SOURCES

*Archival Collections*

American College of Obstetricians and Gynecologists, Washington, DC.
   History Library and Archives.
California State Archives, Sacramento, CA.
   State Board of Medical Examiner Records.
Alan Mason Chesney Medical Archives, Johns Hopkins Medical Institutions, Baltimore, MD.
   Helen B. Taussig Papers.
Helen Keller National Center for Deaf-Blind Youth and Adults, Sands Point, NY.
   Library.
   Rubella Files.
March of Dimes Archives, White Plains, NY.
   Films.
   Medical Program Records.
   Oral History Records.
   Virginia Apgar Papers.
   Minnesota State Law Library, St. Paul, MN.
   Cases and Briefs. (Minnesota) Supreme Court.
Mount Holyoke College Archives and Special Collections, South Hadley, MA.
   Virginia Apgar Collection.
   Virginia Apgar Papers, 1880–1975.
National Archives, College Park, MD.

U.S. Children's Bureau Records, RG 102.

U.S. Food and Drug Administration (FDA) Records, RG 88.

National Library of Medicine, History of Medicine, National Institutes of Health, Bethesda, MD.

Chauncey D. Leake Papers, 1921–1976.

Historical Audiovisuals Program.

New Jersey State Law Library, Law Division, Trenton, NJ.

New York State Library, Albany, NY.

Cases and Briefs.

Office of NIH History, National Institutes of Health, Bethesda, MD.

Historical Resources: Dr. Paul D. Parkman Oral History, 7 June 2005, by Sarah Leavitt.

Social Welfare Archives, University of Minnesota Libraries, Minneapolis, MN.

Leonard Mayo Papers.

Wisconsin State Historical Society, Madison, WI.

*Abortion*, ABC-TV News, 5 June 1969.

Young Research Library, Special Collections, University of California, Los Angeles.

Anthony C. Beilenson Papers.

Anthony C. Beilenson Oral History.

California Committee for Therapeutic Abortion.

David S. Hall Papers.

## Select Newspapers, Periodicals, and Professional Journals

*American Journal of Diseases of Children*
*American Journal of Public Health*
*British Medical Journal*
*CCTA Newsletter*
*Chicago Defender*
*Chicago Tribune*
*Children*
*Children Limited*
*Congressional Record*
*Journal of the American Medical Association*
*Lancet*
*Los Angeles Times*
*Medical Journal of Australia*
*New England Journal of Medicine*
*New York Times*
*NF (National Foundation) News*

Today's Health
Volta Review
Wall Street Journal
Washington Post

## Court Cases

*Berman v. Allan,* 80 NJ 421, 404 A.2d 8 (1979)
*Doe v. Bolton,* 410 U.S. 179 (1973)
*Dumber v. St. Michael's Hospital,* 60 Wis.2d 766, 233 N.W.2d 372 (1975)
*Gleitman v. Cosgrove* 227 A.2d 689 (NJ 1967)
*Gonzales v. Carhart* 550 U.S. 124 (2007)
*Hodgson v. Minnesota,* 295 Minnesota 294 (1970)
*People v. Belous,* 80 Cal.Rptr. 354, 458 P.2d 194 (1969)
*Procanik v. Cillo,* 97 NJ 339, 478 A.2d 755 (1984)
*Shively v. Stewart,* 65 Cal.2d 475, 421 P.2d 65 (1965)
*Stewart v. Long Island College Hospital,* 313 NYS2d 502 (1970)
*Stewart v. Long Island College Hospital,* 30 NY2d 695 (1972)
*Roe v. Wade,* 410 U.S. 479 (1973)

## Articles, Books, Government Documents, and References

Apgar, Virginia, and Joan Beck. *Is My Baby All Right?* New York: Simon and Schuster, 1972.
*Australian Dictionary of Biography Online Edition.* www.adb.online.anu.edu.au.
Beaton, Mary Jean. *The Road to Autonomy.* Enumclaw, WA: Winepress Publishing, Pleasant Word, 2003.
Berill, N. J. *The Person in the Womb.* New York: Dodd, Mead, 1968.
Bullock, Adeline. *Parents Magazine Book for Expectant Mothers,* foreword by Jere B. Faison. New York: McGraw-Hill, 1954.
Burnet, Sir Macfarlane. *Changing Patterns: An Atypical Autobiography.* Melbourne: Heinemann, 1968.
Calderone, Mary Steichen, ed. *Abortion in the United States: A Conference Sponsored by the Planned Parenthood Federation of America, Inc., at Arden House and the New York Academy of Medicine.* New York: Harper Brothers, 1958.
California State Assembly. Interim Committee on Criminal Procedure. *Abortion Hearing (Continued) AB2614, Dec. 17 and 18, 1962.* San Diego, CA.
California State Assembly. Interim Committee on Criminal Procedure. *San Francisco Hearing, July 20, 1964.*
Calvert, Donald R. *Rubella and Deaf Children in California.* San Francisco: San Francisco Hearing and Speech Center, 1967.

Deafness Foundation (Vic.) and Australian Deafness Council. *Maternal Rubella—The Avoidable Tragedy: A Seminar Held at the Royal Children's Hospital, Melbourne, 23rd April, 1976.* Melbourne: Deafness Foundation (Victoria), 1976.

Eastman, Nicholson J. *Expectant Motherhood.* 2nd ed. Boston: Little, Brown, 1947.

———. *Williams Obstetrics.* 10th ed. New York: Appleton-Century-Crofts, 1950.

Eastman, Nicholson J., and Louis M. Hellman. *Williams Obstetrics.* 11th ed. New York: Appleton-Century-Crofts, 1956.

———, eds. *Williams Obstetrics.* 12th ed. New York: Appleton-Century-Crofts, 1961.

Finkbine, Sherri. "The Lesser of Two Evils." In *The Case for Legalized Abortion Now,* edited by Alan F. Guttmacher, 15–25. Berkeley, CA: Diablo Press, 1967.

Fishbein, Morris, ed. *Birth Defects.* Philadelphia: J. B. Lippincott, 1963.

Graves, Judy. *Right From the Start: The Importance of Early Immunization.* Public Affairs Pamphlet No. 350. New York: Public Affairs Committee, 1963.

Guttmacher, Alan F., ed. *The Case for Legalized Abortion Now.* Berkeley, CA: Diablo Press, 1967.

Hodgson, Jane E. "Abortion: The Law and the Reality 1970." *Mayo Alumnus* 6, no. 4 (October 1970): 4.

Keemer, Ed. *Confessions of a Pro-Life Abortionist.* Detroit: Vinco Press, 1980.

Lader, Lawrence. *Abortion.* Boston: Beacon Press, 1966.

Lundstrom, Rolf. *Rubella During Pregnancy: A Follow-Up Study of Children Born after an Epidemic of Rubella in Sweden, 1951, with Additional Investigations on Prophylaxis and Treatment of Maternal Rubella.* Uppsala, Sweden: Appelbergy Boktryckeri, 1962.

Mann, Ida. *The Development of the Human Eye.* 3rd ed. New York: Grune and Stratton, 1964. First published in 1928.

Packer, H. L., and R. J. Gampell. "Therapeutic Abortion: A Problem in Law and Medicine." *Stanford Law Review* 11 (1959): 417–55.

Potter, Edith L. *Pathology of the Fetus and Infant.* 2nd ed. Chicago: Year Book Medical Publishers, 1961. First published in 1953.

Price, Nancy D. *Living With Robbie.* Bloomington, IN: 1st Books Library, 2003.

*Reader's Guide to Periodical Literature.*

Rivera, Geraldo. *Willowbrook: A Report on How It Is and Why It Doesn't Have to Be That Way.* New York: Random House, 1972.

Sanger, Margaret. *Motherhood in Bondage.* New York: Brentano's Publishers, 1928.

U.S. Army. *Index-Catalogue of the Library of the Surgeon-General's Office,* 1880–1961.

———. *The Medical Department of the United States Army in the World War.* Vol. 9, *Communicable and Other Diseases,* edited by Joseph F. Siler. Washington, DC: GPO, 1928.

U.S. Center for Disease Control. *Rubella Surveillance.* Atlanta, GA: CDC, 1971, 1973, 1980.

U.S. Children's Bureau. *The Expectant Mother.* Washington, DC: GPO, 1943.

———. *Infant Care.* Washington, DC: GPO, 1955, 1963.

———. *Prenatal Care*. Washington, DC: GPO, 1915, 1943, 1962.

———. *So You're Expecting a Baby*. Washington, DC: GPO, 1947.

———. *When Your Baby Is on the Way*. Washington, DC: GPO, 1961.

U.S. Department of Health, Education, and Welfare. *Report on Promoting the Health of Mothers and Children*. Washington, DC: GPO, 1972.

———. Public Health Service. *Rubella*. Prepared by Jane S. Lin-Fu. Washington, DC: GPO, 1970.

———. Public Health Service. *Rubella Vaccine*. Washington, DC: GPO, 1969.

———. Public Health Service. *Voluntary Action to Stop Rubella*. Washington, DC: GPO, [1970].

World Health Organization. *Immunization in Practice: A Guide for Health Workers Who Give Vaccines*. Oxford: Oxford University Press, 1989.


*Video/Film/DVD*

*Abortion*. ABC News. June 5, 1969. Print held at Wisconsin State Historical Society, Madison, WI.

*CBS Reports: Abortion and the Law*. Broadcast April 5, 1965. Now distributed as *Before Roe v. Wade: Abortion and the Law, 1965*. Films for the Humanities and Sciences.

*Frontline Reports: Extraordinary People*. PBS. May 2, 1989. Produced by Virginia Storring and Marrie Campbell.

*Paralyzing Fear: The Story of Polio in America*. VHS. Directed by Nina Gilden Seavey. Produced by Nina Gilden Seavey and Paul Wagner. Washington, DC: George Washington University, 1998. Distributed by PBS.

*Voices of Choice*. DVD. Produced by Physicians for Reproductive Choice and Health and Fly on the Wall Productions, 2003.


SECONDARY SOURCES

Abel, Emily K. *Hearts of Wisdom: American Women Caring for Kin, 1850–1940*. Cambridge, MA: Harvard University Press, 2000.

Adams, Rachel. *Sideshow U.S.A.: Freaks and the American Cultural Imagination*. Chicago: University of Chicago Press, 2001.

Albrecht, Gary L., ed. *Encyclopedia of Disability*. Thousand Oaks, CA: Sage Publications, 2006.

Allitt, Patrick. *Catholic Intellectuals and Conservative Politics in America, 1950–1985*. Ithaca, NY: Cornell University Press, 1993.

Apple, Rima D. *Mothers and Medicine: A Social History of Infant Feeding, 1890–1950*. Madison: University of Wisconsin Press, 1987.

———. *Perfect Motherhood: Science and Childrearing in America*. New Brunswick, NJ: Rutgers University Press, 2006.

Baehr, Ninia. *Abortion Without Apology: A Radical History for the 1990s.* Boston: South End Press, 1990.

Bates, Barbara. *Bargaining for Life: A Social History of Tuberculosis, 1876–1938.* Philadelphia: University of Pennsylvania Press, 1992.

Baynton, Douglas C. *Forbidden Signs: American Culture and the Campaign Against Sign.* Chicago: University of Chicago Press, 1996.

Beecher, Henry K. "Ethics and Clinical Research." *New England Journal of Medicine* 274, no. 24 (June 6, 1966): 1354–60.

Bell, Chris. "Introducing White Disability Studies: A Modest Proposal." Chap. 22 in *The Disability Studies Reader,* edited by Lennard J. Davis, 2nd ed., 275–82. New York: Routledge, 2006.

Berke, Jamie. Blog. Information on deafness by About Guide. http://deafness.about .com.

Berkowitz, Edward D. *Disabled Policy: America's Programs for the Handicapped.* A Twentieth Century Fund Report. New York: Cambridge University Press, 1987.

———. "A Historical Preface to the Americans with Disabilities Act." *Journal of Policy History* 6:1 (1994): 96–119.

Bérubé, Michael. *Life As We Know It: A Father, A Family, and an Exceptional Child.* New York: Random House, Vintage Books, 1996.

Brandt, Allan M. *No Magic Bullet: A Social History of Venereal Disease in the United States since 1880.* New York: Oxford University Press, 1987.

———. "Polio, Politics, Publicity, and Duplicity: Ethical Aspects in the Development of the Salk Vaccine." *International Journal of Health Services* 8, no. 2 (1978): 257–70.

Bren, Linda. "Frances Oldham Kelsey: FDA Medical Reviewer Leaves Her Mark on History." *FDA Consumer* 35, no. 2 (March–April 2001): 24–29.

Brian, Amanda M. "Kinderland: Growing Children in Imperial Berlin." PhD diss., University of Illinois, 2009.

Briggs, Laura. *Reproducing Empire: Race, Sex, Science, and U.S. Imperialism in Puerto Rico.* Berkeley: University of California Press, 2002.

Brockley, Janice. "Rearing the Child Who Never Grew: Ideologies of Parenting and Intellectual Disability in American History." In *Mental Retardation in America: A Historical Reader,* edited by Steven Noll and James W. Trent Jr., 130–64. New York: New York University Press, 2004.

Brodie, Janet Farrell. *Contraception and Abortion in Nineteenth-Century America.* Ithaca, NY: Cornell University Press, 1994.

Buchanan, Robert. *Illusions of Equality: Deaf Americans in School and Factory, 1850–1950.* Washington. DC: Gallaudet University Press, 1999.

Burch, Susan. *Signs of Resistance: American Deaf Cultural History, 1900 to World War II.* New York: New York University Press, 2002.

Burgess, Margaret A. "Gregg's Rubella Legacy, 1941–1991." *Medical Journal of Australia* 155, no. 6 (September 16, 1991): 355–57.

Burns, Chester R. "Malpractice Suits in American Medicine Before the Civil War." *Bulletin of the History of Medicine* 43 (1969): 41–56.

Byram, Brad. "A Pupil and a Patient: Hospital Schools in Progressive America." In *The New Disability History: American Perspectives,* edited by Paul K. Longmore and Lauri Unmansky, 133–56. New York: New York University Press, 2001.

Canaday, Margot. "Heterosexuality as a Legal Regime." In *The Cambridge History of Law in America.* Chap. 13 in Vol. 3, *The Twentieth Century and After (1920-),* edited by Michael Grossberg and Christopher Tomlins. Cambridge: Cambridge University Press, 2008.

Carmen, Arlene, and Howard Moody. *Abortion Counseling and Social Change from Illegal Act to Medical Practice: The Story of the Clergy Consultation Service on Abortion.* Valley Forge, PA: Judson Press, 1973.

Carter, Richard. *The Gentle Legions.* Garden City, NY: Doubleday, 1961.

Cartwright, Lisa. "*Mandy* (1952): On Voice and Listening in the (Deaf) Maternal Melodrama." Chap. 5 in *Medicine's Moving Pictures: Medicine, Health, and Bodies in American Film and Television,* edited by Leslie J. Reagan, Nancy Tomes, and Paula A. Treichler. Rochester, NY: Rochester University Press, 2007.

Casper, Monica J. *The Making of the Unborn Patient: A Social Anatomy of Fetal Surgery.* New Brunswick, NJ: Rutgers University Press, 1999.

Castles, Katherine. "'Nice, Average Americans': Postwar Parents' Groups and the Defense of the Normal Family." In *Mental Retardation in America: A Historical Reader,* edited by Steven Noll and James W. Trent Jr., 362–63. New York: New York University Press, 2004.

Chase, Allan. *Magic Shots: A Human and Scientific Account of the Long and Continuing Struggle to Eradicate Infectious Diseases by Vaccination.* New York: William Morrow, 1982.

Chesler, Ellen. *Woman of Valor: Margaret Sanger and the Birth Control Movement in America.* New York: Simon and Schuster, 1992.

Chess, Stella, Sam J. Korn, and Paulina B. Fernandez. *Psychiatric Disorders of Children With Congenital Rubella.* New York: Brunner/Mazel; London: Butterworths, 1971.

Cisler, Lucinda. "Unfinished Business: Birth Control and Women's Liberation." In *Sisterhood Is Powerful: An Anthology of Writings from the Women's Liberation Movement,* edited by Robin Morgan, 274–323. New York: Vintage Books, 1970.

Clarke, Adele E. *Disciplining Reproduction: Modernity, American Life Sciences, and "The Problem of Sex."* Berkeley: University of California Press, 1998.

Clow, Barbara. "'An Illness of Nine Months' Duration': Pregnancy and Thalidomide Use in Canada and the United States." In *Women, Health, and Nation: Canada and the United States since 1945,* edited by Georgina Feldberg et al., 45–66. Montreal: McGill; Kingston, ON: Queen's University Press, 2003.

Colgrove, James. *State of Immunity: The Politics of Vaccination in Twentieth-Century America.* Berkeley: University of California Press, 2006.

Colwell, Stacie. "The End of the Road: Gender, the Dissemination of Knowledge, and the American Campaign Against Venereal Disease During World War I." In *The Visible Woman: Imaging Technology, Science, and Gender,* edited by Paula A. Treichler, Lisa Cartwright, and Constance Penley, 44–82. New York: New York University Press, 1998.

Crenshaw, Kimberle. "Demarginalizing the Intersection of Race and Sex: A Black Feminist Critique of Antidiscrimination Doctrine, Feminist Theory and Antiracist Politics." *University of Chicago Legal Forum* 30 (1989): 139–67.

Cuneo, Michael W. "Life Battles: The Rise of Catholic Militancy within the American Pro-Life Movement." In *Being Right: Conservative Catholics in America,* edited by Mary Jo Weaver and R. Scott Appleby, 270–99. Bloomington: Indiana University Press, 1995.

Curry, Lynne. *Modern Mothers in the Heartland: Gender, Health and Progress in Illinois, 1900–1930.* Columbus: Ohio State University Press, 1999.

Daemmrich, Arthur. *Pharmacopolitics: Drug Regulation in the United States and Germany.* Chapel Hill: University of North Carolina Press, 2002.

———. "A Tale of Two Experts: Thalidomide and Political Engagement in the United States and West Germany." *Social History of Medicine* 15, no. 1 (2002): 137–58.

Daniels, Cynthia R. *At Women's Expense: State Power and the Politics of Fetal Rights.* Cambridge, MA: Harvard University Press, 1993.

———. "Fathers, Mothers, and Fetal Harm: Rethinking Gender Difference and Reproductive Responsibility." In *Fetal Subjects, Feminist Positions,* edited by Lynn M. Morgan and Meredith W. Michaels, 93–96. Philadelphia: University of Pennsylvania Press, 1999.

Davis, Lennard. *Enforcing Normalcy: Disability, Deafness, and the Body.* New York: Verso Press, 1995.

D'Emilio, John, and Estelle Freedman. *Intimate Matters: A History of Sexuality in America.* New York: Harper and Row, 1988.

De Ville, Kenneth Allen. *Medical Malpractice in Nineteenth-Century America.* New York: New York University Press, 1990.

Dowling, Harry F. *Fighting Infection: Conquests of the Twentieth Century.* Cambridge, MA: Harvard University Press, 1977.

Duden, Barbara. "The Fetus on the 'Farther Shore': Toward a History of the Unborn." In *Fetal Subjects, Feminist Positions,* edited by Lynn M. Morgan and Meredith W. Michaels, 13–25. Philadelphia: University of Pennsylvania Press, 1999.

Duden, Barbara. *The Woman Beneath the Skin: A Doctor's Patients in Eighteenth-Century Germany.* Translated by Thomas Dunlap. Cambridge, MA: Harvard University Press, 1991.

Duster, Alfreda M., ed. *Crusade for Justice: The Autobiography of Ida B. Wells.* Chicago: University of Chicago Press, 1991.

Dybwad, Rosemary F. *Perspectives on a Parent Movement: The Revolt of Parents of Children with Intellectual Limitations.* Brookline, MA: Brookline Books, 1990.

Dye, Nancy Schrom, and Daniel Blake Smith. "Mother Love and Infant Death, 1750–1920." *Journal of American History* 73 (September 1986): 329–53.

Edwards, R. A. R. "Speech Has an Extraordinary Humanizing Power: Horace Mann and the Problem of Nineteenth-Century American Deaf Education." Chap. 2 in *The New Disability History: American Perspectives,* edited by Paul K. Longmore and Lauri Umansky. New York: New York University Press, 2001.

Faderman, Lillian. *Odd Girls and Twilight Lovers: A History of Lesbian Life in Twentieth-Century America.* New York: Columbia University Press, 1991.

Featherstone, Lisa. "Surveying the Mother: The Rise of Antenatal Care in Early Twentieth-Century Australia." *Limina* 10 (2004): 16–31.

Fee, Elizabeth, and Daniel M. Fox, eds. *AIDS: The Burdens of History.* Berkeley: University of California Press, 1988.

Feldberg, Georgina, et al., eds. *Women, Health, and Nation: Canada and the United States since 1945.* Montreal: McGill; Kingston, ON: Queen's University Press, 2005.

Feldstein, Ruth. "Antiracism and Maternal Failure in the 1940s and 1950s." In *"Bad" Mothers: The Politics of Blame in Twentieth-Century America,* edited by Molly Ladd-Taylor and Lauri Umansky. New York: New York University Press, 145–90.

———. *Motherhood in Black and White: Race and Sex in American Liberalism, 1930–1965.* Ithaca, NY: Cornell University Press, 2000.

Ferguson, Philip M., Dianne L. Ferguson, and Steven J. Taylor, eds., *Interpreting Disability: A Qualitative Reader.* New York: Columbia University, Teachers College Press, 1992.

Ferraro, Barbara, and Patricia Hussey, with Jane O'Reilly. *Turning Back: Two Nuns' Battle with the Vatican over Women's Right to Choose.* New York: Ivy Books, 1990.

Fissell, Mary E. "Hairy Women and Naked Truths: Gender and the Politics of Knowledge in *Aristotle's Masterpiece,*" *William and Mary Quarterly* 60 (2003): 43–74.

———. *Vernacular Bodies: The Politics of Reproduction in Early Modern England.* New York: Oxford University Press, 2004.

Flood, Dawn. "Proving Rape: Sex, Race, and Representation in Chicago Trials and Society, 1937–1969." PhD diss., University of Illinois, 2003.

———. "'They Didn't Treat Me Good': African American Rape Victims and Chicago Courtroom Strategies during the 1950s." *Journal of Women's History* 17, no. 1 (Spring 2005): 38–61.

Foucault, Michel. *The Birth of the Clinic: An Archaeology of Medical Perception.* New York: Random House, 1994. Previously published 1963; translated 1973.

Fraser, Nancy, and Linda Gordon. "A Genealogy of Dependency: Tracing a Keyword of the U.S. Welfare State." *Signs* 19, no. 2 (Winter 1994): 309–36.

Furrow, Barry R., et al. *Health Law.* Vol. 2. 2nd ed. St. Paul, MN: West Group, 2000.

Galambos, Louis, with Jane Eliot Sewell. *Networks of Innovation: Vaccine Development at Merck, Sharp & Dohme, and Mulford, 1895–1995.* Cambridge: Cambridge University Press, 1995.

Gallagher, Hugh Gregory. *FDR's Splendid Deception.* New York: Dodd, Mead, 1985.

Gamble, Vanessa Northington. "Under the Shadow of Tuskegee: African Americans and Health Care." *American Journal of Public Health* 87, no. 11 (November 1997): 1773–78.

Garrow, David J. *Liberty and Sexuality: The Right to Privacy and the Making of Roe v. Wade.* New York: Macmillan, 1994.

Geison, Gerald L. *The Private Science of Louis Pasteur.* Princeton, NJ: Princeton University Press, 1995.

Ginsburg, Faye D. *Contested Lives: The Abortion Debate in an American Community.* Berkeley: University of California Press, 1998.

Ginsburg, Faye, and Rayna Rapp. "Fetal Reflections: Confessions of Two Feminist Anthropologists as Mutual Informants." Chap. 14 in *Fetal Subjects, Feminist Positions,* edited by Lynn M. Morgan and Meredith W. Michaels. Philadelphia: University of Pennsylvania Press, 1999.

Golden, Janet. "'An Argument That Goes Back to the Womb': The Demedicalization of Fetal Alcohol Syndrome, 1973–1992." *Journal of Social History* 33 (1999): 269–98.

———. *Message in a Bottle: The Making of Fetal Alcohol Syndrome.* Cambridge, MA: Harvard University Press, 2005.

Gordon, Linda. *The Great Arizona Orphan Abduction.* Cambridge, MA: Harvard University Press, 2001.

———. *Heroes of Their Own Lives: The Politics and History of Family Violence—Boston, 1880–1960.* New York: Viking Press, 1988.

———. *Pitied But Not Entitled: Single Mothers and the History of Welfare, 1890–1935.* New York: Free Press, 1994.

———. *Woman's Body, Woman's Right: Birth Control in America.* Rev. and updated ed. New York: Penguin Books, 1999.

Gould, Tony. *A Summer Plague: Polio and Its Survivors.* New Haven, CT: Yale University Press, 1995.

Granchi, Jennifer R. "The Wrongful Birth Tort: A Policy Analysis and the Right to Sue for an Inconvenient Child." *South Texas Law Review* 43 (Fall 2002): 1261–87.

Green, Laurie, "'Saving Babies for Two Dimes a Day': Race, Hunger, and Health Activism During the War on Poverty." Unpublished paper presented at Conference on Making Race, Making Health, University of Texas, Austin, November 15, 2008.

Griswold, Robert L. *Fatherhood in America: A History.* New York: Basic Books, 1994.

Grob, Gerald N. *From Asylum to Community: Mental Health Policy in Modern America.* Princeton, NJ: Princeton University Press, 1991.

Grossberg, Michael. "A Protected Childhood: The Emergence of Child Protection in America." In *American Public Life and the Historical Imagination,* edited by

Wendy Gamber, Michael Grossberg, and Hendrik Hartog. Notre Dame, IN: Notre Dame Press, 2003.

Gutierrez, Elena R. "Policing 'Pregnant Pilgrims': Situating the Sterilization Abuse of Mexican-Origin Women in Los Angeles County." In *Women, Health, and Nation: Canada and the United States since 1945,* edited by Georgina Feldberg et al., 378–403. Montreal: McGill; Kingston, ON: Queen's University Press, 2003.

Hall, Stuart, ed. *Representation: Cultural Representations and Signifying Practices.* London: Sage Publications, 1997.

Halpern, Sydney. *Lesser Harms: The Morality of Risk in Medical Research.* Chicago: University of Chicago Press, 2004.

Harkness, John, Susan E. Lederer, and Daniel Wickler. "Public Health Classics: Laying Ethical Foundations for Research." *Bulletin of the World Health Organization* 79, no. 4 (2001): 365–66.

Hensel, Wendy F. "The Disabling Impact of Wrongful Birth and Wrongful Life Actions." *Harvard Civil Rights and Civil Liberties Law Review* 40, no. 1 (Winter 2005): 141–96.

Hepler, Allison L. *Women in Labor: Mothers, Medicine, and Occupational Health in the United States, 1890–1980.* Columbus: Ohio State University Press, 2000.

Hilts, Philip J. *Protecting America's Health: The FDA, Business, and One Hundred Years of Regulation.* Chapel Hill: University of North Carolina Press, 2003.

Hine, Darlene Clark. "Rape and the Inner Lives of Black Women in the Middle West," *Signs* 14, no. 4 (Summer 1989): 919–20.

Hole, Judith, and Ellen Levine. *Rebirth of Feminism.* New York: Quadrangle Books, 1971.

Holz, Rose. "The Birth Control Clinic in America: Life Within, Life Without, 1923–1973." PhD diss., University of Illinois, 2002.

Horowitz, Daniel. *Betty Friedan and the Making of The Feminine Mystique: The American Left, the Cold War, and Modern Feminism.* Amherst: University of Massachusetts Press, 1998.

Hunter, Tera W. *To 'Joy My Freedom: Southern Black Women's Lives and Labors After the Civil War.* Cambridge, MA: Harvard University Press, 1997.

Hyde, Alan. *Bodies of Law.* Princeton, NJ: Princeton University Press, 1997.

Hyman, David A., and Charles Silver. "Medical Malpractice Litigation and Tort Reform: It's the Incentives, Stupid." *Vanderbilt Law Review* 59 (May 2006): 1085–1136.

Inbau, Fred E. "Self-Incrimination—What Can an Accused Person Be Compelled to Do? *Journal of the American Institute of Criminal Law and Criminology* 28, no. 3 (1937–1938): 261–92.

Insight Team of the *(London) Sunday Times. Suffer the Children: The Story of Thalidomide.* New York: Viking Press, 1979.

Irons, Peter. *The Courage of Their Convictions.* New York: Free Press, 1988.

Jensen, Robin E. "The Birth of Public Sexual Education in the United States: Women, Rhetoric, and the Progressive Era." PhD diss. University of Illinois, 2007.

Joffe, Carole. *Doctors of Conscience: The Struggle to Provide Abortion before and after Roe v. Wade.* Boston: Beacon Press, 1996.

———. "The Unending Struggle for Legal Abortion: Conversations with Jane Hodgson." *JAMWA* 49, no. 5 (September/October 1994): 160–64.

Johnston, Robert D. "Contemporary Anti-Vaccination Movements in Historical Perspective." In *The Politics of Healing: Histories of Alternative Medicine in Twentieth-Century North America,* edited by Robert D. Johnston, 259–86. New York: Routledge, 2004.

———, ed. *The Politics of Healing: Histories of Alternative Medicine in Twentieth-Century North America.* New York: Routledge, 2004.

Kane, Paula M. *Separatism and Subculture: Boston Catholicism, 1900–1920.* Chapel Hill: University of North Carolina Pres, 1994.

Kaplan, Laura. *The Story of Jane: The Legendary Underground Feminist Abortion Service.* New York: Pantheon Books, 1995.

Kennedy, David M. *Birth Control in America: The Career of Margaret Sanger.* New Haven, CT: Yale University Press, 1970.

Klaus, Alisa. *Every Child a Lion: The Origins of Maternal and Infant Health Policy in the United States and France, 1890–1920.* Ithaca, NY: Cornell University Press, 1993.

Kline, Wendy. *Building a Better Race: Gender, Sexuality, and Eugenics from the Turn of the Century to the Baby Boom.* Berkeley: University of California Press, 2001.

Kohler-Hausman, Jullilly. "Militarizing the Police: Officer Jon Burge, the 'Vietnamese Treatment,' and Vigilantism in the 'Urban Jungle.'" In *Challenging the Prison-Industrial Complex: Activism, Arts, and Educational Alternatives,* edited by Stephen Hartnett. Urbana: University of Illinois Press, forthcoming 2010.

Kornbluh, Felicia. *The Battle for Welfare Rights: Politics and Poverty in Modern America.* Philadelphia: University of Pennsylvania Press, 2007.

Kraut, Alan M. *Silent Travelers: Germs, Genes, and the "Immigrant Menace."* Baltimore: Johns Hopkins University Press, 1995.

Kruse, Kevin M., and Thomas J. Sugrue, eds. *New Suburban History.* Chicago: University of Chicago Press, 2006.

Kudlick, Catherine J. "Disability History: Why We Need Another 'Other.'" *American Historical Review* 1083 (June 2003): 763–93.

———. "The Outlook of *The Problem* and the Problem with the *Outlook:* Two Advocacy Journals Reinvent Blind People in Turn-of-the-Century America." Chap. 7 in *The New Disability History: American Perspectives,* edited by Paul K. Longmore and Lauri Umansky. New York: New York University Press, 2001.

Kunzel, Regina G. *Fallen Women, Problem Girls: Unmarried Mothers and the Professionalization of Social Work, 1890–1945.* New Haven, CT: Yale University Press, 1995.

———. "Pulp Fictions and Problem Girls: Reading and Rewriting Single Pregnancy in the Postwar United States," *American Historical Review* 100, no. 5 (December 1995): 1465–87.

———. "White Neurosis, Black Pathology: Constructing Out-of-Wedlock Pregnancy in the Wartime and Postwar United States." In *Not June Cleaver: Women and Gender in Postwar America, 1945–1960,* edited by Joanne Meyerowitz, 304–31. Philadelphia: Temple University Press, 1994.

Ladd-Taylor, Molly. *Mother-Work: Women, Child Welfare, and the State, 1890–1930.* Urbana: University of Illinois Press, 1994.

———. *Raising a Baby the Government Way: Mothers' Letters to the Children's Bureau, 1915–1932.* New Brunswick, NJ: Rutgers University Press, 1986.

———. "Who is 'Defective' and Who Decides? The 'Feebleminded' and the Courts." Unpublished paper presented at the annual meeting of the American Association of the History of Medicine, 2003.

Ladd-Taylor, Molly, and Lauri Umansky, eds. *"Bad" Mothers: The Politics of Blame in Twentieth-Century America.* New York: New York University Press, 1998.

Lader, Lawrence. *Politics, Power, and the Church: The Catholic Crisis and Its Challenge to American Pluralism.* New York: Macmillan, 1987.

Lancaster, Paul A. L. "Gregg, Sir Norman McAlister (1892–1966)." *Australian Dictionary of Biography.* Vol. 14, 325–27. Melbourne: Melbourne University Press, 1996.

Layne, Linda. *Motherhood Lost: A Feminist Account of Pregnancy Loss in America.* New York: Routledge, 2002.

Leavitt, Judith Walzer. "'Be Safe. Be Sure.' New York City's Experience with Epidemic Smallpox." Chap. 25 in *Sickness and Health in America: Readings in the History of Medicine and Public Health,* edited by Judith Walzer Leavitt and Ronald L. Numbers. 3rd ed. rev. Madison: University of Wisconsin Press, 1997.

———. *Brought to Bed: Childbearing in America, 1750–1950.* New York: Oxford University Press, 1986.

———. "Politics and Public Health: Smallpox in Milwaukee, 1894–1895." *Bulletin of the History of Medicine* 50 (1976): 553–68.

———. *Typhoid Mary: Captive to the Public's Health.* Boston: Beacon Press, 1996.

———, ed. *Women and Health in America: Historical Readings.* Madison: University of Wisconsin Press, 1984.

Leavitt, Judith Walzer, and Ronald L. Numbers, eds. *Sickness and Health in America: Readings in the History of Medicine and Public Health.* 3rd ed. rev. Madison: University of Wisconsin Press, 1997.

Leavitt, Judith Walzer, and Whitney Walton. "'Down to Death's Door': Women's Perceptions of Childbirth in America." In *Women and Health in America: Historical Readings,* edited by Judith Walzer Leavitt, 155–65. Madison: University of Wisconsin Press, 1984.

Leavitt, Sarah. "'Something to Think About When I Can't Sleep': The Development of Rubella Vaccine." Unpublished paper presented at the American Association for the History of Medicine annual meeting, Halifax, Nova Scotia, May 2006.

Lederer, Susan E. *Subjected to Science: Human Experimentation in America before the Second World War.* Baltimore: Johns Hopkins University Press, 1995.

Lederer, Susan E., and Naomi Rogers. "Media." In *Medicine in the Twentieth Century,* edited by Roger Cooter and John Pickstone, 487–502. Amsterdam: Harwood Academic Publishers, 2000.

Lemons, J. Stanley. *The Woman Citizen: Social Feminism in the 1920s.* Urbana: University of Illinois Press, 1973.

Lerner, Barron H. *The Breast Cancer Wars: Hope, Fear, and the Pursuit of a Cure in Twentieth-Century America.* New York: Oxford University Press, 2001.

———. *Contagion and Confinement: Controlling Tuberculosis Along the Skid Road.* Baltimore: Johns Hopkins University Press, 1998.

Lewis, Jane. *The Politics of Motherhood: Child and Maternal Welfare in England, 1900–1939.* London: Croom Helm, 1980.

Lindee, Susan. *Moments of Truth in Genetic Medicine.* Baltimore: Johns Hopkins University Press, 2005.

Lipsitz, George. *The Possessive Investment in Whiteness: How White People Profit from Identity Politics.* Philadelphia: Temple University Press, 1998.

Longmore, Paul K. *Why I Burned My Book and Other Essays on Disability.* Philadelphia: Temple University Press, 2003.

Longmore, Paul K., and Lauri Umansky. *The New Disability History: American Perspectives.* New York: New York University Press, 2001.

Luker, Kristin. *Abortion and the Politics of Motherhood.* Berkeley: University of California Press, 1985.

Lyon, Janet, and Michael Bérubé. "Living on Disability: Language and Social Policy in the Wake of the ADA." Chap. 9 in *The Visible Woman: Imaging Technologies, Gender, and Science,* edited by Paula A. Treichler, Lisa Cartwright, and Constance Penley. New York: New York University Press, 1998.

Markel, Howard. *Quarantine! East European Jewish Immigrants and the New York City Epidemics of 1892.* Baltimore: Johns Hopkins University Press, 1997.

Marks, Harry. *The Progress of Experiment: Science and Therapeutic Reform in the United States, 1900–1990.* Baltimore: Johns Hopkins University, 2000.

Marks, Lara V. *Sexual Chemistry: A History of the Contraceptive Pill.* New Haven, CT: Yale University Press, 2001.

Marsden, George. "Fundamentalism Yesterday and Today." Paper presented at the University of Illinois, Urbana-Champaign, April 2005.

Marsh, Margaret, and Wanda Ronner. *The Empty Cradle: Infertility in America from Colonial Times to the Present.* Baltimore: Johns Hopkins University Press, 1996.

———. *The Fertility Doctor: John Rock and the Reproductive Revolution.* Baltimore: Johns Hopkins University Press, 2008.

Mason, Carol. *Killing for Life: The Apocalyptic Narrative of Pro-Life Politics.* Ithaca, NY: Cornell University Press, 2002.

Mason, Carol. "Minority Unborn." In *Fetal Subjects, Feminist Positions,* edited by Lynn M. Morgan and Meredith W. Michaels, 159–74. Philadelphia: University of Pennsylvania Press, 1999.

May, Elaine Tyler. *Barren in the Promised Land: Childless Americans and the Pursuit of Happiness.* New York: Basic Books, 1995.

McDonnell, Jane Taylor. "On Being the 'Bad' Mother of an Autistic Child." In *"Bad" Mothers: The Politics of Blame in Twentieth-Century America,* edited by Molly Ladd-Taylor and Lauri Umansky, 220–29. New York: New York University Press, 1998.

McGirr, Lisa. *Suburban Warriors: The Origins of the New Right.* Princeton, NJ: Princeton University Press, 2001.

McLaughlin, Loretta. *The Pill, John Rock and the Church: The Biography of a Revolution.* Boston: Little, Brown, 1982.

Meckel, Richard A. *Save the Babies: American Public Health Reform and the Prevention of Infant Mortality.* Baltimore: Johns Hopkins University Press, 1990.

Melosh, Barbara. *Strangers and Kin: The American Way of Adoption.* Cambridge, MA: Harvard University Press, 2006.

Meyerowitz, Joanne. "Beyond the Feminine Mystique: A Reassessment of Postwar Mass Culture, 1946–1958." In *Not June Cleaver: Women and Gender in Postwar America, 1945–1960,* edited by Joanne Meyerowitz, 229–62. Philadelphia: Temple University Press, 1994.

Mink, Gwendolyn, with Samantha Ann Majic and Leandra Zarnow. "Poverty Law and Income Support: From the Progressive Era to the War on Welfare." In *The Cambridge History of Law in America.* Chap. 10 in Vol. 3, *The Twentieth Century and After (1920-),* edited by Michael Grossberg and Christopher Tomlins. Cambridge: Cambridge University Press, 2008.

Mitchell, Michele. *Righteous Propagation: African Americans and the Politics of Racial Destiny After Reconstruction.* Chapel Hill: University of North Carolina Press, 2005.

Mohr, James C. *Abortion in America: The Origins and Evolution of National Policy, 1800–1900.* New York: Oxford University Press, 1978.

———. *Doctors and the Law: Medical Jurisprudence in Nineteenth-Century America.* New York: Oxford University Press, 1993.

Moran, Michelle T. *Colonizing Leprosy: Imperialism and the Politics of Public Health in the United States.* Chapel Hill: University of North Carolina Press, 2007.

Morantz-Sanchez, Regina. *Conduct Unbecoming a Woman: Medicine on Trial in Turn-of-the-Century Brooklyn.* New York: Oxford University Press, 1999.

Morgan, Jennifer. *Laboring Women: Reproduction and Gender in New World Slavery.* Philadelphia: University of Pennsylvania Press, 2004.

Morgan, Lynn M., and Meredith W. Michaels. *Fetal Subjects, Feminist Positions.* Philadelphia: University of Pennsylvania Press, 1999.

Museum of DisABILITY History. www.museumofdisability.org.

Nelson, Jennifer. *Women of Color and the Reproductive Rights Movement.* New York: New York University Press, 2003.

Nickerson, Michelle. "Women, Domesticity, and Postwar Conservatism." *OAH Magazine of History* 17 (January 2003): 17–21.

Noll, Steven, and James W. Trent Jr. *Mental Retardation in America: A Historical Reader.* New York: New York University Press, 2004.

Odem, Mary E. *Delinquent Daughters: Protecting and Policing Adolescent Female Sexuality in the United States, 1885–1920.* Chapel Hill: University of North Carolina Press, 1995.

Oshinsky, David M. *Polio: An American Story.* New York: Oxford University Press, 2005.

Ossorio, Pilar N. "Prenatal Genetic Testing and the Courts." In *Prenatal Testing and Disability Rights,* edited by Erik Parens and Adrienne Asch, 308–33. Washington, DC: Georgetown University Press, 2000.

Parascandola, John. "Syphilis at the Cinema: Medicine and Morals in VD Films of the U.S. Public Health Service in World War II." Chap. 3 in *Medicine's Moving Pictures: Medicine, Health, and Bodies in American Film and Television,* edited by Leslie J. Reagan, Nancy Tomes, and Paula A. Treichler. Rochester, NY: Rochester University Press, 2007.

Parens, Erik, and Adrienne Asch. *Prenatal Testing and Disability Rights.* Washington, DC: Georgetown University Press, 2000.

Pascoe, Peggy. "Miscegenation Law, Court Cases, and Ideologies of 'Race' in Twentieth-Century America." *Journal of American History* 83, no. 1 (June 1996): 44–69.

Patterson, James T. *The Dread Disease: Cancer and Modern American Culture.* Cambridge, MA: Harvard University Press, 1987.

Paul, John R. *A History of Poliomyelitis.* New Haven, CT: Yale University Press, 1971.

Pelka, Fred. *The ABC-CLIO Companion to The Disability Rights Movement.* Santa Barbara, CA: ABC-CLIO, 1997.

Pernick, Martin S. *The Black Stork: Eugenics and the Death of "Defective" Babies in American Medicine and Motion Pictures Since 1915.* New York: Oxford University Press, 1996.

———. "Politics, Parties, and Pestilence: Epidemic Yellow Fever in Philadelphia and the Rise of the First Party System." *William and Mary Quarterly* 29 (1972): 559–86. Revised and reprinted in *Sickness and Health: Readings in the History of Medicine and Public Health,* edited by Judith Walzer Leavitt and Ronald L. Numbers, 356–71. 2nd ed. rev. Madison: University of Wisconsin Press, 1985.

Petchesky, Rosalind Pollack. *Abortion and Woman's Choice: The State, Sexuality, and Reproductive Freedom.* Boston: Northeastern University Press, 1984.

———. "Reproduction, Ethics, and Public Policy: The Federal Sterilization Regulations." *Hastings Center Report* 9, no. 5 (October 1977): 29–42.

Philips, Marilynn J. " 'Try Harder': The Experience of Disability and the Dilemma of Normalization." In *Interpreting Disability: A Qualitative Reader,* edited by Philip M. Ferguson, Dianne L. Ferguson, and Steven J. Taylor, 213–32. New York: Columbia University, Teachers College Press, 1992.

Pivar, David J. *Purity and Hygiene: Women, Prostitution, and the "American Plan," 1900–1930*. Westport, CT: Greenwood Press, 2002.

Pleck, Elizabeth. "The Stigma of Cohabitation in the United States, 1960–1990." Forthcoming.

Plotkin, Stanley A., and Edward A. Mortimer Jr., eds. *Vaccines*. 2nd ed. Philadelphia: W. B. Saunders, 1998.

Poirier, Suzanne. *Chicago's War on Syphilis, 1937–1940*. Urbana: University of Illinois Press, 1995.

Pollard, Deana A. "Wrongful Analysis in Wrongful Life Jurisprudence." *Alabama Law Review* 55 (Winter 2004): 327–75.

Quinn, Roswell. "Broader Spectrum: A History of Antibiotic R&D." PhD diss., University of Illinois, 2008.

Rapp, Rayna. *Testing Women, Testing the Fetus: The Social Impact of Amniocentesis in America*. New York: Routledge, 1999.

Rapp, Rayna, and Faye Ginsburg. "Enabling Disability: Rewriting Kinship, Reimagining Citizenship." *Public Culture* 13, no. 3 (2001): 533–56.

Reagan, Leslie J. "Crossing the Border for Abortions: California Activists, Mexican Clinics, and the Creation of a Feminist Health Agency in the 1960s." *Feminist Studies* 26, no. 2 (Summer 2000): 323–48.

———. "Engendering the Dread Disease: Women, Men, and Cancer." *American Journal of Public Health* 87, no. 11 (November 1997): 1779–87.

———. "From Hazard to Blessing to Tragedy: Representations of Miscarriage in Twentieth-Century America." *Feminist Studies* 29, no. 2 (Summer 2003): 356–78.

———. "Law and Medicine." In *The Cambridge History of Law in America*. Chap. 7 in Vol. 3, *The Twentieth Century and After (1920-)*, edited by Michael Grossberg and Christopher Tomlins. Cambridge: Cambridge University Press, 2008.

———. "Medicine, Law, and the State: The History of Reproduction." Chap. 20 in *A Companion to American Women's History*, edited by Nancy A. Hewitt. New York: Blackwell, 2002.

———. "'Monstrous' Babies in the News: Thalidomide, Birth Defects, and Public Policy in the U.S., 1962." Unpublished paper.

———. "Victim or Accomplice?: Crime, Medical Malpractice, and the Construction of the Aborting Woman in American Case Law, 1860s–1970." *Columbia Journal of Gender and Law* 10, no. 2 (2001): 311–32.

———. *When Abortion Was a Crime: Women, Medicine, and Law in the United States, 1867–1973*. Berkeley: University of California Press, 1997.

Reagan, Leslie J., Nancy Tomes, and Paula A. Treichler. *Medicine's Moving Pictures: Medicine, Health, and Bodies in American Film and Television*. Rochester, NY: Rochester University Press, 2007.

Reilly, Philip R. *The Surgical Solution: A History of Involuntary Sterilization in the United States*. Baltimore: Johns Hopkins University Press, 1991.

Reverby, Susan M., ed. *Tuskegee's Truths: Rethinking the Tuskegee Syphilis Study.* Chapel Hill: University of North Carolina Press, 2000.

Richmond, Phyllis Allen. "American Attitudes Toward the Germ Theory of Disease." *Journal of the History of Medicine and the Allied Sciences* 9 (October 1954): 428–54.

Ritter, Gretchen. "Jury Service and Women's Citizenship before and after the Nineteenth Amendment." *Law and History Review* 20, no. 3 (Fall 2002), 479–516.

Roberts, Dorothy. *Killing the Black Body: Race, Reproduction, and the Meaning of Liberty.* New York: Random House, Vintage Books, 1997.

Robertson, Stephen. "Signs, Marks and Private Parts: Doctors, Legal Discourses, and Evidence of Rape in the United States, 1823–1930." *Journal of the History of Sexuality* 8, no. 3 (January 1998): 345–88.

Roediger, David R. *How Race Survived U.S. History: From the American Revolution to the Present.* New York: Verso, 2008.

———. *The Wages of Whiteness: Race and the Making of the American Working Class.* Rev. and exp. ed. New York: Verso, 2007.

Rogers, Naomi. *Dirt and Disease: Polio Before FDR.* New Brunswick, NJ: Rutgers University Press, 1992.

———. *The Polio Wars: Elizabeth Kenny and the Golden Age of American Medicine.* New York: Oxford University Press, forthcoming.

Rohrer, Judy. "Toward a Full-Inclusion Feminism: A Feminist Deployment of Disability Analysis." *Feminist Studies* 31, no. 1 (Spring 2005): 54–58.

Rosenberg, Charles E. *The Cholera Years: The United States in 1832, 1849, and 1866.* Chicago: University of Chicago Press, 1962.

———. "The Therapeutic Revolution: Medicine, Meaning, and Social Change in 19th-Century America." In *The Therapeutic Revolution: Essays in the Social History of American Medicine,* edited by Morris J. Vogel and Charles E. Rosenberg, 3–25. Philadelphia: University of Pennsylvania Press, 1979.

Ross, Ellen. *Love and Toil: Motherhood in Outcast London, 1870–1918.* New York: Oxford University Press, 1993.

Rothman, Barbara Katz. *The Tentative Pregnancy: How Amniocentesis Changes the Experience of Motherhood.* New York: W. W. Norton, 1993.

———. *Weaving a Family: Untangling Race and Adoption.* Boston: Beacon Press, 2005.

Rothman, David J. *Strangers at the Bedside: A History of How Law and Bioethics Transformed Medical Decision Making.* New York: Basic Books, 1991.

Rothman, Sheila M., and David J. Rothman. *The Willowbrook Wars.* New York: Harper and Row, 1984.

Rothstein, William G. *American Physicians in the 19th Century: From Sects to Science.* Baltimore: Johns Hopkins University Press, 1972.

Ruzek, Sheryl Burt. *The Women's Health Movement: Feminist Alternatives to Medical Control.* New York: Praeger, 1978.

Saxton, Marsha. "Disability Rights and Selective Abortion." In *Abortion Wars: A Half-Century of Struggle, 1950–2000,* edited by Rickie Solinger. Berkeley: University of California Press, 1998.

Schlich, Thomas, and Ulrich Trohler, eds. *The Risks of Medical Innovation: Risk Perception and Assessment in Historical Context.* London: Routledge, 2006.

Schoen, Johanna. *Choice and Coercion: Birth Control, Sterilization, and Abortion in Public Health and Welfare.* Chapel Hill: University of North Carolina Press, 2005.

Scotch, Richard K. "American Disability Policy in the Twentieth Century." *The New Disability History: American Perspectives,* edited by Paul K. Longmore and Lauri Umansky, chap. 14. New York: New York University Press, 2001.

———. *From Good Will to Civil Rights: Transforming Federal Disability Policy.* Philadelphia: Temple University Press, 1984.

Self, Robert O. "Prelude to the Tax Revolt: The Politics of the 'Tax Dollar' in Post-War California." Chap. 7 in *New Suburban History,* edited by Kevin M. Kruse and Thomas J. Sugrue. Chicago: University of Chicago Press, 2006.

Seligman, Milton, and Rosalyn Benjamin Darling. *Ordinary Families, Special Children: A Systems Approach to Childhood Disability.* New York: Guilford Press, 1989.

Shah, Nayan. *Contagious Divides: Epidemics and Race in San Francisco's Chinatown.* Berkeley: University of California Press, 2001.

Shapiro, Joseph P. *No Pity: People with Disabilities Forging a New Civil Rights Movement.* New York: Random House, 1994.

Shorter, Edward. *The Kennedy Family and the Story of Mental Retardation.* Philadelphia: Temple University Press, 2000.

Sickham-Searl, Parnel. "Mothers With a Mission." In *Interpreting Disability: A Qualitative Reader,* edited by Philip M. Ferguson, Dianne L. Ferguson, and Steven J. Taylor, 251–74. New York: Columbia University, Teachers College Press, 1992.

Silliman, Jael, Marlene Gerber Fried, Loretta Ross, and Elena R. Gutierrez. *Undivided Rights: Women of Color Organize for Reproductive Justice.* Cambridge, MA: South End Press, 2004.

Sjostrom, Henning, and Robert Nilsson. *Thalidomide and the Power of the Drug Companies.* Middlesex, UK: Penguin Books, 1972.

Smith, Jane S. *Patenting the Sun: Polio and the Salk Vaccine.* New York: William Morrow, 1990.

Smith, Mark M. *Listening to Nineteenth-Century America.* Chapel Hill: University of North Carolina Press, 2000.

Smith, Susan L. *Sick and Tired of Being Sick and Tired: Black Women's Public Health Activism in America, 1890–1950.* Philadelphia: University of Pennsylvania Press, 1995.

Snyder, Sharon L., and David T. Mitchell. *Cultural Locations of Disability.* Chicago: University of Chicago Press, 2006.

Solinger, Rickie. *The Abortionist: A Woman Against the Law*. New York: Free Press, 1994.

————. *Beggars and Choosers: How the Politics of Choice Shapes Adoption, Abortion, and Welfare in the United States*. New York: Hill and Wang, 2001.

————. "'A Complete Disaster': Abortion and the Politics of Hospital Abortion Committees, 1950–1970." *Feminist Studies* 19, no. 2 (Summer 1993): 241–68.

————. "Sherri Finkbine and the Origins of *Roe v. Wade*." Chap. 13 in *True Stories from the American Past*. Vol. 2, *Since 1865*, edited by William Graebner. 3rd ed. New York: McGraw-Hill, 2002.

————. *Wake Up Little Susie: Single Pregnancy and Race Before Roe v. Wade*. New York: Routledge, 1992.

Sontag, Susan. *Illness as Metaphor*. New York: Farrar, Straus and Giroux, 1978.

Speert, Harold. *Obstetrics and Gynecology in America: A History*. Chicago: American College of Obstetricians and Gynecologists, 1980.

Stage, Sarah. *Female Complaints: Lydia Pinkham and the Business of Women's Medicine*. New York: W. W. Norton, 1979.

Steingraber, Sandra. *Having Faith: An Ecologist's Journey to Motherhood*. Cambridge, MA: Perseus Publishing, 2001.

Stephens, Trent, and Rock Brynner. *Dark Remedy: The Impact of Thalidomide and Its Revival as a Vital Medicine*. Cambridge, MA: Perseus Publishing, 2001.

Stern, Alexandra Minna. *Eugenic Nation: Faults and Frontiers of Better Breeding in Modern America*. Berkeley: University of California Press, 2005.

Stone, A. J. "Consti-tortion: Tort Law as an End-Run Around Abortion Rights After *Planned Parenthood v. Casey*." *American University Journal of Gender, Social Policy and the Law* 8 (2000): 471–515.

Strasser, Mark. "Yes, Virginia, There Can Be Wrongful Life: On Consistency, Public Policy, and the Birth-Related Torts." *Georgetown Journal of Gender and the Law* 4 (Summer 2003): 821–61.

Tentler, Leslie Woodcock. *Catholics and Contraception: An American History*. Ithaca, NY: Cornell University Press, 2004.

Thomson, Rosemarie Garland. "Seeing the Disabled: Visual Rhetorics of Disability in Popular Photography." In *The New Disability History: American Perspectives*, edited by Paul K. Longmore and Lauri Umansky, 335–75. New York: New York University Press, 2001.

Tomes, Nancy. *The Gospel of Germs: Men, Women, and the Microbe in American Life, 1870–1930*. Cambridge, MA: Harvard University Press, 1997.

Tone, Andrea. "Contraceptive Consumers: Gender and the Political Economy of Birth Control in the 1930s." In *Women and Health in America: Historical Readings*, edited by Judith Walzer Leavitt, 306–26. 2nd ed. Madison: University of Wisconsin Press, 1999.

————. *Devices and Desires: A History of Contraceptives in America*. New York: Hill and Wang, 2001.

Treichler, Paula A. *How to Have Theory in an Epidemic: Cultural Chronicles of AIDS.* Durham: Duke University Press, 1999.

Treichler, Paula A., Lisa Cartwright, and Constance Penley, eds. *The Visible Woman: Imaging Technologies, Gender, and Science.* New York: New York University Press, 1998.

Trent, James W., Jr. *Inventing the Feeble Mind: A History of Mental Retardation in the United States.* Berkeley: University of California Press, 1994.

Tushnet, Mark. "The Rights Revolution in the Twentieth Century." In *The Cambridge History of Law in America.* Chap. 11 in Vol. 3, *The Twentieth Century and After (1920-),* edited by Michael Grossberg and Christopher Tomlins. Cambridge: Cambridge University Press, 2008.

Ulrich, Laurel Thatcher. *A Midwife's Tale: The Life of Martha Ballard, Based on Her Diary, 1785–1812.* New York: Knopf, 1990.

Wailoo, Keith. *Dying in the City of Blues: Sickle Cell Anemia and the Politics of Race and Health.* Chapel Hill: University of North Carolina Press, 2001.

Wailoo, Keith, and Stephen Pemberton. *The Troubled Dream of Genetic Medicine: Ethnicity and Innovation in Tay-Sachs, Cystic Fibrosis, and Sickle Cell Disease.* Baltimore: Johns Hopkins University Press, 2006.

Warner, John Harley. "From Specificity to Universalism in Medical Therapeutics: Transformation in the 19th-Century United States." In *Sickness and Health in America: Readings in the History of Medicine and Public Health,* edited by Judith Walzer Leavitt and Ronald L. Numbers, 3rd rev. ed., 87–101. Madison: University of Wisconsin Press, 1997.

Watkins, Elizabeth Siegel. *On the Pill: A Social History of Contraceptives, 1950–1970.* Baltimore: John Hopkins University Press, 2001.

Weaver, Mary Jo, and R. Scott Appleby. *Being Right: Conservative Catholics in America.* Bloomington: Indiana University Press, 1995.

Weisbord, Robert G. *Genocide? Birth Control and the Black American.* Westport, CT: Greenwood Press; New York: Two Continents Publishing Group, 1975.

Wexler, Alice. *Mapping Fate: A Memoir of Family, Risk, and Genetic Research.* Berkeley: University of California Press, 1996.

———. *The Woman Who Walked into the Sea: Huntington's and the Making of a Genetic Disease,* with a foreword by Nancy S. Wexler. New Haven, CT: Yale University Press, 2008.

Williams, Patricia J. *Alchemy of Race and Rights.* Cambridge, MA: Harvard University Press, 1992.

Wilson, Daniel J. *Living with Polio: The Epidemic and Its Survivors.* Chicago: University of Chicago Press, 2005.

Wolf, Jacqueline H. *Don't Kill Your Baby: Public Health and the Decline of Breastfeeding in the Nineteenth and Twentieth Centuries.* Columbus: Ohio State University Press, 2001.

# INDEX

*Italicized page numbers refer to illustrations.*

abortions, 3–6, 102, 169; D&E (dilation
and evacuation), 175; deaths due to,
168, 284–85n23; decriminalization of,
106, 144, 167–69, 174, 219; excluded
from health insurance, 137, 176; illegal, 1, 5, 18–19, 77–80, 93, 94–95,
105, 113, 126–27, 135–36, 142–43, 150,
153–54, 168–69, 171, 183, 232, 275n101,
284–85n23, 293nn9,12, 306n111; and
"Jane," 169; late-term, 5, 175–76; legalization of, 157, 170, 174, 178, 183,
187, 221–22, 224, 301n72, 314n29; and
"the List," 156–57, 169, 299n60; and
parental consent for abortion for minor, 174, 176; politics of, 104, 117; representations of, 6, 57, 80, 100, 104; as
sexually deviant practice, 57, 78–80,
104, 275n101; and underground practitioners of, 143, 153, 159, 168–69,
171–73, 293n12, 306n111. See also therapeutic abortions; entries beginning
with abortion
abstinence, sexual, 15, 102, 186, 250n52
addiction programs, 231–32
adolescent girls, 186–87, 313nn22,23
adoption, 4, 78
advertisements, 11, 187–88, 193, 195, 209–11,
210, 212, 219, 237, 320nb77,78
advice columns, medical, 8, 51–54, 64, 74;
and criminalization of pregnant
women, 233; and decisions about therapeutic abortions, 81–84, 276n111,
277–78n130; and exposure of daughters to rubella, 84; and rubella vac-
cine/vaccinations, 194
African Americans, 5, 14, 66, 81; and abortion law, 149, 161, 177; and abortions,
77–79, 275n101, 276n104, 277–
78n130; Catholic community of, 160;
and lack of public education for disabled children, 217; and rubella vac-
cine/vaccinations, 182, 188–89, 190,
195, 202; and suspicions about pregnant women, 227–29, 228; and venereal diseases, 15; and voting rights, 141;
and wrongful birth lawsuits, 114–17,
131, 285–86n34, 288n64
Alaskan abortion law, 167

alcohol use, 5, 227, 228, 231–32, 249n42,
326n15
America (Jesuit magazine), 90
American Academy of Pediatrics, 186,
298–99n56, 316n43
American Association for the Advancement
of Science, 163
American Association of University
Women (AAUW), 155–56
American Bar Association, 298–99n56
American Civil Liberties Union, 168
American College of Obstetricians and
Gynecologists (ACOG), 147, 169, 175
American Dermatological Association,
254n30
American Journal of Diseases of Children,
311nn9,11, 313n23
American Journal of Public Health, 45,
262n119
American Law Institute (ALI), 142, 145,
154, 164, 298n53
American Medical Association, 17,
298–99n56
American Pediatric Society, 311n9
Americans with Disabilities Act, 239
amici briefs, 163–64, 168, 304–5nn97,98
amniocentesis, 4–5, 103, 109, 223, 282n4,
291n106, 320n75
Anderson, Viola Russell, 9–10, 15–16
antiabortion movement. See abortion oppo-
nents
antibiotics, 2, 59
Apgar, Virginia, 63, 84, 193–95, 246n14,
313n24, 320n73
aphasia, 72
Archives of Dermatology, 29
Arkansas Children's Colony (Conway,
Ark.), 213, 321n85
Arlington (Va.) County Medical Society,
315n35
Artenstein, Malcolm, 311n10
arthritis, 33, 186
Ashcroft, John, 175
Asian children, 191, 192
Association for the Study of Abortion
(ASA), 127
Association of Retarded Citizens (ARC),
304n91

eugenics, 4, 20, 64, 188, 211
*Expectant Motherhood* (Eastman), 53
Eyman, Andrew J., 167

families, 2, 6, 18, 222; and abortion law,
142, 154, 156, 160, 162, 164, 167, 171–73,
177–79, 298n54; and criminalization
of pregnant women, 232; and discovery of effects of maternal rubella,
41–42, 46–47, 56–57; and exposure of
daughters to rubella, 84; faulted for
hereditary traits, 64, 269n39; and fear
of maternal marking, 12–13, 249n38;
financial crises of, 68–69, 73, 87, 135,
137–38, 215, 272–73n73; health records
of, 73–74, 273n75; and rubella vac-
cine/vaccinations, 182–84, 196, *198,*
199, *200,* 204, 208–9, 211, 220, 235,
316n44, 317n51; shame/guilt/secrecy
of, 64, 66–69, 152, 270n45, 291n106,
297n45; and women's decisions about
therapeutic abortions, 76, 81–88, *87,*
99–104, 223, 274nn89,90, 281n162,
282n171; and wrongful birth lawsuits,
108, 115, 117, 134–36
family planning, 57, 102–3, 281n169
fathers, 7, 71, 222; and abortion law, 142,
155, 160–61, 178–79, 303n84, 309n136;
and child care, 71, 75; and decisions
about therapeutic abortions, 100,
281n162; and exposure of daughters to
rubella, 84, *85;* fear of maternal marking, 15; and hereditary traits, 13, 46;
and rubella vaccine/vaccinations, 194,
204, 207, 316n44; and venereal diseases, 65
"feeble-minded" children, 12, 53, 65, 67,
79. *See also* mental retardation
*Feminine Mystique, The* (Friedan), 90–91
feminists, 16, 78, 124; and abortion law,
157, *165,* 169, 174, 176, 178, 293–94n14
Ferguson, Ora, *190*
fetal alcohol syndrome (FAS), 229, 326n15
fetuses, 1, 5, 13, 223; and abortion law, 154,
158–59, 162–64, 166–67, 170, 174–76,
178–79, 300–301n67; and criminalization of pregnant women, 232–33;
harmed by teratogens, 22–23, 37, 43,

45, 221, 263n126; harmed by thalidomide, 56, 59; and rubella vaccine/vac-
cinations, 184–85, 187–88, 219; and
suspicions about pregnant women,
225–31, *226, 228, 230;* and wrongful
birth lawsuits, 126–27
fever, 17, 24, 26, 32, 73–74
financial crises, 68–69, 73, 87, 272–73n73
Finkbine, Sherri, 58–59, 85–88, *87, 88,* 91,
171–72, 229, 266n16, 277n124
Food and Drug Administration, U.S., 56,
59, 181, 266n15
food preservatives, 58
Foster, Philip, 160
Foucault, Michel, 23
Franzi, Antonio, 297n48
"freaks," 4, 60, *61,* 71–72
freak shows, 126
freedom of religion, 5, 117, 161
free speech movement, 91
Friedan, Betty, 90–91

Gallaudet University, 240
gamma globulin, 141–42, 292–93n5
Gampell, Ralph J., 143
Garcia, Lynn, 135
Garrow, David, 295n30, 306n111
gastrointestinal problems, 236, 328–29n34
gender, 7, 17–19, 24, 40, 222; and care of
disabled children, 41–42, 66–67, 71,
75, 270n45; and criminalization of
pregnant women, 232–34; and decisions about therapeutic abortions, 76,
81–84, 86, 100, 274nn89,90; and exposure of daughters to rubella, 83–84,
*85;* and interracial sexual relations,
78–80; and rubella vaccine/vaccina-
tions, 182, 194, 199, 202, *203,* 204–5,
207, 219, 316n44, 318n55; and sex-
specific medicine, 28, 254n18; and voting rights, 141; and wrongful birth
lawsuits, 130
general practitioners, 111–12
genetic testing, 4–5, 103, 133, 222–23, 282n4
Gerber baby, 191, *193*
German measles, 1–6, 17–18, 320n73; and
abortion law, 142–43, 146–49, 151–54,
159, 161, 163, 166, 169–72, 174, 176,

German measles *(continued)*
178, 295n32; antibodies for, 292–93n5; blood tests for, 90–93, *92*, 96, 103; as "the crippler," 55–56; diagnosis of, 24–32, 114–16, 208; discovery of effects of maternal rubella, 36–54, 257n65, 260n98, 261–62nn109,115,122, 263n127; epidemic (1853), 29; epidemic (1866: Bombay boarding school), 25–27; epidemic (1871: Massachusetts), 28–29; epidemic (1873: New York City), 29–30; epidemic (1881), 30; epidemic (1940: Australia), 35–36; epidemic (1942: Chicago), 35; epidemic (1958), 57; epidemic (1963–1965), 1–4, 6, 18, 20, 55–104, *92*, 106, 108, 115, 139–79, *140*, 185, 191, 194, 216–17, 243n1, 268–69nn31,35, 278n131, 292–93nn3–5, 314nn30,32, 320n74; epidemics (World War I), 33–34; epidemics (World War II), 33–35, 37, 44, 261n109; epidemics, recurrence of, 181, 183, 199, 202; as foreign disease, 29–30; health department verification for, 109, 111, 125; incubation period for, 26, 32; jokes about, 34–35; as "menace," 44, 52–53; mild symptoms of, 22, 27, 31, 52–53, 73, 255n44; naming of, 19–20, 25, 28–31, 33–34, 254n30, 255n44; not reported disease, 208, 292n4; parties for, 84, *85*, 196, 199; politics of, 19, 143–44, 293–94n14, 319n66; use of military metaphors to describe, 33–34, 264n4; vaccine for, 18–19, 141, 180–220 (*see also under* vaccines); as viral infection, 292n2; and voting, 139–41, *140*, 234, 292n1; and wrongful birth lawsuits, 105–9, 111–19, 121, 123–24, 287n56. *See also* maternal rubella; rubella
germ theory, 28
glasses, 20, 70–72, 196, *197*, 209, *210*, 211–12
glaucoma, 70, 236–37, 328–29n34
Gleitman, Jeffrey, 118, 131
Gleitman, Sandra and Irwin, 105–6, 117–23, 131–32, 135, 172, 284n8

*Gleitman v. Cosgrove,* 105, 107, 117–23, 131–36, 138, 282n4, 284n8, 287n56, 290n91, 291nn110,111
Golden, Janet, 326n15
Goldwater, Barry, 301n72
gonorrhea, 15
*Gonzales v. Carhart,* 175
*Good Housekeeping,* 64–65, 97, 99–101, 199, 281n162
Gordon, Linda, 102
Gordon, Robert, 110–11, 115–16, 118, 128
Grant, Donald Kerr, 136
Great Depression, 35, 77
Gregg, Norman McAlister, Sir, 36–45, 47–52, *50*, 54, 76, 236, 256n38, 257nn64,65, 258n83, 259n88, 262n122, 266n13, 328–29n34; and therapeutic abortions, 273–74nn88,89
*Griswold v. Connecticut,* 105, 158, 164, 173
Grossberg, Michael, 265n8
Grutman, Norman Roy, 115, 126–29, 285n33
Guild of Catholic Psychiatrists, 300–301n67
Guinée, Vincent, 205
Guttmacher, Alan, 147
gynecology/gynecologists, 4, 112–13, 153, 168–71, 176

Hall, Robert E., 77, 109, 114, 127
handicapped children, 20, 63, 68–69, 101, 162, 183, 188, 208, 215. *See also* disabled children
harassment, 95, 164, 176–77
harelip, 260n98
*Harper's Magazine,* 116–17, 130–31
Harvard School of Public Health, 45, 185, 311n10
Hawaiian abortion law, 167, 293–94n14
Hayes, James, 126–28
Head Start programs, 187
Health, Education, and Welfare Department, U.S. (HEW), 185, 207, 313n25
healthcare workers, infected by "rubella babies," 76, 273n84
health clinics, 17, 23, 36, 54, 103, 112, 202; and rubella vaccine/vaccinations, 186, 189, *192*, 196, 218, 315n35

health education materials, 182, 195–214, *197, 198, 210,* 219, 233, 318n55, 319n66; and suspicions about pregnant women, 225–31, *226, 228, 230. See also* pamphlets; *names of publications*

health insurance, 73, 114, 117, 134, 137, 175–76, 218

health reformers, 7, 9, 15, 17, 169

hearing aids, 135, 196, *197,* 205, 209, *210,* 211–12, 215, 317n52, 320n77

heart defects, 23, 36, 40, 44–47, 97, 260n98, 261n109; caused by thalidomide, 60; and rubella vaccine/vaccinations, 180, 184, 201, 317–18n54; surgery for, 60, 70, 72, 121; and wrongful birth lawsuits, 110, 121, 134–35

Helen Keller National Center for Deaf-Blind Youths and Adults (HKNC), *238,* 239, 328–29n34

hemophilia, 103

hereditary traits, 13, 15, 46, 49, 64, 67, 103, 269n39

Herzog, George K., 163, 304n93

heterosexuality, 6, 84, 86, 104, 173

HIPAA (Health Insurance Portability and Accountability Act), 175

Hodgson, Jane, 170–74, 307–8nn118,127,131

*Hodgson v. Minnesota,* 172–74, 308n131

Holocaust, 159, 301n72

home ownership, 172, 246n12

hormone imbalances, 236, 328–29n34

hospitals, 27, 66, 68, 72; and abortion law, 143–51, 153, 164, 167, 175, 295n32, 296n35, 297n48; abortion review committees at, 77, 99–100, 106, 108, 110–13, 123, 137, 145–46, 153, 164, *165,* 168, 170–71, 224, 284–85n23, 307n233; limiting number of therapeutic abortions, 77, 105, 109–23, 128, 148, 167, 284–85nn24,25, 287nn55,56, 295n32; and women's decisions about therapeutic abortions, 89, 95–96, 99–100, 103, 280n154. *See also* institutionalization

*Humanae Vitae* encyclical, 160

Humane Abortion Act (Calif.), 145, 147, 154–56, 160–62, 164, 298n54. *See also* abortion law reform movement; Therapeutic Abortion Act (Calif.)

Humanist Association (San Francisco), 299n60

human rights, 127, 314n29

human subject research, 214

IDEA, 218

illegitimate children, 79

immigrants, 5, 17, 34, 112, 140–41, 201

immunity, 32; blood tests to check for, 73, 90–93, *92,* 96, 103; and decisions about therapeutic abortions, 81, 90; and exposure of daughters to rubella, 83–84; herd immunity, 187, 234, 326n22; lack of family health records, 73–74, 273n75, 313n23; passive, 182

immunization, 17, 19, 48, 180–220; costs of rubella campaign, 188–89, 314n30, 315n35; global immunization campaigns, 316n44; 1969–1970 campaign for, 182–83, 185–214, *190, 192, 193, 197, 198,* 318n58; volunteers for campaigns, 188–89, *190,* 191, *192,* 201, 315–16n38. *See also* vaccines

incest, 149, 156, 164, 174

*Index-Catalogue of the Library of the Surgeon-General's Office,* 30

individual educational plans (IEPs), 235

industrial pollution, 229

*Infant Care* (Children's Bureau), 247n16

infant health, 7, 10, 13–14, 16–17, 37–38; and rubella vaccine/vaccinations, 181, 188, 199, 207

infanticide, 126–27

infant mortality, 2, 23, 36, 46–47, 261n109, 268–69n35; caused by thalidomide, 56, 58, 89, 266n15, 268n32; caused by venereal disease, 65; fear of used in immunization campaigns, 180, 182–83, 208–9, 220, 320nn73,74; questionable statistics for, 208–9, 320nn73,74; and suspicions about pregnant women, 229, 231

infectious diseases, 2–3, 5–6, 26–27, 32–35, 48, 75–76; and health inequalities, 182, 310n2; and immigrants, 140–41; and quarantine, 33–35, 75; "rubella babies" infectious months after birth, 76, 273n84. *See also names of infectious diseases*

rubella vaccine/vaccinations, 187–88, 209–11, *210*

Lindee, Susan, 252n2

lipreading, 317n52, 320n77

"the List," 156, 299n60

listening, medical, 23, 37–38, 40–41, 48, *50*

Little Mothers' Clubs, 207

Long Beach (Calif.) immunization campaign, 319n64

Long Island College Hospital, 110–12, 115, 118, 127, 129

*Look* magazine, 271n54

*Los Angeles Times,* 135, 145, 266n16

*Loving v. Virginia,* 173

Lowell, Edgar, 215

Luker, Kristin, 144, 266n16, 293n13, 295n30, 300–301n67

lymph glands, swollen, 186

lynching, 79, 159

Mafia, 77

magazines, 3, 7–8, 18; coverage of abortion law, 142, 146–48; coverage of abortions, 77–80, 276n104; coverage of blood tests, 90–93, *92;* coverage of decisions about therapeutic abortions, 81–83, 86, *87, 88,* 90–101, *92, 98,* 276n111, 279nn146,147; coverage of German measles epidemic, 67–70; coverage of German measles parties, 84, *85;* coverage of institutionalization, 67, 271n52; coverage of maternal rubella, 45–46, 52–54, 81–83, 262nn118,119,122, 276n111; coverage of rubella vaccine/vaccinations, 187–88, 194, 209–11, *210;* coverage of wrongful birth suits, 116–17, 130–31; coverage of wrongful life suits, 107–9, 116–17; and suspicions about pregnant women, 225. *See also names of magazines*

Maginnis, Patricia T., 156–57, 160, 164, *165,* 166–67, 169, 299n60

"malformed" babies, 55, 64–65, 102–3; and abortion law, 150–52, 167, 296n35; caused by thalidomide, 58, 60, *61, 62,* 89, 268n26; likelihood of having, 82–83, 89, 93–94, 99, 119–21, 130, 132, 276n111; and rubella vaccine/vaccina-

tions, 184, 317–18n54; and wrongful birth lawsuits, 105–6, 108, 119–21, 123–29, 131, 133, 135–36. *See also* birth defects; deformities

Mallon, Mary ("Typhoid Mary"), 32, 273n82

malpractice suits, 4, 19, 105–9, 117, 133–34, 137–38, 167, 174, 284n8. *See also names of lawsuits*

Mann, Ida, 43–44, 259n88

March of Dimes (MOD), 84, 102, 126, 312n14; and rubella vaccine/vaccinations, 185, 191, 194, 199, 201, 204–6, 213, 315–18n54, 320n73; and suspicions about pregnant women, 225–31, *226, 228, 230. See also* National Foundation–March of Dimes

Maremont, Alan S., 303n84, 309n136

Margaret Hague Hospital, 120, 122, 287nn55,56

Marsden, George, 293–94n14

Martin, John, 78

Mason, Carol, 301n72

materialism, 16, 251n58

maternal health, 7–8, 10, 13–14, 16–17; and abortion law, 147, 154, 156, 163–64, 168, 171, 175, 178, 298n54; and rubella vaccine/vaccinations, 181–82, 188, 199

maternal instinct, 233–34

maternalists, 7, 17

maternal marking, 7–18, 21, 35, 43, 46, 48, 53–54, 247–48n19, 263n126

maternal mortality, 2, 47; and abortions, 77–78, 149

maternal responsibility, 9, 13, 17, 24, 38, 54; and abortion law, 154, 161, 177; and criminalization of pregnant women, 233–34; and decisions about therapeutic abortions, 57, 83, 100, 103–4, 224; and exposure of daughters to rubella, 84, 196, 199; and rubella vaccine/vaccinations, 183–84, 187, 194, 202, 207, 218–19, 316n44; and wrongful birth lawsuits, 130, 135, 288n64

maternal rubella: and abortion law, 144–45, 148–52, 166, 170, 174, 179, 295n32; discovery of effects of, 36–52, 257n65, 260n98, 261–62nn109,115,122; and

maternal rubella *(continued)*
rubella vaccine/vaccinations, 180, 183–85,
194–96, 209, 212, 317–18n54; as tragedy, 40–41, 46–47, 63–64, 73, 114,
129, 160, 164, 172, 177, 181, 184, 195–96,
*197,* 199, 201, 291n110, 317n51; and
women's decisions about therapeutic
abortions, 80–104; and wrongful birth
lawsuits, 109–11, 115–20, 123, 132,
291n110
Mayo Clinic, 171
McBride, W. G., 266n13
McHugh, James, 301n69
McKnight, Regina, 231
McNaught, J. G., 33
McNulty, James V., 147–48, 295n25
measles, 24–26, 28–35, 74, 185, 191, 194–95,
208, 212, 214, 218, 259n88, 316n43,
319n66
media, 2–4, 6, 18–20, 32, 34–35; coverage
of abortion law, 142, 144–46, 153, 155,
157, 172–73, 178, 180, 222, 294n19,
295n32, 298n55, 307–8n127; coverage
of abortions, 77–78, 80; coverage of
autism, 327n27; coverage of blood
tests, 90–93, *92;* coverage of decisions
about therapeutic abortions, 81–101, *87,*
*88, 92, 98,* 104, 276n111, 277–78n130,
279nn146,147; coverage of education
for disabled children, 216; coverage of
German measles epidemic, 55–57, 61,
63, 67–68, 70–71, 268n31; coverage of
German measles parties, 84, *85;* coverage of institutionalization, 67, 271n52;
coverage of maternal rubella, 36, 45,
49–54, 81–83, 261–62nn115,118,119,122,
276n111; coverage of rubella
vaccine/vaccinations, 180, 182–83, 185,
187–88, *190,* 194, 205, 207–11, *210,* 219;
coverage of thalidomide, 58–61, *61,*
63, 266n16, 267n20; coverage of
wrongful life suits, 106–9, 111, 114,
116–17, 130; and suspicions about
pregnant women, 225; and wrongful
birth lawsuits, 116–17, 123, 130–31, 133
medical ethics, 5, 146, 174
medical expenses, prospective, 111, 188–89,
217, 315n35

*Medical Journal of Australia,* 44, 121, 257n64
medical licensing, 143, 153, 166, 173–74
medical model, 64–65, 71
medical records, 110, 175
medical schools, 143, 147–48, 153, 163,
166–67, 168, 170
medical surveillance, 53–54
medical textbooks, 18–19
menopause, 236
menstruation, 15–16
mental retardation, 20–21, 23, 46–47, 70,
103, 264n4; and abortion law, 149,
152, 161–62, 297n45, 304n91; and institutionalization, 42, 63, 67–68,
271nn46,52; lack of public education
for, 66, 68–69, 101; as punishment for
deviant sexuality, 65; and rubella vac-
cine/vaccinations, 184, 188–89, 209,
211–14; and suspicions about pregnant
women, 227; treated as inherited trait,
64; and wrongful birth lawsuits, 121,
123–24, 126–27, 135–36, 291n102. *See
also* intellectual impairment
methamphetamine, 231–32
Metropolitan Life Insurance advertisement,
209–11, *210*
Meyer, Harry M. Jr., 213, 311–12n12
Meyerowitz, Joanne, 309n137
Michael, May, 27, 31
microcephaly, 39
middle-classness, 6, 17, 57, 68, 246n12,
281n169; and abortion law, 156, 172,
177–78, 222; and criminalization of
pregnant women, 232; and lack of
public education for disabled children, 217; and rubella vaccine/vacci-
nations, 194, 201; and therapeutic
abortions, 81, 86, 104, 112; and wrongful birth lawsuits, 112, 114, 134–35
midwives, 7, 171, 233
military medicine, 24, 36
military metaphors, 33–34, 264n4
military training camps, 27, 33–35, 37, 44,
234, 255n44, 326n22
Minneapolis (Minn.) immunization campaign, 201, 318n58
Minnesota abortion law, 170–74, 307n118,
308n131

Minnesota Obstetrics/Gynecology Society, 170

Minnesota Supreme Court, 173

*Mirror Crack'd from Side to Side, The* (Christie), 20

miscarriages, 1–2, 10, 12, 15–16, 23, 46, 48, 247–48n19, 250n52; and abortion law, 162; as "blessings," 162, 209, 320n75; caused by thalidomide, 58, 60, 266n15, 268n32; and criminalization of pregnant women, 232–33; and cross-cultural comparisons, 232; and psychological problems, 78; and rubella vaccine/vaccinations, 180, 208–9, 320nn74,75; and wrongful birth lawsuits, 119, 128

MMR (measles, mumps, rubella) vaccine, 19–20, 220, 235, 313n23, 323–24n106

"Mommy, don't" (March of Dimes campaign), 225–31, *226, 228, 230*

mongolism, 162, 260n98, 303–4n90. *See also* Down syndrome

Montgomery (Ala.) bus boycott, 173

Moody, Howard, 157

Mormons, 157

Moss, Alan, 297n48

motherhood, 3, 13, 51, 81, 86, 104, 178, 207, 222–23, 232, 251n58

mothers, 4, 6, 17; and abortion law, 142, 149–50, 152, 154–55, 159–62, 167, 170–72, 177–79, 222; and autism, 235; and child-mother bond, 81, 195; and decisions about therapeutic abortions, 86–88, *87, 88,* 94, 96–97, 99–101, 279nn146,147, 280n155; difficulty of isolating from rubella, 75–76, 81, 84, 94, 97, 108; discovery of effects of maternal rubella, 36–52, 257n65; and exposure of daughters to rubella, 83–84; and hereditary traits, 13, 46; and lack of public education for disabled children, 217; observations by, 18, 23–24, 31–32, 36–40, 48–52, 54, 256n38, 257n64, 261–62n115, 263n129; and rubella vaccine/vaccinations, 183–84, 194–96, 199, 201–2, 204–7, 218–20, 316n44, 319n65; seen as overpowering/overprotective, 69–70, 78;

strain of caring for disabled child, 41–42, 66–70, 111, 130, 222, 235, 270n45, 280n155, 324n1; suspicions about, 225–31, *226, 228, 230;* Widmyer as "model mother," 172, 307–8n127; and wrongful birth lawsuits, 107–8, 110–11, 115, 118. *See also* pregnant women; *entries beginning with* maternal

mother-work, 222, 324n1

multi-handicapped children, 123, 184–85, 215, 217. *See also* congenital rubella syndrome (CRS)

mumps, 35, 53, 193–94, 259n88

Murphy, Freda, 139

National Advocates for Pregnant Women (NAPW), 326n20

National Association for Retarded Children (NARC), 162, 212–13, 304n91

National Communicable Disease Center, 320n74

National Council of Catholic Women, 189

*National Enquirer,* 60

National Foundation–March of Dimes, 63, 189, 191, 199, 243n1, 246n14, 315–16n38

National Institute of Allergy and Infectious Diseases, 185

Native American women, 149, 229

*New England Journal of Medicine,* 45, 267n20

New Jersey Supreme Court, 131–32, 290n91

New Right, 293–94nn14,23, 309n137

newspapers, 3, 18, 36–37, 49, 257n64; coverage of abortion law, 145–46, 148, 155, 158, 170, 294n19, 298n55; coverage of abortions, 77–78; coverage of blood tests, 91, 93; coverage of German measles epidemic, 70–71; coverage of maternal rubella, 50–54, 261–62n115; coverage of voting during epidemic, 139, *140,* 292n1; coverage of wrongful life suits, 109, 111; and rubella vaccine/vaccinations, *190,* 207–8. *See also names of newspapers*

*Newsweek,* 45, 52, 72, 108, 262n118, 273–74n88

New York abortion law, 158, 167, 183

New York Academy of Medicine, 262n122

and criminalization of pregnant
women, 232; general practitioners as,
111–12; as legal pioneers, 153–54, 157,
171–74; as moral pioneers, 5, 176;
murder of, 175–77; refusal to provide
therapeutic abortions, 82–85, 89, 99,
105, 109–13, 117–19, 184; and rubella
vaccine/vaccinations, 186, *200*, 201–2,
*206*, 208
Pike, James, 157, 300n62
Pinkham, Lydia, 8
PKU, 212
Planned Parenthood, 102, 147, 175
Plotkin, Stanley A., 91, 313n23
Plunkett, J. Jerome, 173
police crackdowns/raids, 77, 111, 143, 154,
293n12
polio, 2, 55–56, 63–64, 101, 181, 184, 191,
193–94, 205, 207–8, 211–12, 214, 218,
220, 258n86
political cartoons, 34–35, *165*
political metaphors, 159, 301n72
poor/poverty, 5, 17, 281n169; and abortion
law, 167; and abortions, 79, 81; and
criminalization of pregnant women,
232; and rubella vaccine/vaccinations,
182, 187–88, *190*, 194–95, 310n2,
313n25; and suspicions about pregnant
women, 229; and wrongful birth lawsuits, 114, 136
Pope Paul VI, 160–61
poster children, 205, 211, 237
post-polio-syndrome (PPS), 237
post-rubella syndrome (PRS), 237
Potter, Edith L., 45, 259n88
power, rules of, 107, 119, 159
Pratt, Joseph, 171
pregnancy loss movement, 232–33
pregnant women, 1–5; and abortion law,
148–53, 156, 159, 161, 163, *165*, 166, 168,
170–73, 175–76, 179, 307–8n127; and
blood tests, 90–93, *92*; as conduits for
protecting children's health, 16–17,
225, *226*, 227, *228*, 229, *230*, 231; criminalization of, 231–34; and decisions
about therapeutic abortions, 18–19, 57,
76–104, *92*, 221–24, 280n155, 324n3;
difficulty of isolating from rubella,

75–76, 81, 84, 94, 108, 152, 171, 184,
195–96, 199–204, *200*, 209, 317–18n54;
and discovery of maternal rubella effects, 36–52, 257n65; fear of maternal
marking, 7–18, 21, 35, 43, 46, 48, 53–
54, 65, 247–48n19, 249n42, 263n126;
interviewed in California investigation, 151–52; as legal pioneers, 105,
138, 172; as moral pioneers, 5, 103–5,
177–78; as murderers, 159, 231, 233; reactions to discovery of maternal
rubella effects, 57, 60, 63, 68, 73–76,
80–104, 269n39; and rubella
vaccine/vaccinations, 181, 183–84,
186–88, 194–95, *200*, 201, 204, 208–9,
219–20, 320n73, 321n85; suicidal tendencies of, 150–51, 296n39; suspicions
about, 13–14, 113–14, 225–31, *226*, *228*,
*230*; and thalidomide, 58–60, 85–86,
266n15; and wrongful birth lawsuits,
108–20. *See also* mothers
prenatal care, 12–13, 16–17, 179, 182, 207,
225, 227, 229, *230*
*Prenatal Care* (Children's Bureau), 247n16,
263n127
privacy, right to, 3–4, 106, 158, 168–69,
173–75, 178, 231, 324n3
private patients, 112, 114, 285n25
pro-life movement, 95, 144, 232,
300–301nn62,67,69,72, 326n20. *See
also* abortion opponents; right-to-life
movement
pronatalism, 46, 48, 77
prophylaxis, 40
prosecutors, 79; and abortion law, 143–44,
146–47, 150–53, 166–67, 171–72, 176,
299n57; and criminalization of pregnant women, 231–33
prosthetic limbs, 61, *62*, 63
prostitution, 5, 77
Protestantism, 59, 157–58, 277n124,
297n46, 300nn62,63
psychiatrists, 150, 169
public health, 1–3, 6, 15, 38, 59, 181–82
public health officers/workers, 15, 17, 79,
169, 292n3; and rubella vaccine/
vaccinations, 186, 188, 194–95,
206–7, 220

Text:    11.25/13.5 Adobe Garamond
Display:    Perpetua and Adobe Garamond
Compositor:    Westchester Book Group
Indexer:    Sharon Sweeney
Printer and binder:    Maple-Vail Book Manufacturing Group

Made in the USA
Middletown, DE
16 September 2018